Chinese Society

'In a timely shift away from China's record of economic growth, this original volume looks at the diverse facets of social conflict and popular resistance against state power which have appeared in the wake of the economic reforms. It presents rich evidence of growing dissatisfaction with a system which benefits the few while it frustrates the many. This book should be required reading for any critically inclined scholar with an interest in contemporary China.' **Dr Frank Dikötter, Director of the Contemporary China Institute at SOAS, University of London.**

Conventional images of contemporary China present a picture of stunningly successful economic reform, buttressed by a repressive and inflexible political system. Such portraits, whilst not entirely inaccurate, fail to recognize the sophistication of the Chinese state; leave little room for grassroots resistance; and ignore volatile elements of change in Chinese society. The legacy of reform policies includes mounting discontent leading to a surprising amount of popular unrest. The volume explores a wide range of social, political and cultural strife that has accompanied China's contemporary reform effort; the state's attempts to channel and control it; and the tactical innovations of diverse resistance movements.

Written by an interdisciplinary and international team of China scholars – including anthropologists, historians, sociologists, political scientists, political economists, and psychiatrists – this book offers an authoritative analysis of contemporary Chinese society, protest and resistance. It covers topics such as labour and environmental disputes, rural and ethnic conflict, migration, legal challenges, intellectual and religious dissidence, opposition to family planning, and suicides. This volume is an up-to-date resource for undergraduates as well as specialists.

Elizabeth J. Perry is Henry Rosovsky Professor of Government and Director of the Fairbank Center for East Asian Research at Harvard University. Her previous books include *Rebels and Revolutionaries in North China*, *Shanghai on Strike: The Politics of Chinese Labor*, and *Proletarian Power: Shanghai in the Cultural Revolution*. **Mark Selden** is Professor of Sociology at Binghamton University. His previous books include *China in Revolution: The Yenan Way Revisited*, *Chinese Village, Socialist State*, and *The Political Economy of Chinese Socialism*.

Routledge Studies in Asia's Transformations
Edited by Mark Selden
Binghamton and Cornell Universities

The books in this series explore the political, social, economic and cultural consequences of Asia's twentieth-century transformations. The series emphasizes the tumultuous interplay of local, national, regional and global forces as Asia bids to become the hub of the world economy. While focusing on the contemporary, it also looks back to analyse the antecedents of Asia's contested rise.

This series comprises two strands:

Routledge Studies in Asia's Transformations is a forum for innovative new research intended for a high-level specialist readership, and the titles will be available in hardback only. Titles include:

1. **The American Occupation of Japan and Okinawa**
Literature and memory
Michael Molasky

2. **Koreans in Japan**
Critical voices from the margin
Edited by Sonia Ryang

Asia's Transformations aims to address the needs of students and teachers, and the titles will be published in hardback and paperback. Titles include:

Debating Human Rights
Critical essays from the United States and Asia
Edited by Peter Van Ness

Hong Kong's History
State and society under colonial rule
Edited by Tak-Wing Ngo

Japan's Comfort Women
Yuki Tanaka

Opium, Empire and the Global Political Economy
Carl A. Trocki

Chinese Society
Change, conflict and resistance
Edited by Elizabeth J. Perry and Mark Selden

Mao's Children of the New China
Voices from the red guard generation
Yarong Jiang and David Ashley

Chinese Society

Change, Conflict and Resistance

**Edited by Elizabeth J. Perry
and Mark Selden**

London and New York

First published 2000
by Routledge
11 New Fetter Lane, London EC4P 4EE

Simultaneously published in the USA and Canada
by Routledge
29 West 35th Street, New York, NY 10001

Routledge is an imprint of the Taylor & Francis Group

© 2000 Elizabeth J. Perry and Mark Selden for selection and editorial matter

Typeset in Baskerville by
BOOK NOW Ltd
Printed and bound in Great Britain by
Biddles Ltd, Guildford and King's Lynn

British Library Cataloguing in Publication Data
A catalogue record for this book is available from the British Library

Library of Congress Cataloging-in-Publication Data
Chinese society : change, conflict and resistance /
    edited by Elizabeth J. Perry and Mark Selden.
        p.   cm. – (Asia's transformations)
    Includes bibliographical references and index.
    1. China–Social conditions–1976–   . 2. China–Politics and
government – 1976–   I. Perry, Elizabeth J. II. Selden, Mark.
III. Series.
HN733.5.C69   1999
306′.0951 – dc21   99–38813
                                                                      CIP

ISBN 0-415-20490-9 hbk
ISBN 0-415-22334-2 pbk

To those who resist injustice, whether loudly or softly

Contents

Dedication   v
Illustrations   ix
List of contributors   xi

**Introduction: reform and resistance in contemporary
China**   1
ELIZABETH J. PERRY AND MARK SELDEN

1 **Rights and resistance: the changing contexts of the dissident
   movement**   20
   MINXIN PEI

2 **Pathways of labor insurgency**   41
   CHING KWAN LEE

3 **Gender, employment and women's resistance**   62
   WANG ZHENG

4 **Migration, hukou and resistance in reform China**   83
   HEIN MALLEE

5 **Domination, resistance and accommodation in China's
   one-child campaign**   102
   TYRENE WHITE

6 **The 'externalities of development': can new political
   institutions manage rural conflict?**   120
   DAVID ZWEIG

7 **Environmental protests in rural China**   143
   JUN JING

 8 **Religion as resistance**   161
    STEPHAN FEUCHTWANG

 9 **Ethnic resistance with socialist characteristics**   178
    URADYN E. BULAG

10 **The revolution of resistance**   198
    GEREMIE R. BARMÉ

11 **Suicide as resistance in Chinese society**   221
    SING LEE AND ARTHUR KLEINMAN

    Index   241

Illustrations

Tables

1.1   An analysis of collective ordinary resistance in September and
      October 1998 (25 reported incidents)   26
1.2   An analysis of dissident resistance in September and October
      1998 (49 reported incidents)   27
1.3   International treaties/organizations China has signed/joined
      since 1980   32
1.4   Growth of litigation in China, 1978–1997 (cases accepted by
      the courts of first instance)   34
1.5   Civil lawsuits filed against violation of personal rights   36
1.6   Conception of sources of basic rights   37
6.1   Content of 30 cases of protest activity, 1989–1997   126

Boxes

4.1   The battle of words   86
4.2   'Seesaw warfare': the turbulent history of 'Zhejiang Village'   94

Contributors

Geremie R. Barmé is a Senior Fellow in the Division of Pacific and Asian History, Research School of Pacific and Asian Studies, The Australian National University. His most recent books are *In the Red, On Contemporary Chinese Culture* and *Shades of Mao: the Posthumous Cult of the Great Leader*. He was also an associate director and co-writer with John Crowley of the three-hour documentary on the events of 1989 in Beijing, 'The Gate of Heavenly Peace'.

Uradyn E. Bulag is Assistant Professor of Anthropology at Hunter College of the City University of New York. He is author of *Nationalism and Hybridity in Mongolia*.

Ching Kwan Lee is an Assistant Professor of Sociology at the University of Michigan, Ann Arbor. Her research interests focus on labor, gender, China and East Asia. She is author of *Gender and the South China Miracle* and is now working on a book on the remaking of the Chinese working class.

Stephan Feuchtwang is a Principal Research Associate in the Department of Anthropology, London School of Economics, University of London. He has published 30 articles and chapters on various topics in the anthropology of China and edited three volumes on economic reforms in China, but his main work to date has been *The Imperial Metaphor; Popular Religion in China*. He is currently completing a book with Wang Mingming on 'Grassroots Charisma in Rural China and Taiwan'.

Jun Jing is an Assistant Professor in the Department of Anthropology at the City College of the City University of New York. He is author of *The Temple of Memories: History, Power, and Morality in a Chinese Village*. A native of Beijing, he holds a PhD in Social Anthropology from Harvard University.

Arthur Kleinman is an anthropologist and psychiatrist who is Maude and Lillian Presley Professor of Medical Anthropology & Psychiatry and Chair, Department of Social Medicine, Harvard Medical School, and Professor of Social and Cultural Anthropology, Department of Anthropology, Harvard University. Kleinman has conducted field research in Chinese society for over 30 years, studying illness and health care in Taiwan (1968–79) and mental and social health problems in China (1978–present), including one of the first studies of survivors of China's Cultural Revolution. He recently co-edited (with Sing Lee and Joan Kleinman) an issue of *Culture, Medicine and Psychiatry* on 'Transformation of Everyday Social Experience in Chinese Communities' (Spring, 1999).

Hein Mallee completed a PhD dissertation on 'The Expanded Family: Rural Labour Circulation in Reform China' at Leiden University. He has worked for an NGO in China since 1997.

Minxin Pei is a Senior Associate at the Carnegie Endowment for International Peace in Washington, DC. He is the author of *From Reform to Revolution: The Demise of Communism in China and the Soviet Union*, and numerous articles on Chinese politics.

Elizabeth J. Perry is Henry Rosovsky Professor of Government and Director of the Fairbank Center for East Asian Research at Harvard University. She is the author of a number of books on popular protest in modern and contemporary China.

Mark Selden is Professor of Sociology at Binghamton University. His books include *China in Revolution: The Yenan Way Revisited, Chinese Village, Socialist State* and *The Political Economy of Chinese Socialism*.

Sing Lee is Senior Lecturer at the Department of Psychiatry, The Chinese University of Hong Kong, and Lecturer at the Department of Social Medicine, Harvard University. He is a psychiatrist with an anthropological orientation. His research interests include eating disorders, the social construction of psychiatric diagnosis, neurasthenia, lithium therapy, suicide, and other mental health problems and social change in Chinese society.

Wang Zheng received her college education in Shanghai and her PhD from the history department at UC Davis. She is the author of *Women in the Chinese Enlightenment: Oral and Textual Histories*. She is an Affiliated Scholar at the Institute for Research on Women and Gender at Stanford University.

Tyrene White is an Associate Professor of Political Science at Swarthmore College, Swarthmore PA. She has written widely on China's population policy and rural politics, and is co-editor, along with Christina Gilmartin, Gail Hershatter, and Lisa Rofel, of *Engendering China: Women, Culture and the State*.

David Zweig is Associate Professor in the Division of Social Science, Hong Kong University of Science and Technology and Research Associate of the Joint Centre on Asia–Pacific Studies, York University–University of Toronto. His books include: *Freeing China's Farmers: Restructuring Rural China in the Reform Era* and *Agrarian Radicalism in China, 1968–1981*. He co-edited *China's Search for Democracy: The Student and Mass Movement of 1989* and *New Perspectives on China's Cultural Revolution*. His current book project is tentatively titled *Linking China with the World: The Political Economy of Internationalization*.

Introduction

Reform and resistance in contemporary China

Elizabeth J. Perry and Mark Selden

Throughout the 1980s and 1990s, China has defied the best predictions of development economists and sinologists alike in compiling a stunning record of economic growth. This was accomplished in the face of formidable obstacles including inefficient state enterprises, ambiguous property rights, irrational prices, primitive transportation, and outmoded banking and securities facilities. Whether measured in per capita GDP, exports, income or induction of foreign capital, China's sustained double-digit growth since the late 1970s has been the world's envy. The result is that China was able to join a select group, including the East Asian Newly Industrializing Economies, which significantly improved their position in the world economy. And it did so at the very time when the former socialist economies of the Soviet Union and Eastern Europe were in ruins, even continuing its advance in the late 1990s, when other high-flying Asian economies experienced severe setbacks.

These achievements were not the product of some clear blueprint designed at the outset; rather, Chinese leaders aptly liken their approach to economic reform to 'crossing a river by groping for stones' – or improvising as they go. While economists have marveled at the growth achievements this flexible strategy has produced, rather less scholarly concern has been devoted to the social and political consequences and 'externalities' of the reform agenda, including galloping spatial and class inequality, the explosive growth of migrant labor, and loss of security and jobs for many state sector employees. Still less attention has been drawn to the conflicts that reform engendered, and the myriad arenas of resistance that have been its byproduct at every stage.[1] Ongoing patterns of conflict and resistance are not simply responses to reform initiatives; they have also stimulated and shaped significant dimensions of the reform program.

China's reform effort is a multifaceted process whose key elements include greater latitude for market, mobility, modernization, and internationalization. Viewed from the center, these policies are intended to transform Chinese socialism in ways that will accelerate economic growth, bolster Party authority, and strengthen China's international position. Viewed from the perspective of the diverse social forces promoting the reforms, they afford an opportunity to expand autonomy and facilitate a range of activities previously circumscribed by the party-state. For those who are disadvantaged or disappointed by elements of the reform program, however, the object is often to preserve the benefits and ideals of a bygone era. In sum, reforms generated both from above and from below have brought far-reaching, even revolutionary, changes to the economy, society, politics and culture, changes that touch every citizen and extend to every corner of the land and beyond to redefine China's place in the world.

Diverse patterns of conflict and resistance are directly attributable to the reforms, yet they are frequently rooted in historic contests and display time-honored beliefs and behaviors. Contention during the reform era has ranged from tax riots, labor strikes, and inter-ethnic riots, to pro-democracy demonstrations, environmental, anticorruption, and gender protests, local electoral challenges, and even mass suicides. In addition to overt conflicts that directly challenge the power, authority, and reach of the state, and increasingly that of capital as well, much everyday resistance is invisible.[2] It takes such forms as private acts of evasion, flight and foot dragging, which, in the absence of manifestos or marches, may nevertheless effectively enlarge the terrain of social rights. These acts, as well as direct legal challenges in growing numbers of court cases, persistently press at the margins of official power and raise the costs of state controls. In some instances, they may also strengthen the reform agenda, as in pressures to expand markets and mobility. The cumulative weight of these challenges has forced significant changes in law and social praxis in contemporary China, developments that have been largely missed by analysts whose vision is limited to the search for American-style democracy. The most striking of these shifts have taken place in economic, social and cultural realms, but the effects also extend to the political sphere.

This volume introduces contemporary Chinese society in the era of reform through examination of some of the dominant modes of resistance. Individual chapters trace the origins of different patterns of conflict to diverse sources: old and new, foreign and domestic, socialist and capitalist. Since much of this ferment is a product of the contemporary environment, we begin with a brief consideration of the main features of the reform effort.

Reform agendas and consequences

China's post-Mao reforms began officially with the Third Plenum of the Eleventh Party Congress in December of 1978 when the new leadership gave its blessing to the initial stages of the decollectivization of agriculture and the expanded scope of the market. Significant roots of reform can, however, be traced back to the years 1970–78, not only in the US–China diplomatic breakthrough and China's resumption of its place in the UN Security Council in 1970–71, but also in the rapid expansion of China's foreign trade, an agricultural modernization agenda from the 1970 North China Agricultural Conference, and the putative end of the Cultural Revolution with the 1971 death of Defense Minister Lin Biao, Mao's designated successor.

The centerpiece of post-Mao reform nevertheless was agricultural decollectivization and market opening, which proceeded by fits and starts between 1978 and 1982. Although land ownership has remained in collective hands to this day, individual households were permitted to sign contracts that afforded them effective control over the management, output, and marketing of agricultural production in exchange for payments in the form of crops and labor to the village, and taxes in kind to the state. China's 30-year experiment in collective farming was in essence repudiated in favor of a return to family farming, officially styled the Household Responsibility System (HRS). With pressures from below from villagers and some cadres to expand the scope of market, mobility, and household activity, and with increasing doubts at the center concerning the viability of collective agriculture, in just a few years virtually the entire countryside had dismantled collective agriculture in favor of some form of household contracting that restored the primacy of the family farm. In 1984, these contracts were deemed valid for 15 years; in 1993, they were extended to 30 years; and in 1998, President Jiang Zemin announced that contracts would remain in effect for at least an additional 30 years.

Alongside the HRS, the state sanctioned free markets, encouraged diversification of rural enterprises in the form of small-scale industry and handicrafts, relaxed restrictions on rural–urban migration, and substantially boosted state procurement prices for agricultural products in an effort to jump-start the rural economy. In each of these instances, the state now responded positively to pressures from below for the expanded scope of household and market that had built throughout the era of anti-market collective agriculture. The immediate result of this policy package, which included far more than decollectivization, was a huge spurt in agricultural output and the first major gains in rural income since the start of the collective era a quarter-century earlier. As farmers regained control of their labor power and the state relaxed prohibitions on markets and sideline production, rural labor and capital swiftly flowed in new channels and villagers experienced new earning opportunities.[3]

This did not constitute a complete break with the revolutionary era. Not only did land ownership continue to reside in collective hands, but there was also continuity in the managerial role of collectives, notably in directing rural industry and sideline production. The household economy had in fact never completely disappeared in Mao's China, as most families continued to cultivate individual plots of land. Hence foundations for reform existed in embryonic form throughout the countryside.

Perhaps the most dynamic response to the new opportunities presented by reform was the growth of township and village enterprises (TVEs) that mushroomed across the countryside. Many of the TVEs had their roots in earlier commune and brigade industries, but in the reform era under relatively open market conditions – including access to international markets and capital and with the infusion of migrant labor – they injected unprecedented dynamism into rural industry, notably in coastal and suburban regions. Over time, many of these collectively owned and operated enterprises have converted into share-holding companies (*gufen gongsi*) or private firms or joint ventures, including some with foreign investment.

Demand for labor mobility went hand in hand with pressures to relax the household registration (*hukou*) system that had segregated citizens by rigid categories designed to forestall rural-to-urban migration as well as to deter movement up the hierarchy of urban centers. Reform generally has allowed people the freedom to change their place of work and residence. But as 'outsiders' in the city or in richer agricultural areas, migrants face formidable official and unofficial restrictions in their new domicile and remain ineligible for many benefits enjoyed by those with legal urban registration. Despite the important contributions that migrant workers have made to China's economic growth, the state continues to view them as second class citizens, a 'floating population' and a potential source of unrest, and therefore denies them most of the benefits of urban registration. As their numbers soared into the range of fifty to one hundred million people, permanent urban residents also came to see the floaters as a source of crime and, increasingly, as a threat to their own jobs.

While economic and social transformations in much of the countryside were remarkably swift and far-reaching, urban industry proved more resistant to change. Because the state, rather than lower-level collectives, owned and operated the major urban factories, and depended heavily upon them as its primary source of revenue, it was wary of changes that might undermine its power economically and politically or call into question its important social base among the urban workers who had been among the major beneficiaries of the revolution. In particular, state leaders feared that moves which jeopardized the security and welfare benefits of workers at state-owned enterprises (SOEs), could precipitate widespread labor unrest. By contrast, villagers had enjoyed comparatively few state or other welfare benefits and were tightly controlled under the collective. From the late 1970s, as pressures mounted across the countryside to expand the scope of market and mobility and to curb the collective, workers in the city frequently resisted tendencies associated with reform as a direct threat to their income, security, and prestige.

Comparable phenomena of reform pressures emanating from the rural collective sector, accompanied by a coolness toward reform in state enterprises and cities, was evident in Vietnam in the 1980s and 1990s. By contrast, Soviet collective farm workers, who had gained the security and welfare benefits of industrial workers, staunchly resisted reforms that would weaken or eliminate collective farming.[4]

The initial suspicions of Chinese labor proved prescient. Not only did reform bring few gains to SOE workers, it also meant that industrial laborers lost status to rising entrepreneurs and eventually millions lost lifetime employment and even such welfare benefits as pensions that they had worked a lifetime to secure. Many who retained their jobs were required to sign contracts with their employers, frequently for 5 years, thereby severing the promise of lifetime employment. Neither the long-promised conversion of SOEs to shareholding corporations nor the forced bankruptcies of inefficient enterprises have yet to materialize fully, but with economic growth slowing in the late 1990s, massive layoffs have ensued nonetheless. Older and women workers have borne the brunt of dislocation and unemployment among SOE workers. Competition with joint ventures and private companies has further threatened the once hegemonic status of state industry.

The gap separating rich and poor, both between and within regions, has grown apace under the reforms. In contrast to industrial relocation to poorer and peripheral regions during the Mao era, Deng Xiaoping's reform heavily favored coastal over inland areas with state investment and privileged access to international capital and markets. And in contrast to earlier class leveling, reformers promoted and exalted the new rich. Indeed, by the 1990s some analysts concluded that China in the course of a few decades had moved from the ranks of the world's most egalitarian societies to one of the most unequal in its distribution of income, wealth, and opportunity.[5] Deng Xiaoping's famous adage that 'to get rich first is glorious,' has left many of the less fortunate distraught, angry, and wondering if their time will ever come. Such economic and social inequalities may be multiplied by distinctions of gender and ethnicity. In a context where increased mobility and greater media access have heightened awareness of income differentials and lavish conspicuous consumption, these disparities may prove explosive.

Reform has been accompanied by a relaxation of controls over economy and society in many, but not all, spheres. To ensure that economic gains are not entirely consumed by an ever burgeoning population, the state has imposed strict birth-control regulations, thus reaching directly into the nuclear family to regulate reproduction. In the face of an age-old preference for many children, especially sons whose responsibility is to assure the welfare of parents in their old age, the state insisted that couples limit themselves to a single offspring. The single-child policy is fraught with profound implications and complications for a society whose core cultural values are based largely on kinship relations and an emphasis on the filial obligation to assure family continuity through future generations, an act that requires a male offspring. The single-child policy achieved considerable success in the cities where most families could rely on state or collective welfare to provide for them in retirement. But in the countryside, where no such welfare regime existed, the one-child policy posed agonizing choices for households, generating fierce resistance that took such forms as flight to give birth to a second or higher child, female infanticide and, at times, murder of cadres or family members of cadres who had imposed forced abortions or sterilizations.

It is commonly asserted that, despite far-reaching economic and social reform, China's political system remains frozen. Many of the contributions to this volume suggest otherwise. In part to alleviate the uncertainties and anxieties that accompanied head-spinning changes in both the economic and social arenas, the state initiated sweeping legal reforms. A revised constitution promulgated in 1982, was followed by codes that provide guidelines on a host of issues ranging from labor relations to intellectual property rights, to the environment and commerce. A massive education campaign has been launched to publicize the new regulations. Mediation and arbitration offices, as well as the courts, have been beefed up to handle the escalating number of disputes in an effort to defuse conflicts that might otherwise produce violent confrontation. This is but one important sphere in which political and social relations are being redefined.

In keeping with its professed commitment to honor legal claims, symbolized by China's signing of international covenants on economic, social, and cultural rights as well as on civil and political rights, the state has announced support for religious freedom (albeit only for officially recognized and registered groups) and cultural autonomy for ethnic minorities (that is, for officially classified nationalities). It has also enlarged the scope of official tolerance for intellectual activities in literature, the arts, scholarship and journalism. In practice, official guarantees are periodically circumscribed, at times harshly, primarily out of security concerns, but also in response to concerns over 'cultural pollution' – the importing of deleterious alien concepts and ideas that might undermine officially approved values. Suspicion of subversive, separatist, sectarian, or even 'superstitious' activities has repeatedly elicited draconian state responses. Nevertheless, the combination of broad new legislation, changing social relations, and the thrust and counterthrust of resistance and repression, exert a significant political impact. And what are arguably the two most far-reaching political changes are largely invisible. First, since the late 1970s, the state has abandoned the mass mobilization political campaigns that were the hallmark of Chinese politics in the Mao era. Second, the state has withdrawn from direct control of large areas of the economy, thereby sharply reducing its ability to dominate the lives of ordinary people.

The highly touted elections for village committees illustrate both the logic and limits of political reform. Centrally sponsored democratic elections have apparently been successfully conducted in about half of China's nearly one million rural villages. But in a context in which opposition parties remain illegal, and the nomination process is closely monitored by Communist officials, such grassroots experiments exert minimal influence on the basic structure of power. Moreover, party secretaries, more than village committees, still rule. The Communist Party retains a monopoly over key instruments of control: propaganda, personnel, military, and police. The small officially sanctioned minority parties cultivated by the Communist Party throughout the People's Republic are pledged to loyalty to the ruling party. Publications are restricted by an elaborate system of party censorship, while the official ideology remains Marxism–Leninism–Mao Zedong Thought guided in practice by Deng Xiaoping Theory. And in the wake of the party's crackdown on the protests of 1989, it has moved aggressively to control signs of the emergence of political opposition, for example in its banning a decade later attempts to register a newly founded Democratic Party.

Despite significant changes, an apparent disjuncture remains between the free-wheeling economic expansion, on the one hand, and the still highly circumscribed political climate, on the other. Bustling stock exchanges, bountiful supermarkets, shimmering skyscrapers, and *au courant* electronic modes of communication, have not broken the grip of the omnipresent security system. In the decade since 1989, despite a plethora of strikes, protests, and everyday resistance, no largescale political movements have challenged Party rule. In fact, the forces of repression have grown in tandem with modernization, internationalization, and the new prosperity *for some*. The institution of the armed police (*wujing*) augments the public security bureau in maintaining order, and an espionage service once reserved for international assignments is now being deployed domestically down to the county level.

Conflict, cleavage, and contention

It is not surprising that the current situation, in which Maoist precepts are often neglected in practice but rarely formally negated, has seen the emergence of a polyphony of conflict and contention – among and between state authorities and elements of the populace. Although Maoism shared many features with Leninism and Stalinism, it was also distinctive in its avowed egalitarianism and populism, and in the contentious mobilization politics that it fostered in such periods as the Hundred Flowers Movement of 1956–57 and the Cultural Revolution (1966–76). The mass campaigns for which Maoist China was renowned have long since ended, but not without bequeathing a residual sense of entitlement and a repertoire of protest strategies that extend to even the most remote parts of the countryside and to people of all nationalities.

Of course, popular protest long predated the initiatives of Chairman Mao. Chinese history boasts a record of resistance and rebellion second to none. Whether we survey Imperial, Republican, or Communist periods, we can find ample evidence of defiance and dissent shading into rebellion and revolution. An intriguing question, therefore, concerns the degree to which recent events build (consciously or unconsciously) on earlier precedents. To what extent do the wellsprings of conflict and resistance in China today draw on patterns and practices of bygone days? To what extent have they changed in response to the imperatives of the reform era?

One important basis of comparison concerns the social composition of the participants. Although historians in the People's Republic during the Mao years celebrated the class nature of popular protest in China going back to the earliest recorded peasant uprisings (3rd century BC), analyses of Imperial-era protests by Western and some Chinese scholars have demonstrated the significance of kinship, village, and religious communities in structuring patterns of resistance. A debate has recently developed over whether new forms of community began to emerge in the late Imperial and early Republican periods (and whether they have re-emerged in the post-Mao era) as part of a nascent civil society. Some stress a growing sense of citizenship among ordinary Chinese, particularly urbanites. Others argue that, under the influence of Western imperialism and domestic capitalism, a proto-class consciousness developed that helped to fuel the Communist revolution.[6]

In the post-1949 period, Mao insisted, class continued to command center stage. He justified his Great Proletarian Cultural Revolution on the basis of the continued imperative of class struggle, but this was a class struggle of his own distinctive formulation, one necessary to topple 'those in authority taking the capitalist road'; that is, the enemies of Mao and of socialism as he construed it.

In exploring the roots of cleavages and conflicts in the reform era, the authors of this volume break with stereotypical categories drawn from pre-land reform society to analyze anew the bases and structures of inequality within the People's Republic. They find that not only class, but also gender, ethnicity, generation, and regional location constitute powerful sources of conflict and spurs to resistance in the reform era. These axes of contention intersect in ever changing and volatile ways. For example, as Wang Zheng points out, largescale layoffs of workers in state-owned enterprises in the 1990s have been disproportionately directed against older women, while Hein Mallee underscores the discriminatory treatment of rural migrants to the city. The chapters reveal how multiple intertwined factors shape social tensions and patterns of resistance.

This is not to suggest that the bases for conflict have been entirely reconfigured in the contemporary era. As Jun Jing, Stephan Feuchtwang, and David Zweig show, longstanding village and lineage loyalties continue to shape insurgent identities in rural China as social movements draw on themes and images sanctified by tradition even as they engage the consequences of reform. Popular religion and folk ideologies play pivotal roles in this process, with the beliefs and rituals surrounding local temples, deities, ancestral halls, and festivals often providing inspiration for collective mobilization. This may be the case even when the precipitant of protest, e.g., population relocation occasioned by the massive Three Gorges Dam project, is imbricated within a modernizing agenda associated with construction of the world's largest dam. In other words, traditional forms of contention are being revitalized in a new sociopolitical context, sometimes creating new public spaces with new economic bases.

The recourse to claims rooted in history can take many forms. In the conflict between Mongols and Han Chinese, as Uradyn Bulag demonstrates, the clash over land usage has been a continuing theme for more than a century. Mongol pastoralism has long been pitted against Chinese agrarianism and, more recently, industrialism. To buttress their competing positions, both groups have staked claims to indigenous status in the area that is now Inner Mongolia. Countering Han claims to represent a modern 'civilizing mission', Mongols have turned to their own linguistic, cultural, and historical traditions as weapons of resistance. Yet this longstanding dispute, which resonates with conflicts in other autonomous regions with large minority populations, has undergone substantial change in recent times as Chinese industries cast a covetous eye toward the natural resources hidden beneath the steppes and Mongols find themselves marginalized in proliferating industries in their autonomous region. The widening economic gap between coastal cities and the interior provinces further inflames resentment that includes, but is not limited to, minority peoples.

Significant strains in contemporary popular protest can be traced back to Imperial and Republican era precedents. There are, however, compelling models much closer at hand. Given the stark contrasts between the Maoist and post-Mao eras, the former has come to stand as a convenient foil for many of the disappointments of the latter, and protests often draw on themes and approaches honed during the land reform and Cultural Revolution.

Thus, when workers and women find themselves disadvantaged by the industrial reforms, they are quick to remind authorities (with considerable irony) of Cultural Revolution slogans and promises: 'The working-class must lead in everything!' and 'Women hold up half the sky!' On occasion, as Ching Kwan Lee describes, workers even adopt Cultural Revolution-style struggle tactics to press their demands against brutal or corrupt factory managers. And people of all classes, in bemoaning the rampant corruption of the present era, often recall nostalgically the high ethical standards and plain living of an earlier generation of revolutionaries.

The combination of seemingly ancient styles of protest with Maoist principles and practices can result in some extraordinary expressions of discontent.[7] Take a case which occurred a few years ago in several provinces in Southwest China. A group known as the 'Heavenly Soldiers Fraternal Army' (*tianbing dizijun*) recruited thousands of followers from more than one hundred villages. The group's leader, declaring himself a reincarnation of the Jade Emperor (a Daoist deity), practiced shamanistic rituals of spirit possession and exorcism. His disciples pledged to fight for a new, divine regime free from social classes, authorities, grades and ranks, and the like. If the popular religious elements have a seemingly venerable pedigree, the commitment to rid China of all forms of inequality is an obvious throwback to Cultural Revolution rhetoric.

In another intriguing resistance movement, the 29-year-old peasant leader claimed to be Mao Zedong's son who had come to lead a rural uprising. The would-be Mao penned treatises on the 'thirty great relationships' (Mao Zedong had limited himself to ten) and assumed the titles of party chairman, military commission chair, state chairman, political consultative conference chair, and premier, again surpassing Mao in the range of his official titles. He also sent letters to various government offices praising the radical ideas of the Gang of Four, attacking Deng Xiaoping's market socialism, and calling for armed rebellion, student boycotts and workers' strikes.

Even in what would appear to be the most 'traditional' of peasant uprisings, the slogans have a distinctly 'modern' ring to them. Take the case of a rebellion which got underway in the mid-1980s along the Yunnan–Guizhou border after its leader claimed, in the manner of Hong Xiuquan, commander of the Taiping Rebellion, the great millenarian uprising that rocked China in the mid-nineteenth century, that he had dreamed of an old man with a white beard who lent him a sacred sword. The contemporary insurgents slaughtered a chicken and swore a blood oath in the ancient manner of Chinese rebels, but alongside the age-old slogan of 'Steal from the rich to aid the poor,' they emblazoned their battle banners with new mottos: 'Support the left and oppose the right!' and 'Down with birth control!'

The syncretism of these recent movements is surely due in part to the quasi-religious dimensions assumed by the cult of Mao during the Cultural Revolution. As Feuchtwang emphasizes, political rituals of that era, such as recitation of the *Little Red Book of Mao Quotations* and performance of loyalty dances, helped to blur the distinction between older forms of worship and new Communist practices. Moreover, collective loyalties fostered in that period can serve today as bases for resistance to higher-level state demands.

A theme that runs through many of the chapters in this volume is the pivotal – and often contradictory – role played by local authorities in relation to popular resistance. We find party officials articulating and defending the interests of retirees in their village (Zweig), union officials siding with disgruntled workers (C. K. Lee), birth control officials colluding with prospective parents (Tyrene White), Mongol officials defending indigenous rights against the claims of Chinese migrants (Bulag), local officials leading villagers in demanding compensation from polluting enterprises (Jing), and so on. In short, while local officials frequently crack down on popular resistance, in numerous cases their leadership is instrumental in shaping, legitimating and articulating the demands of social movements. It was, of course, precisely such leadership bifurcations that made possible the persistence and violence of the Cultural Revolution, and that lent strength to earlier rebel and revolutionary movements. Breaches in the loyalties of grassroots authorities are of enormous concern to the central government. Indeed, fears on the part of central leaders about renegade local officials help to explain Beijing's adoption of such policies as legal reform, anticorruption drives, and village elections that provide legitimate state-sanctioned channels to vent and adjudicate grievances. Yet, as Zweig reports, grassroots officials are often loath to respond to such institutional initiatives.

The dramatic recrudescence of organized crime, often with police complicity, is another symptom of the contradictions and contentions that are products of reform. Active in both urban and rural areas on a scale unknown in the early decades of the People's Republic, criminal gangs oversee drug smuggling, trafficking of people, gambling and prostitution rings, extortion, robbery, and more. The upsurge in such activities is attributable to several factors attendant upon the reforms: increased population mobility, high levels of surplus labor and unemployment, growing income disparities, access to previously unavailable economic resources, and declining civic values. Independent financial bases for criminals render government efforts at repression increasingly difficult.

Reform and the future of Chinese communism

Does the rich and multi-faceted history of contemporary resistance augur the demise of China's reform-minded Communist Party? It is difficult to know whether 'liberal' initiatives, from economic reform to judicial reform to village elections, are serving to shore up, or to further erode, central government and party control. What is certain is that they are transforming the nature and terrain of state-society relations, leading some analysts to see the emergence of a 'soft authoritarianism' and even to speak of the advance of democratizing processes within the Chinese polity. Despite the fact that the Communist Party retains *de facto* veto and *de jure* power over the enforcement of laws and electoral results, reform measures have opened new space for expressing local interests and checking arbitrary abuses.

Particularly telling is the retreat of the state from direct control over many aspects of life and labor. The day-to-day economic activities of one billion villagers are no longer closely regulated by collective and commune officials as people turn their energies to farming, industrial or sideline activities, undertake to organize family or joint enterprises, or migrate far from home.

As Minxin Pei and David Zweig explain, legal reforms have set limits on state prerogatives at the same time that they have encouraged greater expectations about, and provided an institutional framework for, the protection of rights among the populace at large. The growing numbers of lawsuits filed against government and party officials in the 1990s are symptomatic of this emergent sense of entitlement. Moreover, the significant number of strikes and other clashes notwithstanding, labor and many other disputes are most commonly settled in newly established arbitration committees rather than in the streets. But laws, of course, are at least as useful to state authorities as to dissidents. The state security law, for example, sanctions the arbitrary arrest of anyone suspected of subversive motives.

Grassroots elections are also a two-edged sword for the state. State leaders hope that such procedures will help curb the corrupt excesses of local tyrants and thereby dampen the fires of rebellion in the countryside. Yet giving villagers an enlarged sense of their own political efficacy, and providing a public forum for open discussion of civic affairs, can also act to stimulate local resistance to higher-level dictates. At a 1999 local election monitored by the Carter Center, for example, voters vociferously protested a nomination process that they considered to have been rigged by party authorities.

While official elections have been closely watched in the West, the more important village activities are probably those sparked by the numerous new associations ranging from religious and sectarian groups to credit societies and cultural associations that operate quite independent of the state. In the cities as well, as Geremie Barmé suggests, intellectuals who were preoccupied with issues of democratic transition and state authority in the late 1980s, by the 1990s had turned their attention to cultural discussions that seem quite removed from direct political confrontation. Yet such debates may of course also work to undercut Party hegemony.

Internationalization

One of the most striking aspects of the reform era is the depth and multiplicity of China's engagement with the world. Whereas Cultural Revolution China was a relatively autarkic society, today the links to the rest of the globe are extra-ordinarily dense. Foreign television programs dominate the air waves in even remote reaches of the countryside and American fast food franchises dot the urban landscape. International capital defines leading sectors of economy and finance. Global fashions in everything from designer jeans to perfume to appliances make their presence felt in town and countryside alike. And pop music reverberates to the beat of Hong Kong and Taiwan musicians.

The implications of internationalization are far reaching and contradictory. Access to the global market has equipped the military and public security agencies with state-of-the-art electronic and communications technology. At the same time, however, the reforms have brought fax machines, personal computers, and internet access not only to state and businesses but also to intellectuals and activists, thereby facilitating contacts with foreign scholars, human rights organizations, and the international media. Such ties, of course, expand the information available to outsiders concerning Chinese domestic affairs while facilitating dissident communications. The role of the international community in publicizing Chinese human rights abuses has been one outcome. But this does not begin to exhaust the implications. As Barmé indicates, the debates among domestic intellectuals and critics have been profoundly shaped by their exposure to international discourse.

As foreigners assume a higher profile in China – whether as suppliers of capital and technology and purveyors of cultural and consumer styles, as human rights advocates, or simply as tourists – they inevitably alter the balance of power. Foreigners as well as Chinese sightseers streaming to religious centers, Feuchtwang suggests, can trigger conflict within the state between public security officials concerned about maintaining social order and a cultural apparatus intent on promoting local traditions for economic as well as aesthetic reasons.

Contradictions of reform

In short, the reforms have stimulated contradictory currents that elicit a melange of old and new responses. Strict birth control policies gave rise initially to tragic, yet historically familiar, practices of female infanticide and abandonment as desperate villagers sought to ensure that their one child would be a boy. However, as White shows, these tactics have been largely supplanted by new strategies such as sex-selective abortion, enabled by state-of-the-art ultra-sound technology. Similarly the protest against a dangerously polluting fertilizer factory, detailed by Jing, erupted only after a government medical team educated the villagers about the link between water pollution and birth defects. Sympathetic township officials not only sanctioned the worship of fertility goddesses to combat the pollutants, they also allowed village cadres to mobilize demonstrations forcing the fertilizer factory to solve the problems resulting from its wanton discharge of toxic waste and compensate the community for damages.

Relaxation of the household registration system, complementing the reform of agriculture and industry, has greatly complicated state control. Since the 1980s, migrant workers have provided the labor for many of the most productive and income-producing industries (Mallee). The option of flight from local authorities makes it much easier to evade the family planning policy (White). Migrant workers constitute a new source of labor unrest, notably in Special Economic Zones, like Shenzhen, where their numbers have skyrocketed (C. K. Lee). And the continued growth in the number of migrant workers at a time of rising urban unemployment brings into direct conflict the interests of urban and rural workers who once occupied different niches on the employment ladder with migrants assuming jobs disdained by urban residents (Mallee, Wang).

Whether using tested tactics from bygone days or innovative strategies of a new era, protests are seldom undertaken lightheartedly in contemporary China. The tremendous personal risk implicit in any confrontation with authority is a serious deterrent. Perhaps no action demonstrates this dilemma more poignantly than the ultimate recourse: suicide. Sing Lee and Arthur Kleinman report that the number of suicides in reform-era China is extremely high. While the rate of suicides among certain categories of people almost certainly reached even more dizzying heights during the Cultural Revolution, the current figures – based for the first time on valid data – are of particular concern inasmuch as they indicate patterns rarely found elsewhere in the world. The victims fall into two high risk groups: young, rural females; and elderly men and women. It cannot be determined on current evidence alone whether this is a new pattern or a continuation of one found in earlier Chinese history; but the contemporary precipitants of suicide do seem to be closely connected to local social problems brought on or intensified by the reform era.

Resistance, revolution, and China's future

Along with rising per capita incomes and remarkable affluence for some, China's reforms and their attendant economic growth have brought anxiety and anguish to many. What does this situation augur for the future of state-society relations? Is Chinese society a ticking time bomb, about to detonate the Communist state? Have the wide-ranging patterns of resistance and pressures for change from below generated a fundamental transformation in popular consciousness or in the state–society relationship? Or are the signs of discontent so small, scattered, and (in some cases, literally) suicidal as to pose little threat to the survival of the political system?

Social science theories provide few signposts that allow us to specify with confidence the conditions under which social conflict may become politically destabilizing and even regime threatening. Individual personalities and historical contingencies – factors which remain stubbornly immune to the best predictive efforts of social scientists – play a decisive role in translating popular unrest into political challenge or political and social transformation.

As this volume indicates, there is plenty of dissatisfaction in contemporary China, some of it attributable to grievances built up during the earlier Mao era, but much traceable directly or indirectly to the effects of the reform policies. The very economic successes of these policies have encouraged 'rising expectations' that could (*à la* Crane Brinton) not only spark protest but might ultimately prove revolutionary.[8] Moreover, the growing gap between greater and lesser beneficiaries of the reforms has clearly fostered among the less fortunate a sense of 'relative deprivation' (*à la* Ted Robert Gurr)[9] that generates not only individual frustration but may also, at times, lead to collective violence. If the economy were to suffer a sudden downturn after its steep gains of recent years, as eventually it surely will if history is any guide, it would then resemble James Davies' 'J-Curve'[10] – a situation said to be replete with revolutionary potential. And China's high–speed growth has produced deepening class polarization, the very outcomes that Karl Marx pinpointed as the prerequisites for resistance and revolution.

The chapters in this volume present evidence of all of these patterns at work, giving rise to diverse forms of everyday resistance as well as strikes, protests, riots and other types of organized and unorganized protest. Does this mean that China stands poised at the brink of revolution, auguring the overthrow of the Chinese Communist Party and a passage either into system disintegration and civil war or reunification under another political banner? The problem with the diverse theories sketched briefly above is that, while suggestive for analyzing the psychological and material roots of protest, resistance, rebellion and revolution, none specifies the threshold point at which popular aspirations and grievances gain sufficient momentum to become politically threatening. Thus, however useful the theories may be in offering explanations for what occurred after the fact, they offer little predictive value.

Approaches that focus on the state, more than the societal, side of the revolutionary equation (Charles Tilly, Theda Skocpol, Jack Goldstone, Mark Lupher)[11] direct our attention to critical issues of state capacity to administer and to repress. Revolution is contingent not only on social discontent, but also on the ability to mobilize people and resources effectively to exploit state weakness and ineptitude, and state capacity to counter such challenges. Here we move beyond the psychological to the political arena, but still without a clear vision – until we attain the vantage point of twenty-twenty hindsight – of the actual dividing line between state capacity and incapacity.

What is striking is the fact that for all the popular anguish and the variety and depth of contemporary protest, to date no significant organizational focus, whether enshrined in a political party or social movement, has emerged at the regional, national, or even local level to effectively challenge Communist Party leadership. Moreover, the Chinese state has important residual strengths. In contrast, for example, to the Soviet-imposed regimes of much of Eastern Europe, China's Communist Party led a popular resistance against Japanese invasion en route to the founding of the People's Republic. And in contrast to the Communist-led regimes that collapsed or were overthrown in Eastern Europe in the late 1980s and 1990s, China's Communist Party can claim credit for several decades of rapid economic growth and income gains. The result has been growing international power and prestige as China assumes a wider role as a regional and in certain respects even a global power.

Equally important has been the Communist Party's ability to absorb some of the most powerful complaints of its critics without yielding its grip on state power. The state has accommodated demands for expanding the market and the private sector as well as enlarging the scope of the legal system, and has even sponsored elections at the grassroots levels. Nevertheless, far from quelling social protest, these achievements have arguably stimulated it.

Recently, analysts have advanced a tripod of concepts to account for the emergence of powerful social movements: political opportunity structure, mobilizational networks, and collective action 'framing' (or cultural/symbolic interpretation).[12] This 'political process approach' has sensitized scholars to a wider array of relevant factors in generating social movements, ranging from the political climate to social connections to symbolic constructions. Like earlier theories, it offers scant likelihood of forecasting the outcomes of social protest. It does, however, draw attention, in assessing the salience of social movements, to the need to examine not only the nature and levels of discontent in society or the strength, resources, and flexibility of the state, but also the concrete opportunities, organizations, and outlook of would-be protesters.

The chapters of this volume provide insight into all of these dimensions. In terms of opportunities, we learn for example about ways in which ordinary people have taken advantage of new openings afforded by the legal reforms to press previously untenable claims against officials. In terms of organization, we discover the continuing importance of lineage and village membership in structuring a range of activities from environmental protests to tax riots, ethnic protests, and demands for relocation compensation. In terms of outlook, we find that popular religion and historical myths, Maoist ideology, and international discourse, sometimes intertwined in unexpected combinations, all play significant roles in inspiring and sustaining resistance and in creating spaces autonomous from, and at times directly challenging, state power and discursive formulations (Bulag, Jing, Zweig, Feuchtwang, Barmé).

At present these diverse strains of resistance take the form of single issue conflicts. Resistance movements are for the most part quite isolated from one another, lacking interconnective ideological and organizational bonds. The fragmentation of the Chinese economy, with the decollectivization of agriculture and the increasing privatization of industry, has brought greater social segmentation as well. As the living and working conditions of various groups of Chinese citizens become increasingly heterogeneous, their relations to – and dissatisfactions with – the demands of state and market diverge accordingly. Consequently, the laments of laid-off workers do not readily resonate with the outcries of over-taxed farmers or the complaints of critical intellectuals, or the protests of minority nationalities or women. Facing very different dilemmas, these diverse groups among today's protesters frame their grievances and demands in distinctive terms that do not easily transcend the barriers of class, region, gender, nationality, or educational level. Still less has resistance taken the form of a significant political party or social movement that transcends a single locality or addresses multiple issues, or offers a comprehensive ideological or organization challenge to Communist Party rule.

New Social Movement theory (as developed by Alberto Melucci, Alain Touraine, and others) celebrates the cultural creativity and tactical virtuosity born of such diversity.[13] The post-modern condition, they tell us, is inherently fragmented. Even globalization, indeed precisely globalization, breeds local-ization. At the same time, however, the annals of Chinese history stand as a reminder of the power of social cooperation. Alliances among previously disparate categories of intellectuals, farmers, workers, women, youths, minorities, and so forth have served as the building blocks for influential protests, some of which eventually toppled the reigning order from imperial rebellions through the revolution of 1911 to the Communist revolution of 1949.

To be sure, such mergers may harbor the seeds of hegemony in which 'liber-ation' from the ancient regime can mean an even more repressive and preemptive fate in the hands of the victors. A party that rides to power on the waves of mass mobilization, while claiming to represent the will of the people, may rule in the interests of a limited few. Nor is revolutionary victory any guarantee that a nation locked in the grip of poverty will improve its position within the hierarchical order of inequality of the world economy, still less that it will shake that international order to its roots. Nevertheless, diverse alliances are the *sine qua non* of politically consequential social movements. And the paucity of such connective webs in the case of recent Chinese protests bespeaks a fundamental weakness in their capacity to challenge state power beyond the realm of the single issues and local grievances that remain their strength.

Of course, the absence of ecumenical movements in contemporary China is hardly accidental. As astute students of their own history, Chinese leaders are perfectly aware of the dangers inherent in cross-class, cross-nationality, and cross-regional associations. Since the founding of the People's Republic, attempts to forge such bonds have been dealt with swiftly and severely. The crackdown against the Falungong movement in 1999 is only the latest in a series of suppression efforts that includes the Anti-Rightist Campaign of 1957, the crushing of Cultural Revolution rebels in 1967–68, the closing of Democracy Wall in 1979, and the June Fourth Massacre of 1989 among others. In all of these instances, repression was a response to state fears that protest could give rise to inter-class and inter-regional connections.

This is not to say that state–society relations have remained frozen throughout the duration of the Communist era. Far from it. The revolution itself generated fundamental social changes, destroying the power of landlord, merchant, and industrial classes, undermining the status and influence of intellectuals, raising the status of the industrial working class while curbing its political autonomy, and elevating the new cadre class, dividing city from countryside, and reorgan-izing agriculture on collective foundations and industry on state foundations, to the detriment of China's villagers. The socioeconomic transformations of the reform era have been equally powerful. Despite the survival of the single party system, the situation today differs markedly from that which prevailed during the Mao era. And nowhere is this difference more obvious than in the realm of popular protest. A 1998 press account captured the distinction in an article whose headline read 'Emboldened Chinese take their complaints to the streets':

About 200 demonstrators blocked traffic in the central Chinese city of Changsha this week protesting over not getting paid in the past six months by a local, formerly state-owned company. The police showed up to help unsnarl traffic, but not to intervene in the demonstrations.

Last week 200 angry investors who lost their savings in a government-linked futures trading scheme marched to Tiananmen Square and demanded their money back. Police formed a line between them and the square, but allowed them to pass peacefully.

. . . From striking cab drivers to disgruntled farmers, more and more people are taking their economic frustrations to the streets of China . . . Instead of beating and arresting protesters as they might have some years ago, officials seem more willing these days to accommodate, negotiate or simply pay them off. As long as demonstrators don't make personal attacks against top leaders or demand political change, they are often free to vent their anger.[14]

As the chapters in this volume make clear, demonstrations are but one weapon in a vast arsenal of resistance and protest techniques that include legal challenges and silent pressures on the sociopolitical system in defense of enlarged claims by diverse groups. In recent years incidents of worker protest have been legion, and in some instances the state has permitted and legitimated protest directed toward local officials and private capital even as it seeks to create non-confrontational channels for resolving conflicts.

Under the reforms, economic protests have become increasingly routinized. As the state assumes less responsibility for running the economy, it has become more willing to tolerate economic criticism and worker protest. Demonstrations over back wages, lost investments, and so forth are less apt to elicit harsh state repression and more likely to gain a sympathetic hearing from concerned authorities than was true in Mao's China. Such public outbursts serve as important signals to a government whose reform program is very much a work in progress, seeking to navigate the shoals of sharply conflicting and potentially destablilizing class and group interests in a period of explosive social change.

The establishment in recent years of hundreds of thousands of arbitration committees to resolve labor disputes is an important sign of the state's attempt to regularize channels of economic conflict. Advocates of moderation in the All-China Federation of Trade Unions, the Ministry of Civil Affairs, and other official agencies have argued that demonstrations, arbitrations, and village elections not only provide a safety-valve for disgruntled citizens, but also serve as correctives to misguided policies and corrupt administration. Nonetheless, the Communist Party's virtual monopoly on power and the weak institutional foundations for citizens' rights to assemble and organize, produce a situation in which the state periodically expands and contracts the terrain of protest and resistance.

The past 150 years of Chinese history, not least the half century of the People's

Republic, has been a period of extraordinary contention. These years have witnessed the growth of diverse organized and unorganized challenges to state power, ranging from democratic, communist and anarchist movements to labor, peasant and nationality protests, and from religiously inspired uprisings to individual and private acts of everyday resistance. For their part, successive states have sought to maintain power by means of strategies ranging from fierce repression to cooptation and institutional adaptation. Periods of repression have often alternated with periods of relaxation, a pattern that has continued through the reform era.

China's reform leadership has presided over an era of rapid and far-reaching economic growth and equally profound social change. The pluralization of channels to wealth and power has given rise to new social formations and new political channels both independent of and interacting with the Communist Party. Diverse new social movements have responded to the imperatives of the day with new claims on the state and on private capital, some of which pose direct challenges to Communist Party rule. Like earlier regimes, China's reform leaders oscillate between the extremes of political repression and a willingness to tolerate local protest and social movements that do not directly challenge their own claims to power. But as they grope their way across the river of reform, the stones underfoot appear ever more slippery.

Notes

1 But see, in addition to the other contributions of authors in the present volume, Greg O'Leary (ed.), *Adjusting to Capitalism. Chinese Worker and the State* (Armonk: M.E. Sharpe, 1998), Xiaobo Lu and Elizabeth J. Perry (eds), *Danwei: The Changing Chinese Workplace in Historical and Comparative Perspective* (Armonk: M.E. Sharpe, 1997); David Zweig, *Freeing China's Farmers. Rural Restructuring in the Reform Era* (Armonk: M.E. Sharpe, 1997); Mark Selden, *The Political Economy of Chinese Development* (Armonk: M.E. Sharpe, 1993); Barrett McCormick and Jonathan Unger (eds), *China After Socialism. In the Footsteps of Eastern Europe or East Asia?* (Armonk: M.E. Sharpe, 1996); and Merle Goldman and Roderick MacFarquhar (eds), *The Paradox of China's Post-Mao Reforms* (Cambridge, MA: Harvard University Press, 1999).
2 See James C. Scott, *Weapons of the Weak. Everyday Forms of Peasant Resistance* (New Haven: Yale University Press, 1985) and *Domination and the Arts of Resistance: Hidden Transcripts* (New Haven: Yale University Press, 1990); Forrest Colburn (ed.), *Everyday Forms of Peasant Resistance* (Armonk: M. E. Sharpe, 1989).
3 On the nature and impact of the reform see, in addition to works cited above, Elizabeth J. Perry and Christine Wong (eds), *The Political Economy of Reform in Post-Mao China* (Cambridge: The Council on East Asian Studies/Harvard University, 1985); Joseph Fewsmith, *Dilemmas of Reform in China. Political Conflict and Economic Debate* (Armonk: M.E. Sharpe, 1994); Barry Naughton, *Growing Out of the Plan. Chinese Economic Reform 1978–1993* (Cambridge: Cambridge University Press, 1995); Deborah Davis and Ezra Vogel (eds), *Chinese Society on the Eve of Tiananmen. The Impact of Reform* (Cambridge: The Council on East Asian Studies/Harvard University, 1990); Stephan Feuchtwang, Athar Hussain and Thierry Pairault (eds), *Transforming China's Economy in the Eighties* (Boulder: Westview, 1988) 2 vols.
4 Mark Selden, 'After Collectivization: Continuity and Change in Rural China,' in Ivan Szelenyi (ed.), *Privatizing the Land: Rural Political Economy in Post-Communist Societies*

(London: Routledge, 1998); Benedict Kerkvliet and Mark Selden, 'Agrarian Trans-formations in China and Vietnam,' in Anita Chan, Benedict Kerkvliet and Jonathan Unger (eds), *Transforming Asian Socialism: China and Vietnam Compared* (Melbourne: Allen and Unwin, 1999); Mark Selden, 'Pathways From Collectivization: Post-Socialist Agrarian Alternatives in Russia and China,' in Barrett McCormick and Jonathan Unger (eds), *China After Socialism: In the Footsteps of Eastern Europe or East Asia?*

5 *China: National Human Development Report. Human Development and Poverty Alleviation 1997* (Beijing: United Nations Development Programme, 1998).

6 See for example the contributions to the symposium '"Public Sphere"/"Civil Society" in China?', *Modern China*, 19, 3 April 1993; Jeffrey Wasserstrom and Elizabeth J. Perry (eds), *Popular Protest and Political Culture in Modern China* 2nd edition (Boulder: Westview, 1994); Deborah Davis, *et al.* (eds), *Urban Spaces in Contemporary China: The Potential for Autonomy and Community* (Cambridge: Cambridge University Press, 1995). The debate was in part sparked by Jurgen Habermas' influential *The Structural Transformation of the Public Sphere: An Inquiry into a Category of Bourgeois Society* (Cambridge: MIT Press, 1989) and by the movements of 1989 in China.

7 The following cases are drawn from Li Kaifu (ed), *Xingshi fanzui anli congshu – fangeming zui* (Compilation of criminal cases – counterrevolutionary crimes) (Beijing: Chinese Procuracy Press, 1992).

8 Crane Brinton, *The Anatomy of Revolution* (New York: Vintage, [1938] 1965).

9 Ted Robert Gurr, *Why Men Rebel* (Princeton: Princeton University Press, 1970).

10 James C. Davies, *When Men Revolt and Why* (New Brunswick: Transaction, 1997).

11 Charles Tilly, *From Mobilization to Revolution* (Reading, MA: Addison-Wesley, 1978); Theda Skocpol, *States and Social Revolutions* (Cambridge: Cambridge University Press, 1979); Jack A. Goldstone, *Revolution and Rebellion in the Early Modern World* (Berkeley: University of California Press, 1991); Mark Lupher, *Power Restructuring in China and Russia* (Boulder: Westview, 1996).

12 Doug McAdam, John D. McCarthy, and Mayer N. Zald (eds), *Comparative Perspectives on Social Movements: Political Opportunities, Mobilizing Structures, and Cultural Framings* (Cambridge: Cambridge University Press, 1996.)

13 Alberto Melucci, *Nomads of the Present: Social Movements and Individual Needs in Contemporary Society* (Philadelphia: Temple University Press, 1989).

14 *Baltimore Sun*, November 20, 1998, p. 34A.

1   Rights and resistance

The changing contexts of the dissident movement

Minxin Pei

This study of the dissident movement in post-Mao China shows that the level of rights conciousness may be an important underlying cause of the increasing resistance waged by China's small but resilient dissident community. It further contends that rights consciousness rises as repression ebbs. Rights consciousness not only increases the frequency of resistance, but changes the forms of such resistance. In the Chinese case, the forms and tactics of democratic resistance have undergone significant changes since the late 1970s. While the dissident movement in the 1980s favored direct and confrontational methods of resistance, the same movement in the late 1990s began to rely increasingly on indirect and legal means.

Although it is premature to evaluate the effectiveness of the new tactics, this chapter attempts to place the newly transformed dissident movement in political, institutional, and social context. Politically, China's extensive and deepening integration into the international system in general, and its various commitments to international laws and institutions in particular, have placed leaders under new constraints and provided dissidents with new sources of moral support. Legal reform has also created a new legitimate political arena in which the dissident movement can challenge the regime, and the rising level of rights consciousness in Chinese society provides a more hospitable social milieu within which invocations of rights are more likely to gain broad-based support.

Oppression and resistance are symbiotic political acts – one almost never occurs without the other. Even the most oppressive regime, such as the one portrayed in George Orwell's *1984*, fails to eradicate resistance completely. Although resistance – ranging from dramatic and sometimes violent confrontations with the authorities to 'everyday forms of resistance' may not succeed in overthrowing oppressive regimes, such acts of defiance help preserve individual dignity and set limits to oppression.[1] Those whose works celebrate resistance in all forms may have bolstered our faith in the strength of the human spirit. But at the empirical level, the scholarship on resistance has not shed much light on the precise relationship between oppression and resistance. We are not sure, for example, about whether more oppression elicits greater resistance or vice versa; we know still less about the conditions that produce successful resistance.

This relationship poses an especially intriguing problem for social scientists because it is central to understanding the politics of reform in a liberalizing authoritarian regime. The most insightful observer of the French Revolution, Alexis de Tocqueville, was perhaps the first to hint at a possible connection between declining oppression and growing resistance. In one of his most quoted passages in *The Old Regime and the French Revolution*, de Tocqueville wrote:

> The social order overthrown by a revolution is almost always better than the one immediately preceding it. Only consummate statecraft can enable a King to save his throne when after a long spell of oppressive rule he sets to improving the lot of his subjects. Patiently endured so long as it seemed beyond redress, a grievance comes to appear intolerable once the possibility of removing it crosses men's minds. For the mere fact that certain abuses have been remedied draws attention to the others and they now appear more galling; people may suffer less, but their sensibility is exacerbated.[2]

Tocqueville's formulation identifies a sudden change in the sensibility of the people as the cause for a dramatic fall in the public tolerance of the practices of the regime that used to be accepted with resignation. What de Tocqueville called 'sensibility' seems very similar to 'rights consciousness' in the parlance of social scientists. Unfortunately, although he alerted us to the paradoxical effects of political opening by a softening autocracy, de Tocqueville's own analysis overlooked other important issues on oppression and resistance: why rights consciousness rises quickly in an autocratic regime undergoing partial political opening; which specific factors contribute to this change; how changes in rights consciousness affect the forms and tactics of resistance; how changes in the balance of power or control of resources between the state and society may result from regime-initiated reform to produce a more favorable outcome in the contest between the regime and its societal opponents.

It is of theoretical and practical importance to raise these questions in analyzing the changing relationship between the Chinese government and its citizens in general, and the evolving patterns of conflict between the ruling Chinese Communist Party (CCP) and its domestic critics in particular. For many students of Chinese politics have observed that, despite a considerable fall in the level of overt political repression since the late 1970s, the degree of resistance against the postcommunist authoritarian regime appears to have risen steadily over the same period.[3] The most dramatic expression of resistance was, without doubt, the Tiananmen Square demonstrations in 1989 that posed the most serious threat to the survival of the regime in the post-Mao era. But Tiananmen 1989 was a rare event (as was the violent repression unleashed by the regime in response). Most forms of the post-Mao resistance did not directly endanger the existence of the ruling regime. There are few signs suggesting that popular resistance has reached such a level as to portend an imminent revolution. Nevertheless, despite the absence of revolution, China's limited reform has created enough public space to permit a small but tenacious dissident movement persistently to challenge the political legitimacy of the ruling regime.[4]

This chapter explores the factors that have indirectly contributed to the endurance, growth, and change in resistance by China's pro-democracy activists. Such resistance must be understood in the overall context of the dramatic institutional, socioeconomic, and political changes that China has experienced since the 1980s. While no single cause should be credited with increasing the degree of rights consciousness of the Chinese people in general, and that of the dissident community in particular, I argue that a multiplicity of factors has decidedly reshaped the contexts within which rights consciousness is engendered. More importantly, the changing contextual factors have not only influenced the emergence of new norms that give more specific meanings to certain rights, but reduced the institutional and structural barriers that previously impeded the full protection and exercise of such human rights, enabling resisters to adopt novel means of defiance. In the first section of this study, I briefly discuss the idea of rights and the relationship between rights and resistance in the Chinese context. Then I trace the evolution of dissident resistance since reform began in 1979. Finally, I analyze the socioeconomic, legal, international, and political–psychological contexts within which such resistance has been waged.

Rights and resistance

In theory, the relationship between rights and resistance appears straightforward: individuals or groups of individuals who feel either entitled to and/or endowed with certain fundamental rights may be expected to put up resistance when such rights are violated or perceived to be violated. The stronger the feeling of entitlement and/or endowment, the stronger the resistance. The more rights are claimed by individuals or groups, the more likely resistance will be triggered as government action infringes on them. In reality, however, both the definition of rights and the degree of rights consciousness are problematic and contingent on historical, cultural, and political contexts within which such concepts are invoked. Students of Chinese politics and legal history, for example, have long noted some of the important differences in the meaning, nature, scope, and utility of rights. According to Andrew Nathan, rights in China are derived from citizenship/membership instead of humanity, treated as programmatic goals instead of claims on government, restricted by state power, and unprotected by independent judicial review.[5] This restrictive conceptualization of rights creates apparent inconsistencies in rights practices. For example, even though Chinese constitutions grant extensive rights in theory, the state has maintained tight control over how these rights are exercised in reality.[6] The central goal of the extension of rights to individuals, moreover, is not the protection of individuals against the state, but the better fulfilment of duties to the state by individuals. This state-centered notion of rights, Nathan argues, is a product of Chinese obsession with a weak state since the mid-nineteenth century. Consequently, the strengthening of the state and the restoration of political order were viewed by Chinese rights thinkers as the more important collective goal.[7]

Other scholars have detected a strong influence of utilitarianism and collectivism on the Chinese conceptualization of rights. Chinese often conceive of rights as interests. An important political consequence of this conception is that political legitimacy does not derive from popular sovereignty but from the government's ability to serve the interests of the people. Another consequence is the inherent bias in this conception in favor of collective interests (rights) over individual rights (interests), especially if the two should come into conflict.[8] Thus, reciprocity becomes a central principle: an individual may possess and enjoy certain rights only to the extent that he or she has fulfilled certain duties to the community and the ruler.[9]

The conceptual differences between Chinese and Western notions of rights, however, must not be exaggerated. Even though such differences may influence rights practices, the extent to which rights are respected and protected may depend more on political conditions than on concepts of rights. In particular, the political milieu of a society may profoundly affect the degree of rights consciousness. Since rights consciousness is never static, individuals may assess the extent of the protection, exercise and enjoyment of rights on the basis of various political signals they receive from the governing élite, from the international environment, and from society in general. Therefore, the level of rights consciousness may be low when the possibility of rights protection and enjoyment is judged to be dim, and high when the same possibility improves. This reasoning may explain the paradoxical relationship between falling repression and rising resistance observed first by Tocqueville, whose insights provide a persuasive explanation for the patterns of repression and resistance in contemporary China.

If the Maoist era is identified with the most massive and systematic violation and curtailment of civil and political rights in Chinese history, the post-Mao reform era is a period in which the regime has tried to remedy its past excesses and restored some basic rights to people. Formally, some of these rights were re-granted or reiterated in the revised Chinese Constitution (1982) and in many other laws. Informally, the regime has significantly expanded certain individual rights (such as most personal freedoms) while severely restricting some of the most important political rights (such as the freedom of political speech and association). Despite the limited nature of the improvement in the expansion and protection of rights, the enumeration of legal rights and promulgation of public policies have provided Chinese citizens important instruments of resistance against the government and its agents. The pioneering research by Kevin O'Brien and Lianjiang Li reported that peasants knowledgeable about specific government tax and procurement policies were able to protect their rights and interests more effectively.[10] Over time, out of China's new laws and policies have evolved implicit rules and norms that limit the scope and degree of oppression and abuse of power. For instance, persecution (such as imprisonment and physical abuse) of dissidents may occur routinely, but persecution of family members of dissidents has become almost taboo. This new norm enables family members of jailed dissidents to become open advocates of their personal causes and gain public and international support. Another newly established norm protects ordinary citizens who publicly protest against government administrative failures, abuse of power by lower-level officials, economic hardships and other shortcomings for which the government is held responsible (such as unemployment and financial scams). Citizens involved in these protests are not branded, as they once were, anti-government elements. Instead, their collective acts are tolerated. They sometimes succeed in attracting high-level attention and obtaining at least a partial resolution of the problems that triggered the protests initially. This may explain why collective protests by ordinary citizens increased dramatically in the late 1990s.

Dissident resistance in post-Mao China

Dissident movements in post-Mao China emerged and persevered in this dynamic environment. Democratic resistance accompanied Deng Xiaoping's reform in the late 1970s. To be sure, acts of defiance against the ultra-leftist Maoist regime occurred even during the darkest days of the Cultural Revolution. But dissident resistance in the post-Mao era was qualitatively different. While most acts of democratic resistance against the Mao regime were individual and non-public in nature,[11] post-Mao resistance by political dissidents was increasingly collective, organized, public, and evocative of new laws and procedures.[12] Moreover, dissident resistance in the post-Mao era has also evolved through several stages, each of which displayed subtle but important differences.

Dissident resistance: the early years

In the early years of reform, the embryonic dissident movement adopted a more direct and confrontational approach, relying heavily on underground publications and mass demonstrations to challenge the Communist Party's monopoly of power. During this period (1978–89), the first sustained campaign of dissident resistance was the Democracy Wall movement in 1978–81. Although the movement initially began in Beijing, it soon spread to more than twenty major cities and continued for slightly more than two years. According to a veteran participant of the Democracy Wall movement, Hu Ping, underground publications mushroomed in these cities. At the peak of the movement, Beijing alone had over forty such publications, involving more than 2,000 people.[13] The crackdown on the Democracy Wall movement and the imprisonment of several of its main leaders (such as Wei Jingsheng and Xu Wenli) left the dissident community temporarily without leaders. In the hiatus between 1981 and 1986, dissident resistance was waged mostly under the protection of official covers. Pro-democracy activists were able to establish a presence on college campuses and in semi-official publications. Their intellectual influence was instrumental in fomenting the debate on political reform in the summer of 1986, which was soon followed by the student-led pro-democracy demonstrations that rocked several major Chinese cities at the end of 1986 and beginning of 1987.

The 1986–87 movement was quickly, but with little bloodshed, crushed by the authorities. Several political patrons of the liberal intelligentsia, such as CCP General Secretary Hu Yaobang and propaganda chief Zhu Houze, were dismissed. A handful of leading critics of the government (Fang Lizhi, the former vice-president of the Chinese University of Science and Technology) were blamed by the government for instigating student unrest and stripped of their party membership. In retrospect, however, the crackdown in early 1987 was both short-lived and limited in scope. The majority of liberal intellectuals and dissidents were unaffected. Two years later, they launched a third, and more costly, direct political challenge against the regime: the Tiananmen Square movement in the spring of 1989. The bloody end to the episode and, more importantly, the subsequent imprisonment and exile of many leaders of the Tiananmen movement dealt a severe, albeit temporary, blow to China's dissident community. In fact, it did not recover from the Tiananmen setback until the mid-1990s.

Dissent in the 1990s

The revival of the dissident movement in the mid-1990s may be attributed to many factors. Most importantly, the conservative attempt to reverse China's economic reform failed miserably and decisively in 1992 after Deng Xiaoping toured southern China and re-ignited economic reform. The decline of conservative élites and strengthening of moderate reformers in Beijing created a more relaxed political atmosphere. Internal political considerations and external pressures led to the release of most of the leading dissidents (although some of the more prominent ones were forced into exile). Chinese society in the 1990s also became much more open and, as we shall see later, contained an increasing number of autonomous enclaves where resistance could be waged.

However, the renewed dissident resistance differed in important ways both from popular resistance by ordinary people (workers, peasants, and urban residents) and from previous dissident resistance. Ordinary resistance in contemporary China seeks redress of routine instances of injustice for which the government and its agents are responsible. Such resistance may take several forms. Individual acts of defiance may consist of filing petitions, staging sit-ins, lodging complaints, taking the government to court, and refusing to comply with official rules and policies.[14] While this type of resistance is observed daily and everywhere, there are no good data to measure its size, variety, causes, and effects chiefly because routine resistance seldom gets the type of media attention that is typically accorded to collective resistance by individuals and dissident resistance. A partial comparison between ordinary resistance and dissident resistance may thus be made by examining only the reported instances of resistance of both types. Official reports indicate that the number of collective protests was high – more than 5,000 such protests took place throughout China in 1998, even though only a small percentage of these incidents received media coverage.[15] To help us understand the causes, forms, and size of collective resistance waged by ordinary people, Table 1.1 provides some of the essential details of the reported instances of collective protests during September and October 1998. It should be noted, however, that this table certainly does not capture unreported, and mostly individual, acts of routine resistance. The selection bias may also be significant because these incidents were collected by a US-based dissident magazine, which tends to give prominence to collective resistance as a sign of the regime's weakness and unpopularity. Such limitations aside, the information presented in Table 1.1 may offer some useful clues about collective resistance in China today. For example, this type of resistance is quite large (with more than 100 participants in most cases). Ordinary resisters are likely to employ simple and direct forms of defiance. Their weapon of choice is street demonstrations. The targets of their protest are mostly local governments and state-owned enterprises. But the potential for violence is high for ordinary resisters because their tactics focus on direct protest in public places and involve confrontation with the police and security forces in most instances.

In comparison, dissident resistance was characterized by its peaceful nature. An analysis of the forty-nine reported instances of incidents from September to October 1998 (Table 1.2) shows that, as a sign of growing solidarity within the dissident community, nearly 40 percent of the protest events were precipitated by the persecution of fellow dissidents. About 25 percent of the incidents involved the declaration of rights and positions on major political issues. It should be

Table 1.1 An analysis of collective ordinary resistance in September and October 1998 (25 reported incidents)

Causes of incidents	Number of participants	Type of participants	Forms of resistance	Targets of resistance
Unpaid wages/ pensions (8)	Fewer than 100 (3)	Workers (14)	Demonstrations (9)	State-owned enterprises (11)
Corruption (4)	100–500 (10)	Urban residents (5)	Demonstration in front of government offices (7)	Local governments (10)
Financial scams (3)	Over 500 (6)	Peasants (4)		Police (2)
Government restrictions (2)	Unknown (6)	Private businessmen (2)	Blocking highways and railways (4)	Other (2)
Detention of fellow citizens (2)			Sit-ins (3)	
Other (6)			Other (2)	

Source: *Beijing Spring*, No. 63 (August 1998), pp. 100–105

Table 1.2 An analysis of dissident resistance in September and October 1998
(49 reported incidents)

Causes of incidents	Number of participants	Type of participants	Forms of resistance	Targets/intended audience
Persecution of fellow dissidents (20)	Fewer than 50 (35)	Known dissidents (39)	Open letter, appeals, declaration, and protest (37)	Local government agencies (14)
Rights/policy announcement (13)	50–100 (5)	Organized dissident groups (6)		Central government leaders (13)
Registration of opposition groups (11)	Unknown (6)	Family members of dissidents (4)	Formal application (12)	Police/courts (10)
Declaration of candidacy (3)			Hunger strike (1)	International community and world leaders (6)
Other (2)				N/A (6)

Source: *Beijing Spring*, No. 63 (August 1998), pp. 100–105; other press accounts.

noted that dissidents were also less fearful of waging organized resistance, as shown by the fact that attempts to register their opposition party and other groups comprised 20 percent of the protest events. Even though most dissident protests involved a small number of participants (fewer than fifty), about one in five protests had over fifty participants. While street demonstrations were a favored form of ordinary resistance, issuing open letters, appeals, and declarations was the preferred tool of protest for dissidents. Filing formal applications was another frequently used tactic. Notably, dissidents eschewed the tactics of street politics and none of the protests was violent. Finally, dissident protests targeted not only central and local political leaders, but also an international audience.

This analysis suggests that Chinese dissident resistance toward the late 1990s was waged non-violently in the arenas of public relations and legal procedures. The immediate effects of dissident resistance were, however, not obvious, mainly because dissidents remained unable to expand their social bases of support or mobilize workers and peasants. Even college students, who had been among the strongest supporters of the pro-democracy causes, had withdrawn from politics by the late 1990s. These adverse conditions did not appear to have discouraged the dissident community from continuing its resistance. Indeed, toward the end of the 1990s, Chinese dissidents had acquired more creative and sophisticated tactics, apparently to offset the disadvantages of relative political and social isolation that was caused both by the regime's repressive measures and by a more consumerist and less politicized society. In the 1980s, Chinese dissidents tended to discuss and promote democracy at relatively abstract levels that appeared remote to the concerns of ordinary Chinese citizens. That élitist approach did not gain much sympathy or support from the working class even though it did attract significant support from the intelligentsia and college students (largely because these social élites were much more politicized in the 1980s than in the 1990s).

That is perhaps why, in the 1990s, the same dissidents began to pursue a two-pronged strategy: combining direct challenges to the regime with the adoption of certain populist causes (such as workers' rights, anti-corruption, and environmental protection) to gain public sympathy. Therefore, on the one hand, dissidents continued to show their defiance directly, such as by declaring candidacy for local electoral offices (local people's congresses and village committees) and by attempting to register dissident groups.[16] Such efforts culminated in the formal declaration of the formation of China's first open opposition party, the China Democracy Party (CDP), in the summer of 1998. The 'provisional party charter' explicitly called for an end to the 'one-party dictatorship' of the Communist Party and advocated the promotion of justice, human rights, market reforms, freedom of religion, and autonomy for ethnic minorities. Within 4 months, CDP claimed to have about 200 members in a dozen branches around the country (Guizhou, Henan, Beijing, Tianjin, Zhejiang, Shanghai, Liaoning, Jilin, Heilongjiang, Hubei, and Shandong) and had secured broad and sympathetic international press in the US and other democratic nations.[17]

In their efforts to win public support, dissidents focused on three issues: corruption, patriotic causes, and environmental protection. Capitalizing on public anger at rampant official corruption, some dissidents attempted to organize anti-corruption civic groups. In November 1998, a self-styled anti-corruption fighter, Xiong Zhifu, announced a plan to visit several provinces to collect signatures on an anti-corruption petition. After the former Politburo member Chen Xitong was secretly tried and sentenced to 16 years in jail for corruption, seven dissidents in Zhejiang wrote an open letter to the People's Supreme Court demanding a live TV re-trial and a death sentence for Chen upon conviction.

Sometimes dissidents presented their anti-government activities as patriotic acts. The most famous examples were their efforts to organize an unofficial movement to seek war compensation from Japan, to protest against Japan's occupation of the Diaoyutai Islands over which China claimed sovereignty, and to demonstrate against the persecution of ethnic Chinese in Indonesia in 1998. In each case, the Chinese government was forced into a political dilemma because diplomatic considerations dictated a softer stance, which made it look weak and incapable of defending China's national interests. This created a rare opportunity for democratic resisters to score political points. While the Chinese government remained silent on the violence against ethnic Chinese in Indonesia in May 1998, forty-four dissidents signed a letter in July demanding that the Chinese government take a tough stand. In August 1998, several hundred people staged demonstrations – the largest post-Tiananmen rallies – every day for 2 weeks in front of the Indonesian Embassy in Beijing to protest against Indonesia's treatment of ethnic Chinese. A written protest, signed by 240 people, was delivered to the Indonesian Embassy. It turned out that one fourth of the signers were relatives of the victims of the Tiananmen Square crackdown.[18] Embarrassing the government was an obvious objective. A hidden agenda of the dissidents was to use these unofficial patriotic events to develop an organizational base. This effort began with Bao Ge of Shanghai, who formed the 'All-China Alliance for Seeking Civil Damages from Japan' with several activists in Hubei, Fujian, and Nanjing in 1988. Its branch organizations sought, unsuccessfully, to register as civic organizations in Shanghai, Hubei, and Nanjing. During the annual National People's Congress session in March 1993, Bao issued an open letter calling for a national referendum on the issue of seeking civilian war damages from Japan. Recounting this experience several years later, Bao said,

> On this issue (seeking war damages from Japan), we could hold public lectures at universities, conduct debates and invite international law special-ists to answer legal questions. Eventually we would ask various places to send special petition groups to Beijing to ask the NPC to hold a national referendum on this important issue. This perhaps could have become an opportunity to rekindle China's democracy movement.[19]

Dissidents were also quick to champion the cause of environmental protection. After disastrous floods ravaged central China in August 1998, 309 prominent intellectuals and dissidents signed a letter openly blaming the government's policy for the floods. They called on the government to protect the environment along the Yangzi River, to publish accurate figures on the disaster (such as casualties and economic losses), and to punish the officials responsible for the disaster.[20] Fifteen dissidents donated 1,000 yuan to the flood victims.

The contexts of resistance

That Chinese pro-democracy activists were able to adopt various means of resistance owed significantly to the dramatic changes in the socioeconomic, legal, and international context. Despite the tight control the regime maintained over the political sphere, market-oriented reforms and relaxation of restrictions on personal freedom provided dissidents modest but valuable resources to sustain their efforts of political resistance. Financially, dissidents received support from overseas exiles and domestic private businessmen, allowing them to purchase much-needed equipment such as fax machines and personal computers. (The Chinese police claimed that the money for the Shanghai branch of the China Democracy Party – $1,000 – was sent from Fu Shenqi, an exiled dissident based in New York City.) Guo Ruoji, a professor of philosophy in Nanjing who filed China's first lawsuit against the Communist Party, wrote his legal documents on an IBM computer which a private vendor sold him at a discount as a gesture of solidarity); the money paid for the computer was a $600 payment for an article Guo wrote for the Taiwan-based China Times Publishing Company.[21] Some dissidents operated commercial businesses to support themselves. Qin Yongmin, a Wuhan dissident, ran a small street stand. Peng Ming, who founded the China Development Union, was a successful private entrepreneur. Lin Hai, who was sentenced to 2 years in prison after he was convicted of illegally collecting and sending more than 30,000 e-mail addresses in China to a New York-based dissident Internet publication, owned his own software company in Shanghai.

Access to modern communications also enabled China's dissidents to maintain contact with each other and their overseas supporters. Many dissidents had home telephones, personal computers, fax machines and even Internet connections (in a country where, in urban areas, there were only about twelve telephone lines for 100 residents in 1996).[22] Qin Yongmin, a former skilled laborer who spent 8 years in prison for dissident activities in the early 1980s, published a fax newsletter called *China Human Rights Observer* (the country's first human rights newsletter) at home. Before he was arrested on charges of 'subverting state security' and sentenced to twelve years in jail at the end of 1998, Qin was able to put out 362 issues.[23] Peng Ming claimed that he transmitted e-mail notices to hundreds of people within China every day. Chinese dissidents frequently faxed their messages and political manifestos to overseas Chinese groups to gain exposure in the international media. For example, when a group of veteran dissidents, families of Tiananmen Square victims, and former CCP officials issued two manifestos ('Declaration on Civil Rights and Freedom' and 'Declaration on Civil Rights and Social Justice') at the end of September 1998, they first faxed the documents to Chinese dissident groups in New York for translation into English and then posted them on the Internet.[24] Having home telephones also enabled dissidents to reach the international media, give interviews, and report instances of human rights abuse. Overseas dissident groups used the Internet to reach China's rapidly increasing population of netizens (about 2.4 million Internet users at the end of 1998, according to one account). *Dacankao* (*VIP Reference*), an Internet magazine published by a New York overseas Chinese group, claimed to be able to send its on-line publication to 120,000 Chinese e-mail addresses every ten days.[25]

The international context

One of the favorable contextual factors contributing to the increasing level of dissident resistance has been China's growing economic and political integration into the international community. Obviously, the post-Mao ruling élite pursued an 'open-door' policy primarily to gain Western investment, markets, and technology; its expansion of political ties with international organizations and major Western governments also served to increase the status and respectability of the regime. While the economic and political gains of the 'open-door' policy were considerable, the regime has also paid a hidden price: its domestic behavior has been subjected to the scrutiny and criticisms of most industrial democracies. While Beijing's leaders often reacted furiously to such outside pressures, China's growing economic and political ties with the international community indirectly and, sometimes, directly, constrained its leaders' domestic policies and created new opportunities for dissident resistance.

There are numerous examples of how access to external material and moral support strengthened the dissident community. Overseas dissident groups routinely sent money to China-based dissidents, who frequently contacted the foreign media and their overseas supporters to mobilize international pressures. For some leading dissidents, Western pressures have become an integral part of their resistance. In an essay published in December 1998, Xu Wenli wrote, 'Now, through the help and pressure of the international community, the CCP has recognized that human rights is a very serious problem, which has at times caused China to 'lose face' and damaged its international image.'[26] Xu believed that Western coverage of the human rights conditions in China

> forced the Communist Party to gain a bit of understanding of the issue of human rights . . . in particular, I believe that during Jiang Zemin's numerous visits abroad, he must have deeply felt the international criticisms and condemnation of the Chinese government on this issue . . . he perhaps has made some commitments to Western leaders. Now it appears that there is some progress, for example, the CCP has pledged to sign the two inter-national covenants on human rights . . . we should take advantage of the opportunities the CCP is forced to give us.'[27]

Chinese dissidents frequently timed their protest activities to coincide with important visits by major Western leaders, to put the government in an embarrassing situation. Zhejiang-based Wang Youcai, a veteran of the 1989 Tiananmen Square movement, chose to announce the founding of the China Democracy Party the day before the arrival of President Bill Clinton at the end of June in 1998. When the United Nations Human Rights Commissioner, Mary Robinson, paid her landmark visit to China in September 1998, leading dissidents openly challenged the government by requesting meetings with Robinson and attempting to present her with petitions for releasing jailed dissidents. Dissidents made similar attempts during the visits by British Prime Minister Tony Blair and French Prime Minister Lionel Jospin in October 1998.

In addition, China has signed a large number of international treaties and joined many international organizations since the late 1970s (Table 1.3). Most significantly, Beijing signed two critical human rights covenants under Western pressure – the international covenant on social, economic, and cultural rights (in 1997) and international covenant on civil and political rights (in 1998). According to the stipulations of the covenants, China would be required to report to the UN on its fulfilment of the covenant obligations within 2 years of their ratification by the Chinese National People's Congress. These, and other formal obligations under these treaties, may increasingly limit Chinese leaders'

Table 1.3 International treaties/organizations China has signed/joined since 1980

1980	signed convention on elimination of discrimination against women
1981	signed convention on elimination of racial discrimination
1984	acceded to seven International Labor Organization (ILO) conventions on labor inspection, wage protection, collective bargaining, forced labor, non-discrimination in employment, and breaches of labor contract.
1987	accepted 1951 Hague statute on private international law
1987	ratified 1973 UN convention on punishment of crimes against internationally protected persons
1988	acceded to 1984 convention against torture and other cruel, inhuman, or degrading punishment
1990	acceded to ILO convention on equal pay for male and female workers
1990	ratified ILO convention on consultations to promote implementation of labor standards
1992	signed 1989 convention on the rights of the child
1992	acceded to the 1952 Geneva convention on universal copyright
1992	signed memorandum of understanding with US prohibiting trade in products made with prison labor
1993	signed 1971 Geneva convention protecting producers of phonograms against unauthorized duplication
1993	ratified 1979 convention against taking of hostages
1993	acceded to Bern convention on protection of literary and artistic works
1997	ratified 1964 ILO convention on employment policy
1997	signed international covenant on social, economic, and cultural rights
1998	signed international covenant on civil and political rights

Source: selected from Richard Baum, 'Globalization and Normative Convergence: The Chinese Case' (Department of Political Science, University of California, Los Angeles, 1998) pp. 7–8.

ability to impose repressive measures on pro-democracy activists and provide the latter with greater political legitimacy in their struggle. This potential was certainly not lost on China's dissident community. Wang Youcai, a founder of the CDP, claimed that 'Since the government has signed the international covenant on economic, social, and cultural rights and pledged to sign the international covenant on civil and political rights, a large space has emerged for organizing an opposition party openly and through legal means.'[28]

The changing legal context

A notable trend in the pro-democracy movement in the 1990s was the dissidents' increasing use of China's evolving legal system in asserting rights and putting the government and the ruling party on the defensive. This important shift in the tactics of resistance was made in response to changes brought about by the post-Mao legal reform that gradually expanded individual rights, limited the repressive power of the state, and provided ordinary citizens a limited set of legal tools to challenge the government. The institutional changes embodied in China's law reforms were part of a complex process of political evolution in the Deng era. No longer a monolithic communist regime, the CCP-controlled

party-state in fact consisted of groups and elements of diverse ideological persuasion. Indeed several open-minded reformers, such as Hu Yaobang and Zhao
Ziyang, rose to the highest level of the power hierarchy inside the regime and
used their office to promote a more tolerant political atmosphere. Several
important institutional developments, such as the gradual strengthening of the
National People's Congress and the initiation of village elections, occurred in this
fluid political environment.

The most promising development, one that had a more immediate impact
on the dissident community and the rights consciousness of the general public,
has been China's legal reform. Official data show that the National People's
Congress issued 222 laws and 84 other pieces of legislation between 1979 and
1998.[29] Of these laws, the most important were the administrative litigation law,
the civil procedure law, the revised criminal procedure law, and the new criminal
code that came into effect in 1998. Litigation – commercial, civil, and administrative (suits filed against the government) – exploded as well, indicative of the
growing importance of the legal system in resolving various conflicts (Table 1.4).
China's professional legal community, which was almost non-existent at the end
of the 1970s, grew rapidly in the same period. The number of licensed lawyers
reached 100,000 at the end of 1996.[30] Before a genuine democratic opening,
China's emerging legal system may not become a fully fledged channel for
resolving fundamental political conflicts between the CCP and its opposition.
But the very existence of this channel and the increasing utility and importance of
the courts in the lives of ordinary people should, in the long run, enhance the
legal system's relative institutional autonomy and transform it into a political
arena where democratic resistance is waged publicly and under certain legal
protection.

To a limited extent, this has already occurred. In William Alford's view,
China's legal reform forged a 'double-edged sword.' He observed that

> the regime has not only through its law provided a legal, moral, and political
> vocabulary with which those who wish to take it to task might articulate
> their concerns, but also has proffered these individuals a singular platform
> from which their concerns might be broadcast. In seeking to deploy formal
> legality for highly instrumental purposes, the regime has unwittingly handed
> its opponents a keenly honed instrument through which to seek to accom-
> plish their own, very different ends.[31]

Indeed, as political entrepreneurs quick to detect the potential advantages
embedded in the formal provisions of these laws, some Chinese dissidents took
the lead in invoking the new laws, especially the administrative litigation law, to
test the limits of the regime's tolerance of dissent. The first and most publicized
lawsuit filed by a leading dissident scholar, Guo Ruoji, was a case in point. Guo, a
professor of philosophy at Nanjing University, was stripped of his professorship
and banned from travelling abroad by the Communist Party committee of his
university in 1991. He promptly sued the Communist Party committee. His case

Table 1.4 Growth of litigation in China, 1978–97 (cases accepted by the courts of first instance)

Year	Commercial	Civil	Administrative
1978	–	285,000	–
1984	85,700	–	–
1987	367,156	1,213,219	5,240
1997	1,483,356	3,277,572	90,557

Sources: *Zhongguo falu nianjian*, various years; *Renmin sifa*, No. 4, 1998, p. 13.

attracted intense interest mainly because it was the first time the new administrative litigation law was explicitly used to challenge the power of the ruling party (although, technically, acts of the CCP were immune from administrative litigation). Both the Nanjing Intermediate Court and the Jiangsu Provincial Supreme People's Court ruled against Guo, but the professor believed that he scored a moral victory. Writing about the experience later, Guo said, 'I knew that my lawsuit could not win in court, but it would certainly win morally. My suit was not filed to be read by the judges; it was meant for the people.'[32]

Several other dissidents filed similar lawsuits against the government and the CCP. In 1993, a professor at People's University in Beijing, Yuan Hongbing, sued the university's CCP committee for banning a book he had edited, *The Tide of History*, which attacked leftist orthodox views. In 1998, a Wuhan-based dissident, Li Weiping, used the administrative litigation law to sue the head of the city's public security bureau for the illegal seizure of his passport. In the same year, a Beijing-based dissident, Peng Ming, filed an administrative litigation suit against the Beijing Municipal Civil Affairs Bureau for shutting down an affiliate of his private think-tank (the China Development Union) and confiscating its office equipment. Bao Ge, a former medical student in Shanghai who was sent to a re-education camp for organizing an unofficial movement to seek war compensation from Japan, claimed to have filed more than twenty suits against the government while in camp and against the agency in charge of the camp after his release. 'Each time I filed a suit, I made sure the press knew.'[33] Although none of the dissidents won their suits against the government, the very act of filing these suits achieved important political and symbolic victories. As Alford perceptively noted,

> The mere act of filing a complaint enables litigants to juxtapose publicly the gap between the state's professed ideals and lived reality with a rare drama, clarity, and moral force – whether their goal be to attack particular individuals and institutions without appearing vengeful or to raise more systemic questions about legitimacy. Litigation further poses a profound dilemma for the authorities by requiring, in effect, that the state either provide the litigant a day in court to make his case or appear to be acting in hypocritical disregard of processes that it has labored hard to publicize.[34]

In using the legal system to resist the domination of the state, the Chinese dissident community merely borrowed a time-tested and proven political tactic widely adopted by resisters in other countries. 'Legal institutions are important sites for public performances of resistance by individuals and groups. Telling one's story in court, particularly a story of oppression, can be an important act of resistance.'[35] As an institution of the state, the court is often identified as an instrument of domination. But ironically, under certain conditions the court can be sometimes converted into a forum where acts of resistance may be performed at relatively low cost. Scholars of popular resistance have reported that

> people who are otherwise politically marginal go to court regularly to resist domination . . . they skillfully manipulate legal rhetoric in courts and in a variety of other sites of oppositional practice . . . although governments wield tremendous power to encode and enforce law, a crucial part of the power of law is its very contestability. . . resisting state domination . . . often entails seeking inclusion in legal institutions . . . people regularly appropriate the terms, constructs, and procedures of law in formulating opposition.[36]

To be sure, Chinese dissidents have filed only a handful of lawsuits against the government and these suits had no direct impact on the protection of the rights of dissidents. But the knowledge and experience gained in making use of China's own laws against its rulers seemed to have prompted a shift of emphasis – away from direct acts of protest to the skillful exploitation of existing political procedures and processes. Veteran dissident Xu Wenli openly articulated such a change in tactics. 'We're using the law now, and they (the government) have never dealt with that before on such a scale.'[37] Xu saw great potential in exploiting existing institutional advantages under the current system:

> Our actions should not be covert, but should be open and in conformity with the Chinese constitution. The tactics of so-called 'street politics' or demonstrations should be minimized or be used with great caution . . . we must gradually shift from a 'street politics' approach to parliamentarianism. We must begin now to enter the process of instituting an electoral process and to strive for the participation of democracy activists in that process.[38]

Rights consciousness and resistance

Democratic resistance in China may be better understood as part of a broad trend of increasing rights consciousness among ordinary people. Such resistance is likely to occur more frequently and intensely and gain greater, although not necessarily overt or direct, popular support when the general level of rights consciousness is on the rise. There is evidence that suggests that rights consciousness has gradually risen in the post-Mao era. One of the manifestations of the rise is the number of complaints filed by consumers. In 1996 alone, Chinese consumer associations handled 526,975 complaints from consumers and were able to obtain 304 million yuan in compensation.[39] At the end of 1998, China's Internet subscribers used on-line bulletin boards to threaten a consumer boycott against government-owned Internet service providers for charging excessive monthly fees (although their campaign did not win an immediate victory). Another trend was the increase in the number of lawsuits filed against violations of property rights and personal rights (such as libel, defamation, and unauthorized use of personal portraits). As Table 1.5 shows, the number of personal rights-related civil lawsuits tripled in 8 years (from 1988 to 1996). Although no official data are available, many ordinary citizens have filed collective and individual lawsuits under the administrative litigation law against government agencies for collecting illegal taxes and seizing their private property.

More systematically gathered data, mainly public opinion survey results, similarly show rising rights consciousness. In an extensive survey (financed by the Ford Foundation), Chinese legal scholars interviewed 5,461 individuals in six provinces in 1993 and published some of their findings in a landmark book titled *Zou xiang quanli de shidai: Zhongguo gongmin quanli fazhan yanjiu (Marching Toward the Era of Rights: a study of the development of citizens' rights in China).*[40] This study, the first of its kind undertaken in China, has several limitations, chief of which is its inability to clarify how popular attitudes towards rights have changed over time. Nevertheless, the study provides valuable insight into the current state of rights consciousness. One important finding of the study is that, indeed, popular Chinese conceptions of the source of rights are substantially different from those in the West. As Table 1.6 shows, far more respondents stated that some of the most basic rights are granted by the state rather than given at birth.

Nevertheless, there is evidence suggesting that rights consciousness, especially in the areas of property rights, personal rights, due process, and legal rights, may have risen to relatively high levels. For example, nearly 80 percent of the respondents in the survey agreed with the statement 'Private property is sacred and must not be violated.' (*'siyou caichan shensheng buke qinfan'*)[41] Two-thirds of the respondents also opposed the suggestion that 'The government may confiscate private property under any circumstances in the national interest.'[42] About the same proportion of respondents also rejected the view that 'In a lawsuit involving

Table 1.5 Civil lawsuits filed against violation of personal rights

Year	Number of lawsuits accepted by the courts of first instance
1988	2,434
1990	3,032
1992	3,761
1994	5,655
1995	6,354
1996	7,467

Source: *Law Yearbook of China,* various years.

Table 1.6 Conception of sources of basic rights*

Type of Rights	Granted by the state and government	Given at Birth
Security of life	32.38	8.15
Security of livelihood	36.95	1.34
Elect and dismiss officials	34.82	1.08
Work for wealth	23.38	7.45
Receive primary education	40.92	6.7
No mistreatment of the imprisoned	49.99	2.95

Source: *Era of Rights*, p. 46.
*'According to the Chinese constitution and laws, you enjoy the following rights. Where do you think these rights come from? Choose the principal source of rights from the following choices.' Numbers indicate percentage of respondents

an individual and a collective, the judgment should favor the collective.'[43] Chinese citizens also seemed to be more aware of their rights to due process. When asked whether a law enforcement agency could continue to detain a person for public security even if it was unable to determine his guilt or innocence, nearly 47 percent of the respondents opposed such action while only 27 percent of the 5,456 respondents supported it.[44]

Rising levels of rights consciousness are accompanied by increasing popular awareness of legal recourse. Contrary to the traditional perception that Chinese culture frowns upon confrontational litigation and prefers mediation, Chinese legal researchers reported that more than half of the rural respondents and 70 percent of the urban respondents felt they neither gained nor lost face going to court to resolve conflicts with someone they knew.[45] More importantly, a very large proportion of ordinary citizens selected the legal system as a channel to seek recourse to official injustice. When asked what they would do if they were attacked and injured by the police or local bullies, more than 60 percent of the respondents stated that they would take their cases to judicial authorities and demand punishment. Only 5 to 7 percent of the respondents would acquiesce. About 43 percent would take the same action if they were attacked by their bosses or supervisors.[46]

Conclusion

The preliminary evidence presented in this chapter offers some support for Tocqueville's hypothesis that falling repression produces greater resistance mainly as a result of rising rights consciousness among the oppressed. In China's case, a small but resilient dissident resistance movement has been sustained since the late 1970s because of many important changes in the political, economic, social, and international context within which the movement operates. These changes sometimes provided dissidents with direct means of resistance (such as access to material, legal, and moral support). At other times, the impact of these contextual changes was less direct but no less real, and they created a more favorable political milieu for resistance. Operating within such a milieu, dissidents were likely to gain greater confidence, enjoy more influence, and increase the effectiveness of their acts. Of course, as in most cases of resistance waged by relatively small groups, their acts of defiance such as making public declarations, petitioning the government, protesting against personal persecution, and attempting to register opposition groups have failed to have an immediate and measurable effect. Rarely have they succeeded in visibly weakening the regime or directly changing public opinion or government policy. Over time, however, sustained dissident resistance, even in its most routine forms, may slowly sap the authoritarian regime's legitimacy, authority, and prestige. At the most basic level, such acts reveal most vividly and publicly the vulnerability of the political authority of the regime. They demonstrate that even a government with a considerable repressive capacity may be brought to answer some of the most basic questions about its political legitimacy and governance record: why did it violate its own laws in imprisoning its critics; why did it stop unofficial groups from registering; why did it fail to protect the national interests; why did it fail to protect the environment; why did its own officials commit crimes of corruption?

In short, dissident resistance performs some of the most essential functions of political opposition in political systems where legal opposition does not exist. In the long term, dissident resistance may have important and more direct political consequences. It will likely produce demonstration effects encouraging ordinary resisters to imitate the tactics of dissidents in asserting their rights. Persistent dissident efforts may loosen up parts of the political system (the most likely point of entry is the legal system) and create more favorable political conditions for ordinary resisters. Dissident resistance may lead to the emergence of a freer media which will become a voice for ordinary resisters. Dissidents are also likely to forge direct organizational links with ordinary resisters to develop a stronger and broader social base. If the history of dissident resistance between 1978 and 1998 is to be used as a basis for judging its future potential, China's incipient opposition is likely to become more resilient, sophisticated and adept in challenging the regime as the conditions for democratic resistance further improve.

Notes

1 For the most illuminating account of ordinary resistance against domination, see James Scott, *Weapons of the Weak: Everyday Forms of Peasant Resistance* (New Haven: Yale University Press, 1985).
2 Alexis de Tocqueville, *The Old Regime and the French Revolution* (New York: Anchor Books, 1955), pp. 176–77.
3 See, for example, Craig Calhoun, *Neither Gods Nor Emperors: Students and the Struggle for Democracy in China* (Berkeley: University of California Press, 1994); Jeffrey N. Wasserstrom and Elizabeth J. Perry (eds), *Popular Protest and Political Culture in Modern China* (Boulder: Westview Press, 1994); Kevin O'Brien, 'Rightful resistance,' *World Politics* vol. 49, no. 1 (October 1996), pp. 31–55.
4 Dissidents are individuals who directly oppose the Communist Party's claim to rule and openly offer a political alternative. They are also referred to as pro-democracy activists because the political alternative they offer embodies democratic ideals and

institutions. Their political objective distinguishes them from other protesters who are motivated by non-political issues.

5 Andrew Nathan, 'Sources of Chinese rights thinking,' in R. Randle Edwards, Louis Henkin, and Andrew Nathan (eds), *Human Rights in Contemporary China* (New York: Columbia University Press, 1986), pp. 125–26.
6 Nathan, 'Sources of Chinese Rights Thinking,' p. 161.
7 Nathan, ibid.
8 Randall Peerenboom, 'Rights, interests, and the interest in rights in China,' *Stanford Journal of International Law* vol. 31, no. 2 (Summer 1995), pp. 359–86.
9 Wang Gungwu, 'Power, rights and duties in Chinese history,' *The Australian Journal of Chinese Affairs* no. 3 (January 1980), pp. 1–26.
10 Lianjiang Li and Kevin O'Brien, 'Villagers and popular resistance in contemporary China,' *Modern China* Vol. 22, No. 1 (January 1996), pp. 28–61.
11 One of the most common forms of private resistance during the Cultural Revolution was to keep a secret diary in which resisters wrote what they really thought about the Maoist regime. An exception was the long essay on democracy and law jointly written and posted publicly by Li Yizhe in Guangzhou in the mid-1970s.
12 The protest against the Gang of Four in April 1976 was perhaps an exception. But strictly speaking, that event should not be classified as a pro-democracy act.
13 *Beijing Spring*, No. 66 (November 1998), p. 3.
14 Ordinary resistance described here is different from 'everyday resistance' formulated by James Scott. In this paper, ordinary resistance primarily targets political authorities while in Scott's work, everyday resistance is directed against non-political forces of domination.
15 *Washington Post*, January 21, 1999, A 19.
16 In September 1998, three dissidents in the Chaoyang district in Beijing announced their candidacy for the district's people's congress on a platform of workers' rights and anti-corruption. *AFP*, Sept. 21, 1998.
17 *Wall Street Journal*, November 27, 1998, A9.
18 Reported in *USA Today*, August 31, 1998, p. 4A.
19 Ya Yi, 'Tuijin Zhongguo gongmin quanli yundong' (The movement to promote citizens' rights in China) *Beijing Spring*, No. 57 (February 1998), pp. 66–74.
20 Letter reprinted in *Beijing Spring*, No. 65 (Oct. 1998), pp. 6–7.
21 Guo Ruoji, *Gongchandang weifa an ji shi* (Real stories of the Communist Party's violation of law) (Minzhu daixue chubanshe, Hong Kong, 1997).
22 Calculated from data in *Zhongguo tongji nianjian* 1997, p. 539.
23 *AFP*, November 18, 1998.
24 *New York Times*, September 30, 1998, p. 3.
25 *Washington Post*, December 5, 1998, A20; *South China Morning Post*, January 11, 1999 (Internet edition).
26 Xu Wenli 'Democratic movement in China,' *China Strategic Institute Issue Papers on China*, No. 43, December 3, 1998.
27 *China Spring*, No. 172 (June 1998), pp. 30–34.
28 Wang Youcai, 'Ruhe zhujian quanguoxing gongkai fandui dang' (How to organize an open national opposition party,' *Beijing Spring*, No. 65 (October 1998), pp. 42–43.
29 *Legal Daily*, March 13, 1997, p. 5; the data for 1993–98 are the author's compilation according to official publications.
30 *Zhongguo falu nianjian* 1997, p.1074.
31 William Alford, 'Double-edged swords cut both ways: law and legitimacy in the People's Republic of China,' *Daedalus*, Vol. 122, No. 2 (Spring 1993), p. 62.
32 Guo Ruoji, *Gongchandang weifa an ji shi*, p. 27.
33 Ya Yi, 'Tuijin Zhongguo gongmin quanli yundong' (The movement to promote citizens' rights in China) *Beijing Spring*, No. 57 (February 1998) pp. 66–74.
34 Alford, 'Double-edged swords cut both ways,' p. 58.

35 Susan Hirsch and Mindie Lazarus-Black, 'Introduction,' in Mindie Lazarus-Black and Susan Hirsch (eds), *Contested States: Law Hegemony and Resistance* (London: Routledge,1994), p. 11.
36 Susan Hirsch and Mindie Lazarus-Black, 'Introduction,' *Contested States*, pp. 1–10.
37 Quoted in *AFP*, September 28, 1998.
38 Xu Wenli, 'Democratic movement in China,' *China Strategic Institute Issue Papers on China*, No. 43, December 3, 1998.
39 *Legal Daily*, February 15, 1997, p. 1.
40 Xia Yong (ed.), *Zou xiang quanli de shidai: Zhongguo gongmin quanli fazhan yanjiu* (Marching toward the Era of Rights: a study of the development of citizens' rights in China) (Beijing: Chinese University of Politics and Law Publishing Co., 1995).
41 Xia Yong, *Era of Rights*, p. 376.
42 *Era of Rights*, p. 353.
43 *Era of Rights*, p. 383.
44 *Era of Rights*, p. 464.
45 *Era of Rights*, p. 42.
46 *Era of Rights*, p. 37.

2   Pathways of labor insurgency

Ching Kwan Lee

Will the arrival of the market after 40 years of communism create the conditions for a restive Chinese working class? What makes the national leadership openly and repeatedly declare the labor problem to be the 'biggest threat to social stability'? This chapter traces the twin processes of deepening reforms and gradual radicalization of the Chinese working class. The barrage of reform policies in the last two decades has brought about, on the one hand, massive lay offs and destitution for veteran workers in state owned enterprises and, on the other hand, despotic labor conditions for a new generation of migrant workers employed in the private and foreign-owned sectors. Pursuing different forms of labor struggles – ranging from everyday workplace resistance, petitions, work stoppages and strikes to public protest, violence, independent unionism and political movements – workers have at times extracted concessions from the state in the forms of emergency funds or favorable verdicts in labor dispute arbitration. But they also confront unrelenting state determination to press ahead with reforms and to repress any sign of independent unionism and organized political dissent.

Two decades of market reform have brought on their heels waves of labor insurgency. By the late 1990s, incidents of worker unrest had become so routine that government and party leaders identified labor problems as the 'biggest threat to social stability.' Indeed, state-led economic reforms have paradoxically undercut a major social base of regime support. In targeting the state industrial sector for an overhaul that brings about massive layoffs, reformers have confronted many state workers with a drastic reversal of fortune, from being 'masters' of their enterprises to becoming destitute. By documenting various forms of labor insurgency – ranging from everyday workplace resistance, petitions, work stoppages and strikes to public protests, violence, independent unionism and political movements – this chapter assesses the consequences of reform on labor and its relation with the state. The overall argument is that accelerated reforms have triggered both a proliferation and a deepening of labor activism. The relation between reform and resistance is due, on the one hand, to heightened labor antagonism towards state officials, managers and capitalists;

and on the other hand, to an opening up of new political and institutional spaces for interest and grievance articulation. For instance, labor conflicts in private and foreign-owned factories do not fall readily within the scope of state intervention and preemption, thereby creating greater leeway for labor struggles. Also, new arbitration institutions invite more petitions and complaints from workers, resulting in the dramatic growth of registered conflicts. Although workers have succeeded in extracting some concessions from the regime, the latter has been unrelenting in crushing certain forms of labor action. Thus, on the one hand, emergency funds have been doled out to localities hardest hit by unemployment and protests and a national re-employment campaign has been emphasized. On the other hand, however, the state has continued to press ahead with reform of state-owned enterprises and has shown its determination to repress any sign of independent unionism or political organization involving cross-class alliances among peasants, workers and intellectuals. It seems that as long as workers' actions are not politically oriented, but limited to purely economic and livelihood demands, the state tends toward tolerance and appeasement. However, the arrest and imprisonment of labor activists has continued to send a powerful message concerning what the state designates as a forbidden path of resistance – organized political dissent.

Worker rebellion in a worker's state

Escalation of labor action occurs in the context of a sea change in China's socio-economic system. In the Maoist era of state socialism, the working class as a whole made great strides *vis-à-vis* the peasants, the bourgeoisie, and the intellectuals in terms of political status, wages, welfare and employment security. Thanks to the egalitarian bent of the Maoist road to modernization, which placed dual emphasis on industrialization and socialization, both blue collar and white collar employees in urban China benefited. Maoist ideology also enhanced the position of workers *vis-à-vis* the managerial cadres. The latter were required to engage in productive labor periodically, sometimes being sent to the countryside for this purpose, and their salaries were capped following the Cultural Revolution at only 10–30 percent above those for the highest paid skilled workers. On the other hand, manual laborers were involved in managerial work through innovation and design campaigns, group decision-making, group problem solving, and representation on factory revolutionary committees. In material terms, despite a low wage system, workers' real wage levels in 1970 represented a 35 percent rise above those of 1952. Periodic setbacks notwithstanding, the revolutionary regime made available unmistakable improvements in worker consumption – food, housing, medical care, education and training opportunities.[1] At the top of the labor hierarchy were the permanent workers employed in state owned enterprises. In 1981 when reform began, this labor aristocracy accounted for 42 percent of the entire industrial workforce and produced 75 percent of total industrial output. Their employment conditions epitomized all that was superior about socialism: cradle to grave welfare, permanent job tenure, housing provision, life-long medical and pension benefits, and guaranteed, superior wages. The next group down the industrial rank order consisted of workers in urban collectives, followed by temporary workers in state-owned enterprises and those in rural industries. All these workers were distinguished from those in the state sector by relatively inferior material conditions and political status.[2]

Even in the pre-reform period, when workers were economically dependent on enterprise paternalism, and were politically controlled by well-entrenched party networks extending to each factory shop floor, Chinese labor was not always a docile subject of a totalitarian state. Both state-inspired factionalism and economic inequalities rooted in the socialist industrial system have periodically propelled different segments of the work force to assert political prowess and economic demands. Thus, post-1949 China can claim a history of proletarian rebellion and activism, notably in the strike wave of 1956–57, factional strife and protests during the Cultural Revolution in 1966–67, and workers' participation in the 1976 April Fifth Movement.

Seizing the opportunity of the Hundred Flowers Campaign, when Chairman Mao encouraged dissent from below to pre-empt larger scale revolts similar to the Hungarian ones, workers displaced by the socialization of industries staged more than 1,300 strikes in Shanghai alone between the months of March and June in 1957. Launched most fervently by apprentices and temporary workers and those in joint-ownership enterprises, the strikes demanded higher wages, better welfare, permanent worker status and guaranteed promotion.[3] The Cultural Revolution a decade later offered another political opportunity for labor struggles. Turmoil inside Chinese factories across the nation was partially shaped by factional cleavages created by the Party's network inside the factories, distinguishing the royalists (composed of loyal members of the Party's organization, activists, party members, shop-floor leaders, model workers, etc.) from the rebels (including a diverse group of ordinary workers who were either victimized by the royalists or by factory managers prior to the Cultural Revolution, or those who had criticized Party authority). But labor conflicts during this period were also structured by deep-rooted occupational grievances and inequalities, with apprentices, the unskilled, irregular workers and younger workers figuring most prominently in making economic demands and joining rebel factions across the country.[4] Then, in the spring of 1976, mass demonstrations and riots with a strong contingent of worker participation broke out in more than forty places across the country. The backbone of this uprising was made up of young workers, who had been the basis of mobilization during the Cultural Revolution but had been stigmatized for their bourgeois leanings. They used the occasion of commemorating the late Premier Zhou Enlai to express their dissatisfaction with the Gang of Four, as well as the political persecutions and the injustices they had suffered.[5]

Labor's loss in the reform era has occurred amidst momentous economic growth. During the period 1980–97, China's gross national product attained an average annual growth rate of 10 percent. Industry, while maintaining the same

49 percent share of national output, grew at an even more impressive annual rate of 12 percent.[6] Real annual wage increases for urban employees between 1979–96 averaged 4.4 percent.[7] The influx of foreign investment and liberalization policies towards the private economy have created a national labor market, enhancing labor mobility and autonomy. Employment in these two sectors, which were non-existent at the beginning of reforms, had mushroomed to an estimated 80 million, or 15 percent of total by 1995.[8] A new class of rural, migrant laborers, many of them young women known as *dagong mei* or maiden workers, has emerged in response to these employment opportunities and an estimated 100 million migrant laborers have left the countryside to enter towns and cities in search of non-agricultural jobs. Another important source of employment for these rural laborers is the burgeoning township and village enterprises employing some 170 million workers.[9]

Inequalities across regions, ownership sectors, industries and occupations are concealed behind figures of aggregate growth and prosperity, however. The stark fact remains that relative to other social groups, the working class as a whole is suffering drastic dislocation. Veteran permanent workers and retirees find their employment security, welfare benefits and workplace status vanishing. While a new generation of young migrant workers benefits from substantially improved income and, status that when they find urban jobs they have to confront ruthless exploitation that harks back to labor degradation of nineteenth-century industrial capitalism.

Almost every step along the path of market reform amounts to a setback for state workers' status and livelihood. First came the reform for greater enterprise autonomy and director responsibility in 1984, paving the way for the ascendance of managers' dictatorial power over workers, the union and even the Party. Then the policy of 'labor re-optimization', first implemented in 1988, gave managers the power to render redundant surplus workers in state enterprises. Labor contract reform required that all employees sign contracts of varying duration with employers who now have a legal mandate to dismiss workers. By 1995, the permanent employment system was officially dismantled, giving rise to two groups of unemployed workers: the off-duty and the registered unemployed. What the state has euphemistically called the 'off-duty' (or *xiagang*) workers are those who maintain 'employment relations' with the enterprise, potentially re-employable if business improves, and who receive livelihood allowances amounting to only a tiny fraction of regular income. The 'registered un-employed' workers are those who have completely severed employment relations with the enterprise and are left to their own devices after receiving minimal unemployment allowances. These destitute workers now number more than 20 million nationwide. Unemployment is further aggravated by the rise in the number of enterprise bankruptcies since the early 1990s. By 1996, 11,544 state-owned enterprises had declared bankruptcy, and many more had applied without success for bankruptcy.[10] Finally, for those who are still employed in state factories, the enterprise welfare system has also been gradually eliminated and the retreat of this old system has outpaced the installation of a new societal insurance system.

The pattern of 'organized dependence' and paternalism characteristic of state–labor relations under state socialism has given way to a new despotism. State sector workers who are unable to find alternative employment in private or foreign firms, including large numbers of unskilled, older and particularly women workers, are subordinated to a dictatorial management empowered by labor contract and enterprise reforms, and untrammeled by the Party or the union.[11] With more than 40 percent of state-owned enterprises operating in the red, workers' paychecks have dwindled and these reduced wages now have to cover 'commodified' welfare services like nurseries, clinics, and housing that were until recently provided free or with substantial subsidies. For the millions of migrant laborers in the private sector where state regulations are rarely enforced, despotism is all the more blatant.[12] Local governments, engaged in fierce competition for foreign investments, collude with foreign capital in undermining state labor regulations regarding contracts, minimum wages, overtime pay, rest days, total working hours and industrial safety. Under these oppressive and deteriorating employment conditions, Chinese workers have pursued a variety of collective action.

Everyday resistance

'Everyday resistance' refers to the various forms of power of the weak in the 'hidden realm of political conflict': the nearly continuous, informal, undeclared, disguised forms of autonomous resistance by the lower classes. Although empirical studies on poaching, squatting, tax evasion, desertion and foot dragging behavior have most commonly focused on the peasantry, 'resistance is virtually always a stratagem deployed by a weaker party in thwarting the claims of an institutional or class opponent who dominates the public exercise of power.'[13] Applying James Scott's concept to socialist China, sociologist Xueguang Zhou has emphasized the collective and political nature of everyday resistance. What he calls 'collective inaction' may take the forms of a lack of enthusiasm for participating in state-initiated political campaigns, absenteeism or inefficiency in the workplace, evasion of public duties, and the emergence of subcultures opposing the official ideology. In the institutional context of Chinese state socialism, where the state monopolizes the public sphere, the convergence of such unorganized non-compliant behavior amounts to political actions in that they directly challenge state authority and constrain state capacity to extract resources.[14]

Quotidian resistance is not a novel phenomenon in Chinese factories. During the Cultural Revolution decade (roughly 1966–77), worker discontent with wage austerity and stagnation, decline in living standards, worsened housing shortage and rampant favoritism by cadres found expression in various forms of non-compliance. Andrew Walder's influential study of labor under state socialism reported widespread slow downs, tardiness, absenteeism, appropriation of raw materials from the factory to make household articles, conscious withdrawal of work effort and excessive use of paid sick leave. Managers themselves were demoralized, as there was no material incentive but much political inhibition for them to enforce discipline.[15] Everyday labor resistance continues to plague Chinese industry in the late 1990s, particularly in large and medium size state enterprises. Chinese academics warned that what they described as a widespread 'indolent mentality' among workers had become a major social problem as demoralization was impeding national economic development. National surveys found that workers had lost the sense of being the masters of the enterprise in which they were working now that managers treat workers as 'wage labor'. The official press of the All-China Federation of Trade Unions (ACFTU), *Gongren ribao* (*Worker's Daily*), also made reference to workers' 'rebellious psychology', as manifested in an unwillingness to participate in political study or educational meetings, lack of interest in production and the learning new of skills, slowdowns and theft of enterprise property.

Channeled by the new political economy, workers take up new modes of non-compliant behavior. Investigation of several state enterprises in Guangzhou, a pioneer city of economic reform, revealed spontaneous work stoppages and goldbricking as workers respond to punitive work disciplines. Under market socialism, moreover, there is rampant displacement of work effort from state jobs to second jobs in the non-state sector. Estimates of moonlighters range from 30 to 90 percent of the local industrial workforce. As moonlighting crazes turn skilled workers into part-time technical consultants for village and township enterprises or Sunday self-employed electricians, and as unskilled workers become part-time peddlers or motorbike drivers, productivity of state owned enterprises suffers.[16] Moonlighters put in minimal energy during regular work hours, reserving real effort for private job ventures. The local press condemns second jobs for weakening workers' sense of commitment to the occupation, damaging workers' health and undermining state enterprises' economic performance. Some workers also pilfer work tools and raw materials, products and designs to help their second job ventures. Workers disgruntled by low wages in unprofitable enterprises deliberately defy the piece rate wage system, a linchpin of reform intended to motivate workers, replacing it with an egalitarian redistribution of wages within the work group. Finally, when housing is no longer a welfare entitlement but a commodity and a reward to be selectively given, workers strategically manipulate the rules in order to keep their enterprise apartments. For instance, one family strategy is for wives to continue working in state-owned enterprises to maintain their claim to work unit apartments, while the skilled worker-husband leaves for higher paying jobs. Others simply refuse to move out when they quit the enterprise, claiming that their long years of low-wage labor have earned them 'capital rights' over their apartments.[17]

Practices of resistance like these are clandestine forms taken by the weak and the dispersed. They are tactical and make-shift examples of the creativity of groups or individuals already caught in the net of discipline. These tactics are popular ruses insinuated in the interstices of everyday life, with which workers seek to direct the system to their own ends, deflecting and escaping its power without leaving it. Everyday resistance is primarily the terrain of workers with little bargaining power and few exit options. Without recourse to more open confrontation or explicit bargaining with the authorities, everyday resistance may at least bring a modicum of mundane benefits and respite from abuse.

Labor disputes and arbitration

A new form of labor conflict results from Chinese government efforts to institutionalize conflict resolution. In July 1987, the State Council revived the national labor dispute arbitration system, which had been abolished in 1955. By 1997, some 270,000 labor dispute mediation committees at the enterprise level, and 3,159 labor dispute arbitration committees at county, city and provincial levels had been established. These committees are constituted by a 'tripartite principle', with representatives from the labor bureau administration, the trade union, and economic administrative organs, representing respectively the state, labor, and the employer. In the past decade, enterprise mediation cases amounted to 820,000, while 450,000 cases of labor arbitration were processed. With the promulgation of the 1993 Regulation on Handling Labor Disputes and the 1995 Labor Law, the scope of arbitration and legal actions has been expanded in terms of actionable claims and coverage of enterprise types. The original dispute resolution process only covered contract disputes or cases involving termination of permanent workers in state enterprises. Since 1993, workers in private and collective enterprises can bring their grievances concerning wages, fringe benefits, occupational safety and health as well as termination of contract to obtain legal resolution.[18]

This national hierarchy of labor dispute arbitration mechanism attests to the Chinese state's explicit recognition of an inevitable growth in labor conflicts and the subsequent need to provide institutional channels for resolution, if social stability is to be maintained. The emphasis is on pre-emption and mediation at the enterprise level, with arbitration at the local committee level. Submission of labor disputes to the civil court is the last resort. Workers have seized this institutional space to redress grievances and defend their rights, as statistics register a staggering and continuous increase in the number of petitions and dispute cases. The explosion in the number of arbitrated labor disputes followed the implementation of labor contract reform and the drastic rise in unemployment. The annual rate of increase in formally arbitrated labor disputes nationwide for 1994, 1995, 1996 and the first half of 1997 was 54.5, 73, 45.7 and 59 percent, respectively. These figures do not include informally arbitrated cases and cases mediated at the enterprise committee level.

Beneath this aggregate rise in the volume of arbitrated disputes, certain patterns can be discerned, illustrating the focus and distribution of labor conflicts. Firstly, the most contentious provinces in the 1990s have been Guangdong, Chongqing, Shanghai, Fujian and Jiangsu, regions which experienced the most rapid economic growth. On the other hand, in terms of increase in arbitration, Sichuan, Inner Mongolia, Tianjin, Gansu, Shanxi, and Xinjiang all registered triple digit rates in 1995, reflecting perhaps the rapid deterioration in employment conditions among workers in the state-owned sector. Secondly, in terms of ownership type, and taking the year 1996 as an example, state-owned enterprises account for 34 percent of arbitrated disputes, while foreign invested, collective and private enterprises respectively account for 21, 26 and 10 percent of the total of 48,121 cases, involving 189,120 employees. Thirdly, most disputes are economic in nature, with wages, welfare and social insurance payments being the most common (50 percent) causes of conflicts. Wage arrears are particularly pronounced in private and foreign-invested firms.[19]

Most of these dispute cases originated in petitions by employees. They succeeded in redressing their grievance in 50–80 percent of cases depending on the locality. However, the protection of workers' rights is still wanting, as follow-up studies have revealed many examples of discrimination against the plaintiffs after disputes were formally settled. In a county in Beijing, for instance, of the 441 employees involved in disputes in 1993–94, 66 percent were later dismissed by employers. Moreover, the tripartite principle in the makeup of enterprise mediation committees is often violated. In Hubei for instance, in the enterprise committees studied, management and union representatives always outnumbered worker representatives, who were also mostly appointed rather than elected. Thus, it remains to be seen how effective and genuine these different levels of labor dispute arbitration mechanisms are in protecting workers' rights in the reform era.

Work stoppages and strikes

The entire 20-year period of reform has been punctuated with incidents of work stoppages and strikes of varying durations throughout China. As reform deepened in the 1990s, strikes occurred more frequently, involved more workers, and affected enterprises in more ownership sectors. Although the demands workers made were predominantly material ones, occasions arose when economic grievances evolved into a political critique of regime legitimacy.

Under the regime of Deng Xiaoping, the first wave of strikes emerged in the autumn of 1980. The ascendance of the Polish Solidarity Movement emboldened Chinese workers, already dissatisfied with years of wage stagnation and inadequate housing, to take action. Some twenty to thirty strikes reportedly occurred in the last quarter of 1980 in the industrial cities of Wuhan and Taiyuan. Additional strikes were reported in 1980–81 in Shanghai, Tianjin, Kunming, the Northeastern cities, and in cities in Hubei and Shanxi, involving coal miners, steel workers, tool-and-die workers, workers in machinery and electronics factories. One noteworthy incident at the Taiyuan steel mill in December 1980 was sparked by demands for better housing, rights to family reunion for workers living apart from spouses and election of worker representative to sit in management committees. Demands turned political as more steel workers joined in. The local press reported that, a 'minority of workers'. . . labeling themselves 'the poorest workers in the world,' called for 'breaking down the rusted door of socialism,' the right to decide their own fate, the end to dictatorship, and the overthrow of the system of political bureaucracy'.[20] Poland's Solidarity seemed to have the greatest impact on Shanghai, where the call for independent unions was a recurrent theme in a number of go-slow and strike incidents in 1981. When such demands proliferated across the country, reaching as far as Xinjiang, the Chinese government reacted by striking the 'freedom to strike' clause from the revised 1982 Constitution.[21] Deprived of the constitutional right to strike, Chinese workers have nevertheless remained adamant in using strikes to defend their rights and welfare throughout China's reform transition.

The late 1980s witnessed another period of volatile labor relations, as state workers' discontents intensified due to anxiety fueled by rising unemployment, widening income gaps between managers and workers, and corruption. These grievances resulted from reform measures aimed at increasing the efficiency and competitiveness of state-owned enterprises. Between 1986 and 1988, labor contract reform, the bankruptcy law and the regulation on labor re-optimization were enacted one after another, threatening workers' employment security and livelihood. Coupled with record high inflation rates, climbing to 18.5 percent in 1988 and 25.5 percent in 1989, worker frustration reached a zenith.[22] The official ACFTU counted 97 strikes in 1987, and over 100 in 1988. The largest took place in a cotton mill in Zhejiang Province, where 1,500 workers participated. The longest occurred in the Northwest Medical Instruments Plant in Xi'an, lasting more than 3 months from 1987 to 1988. In the first quarter of 1989 in Shanghai alone, the official union handled fifteen strikes, touched off by worker grievances regarding bonus allocation and lay-offs. Thousands of People's Liberation Army soldiers were reportedly sent to occupy the Daqing oil fields to quell a labor stoppage demanding higher wages and better treatment.[23] Then, in May and June 1989, workers in Beijing, Shanghai and other cities left the confines of factory gates and their collective action took the forms of public protests, independent unionism and political mobilization. Despite the deadly crackdown against the Tiananmen movement, with workers receiving the heaviest sentences, strikes have become an increasingly routine method of labor resistance. For instance, internal reports compiled by the Department of Public Security recorded a national total of 480 strikes in 1992, 1,870 in 1995, and 1,740 in the first nine months of 1996. In the mid-1990s, when massive lay-offs, plant closures and delays in pension payment occurred, strikes gave way to sit-ins and public demonstrations by unemployed and retired workers as the most common forms of protest. Scattered reports of labor strikes have nevertheless continued to surface.

Besides veteran workers dislocated by restructuring of the state industrial sector, labor militancy in the 1980s and 1990s has also been fueled by a new generation of factory workers who waged their own struggles against exploitation in private and foreign-invested companies. Concentrated mostly in the

Special Economic Zones (SEZs) in southern coastal provinces, migrant worker discontent centered on poor working and living conditions, low wages, wage arrears and degrading management practices. As early as 1986–87, Shenzhen (the first SEZ in China) witnessed at least 21 strikes in foreign-funded enterprises and the local trade union received about 1,000 worker complaints. Incidents were triggered by harsh treatment, low wages, wage arrears, extremely long hours of work and unreasonable disciplinary practices involving meal times, toilet breaks and holidays. A typical incident reported by the Chinese press revealed that a Hong Kong-owned toy factory forced young women workers to work up to 18 hours a day 7 days a week without adequate overtime pay and no time off on Sundays. Thirty women went on strike after one pregnant woman collapsed from exhaustion.[24] Even though statistics on work stoppages and strikes are always incomplete, the unmistakable trend is one of increased volume. In Shenzhen alone, where 69 strikes and work stoppages were recorded from June 1989 to the end of 1990, there were 250 such cases in 1992. From mid-1993 to early 1995 a series of strikes were staged by workers in Japanese-owned plants of Canon, Mitsumi, Sanmei and Panasonic in Shenzhen and Zhuhai SEZs. Runaway inflation reaching as high as 20 to 27 percent in these cities caused economic distress among migrant workers who demanded wage hikes of 30 to 35 percent to maintain their livelihood. These work stoppages and strikes varied in duration, from a few hours to several days, and involved up to one to two thousand workers in large factories.

Based on their experience in handling fourteen strikes in Xiamen SEZ in Fujian Province, two labor officials summarized the characteristics of these incidents as short-lived, economically motivated episodes. However, spontaneous as they may be, 'very soon organizers and leaders would emerge from among the foremen, line leaders or shop floor heads'. They also pointed to the importance of native-place ties, noting that eight out of the fourteen strikes occurred in factories with a disproportionate number of workers coming from the same locality, forming regional cliques. 'As relatives or native-place locals, they share strong exclusionary sentiments and solidarity which can easily lead to collective rebellions'.[25] Other reports of similar incidents elsewhere revealed more ambiguous effects of localism in worker resistance. During a go-slow in a Korean factory, workers remarked that regional divisions among them undermined the unity needed for a strike, saying 'if there were no migrant workers, we would be on strike already'.[26]

Striking workers demonstrated a certain level of organizational ability, as accounts of these incidents mentioned organizers writing open letters and printing leaflets and flyers to mobilize workers. One commonly used tactic was to notify journalists and news agencies about their actions, in an effort to arouse public attention and sympathy for their struggles.

A notable feature in most of these strikes is the ambiguous and conciliatory role played by the local ACFTU and Labor Bureau officials. Trade union officials admitted that their double role was one 'of supporting the foreign investors, but also monitoring whether management is abiding by the labor laws'. The Zhuhai ACFTU criticized the 1993 strike at the Canon plant. In a number of cases where striking workers demanded the setting up of enterprise unions, local ACFTU officials urged consultation with management before endorsing their establishment. Union officials were also helpless in defending workers during strikes in foreign-owned enterprises, when public security personnel were often called into the compounds by management to intimidate strikers. Although unionization rates among foreign-invested enterprises reached 40 percent by the end of 1994 in Guangdong, most of these ACFTU-approved unions were led and staffed by management personnel who were mainly responsible for collecting union fees, organizing birthday parties and recreational events. These union leaders were also salaried shop floor supervisors or section heads in the factory administration.[27]

Protests, demonstrations and violence

In the spring of 1989, the mobilization of workers into street protests, many with support and approval from work unit leadership and the official union, raised the specter of labor mobilization against the state. In mid-May 1989, marching workers in Beijing hoisted banners bearing the name of their enterprises including the Capitol Steel Corporation, the main factory of the Beijing Internal Combustion Engines, Beijing Lifting Machinery Factory, etc. At one point before the declaration of martial law, the ACFTU also joined the demonstration with its own banner and even made a 100,000 yuan donation to the student hunger strikers.[28] One observer remarks that this 'distinctive Chinese pattern of (work-unit) protest has come to mirror the distinctive Chinese pattern of work-unit control.'[29] Labor protests in the post-Tiananmen decade have witnessed a heightened tendency for workers to go beyond the confines of their workplace. Bringing their protests into the public, they are often joined by other disgruntled segments of the local community. Labor activism thus not only underlines the erosion of state power at the grass-roots level, and a shift from the enterprise to the state as their target of challenge, it also has the potential to become a rallying point for community-based activism.

In 1995 alone, by official reckoning, protest marches involving more than 20 people rose to a record-high of 1,620, including more than 1.1 million people and occurring in more than thirty cities.[30] Grievances that sparked these public protests reflected the predicaments of debt-ridden state enterprises under reform. Worker opposition was directed against wage and pension arrears, inadequate unemployment and medical allowances, embezzlement of funds by factory managers, plant mergers, restructuring and relocations. Among the first of its kind, the largescale protest staged by workers in the Chongqing Knitting Mill in November 1992 turned out to be representative of similar incidents in the province of Sichuan and other impoverished provinces throughout the 1990s. When this large state enterprise went bankrupt and cut back on pension payments to retired workers, workers took to the street, demanding the 'right to subsistence'. Retirees led the procession and pleaded tearfully with the riot police, arguing that their pension payment was their rightful share of the surplus value they had generated for the state over the years, and that the state and the enterprise had no right to withhold their repayment. Workers on the job also demanded state guarantee of their basic right to live. After 5 days of confrontation, the authorities conceded to workers' demands: pension payments would not be cut while workers on the job were retrained or assigned to new jobs by the enterprise.[31]

Subsistence rights occupy a top priority in the slogans found in many other demonstrations, revealing workers' desperation and outrage. 'We Want To Work', 'Our Children Want to Go To School' (in a Chengdu shoe factory protest in July 1997), 'We Want Jobs' and 'We Want Food' (in a textile mill protest in Baicheng, Jilin in October 1995), 'We Don't Demand Fish or Meat, Just Some Porridge', and 'Not a Yuan in Six Months, We Want Rice to Eat' (a protest in Changsha in November 1998). Corruption was also a major complaint, with slogans targeting cadres: 'Down with the Newly Emerging Nobility' and 'Eradicate the New Bureaucratic Bourgeoisie' (a petition rally by chemical workers in Shenyang in March 1994). Or, in a protest in Ningxia, banners read 'We Need to Eat, We Need to Exist' and 'Save the Factory, Save the People.' Most noteworthy among these slogans were those heard at a 5,000-strong protest march in April 1994 in Anshan, the capital of China's iron and steel industry: 'Workers Are the Masters of the State', 'Down with the New Born Bourgeoisie', 'Yes to Socialism, No to Capitalism' and 'Long Live the Working Class'. Reappropriating what used to be ideological statements from the party-state to launch their political critique, workers' demands have gone beyond strictly economic ones to challenge directly the legitimacy of a self proclaimed socialist state. Increasingly prominent too is an emergent discourse of rights.

In another illustrative incident, the city of Nanchong in Sichuan was the scene of a massive spontaneous labor uprising. Certain features of the incident could be found in milder form in numerous other labor protests. The state-run Jialihua silk factory used to support 10,000 workers, who suffered pay cuts and lay offs as company revenues plunged in the early 1990s. Disgruntled by management's extravagance in hard times, workers held the general manager hostage as he prepared for an official 'inspection tour' in Thailand with his wife.

> They loaded Huang (the manager) into the back of a flatbed truck and forced him into the painful and demeaning 'airplane position' – bent at the waist, arms straight out at the sides. Then they marched 10 kilometers through the rain to downtown Nanchong and paraded him through the street . . . as during the Cultural Revolution. Workers from other factories joined the spontaneous demonstration; in all some 20,000 people took part. The day-long parade ended at the city government building where workers blocked the gates, refusing to let officials out. They took turns making speeches. This stand-off lasted 30 hours, ending peacefully only with the promise of payment. The government ordered the local branch of the state-run Industrial and Commerce Bank of China to lend enough money to Jialihua to cover back wages.[32]

Acts of vengeance like those in the Nanchong incident, sometimes escalating into violence, have characterized many labor actions as furious laid-off workers and retirees blame managers for corruption, profiteering, abuse of power and plundering of state assets. Physical assaults and kidnapping of managers by angry workers have been reported in various provinces. In Liaoning, from January to July 1988, there were 276 reported incidents in which managers were beaten up and a total of 297 managers injured. In the provincial capital Shenyang, a study revealed that 54 percent of managers had been threatened by force or blackmailed.[33] Cases of suicide and attempted murder were also reported: in Fujian, an unemployed worker poured gasoline over himself and ignited a fire after seizing two officials responsible for imposing fines on his peddling business. The worker died and the officials were seriously burned. In many other sit-ins and demonstrations, workers broke through police blockades to occupy main thoroughfares and rail lines, bringing local and inter-provincial traffic to a standstill. Officials have also been alarmed by the rise in violent crime committed by laid-off workers and migrant workers, especially in provinces where unemployment rates are high. Public security officials have found that laid-off workers were ganging up to commit armed robberies and other violent crimes including murder, bombings, and theft. Large-scale factories, steel mills, and mines have been particularly hard-hit by this upsurge in crime. Some 1,900 illegal purchasing centers for steel and metal products, involving more than 300 gangs were found to be buying steel and metal products and raw materials that workers had stolen from factories.

Available accounts indicate that most protests originated at enterprises. After workers took to the streets, they would be joined by laid-off workers from other factories, disgruntled teachers and civil servants in the same locality, all demanding payment of wages, pensions and insurance benefits. In a few cases, workers made deliberate efforts to organize a general strike across enterprises in the same city. Workers in Shenyang reportedly attempted to organize a 10,000-strong protest delegation to Beijing, chartering trains for the petition trip.[34] Local corporatism has developed in areas where the entire neighborhood or city suffers from the effects of reforms. Plant directors, in such localities, rather than being targeted as workers' enemies, have sometimes been the organizers of demonstrations. When a Sichuan munitions factory failed to pay wages, managers led 300–400 elderly retired workers to march downtown, forcing authorities to pay pension arrears.

Leaders and cadres in the impoverished central and northeastern provinces allegedly tried to hold Beijing hostage over the proliferation of labor unrest, in an attempt to demand more central funding for economic development and social insurance. In 1998, an extra 3,000 million yuan was allocated to these provinces as emergency funds.[35] In most cases, public security looked on and cordoned off the protest areas, but arrests were not widespread. One reason for official toleration may have been the central authorities' intention of establishing 'safety valves' whereby protesters could let off steam without targeting the top leadership. More recently, government concession has become so common that workers have entered into a rather 'ritualized' exchange with local officials: demonstrations, especially those taking place before important holidays, e.g. National Day or Chinese New Year, are occasions for pressuring the government to dole out emergency pay.

Geographical variation in the volume of protest dovetails with the uneven regional consequences of reform on Chinese workers. One writer has remarked that the provinces that experienced the most turmoil were mostly interior provinces in central China, including Sichuan, Hunan, Shaanxi, and Henan. These provinces have a high concentration of strategic and heavy industries as a result of the Communist Third Front industrialization and relocation inland of enterprises in the 1960s and 1970s, when heavy industries were moved to avoid possible attacks by the United States and Soviet Union. Of the thirteen provinces where labor turmoil is most pronounced, eleven have more heavy than light industrial firms. Besides, the three northeastern provinces – Liaoning, Jilin and Heilongjiang – have also been prone to worker unrest due to the heavy reliance of their economies on state firms, coal mining and steel production, sectors which have suffered most from economic liberalization.

Although worker insurgencies have been concentrated in coal mining, steel and textile industries, laborers in other economic sectors have also engaged in collective and public actions. Sanitation workers in Beijing, hawkers in Shenzhen, taxi drivers in Beijing, Luzhou (in Sichuan), Changsha, Zhuhai, Shenzhen and Shaoguan (in Guangdong) have protested against low wages, unreasonable hikes in fines and license fees, and arbitrary punishment meted out by police. Many of these service workers were formerly laid-off workers from state-owned enterprises or migrant workers from poverty-stricken rural areas. The most serious turmoil occurred in April 1998, when direct sales agents across the country rioted after a government ban on direct sales firms. At least ten people were killed and more than 100 injured when these agents demanded refunds. Many of the 10 million sales personnel involved in direct marketing were laid-off workers who had to use their savings to pay for training and deposits before joining the companies. Likewise, in November 1998, when the government closed down a number of financial services firms for fraudulent practices, hundreds of workers marched through the streets of Beijing, Zhengzhou and Xinhui. These worker-investors, some of them unemployed, were lured by the promise of interest payment as high as 30 percent a month and some had invested their life savings with these firms.

Overall, only some of these collective protests, demonstrations and strikes have been effective in bringing concrete improvements in workers' livelihood. As mentioned previously, central and local authorities occasionally responded to workers' demands by providing emergency relief funds, or by postponing and revising plant closure or relocation decisions. So far, it seems that economic demands by retirees and unemployed workers in the state sector have been most successful in soliciting sympathetic government responses. But these are at most random and temporary stop-gap measures by the state to silence excessive discontent. The course of enterprise restructuring and market reforms, coupled with China's huge reserve of surplus labor, will likely see a significant segment of the working class continue to suffer from a wholesale commodification of their labor power, well before a societal system of insurance and labor regulation will be effectively in place to protect their rights. This is especially true for the former state workers whose employment status is now legally the same as that of the teeming millions of younger migrant workers, after the universalization of labor contracts in 1995.

Independent unionism and political movement

Organized labor dissent, among all forms of labor resistance, has provoked the most severe repression by the Chinese state. The beleaguered official union, ACFTU, has proved to be too weak to protect worker rights under the combined onslaught of economic reforms and the government decisions to cut back sharply on state enterprises. The 1992 Union Law may have boosted the ACFTU's legal status, and was indicative of top union leaders' striving for a more autonomous role from the party–state. But numerous surveys undertaken by the ACFTU indicate widespread disillusion among rank-and-file workers: over 64 percent of workers in the state sector turn not to the ACFTU but to informal networks for support when their rights are encroached upon. More often than not, official unions are controlled directly by management. Moreover, transmission of funds from lower level unions to the ACFTU has frequently been blocked due to financial difficulty or estrangement of grassroots enterprise unions. In 1993, for instance, the national ACFTU was able to collect only 38 percent of expected contributions.[36] Finally, the laying off of tens of millions of state workers means the loss of the core of the ACFTU membership. These unattached and underprivileged workers have become a potent source of rebellion and protest and perhaps the most serious threat to the party's monopoly on power.

The emergence of autonomous trade unions and their alliance with intellectual and human rights dissidents are particularly threatening to a regime that still proclaims itself the embodiment of the dictatorship of the proletariat. The reform era has marked a period of unprecedented ferment in organized labor dissent in the history of post-1949 China. Political challenge climaxed in the 1989 Democracy Movement, although mobilization for independent unions and cross-class political coalitions have been found both before and since. Demands for forming independent unions *à la* Polish Solidarity first emerged in 1981 in Shanghai, Hangzhou, Tianjin, Wuhan, Anshan, Nanchong, and Zhengzhou. In Chongqing, a mimeographed pamphlet entitled *The Chongqing Democratic Trade Union* accused the provincial ACFTU of being 'a docile instrument of the Party'. In response, the Chinese government decided to allow more workplace democracy by setting up worker's congresses in Chinese state enterprises.[37] The next round of struggle for autonomous unions took place in April 1989. Taking advantage of student agitation and a rebellious social climate, several dozens of young workers who gathered to talk politics in Tiananmen Square gave birth to the Beijing Workers' Autonomous Federation (BWAF), or *gongzilian*. Claiming a registered membership of 20,000 workers before the military crackdown, the BWAF became a model for fifteen other independent unions set up in other major cities. WAFs were organized in Tianjin, Harbin, Shenyang, Huhhot, Xi'an, Wuhan, Nanjing, Shanghai, Jinan, Hangzhou, Suzhou, Changsha, Shaoyang, Fuzhou and Guangzhou during the two months between April and June 1989.[38] An analysis of several WFAs finds that 70 percent of the core organizers came from the blue-collar working class, while 20 percent were members of the intelligentsia, and 10 percent white-collar workers. Despite Beijing students' disdainful stance towards workers' participation in the Tiananmen protests, there were conscious efforts on the part of workers to recruit more educated 'experts' into WAFs, and these people eventually played a key role in drafting memoranda and declarations for their organization. In the BWAF, for instance, two students were among the five core leaders. Significantly, a number of ex-ACFTU cadres were among the core organizers of the Fuzhou WAF. Born at the height of a political movement and state crisis, WAFs were loose, fluid and short lived, with relatively small memberships (ranging from several hundred to several thousand members), and weak organizational linkages among WAFs scattered around the country.[39] However, contacts were maintained among WAFs and other citizen groups in the same region. For instance, there were liaisons between the Beijing WAF and employees of the Capitol Steel Corporation who were organizing their own workers' federation, the Capital Workers Picket Corps, the Flying Tigers Motorcycle Brigade, and the Beijing Citizens Dare-to-Die Corps. Despite its small size and precarious financial conditions, the Beijing WAF played a pivotal role in the mobilization and coordination of street demonstrations after the declaration of martial law on May 1989. It even issued calls for a general strike and maintained a broadcasting system on the Square where news from overseas stations and political statements and complaints from the masses could be heard.[40]

Of lasting significance may be the political consciousness of WAF leaders and the tradition of democratic movements they draw on and keep alive. Walder and Gong have stressed a strong strain of 'working-class populism' in the rhetoric and collective mentality of the Beijing WAF – disrespectful of intellectual authority, doggedly independent, inclusive of and open to all ordinary citizens, capable of linking the idea of working class struggle with the language of democratic opposition to political oligarchy. Thus, not only did this independent union movement demand price stabilization, the right to change jobs, an end to discrimination against women workers, investigation of official incomes and privileges, but it also consciously engaged in a 'fight for democracy', a struggle for the right to 'supervise the Communist Party', and the right to supervise the legal representatives of the company in state and collective enterprises.[41] Elsewhere, Elizabeth Perry has observed a tradition of democratic movements, fueled by worker–student nationalism, which began with the May Fourth Movement in 1919 and continued throughout the Civil War years. In 1989, it was the students' exclusionist and elitist attitude towards ordinary workers which set limits on the potential for an urban coalition of citizens.[42] After the bloody crackdown in June, workers were treated more ruthlessly than any other group and several were swiftly executed or sentenced to life imprisonment for 'counter-revolutionary sabotage'.[43]

Relentless suppression by the Chinese state of autonomous unionism has been met with an equally persistent resolve on the part of some labor activists to keep alive the radical tradition of the 1989 uprising. In 1991, there were reports of government crackdowns on some fourteen underground labor organizations with memberships ranging from twenty to 300 in the capital alone. In the post-Tiananmen decade, several underground unions and initiatives have surfaced, thanks to their strategy of maintaining international connections and communication: the Free Trade Unions of China, the League for the Protection of the Rights of the Working People, the Hired-hands Workers' Federation, China Development Union, among others. Although workers are represented among the core members of these groups, dissident intellectuals – mainly students and university lecturers – account for the majority of organizers. Many of them had participated in the 1979 Democracy Wall Movement and the 1989 Movement, and shared the goal of incorporating an independent union movement into a broad-based political opposition to the CCP regime.[44] In 1997, seizing the opportunity of China's signing the United Nations Convention on Economic, Social and Cultural Rights, dissidents wrote open letters urging Chinese workers to exercise their right to free association and to unite against massive layoffs. They also published and distributed bulletins to workers, released petitions for workers' rights, set up nation-wide networks of activists, and even attempted to register their organizations with the Ministry of Civil Affairs. Appealing to unemployed and migrant workers (and peasants in some cases), and supported by Chinese dissident communities living overseas, activists of these nascent associations increasingly frame labor interests in terms of human rights concerns.[45] Not surprisingly, however, arrests, convictions and imprisonment of labor activists have also continued unabated in different parts of China, including Hubei, Jilin, Guangdong and Shanxi.

The road ahead

Social conflicts between various sectors of labor, on the one hand, and enterprise management, local officials and the state, on the other, have been sharpened by market reforms. A more restive Chinese working class is in the making, as shown by the massive eruption of collective actions over the past two decades. Rice bowl issues have combined with a reappropriation of Marxist and Maoist rhetoric of exploitation and inequality to unite a broad spectrum of veteran laborers in the state sector. Their common interests and cultural frames for action have their roots in almost forty years of state socialist rule with its claims of worker mastery. The young generation of migrant workers, many of them employed in the private sector, share widespread degrading and inhumane treatment. Although they may have weaker awareness of labor rights than their veteran counterparts,[46] migrant workers' agitation has often been energized by localistic solidarity and common experience of exploitation at the point of production. Yet these two generations of workers are not ready allies in forming any class-based movement. Divided by localistic origins (local workers versus outside workers), sociocultural backgrounds (country folk versus urbanites), and age (young versus middle-aged and older), different groups of workers often find themselves in competition for the same unskilled and low paid manufacturing jobs in both the state and non-state sectors, now that labor contract reforms have standardized their employment status and rights. Even when they labor side by side within state-owned factories, conflicts regarding wage rates and work allocation are common.[47]

China has yet to witness the emergence of a labor movement, if movements are defined by 'collective challenges by people with common purposes and solidarity in sustained interaction with elites, opponents and authorities.'[48] The many episodes and pockets of resistance documented in this chapter lack effective social and organizational networks to transform them into sustained challenges. Under reform, Chinese workers and ordinary citizens alike no doubt enjoy greater personal autonomy and a widening public sphere,[49] as market mechanisms and economic decentralization have gradually unbundled their webs of dependence on official units. Yet, the strong grip of the state is also evident in the organization and leadership formation of these newly-emerging societal and civic associations.[50] Attempts to form opposition political parties or independent unions are ruthlessly crushed, as the above discussion shows. The political opportunity structure remains decidedly exclusionary and closed.

One critical factor affecting the possibility of widening the political space for organized labor dissent hinges on elite alignment. Two of the most astute observers of Chinese labor politics agree on the importance of élite cleavage for labor activism. Reviewing the trajectories of labor strife since 1949, Elizabeth Perry concludes that 'Chinese labor activism has, for the better part of a century, been characterized by a complex blend of bottom-up initiatives and top-down mobilization . . . (W)e should not underestimate the extent to which contemporary labor protest is likely to feed into the projects of rival political leaders.'[51] Andrew Walder likewise underlines the interaction between divided élites and social groups:

> The 'Tiananmen protest' was emphatically not a case where an autonomous protest movement from below rose up to challenge and incapacitate a communist regime. . . . Instead, 'Tiananmen' is a classic case in which nascent protests interact with a divided elite and party–state apparatus . . . with impulses for protests from below.[52]

As Sidney Tarrow notes, a political opportunity structure becomes more conducive to sustained collective action during times of shifts in ruling alignments, influential allies or élite cleavages. These conditions have strong precedents in contemporary Chinese politics. And when these conditions do mature in conjunction with labor agitation, forms of unobtrusive struggle and public resistance documented above may prove to be constitutive elements of a 'repertoire of contention' for a Chinese labor movement powerful enough to challenge the government's monopoly of power. But there is an alternative road ahead, one in which the state successfully institutionalizes a new social security net to guarantee the economic survival of the weak, puts in place a system for labor arbitration based on genuine tripartite representation including labor, and sustains economic growth so as to dampen the motivation to rebel collectively. Coupled with state repression of any sprout of independent organizing, these conditions may over time channel labor discontent into the confines of localized and sporadic unrest, or individual forms of resistance.

Notes

1 Charles Hoffmann, *The Chinese Worker* (Albany: State University of New York Press, 1974).
2 Andrew G. Walder, *Communist Neo-traditionalism – Work and Authority in Chinese Industry* (Berkeley: University of California Press, 1986), Chapter two.
3 Elizabeth J. Perry, 'Shanghai's Strike Wave of 1957,' *The China Quarterly* 137 (March 1994), 1–27.
4 Andrew G. Walder, 'The Chinese Cultural Revolution in the Factories: Party-State Structures and Patterns of Conflict,' in Elizabeth J. Perry (ed.), *Putting Class in Its Place: Worker Identities in East Asia* (Berkeley: Institute of East Asian Studies, University of California, China Research Monograph, 1996), pp. 167–98; Elizabeth J. Perry, 'Labor's Love Lost: Worker Militancy in Communist China,' *International Labor and Working-Class History* 50 (Fall, 1996), 64–76; Elizabeth J. Perry and Li Xun, *Proletarian Power: Shanghai in the Cultural Revolution* (Boulder, CO: Westview, 1997).
5 Sebastian Heilmann, 'The Social Context of Mobilization in China: Factions, Work Units, and Activists During the 1976 April Fifth Movement,' *China Information* 8 (Winter 1993–94), 1–19.
6 Renhong Wu, 'China's Macroeconomy: Review and Perspective,' *Journal of Contemporary China* 7 (19), 1998, 443–58.
7 *China Labour Statistical Yearbook 1997,* p. 6.
8 Fei-ling Wang, 'Floaters, Moonlighters, and the Underemployed: a National Labor Market with Chinese Characteristics,' *Journal of Contemporary China* 7 (19), 1998, 459–75.
9 A Statistical Survey of China 1998, p. 32.
10 Russell Smyth, 'Toward "the Modern Corporation": Recent Developments in the Institutional Reform of State-owned Enterprises in Mainland China,' *Issues and Studies* 34 (August 1998), 121.
11 Ching Kwan Lee, 'From Organized Dependence to Disorganized Despotism: Changing Labor Regime in Chinese Factories,' *The China Quarterly*, no. 157 (March 1999), 44–71.
12 Dorothy Solinger, 'The Chinese Work Unit and Transient Labor in the Transition from Socialism,' *Modern China* 21 (April 1995), 155–83.
13 James C. Scott, *Domination and the Arts of Resistance: Hidden Transcripts* (New Haven: Yale University Press, 1985).
14 Xueguang Zhou, 'Unorganized Interests and Collective Action in Communist China,' *American Sociological Review* 58 (February 1993), 54–73.
15 Andrew G. Walder, *Communist Neo-traditionalism*, Chapter 6.
16 This situation differs from conditions studied by David Stark in Hungary in the 1980s. There, core workers formed 'work partnerships' inside state owned factories,

allowing strategic workers to earn extra money and to resolve bottlenecks of raw material supplies for production. Chinese workers' participation in the second economy is not institutionally incorporated into state enterprises and management perceives such moonlighting as detrimental, not supplementary, to firm productivity. See David Stark, 'Co-existing Organizational Forms in Hungary's Emerging Mixed Economy,' in Victor Nee and David Stark (eds), *Remaking the Economic Institutions of Socialism: China and Eastern Europe* (Stanford: Stanford University Press, 1988), pp. 137–68.

17 Ching Kwan Lee, 'The Labor Politics of Market Socialism: Collective Inaction and Class Experiences Among State Workers in Guangzhou,' *Modern China* 24 (January 1998).

18 See *Zhongguo laodongbao*, July 26, 1997; Hilary K. Josephs, 'Labor Law in a "Socialist Market Economy": the Case of China,' *Columbia Journal of Transnational Law* 33 (1995), 559–81; Anita Chan, 'The Emerging Patterns of Industrial Relations in China and the Rise of Two New Labor Movements,' *China Information* 9 (Spring 1995), 36–59.

19 *Laodong Zhengyi Chuli Yu Yanjiu* (*Labor Disputes: Handling and Research*) 1995, 1996, 1997, various articles.

20 Alan Liu, *Mass Politics in the People's Republic* (Boulder, CO: Westview, 1996), p. 105; Jeanne L. Wilson, '"The Polish Lesson": China and Poland, 1980–1990', *Studies in Comparative Communism*, 23 (Autumn/Winter 1990), 263. See also Chen-chang Chiang, 'The Role of the Trade Unions in Mainland China,' *Issues and Studies* 26 (February 1990), 92–93.

21 Chiang, ibid.

22 Shaoguang Wang, 'Deng Xiaoping's Reform and the Chinese Workers' Participation in the Protest Movement of 1989,' *Research in Political Economy* 13, 1992, 163–97.

23 Elizabeth J. Perry, 'Labor's Battle for Political Space: the Role of Worker Associations in Contemporary China,' in Deborah Davis *et al.* (eds), *Urban Spaces in Contemporary China* (Cambridge: Cambridge University Press, 1995), p. 315.

24 Leung Wing-yue, *Smashing the Iron Rice Pot: Workers and Unions in China's Market Socialism* (Hong Kong: Asia Monitor Research Center, 1988), pp. 155–58.

25 Lin Zhengong and Chen Yulin, 'Sanziqiye Gongren Daigong Bagong de Tedian he Duize' (Characteristics and Handling of Slow Downs and Strikes by Workers in Foreign-invested Enterprises) in *Zhongguo Laodong Kexue* (Chinese Labor Science), no. 89 (May 1993), 33–35.

26 China Labor Education and Information Center, *The Flip-Side of Success: The Situation of Workers and Organizing in Foreign-invested Electronics Enterprises in Guangdong* (Hong Kong, 1996), p. 11.

27 Anita Chan, 'Labor Relations in Foreign-funded Ventures: Chinese Trade Unions and the Prospects for Collective Bargaining,' in Greg O'Leary (ed.), *Adjusting to Capitalism* (Armonk, NY: M. E. Sharpe, 1998), pp. 122–49; China Labor Education and Information Center, *The Flip-Side of Success*, 1996, op. cit.; Leung Wing-yue, *Smashing the Iron Rice Pot*, 1988, op. cit., p. 175.

28 Elizabeth J. Perry, 'Labor's Battle for Political Space: the Role of Worker Associations in Contemporary China,' op. cit., pp. 318–19; Andrew G. Walder, 'Urban Industrial Workers: Some Observations on the 1980s,' in Arthur Lewis Rosenbaum (ed.), *State and Society in China: The Consequences of Reform* (Boulder, CO: Westview) 1992, pp. 103–20; Lu Ping, *A Moment of Truth: Workers' Participation in China's 1989 Democracy Movement and the Emergence of Independent Unions* (Hong Kong: Hong Kong Trade Union Education Center, 1990); Jonathan Unger (ed.), *The Pro-Democracy Protests in China: Reports from the Provinces* (Armonk, NY: M. E. Sharpe, 1991).

29 Andrew G. Walder, ibid., p. 116.

30 FBIS-CHI-96-077, 29, April 19, 1996.

31 *Cheng Ming*, April 1993, 37.
32 *Far Eastern Economic Review* June 26, 1997, 15.
33 Shaoguang Wang, 1988, op. cit., p. 187.
34 *Cheng Ming*, April 1994, pp. 30–31; FBIS-CHI-96-028, 34, February 9, 1996.
35 *South China Morning Post*, December 6, 1995; *Ming Pao*, July 24, 1998.
36 Feng Tongqing, 'Workers and Trade Unions Under the Market Economy: Perspectives from Grassroots Union Cadres', *Chinese Sociology and Anthropology* 28 (Spring 1996).
37 Chen-chang Chiang, op. cit., 1990, 92–93.
38 Lu Ping, 1990, op. cit.
39 Trini Wing-yue Leung, 1988, op.cit., chapter 7.
40 Andrew Walder and Gong Xiaoxia, 'Workers in the Tiananmen Protests: the Politics of Beijing Workers' Autonomous Federation,' *The Australian Journal of Chinese Affairs* 29 (January 1993), p. 11.
41 Ibid.
42 Elizabeth J. Perry, 'Casting a Chinese "Democracy" Movement: the Role of Students, Workers, and Entrepreneurs,' in Jeffrey N.Wasserstrom and Elizabeth J. Perry (eds), *Popular Protest and Political Culture in Modern China* (Boulder, CO: Westview, 1994) (second edition), pp. 74–92. David Strand traces a tradition of public critique to the post-Taiping Rebellion of the nineteenth century in his 'Protest in Beijing: Civil Society and Public Sphere in China,' *Problems of Communism* (May–June 1990), pp. 1–19.
43 Lu Ping, op. cit., p. 19.
44 Trini Wing-yue Leung, 1988, op. cit., chapter 8; *South China Morning Post*, October 9, 1998.
45 *New York Times*, December 24, 1997; *South China Morning Post*, December 28, 1997.
46 Cai He, 'Cong Zhigongde Quanli Renshi Kan Feizhengshi Yueshu de Suoyouzhi Cibie jiji Yingxiang' ('From "Rights Congition" to Informal Control Across Types of Enterprise Ownership: Differences and Implications'), paper presented at the International Conference on 'China's Economic Opening and Social Structural Change', May 18, 1998, Hong Kong.
47 Ching Kwan Lee, 'From Organized Dependence to Disorganized Despotism,' op. cit.
48 Sidney Tarrow, *Power in Movement: Social Movements, Collective Action and Politics* (Cambridge: Cambridge University Press, 1994), pp. 3–4.
49 See for example, Deborah Davis *et al.* (eds), *Urban Spaces in Contemporary China: the Potential for Autonomy and Community in Post-Mao China* (Cambridge: Cambridge University Press, 1995).
50 Kin-man Chan and Haixiong Qiu, 'Small Government, Big Society: Social Organizations and Civil Society in China,' *China Area Studies Series* (Japan), no. 8, 1998, 34–47; Margaret Pearson, *China's New Business Elite* (Berkeley: University of California Press, 1997).
51 Elizabeth J. Perry, 1995, op. cit., p. 325.
52 Andrew G. Walder, 'Does China Face an Unstable Future?' in Maurice Brosseau, Kuan Hsin-chi and Y. Y. Kueh (eds), *China Review 1997* (Hong Kong: Chinese University Press, 1997), pp. 344–45.

3 Gender, employment and women's resistance

Wang Zheng

This chapter examines the impact of social and economic transformation on women's lives by delineating changes in urban women's employment. Women's employment has been an intensely contested site that has not only reflected conflicting social interests and revealed gender assumptions, but has also shaped gender identities and class realignment. Women of diverse social groups have deployed differentiated strategies of resistance.

It is often asked 'Has reform improved the condition and status of women, or has it set it back?' Departing from simplistic assumptions concerning the existence of a monolithic Chinese womanhood, and a singular gender relationship, this chapter highlights multiple contradictory social realities experienced by contemporary women positioned differentially across hierarchies of age, urban/rural residence, education, and class. Gender relationships are differentially affected depending on one's position in these and other power-laden hierarchies. Women's resistance, accordingly, takes different forms, employs variegated resources, and aims at diverse goals.

This chapter examines the impact of social and economic transformation on women's lives by delineating changes in urban women's employment. The rapid diversification of the rural economy, development of the market, the rise of industry at the township level as well as of household enterprises, and the opening of urban labor markets have also brought tremendous changes in rural women's employment. Here I focus on changes in employment in the urban setting, including employment of women living in cities whom the state classifies as 'rural.' Beginning with a brief review of Maoist policy on urban women's employment, this chapter explores changing patterns of urban women's employment and women's resistance and negotiation in the rapidly changing social, cultural and political milieu in post-Mao urban China.

Urban employment, gender and inequality in the Mao era

In the socialist, planned economy, the state guaranteed urban employment while prohibiting labor influx from rural areas (see Mallee in this volume). Local governments assigned each resident a permanent job either in a state- or collectively-owned enterprise. Once assigned, mobility was largely restricted to promotion within the work unit. A work unit was not only a production unit but also an all-encompassing welfare institution that covered employees' health care, accident insurance, and maternity leave. Some large work units offered housing and childcare as well. Employee benefits varied in different industries and state run enterprises provided better packages than collective enterprises. But within the same work unit, men and women, old and young, generally received comparable benefits. Employment meant lifetime security.

Women's employment policy in the Mao era was framed within the Engelsian concept of women's liberation and gender equality: only through participation in social production would women achieve liberation. Employment meant socialist construction since the private sector virtually disappeared in the early 1950s. 'Housewife,' by definition not a participant in social production, became a scorned urban social category and increasingly a historic relic. For urban women growing up in the Mao era, employment was taken for granted as an important component of a woman's life, even though far from all women experienced a sense of liberation by participating in social production. Women's employment enhanced their status at home since their income was vitally important to the family in the egalitarian low income system of the Mao era.

Urban women in the Mao era enjoyed equal employment opportunities with men and lifetime security and welfare benefits. This does not mean that they had achieved gender equality as the Cultural Revolution slogan 'Women hold up half the sky' implied. A recent study investigating two state-owned factories in Guangzhou finds that, although the government issued equal employment guidelines from the early 1960s, specific job assignments invariably followed unstated gender lines. In an optical instrument factory, for example, of twenty-five categories of technical work, seven were seen as suitable to women and eighteen to men. In a machinery plant, fewer than twenty of 106 categories were seen as suitable to women. In both factories, service and auxiliary work was always 'female work.' This includes maintenance of tools, cleaning, operating day care centers, dining rooms, and clinics. Men were overwhelmingly assigned to technical jobs and women to non-technical, auxiliary, and service jobs, regardless of educational level. This gendered employment hierarchy established women's subordinate position and shaped women's self-definition.

While job assignment, promotion, and allocation of resources such as housing in the workplace have reinforced both men's and women's identity, differential gendered social expectations also color assessments of performance in the workplace. Women's family responsibilities and their tendency to focus expectations on their husbands' career development are major factors that render women workers less motivated than men to pursue promotion or join the party, a form of political capital and means of networking critical for advancement and other benefits.

Another important factor kept women in subordinate positions. In Maoist egalitarianism, which reached a peak for the cohort entering the workplace during the Cultural Revolution, income differentials, including those based on skill, were relatively small in China's low-income, high welfare, lifetime urban employment system. In line with the slogan that all jobs were equally important to the revolution, gendered job assignments were not perceived as discriminatory to women.

Urban women employees enjoyed pay, benefits and security, of which their rural sisters could only dream. Urban women's substantial gains in the Mao era, often cited by the state as proof of Chinese women's liberation, were inherent in privileging of the urban working class over the peasantry. The huge gap in wages and benefits for working women (and men) in urban areas continues in the post-Mao era even when rural reform has rapidly improved rural people's living standard. A nationwide survey conducted by the Women's Federation in 1990 found that 82.6 percent of urban women had pensions vs. 5.6 percent of rural women; 71 percent of urban women had medical coverage vs. 8 percent of rural women; 79.9 percent of urban women had paid sick leave vs. 9.2 percent of rural women; and 85.3 percent of urban women had paid maternity leave vs. 12.1 percent of rural women.

The reform of the labor system in the 1980s has reduced, but hardly eliminated, the advantages enjoyed by urban workers. The state no longer guarantees urban employment. Indeed, urban employment is no longer an exclusive privilege for urban dwellers. But throughout the 1980s, with rapid expansion of urban employment, workers with urban residence permits maintained their advantages in a two-tier employment structure that disadvantaged rural workers. Under pressure to reduce losses in the 1990s, however, state enterprises have laid off employees or turned to cheaper rural labor. With job creation slowed to a virtual halt, the influx of rural labor has reduced wages in many urban unskilled and service jobs to levels unacceptable to urban workers. Rural labor has thus undermined job prospects for urban workers. While the urban working class experience in general involves dwindling prestige and security from levels enjoyed in the Mao era, the losses suffered by women workers have been greatest.

Moving from job assignment by government to a job market in which different ownership forms coexist and compete, freedom of mobility joins freedom of discrimination, and opportunities blend with insecurity. New employment patterns have broad social ramifications entailing realignment of social classes and gender position. This profoundly affects urban dwellers' relationships to the state and reshapes their identities. This is a gendered process in which urban men and women of diverse social positions engage in contestation at multiple levels.

Gendered layoffs: women workers bear the brunt of reform

Throughout the 1980s, China's high growth economy created millions of jobs annually, with women as well as men sharing in expanded and diversified employment opportunities. Since the 1980s, however, many women workers in the state sector have found themselves in the category of 'surplus labor.' Disproportionate numbers of women were among those laid-off or forced to retire prior to the legal retirement age (60 years of age for men, 55 for women). Gendered layoffs reached new magnitudes in the late 1990s, coinciding with structural changes in China's industry and economic slowdown. At the heart of the employment crisis is China's manufacturing sector, which accounts for almost one-third of urban employees, as many state and collectively owned enterprises, now labeled as a drain on state resources, confront painful choices of technological change, merger, closure, or bankruptcy. Official statistics reveal that by the end of 1997 there were 11.51 million laid-off workers (of which 7.87 million were from state owned enterprises) in China's cities, with 3.5 million more projected for 1998. A survey by the State Statistical Bureau of 15,600 households in 71 cities across the country reveals that women constitute 62.8 percent of the laid-off workers, while they account for less than 39 percent of the total urban workforce. In other words, women have been singled out as special targets of the massive layoffs of the 1990s.

More than any other issue, gendered layoffs reveal the disproportionate burden borne by women as a consequence of the reform. Women's journals and newspapers have paid much attention to the issue by publicizing individual laid-off women's miseries. Many surveys show that although work units are supposed to pay monthly subsidies to laid-off workers (from 150 to over 300 yuan), many laid-off workers receive little or nothing. In order to boost the morale of laid-off women, an editorial in *Women of China* presented a touching analogy. 'The whole society is like a woman in delivery who is enduring the pain of contractions. . . . The piercing pain shaking you is only one step away from the birth of a new life. . . . Sisters, hang on a little bit longer. You will find your own path in your future choice.' The pain of contractions may be a close analogy to the pain that laid-off women are experiencing. But few women suffering the pain of layoffs can expect a joyful new life at the end of 'contractions.' Many have been forced to endure suffering in the form of humiliation and poverty. Many women workers protested:

> Before it was said that we workers were the masters. How come now we are so casually thrown out of the door? Why are our contributions to the state-run enterprises no longer mentioned? The current state of the enterprises was not caused by women workers. Why should we be told to swallow the bitter fruit?

Why has the weight of urban reform in the form of unemployment impinged so heavily, and disproportionately, on women workers? Since the majority of laid-off women are in their thirties and forties with a high-school education or lower, many studies emphasize these women's reproductive role, domestic role, and low education level as key factors disadvantaging them in the labor market. But the gender disparity in layoffs suggests that something deeper is involved.

The discriminatory structure of the socialist workplace disprivileges women workers in a market economy. As noted previously, most women lack the bargaining power that skilled male laborers and technicians have both inside their factories and outside in the job market. A 1998 survey from Chongqing indicates that women comprised 65 percent of all those laid-off and that more than 80 percent of these women held non-technical and service jobs. When state-owned enterprises are being transformed from all-encompassing 'work units' to profit-seeking entities, auxiliary and service components are the first to be cast off. Structural readjustment is profoundly gendered in its implications, if not its goals. Disproportionate numbers of women have been driven out of state industry and into low prestige, low-pay collective or private service sector jobs with few benefits. In short, gendered training and job assignment in the socialist planned economy provided the foundations for widening gender disparities in the reform era.

Although none of the reform policies specifies or rationalizes policies addressing gender, the explicit prioritization of profitability and sheer disregard of gendered consequences are indicative of the state's withdrawal from its previously proclaimed, if weakly implemented, commitment to sexual equality. Abandoning women workers who have long been disadvantaged by gendered practices at workplaces, the state is creating an urban underclass whose predicament is aggravated by widespread gender discrimination.

With the end of state commitment to women's equality, 'freedom' of gender discrimination has become rampant. Where gender stereotypes previously structured job assignments, they now provide the rationale for layoffs. Indeed, there is abundant evidence that in addition to factors such as women's predominance in expendable service positions, gendered stereotyping by overwhelmingly male managers is at the heart of women's disproportionate unemployment. Asked why so many more women than men were laid off, a factory manager replied without hesitation, 'If you lay off men, they will get drunk and make trouble. But if you lay off women, they will just go home and take it quietly by themselves.'[1] This remark may be taken as representative of the mindset of many in power who would put women workers in jeopardy in order to achieve profitability or stability. From the perspective of the state, layoffs which leave most families with one job intact produce a result that is far less explosive than if many families were without even one income earner. From job assignment to layoffs, gender is a critical dimension in labor management and development strategies. But how have women reacted to this transformed social landscape? What resources have women deployed for negotiation or contestation?

Women's employment: a contested site

Long before gendered layoffs became a critical issue, women's employment was hotly debated. Since the early 1980s, intellectuals have crossed swords over the Maoist equal employment policy, relations between women's employment and 'modernity,' patterns of women's employment in the market economy, and the predicament of laid-off women workers. These debates reveal not only conflicting social and economic interests, but also different assumptions concerning gender. In the process of discursive contestation, new demands have emerged to shape policy-making processes, including those affecting employment and gender.

In the early 1980s reformers criticized Maoist gendered employment policies for impeding economic growth. Rather than critiquing the skewed gender structure in the workplace, these critics simply pointed to urban women's high employment rate as a relic of Maoist egalitarianism and a source of inefficiency in enterprises. 'Women return home' was openly advocated in official journals and newspapers as urban reform began to confront unemployment problems compounded by more than ten million 'returned youth' from the countryside. Thus, even before the government issued any reform policies that threatened women's interests, a serious challenge to equal employment loomed in public discourse.

New theories rationalized sending women home. Women's liberation, it was said, exceeded the low level of productivity in China. According to this theory, China's economic development was still at a low level that was incompatible with full employment of women. Because women's physical characteristics made them less adaptable to various job requirements, excessive employment of women reduced enterprise efficiency. The goal of socialism, reformers asserted, is to increase productivity. To contribute to this goal, women should return home. This 'exceeding theory' (*chaoqian lun*) openly blamed women for the low productivity of the socialist planned economy. At a time when urban women activists were beginning to question the myth that 'Chinese women are liberated' and express their discontent with a masculinist Maoist 'gender equality' that taxed women with a double burden, advocates of the 'exceeding theory' claimed that Chinese women were too liberated, or liberated too early.[2]

Many urban educated men seized on the discussion of women's employment to express their long held aversion toward gender equality. As one charged, 'In the name of equality between men and women, the role of men was suppressed in exchange for a relative increase in women's status.' Another complained, 'The helping that women took from the socialist 'big rice pot' exceeded the value of the quantity and quality of their work.' Some simply abandoned gender equality openly and called unabashedly for Chinese women to sacrifice themselves for the sake of national development. Japanese women's domesticity was cited as an example for Chinese women to emulate. Chinese women should likewise return home and sacrifice themselves for the nation.

The anti-gender equality sentiment expressed in the debate over employment was not an isolated case in the 1980s. Throughout the 1980s, urban China was engulfed by a rising discourse of femininity that aimed at combating Maoist perspectives of gender equality and widening gender differences. Beginning as a critique of the ultra-left line of the Cultural Revolution, the discourse of femininity evolved rapidly from condemning such Cultural Revolution era practices as identical clothing and job assignments to a demand for new norms for women. The emerging market economy was quick to produce commodities to enhance femininity. Gender differentiation in dress, social roles, behavior, and occupations became hallmarks of the decade. The challenge to women's equal employment was shaped by, and contributed to, the discourse of femininity.

Feminist voices and strategies

Amidst the rising discourse of femininity in the 1980s, few women or men contested such problematic proposals as 'women should choose feminine jobs.' Fewer disputed new norms of feminine appearance and feminine demeanor that were associated with the image of modernity. But when it came to define women's social roles, sharply opposing views were expressed, often along gender lines. The debate on women's employment and the attack on gender equality in the form of the proposal that 'women return home,' alarmed women activists. The defense of women's equal employment rights became a priority of the Women's Federation as well as of academics engaged in research on women's issues.

The Women's Federation played the most prominent role in blocking the proposal that 'women return home' in the 1980s, drawing on Maoist gender ideology to counterattack. When the suggestion to send women home first appeared in an article in 1980, the Shanghai Women's Federation quickly rejected the proposal as a solution to mitigate Shanghai employment problems. They counterattacked, using unambiguous language of Maoist gender ideology drawn from Engels:

> Women's employment must be linked with women's liberation. Economics is the foundation. Without participation in social production, women would have no economic status. This would in turn undermine the equality between men and women in politics, society and family.

They condemned the proposal that women return home as retrogressive. The 'retrogression' argument was widely repeated and disseminated by Women's Federation representatives throughout the country and by the mainstream media. Women's conscious appeal to 'the Marxist line of women's liberation' in defending employment rights reveals the continuing power of Maoist gender ideology as a source of resistance.

In the reform era, when the party's priority of developing a market economy conflicted with policies upholding gender equality, how could Maoist gender ideology be sustained? To answer this intriguing question, we need to understand that the roots of this discursive power lie deep in China's modern history. From the early twentieth century, especially since the rise of May Fourth feminism in 1919, women's liberation has been linked with the modernity project in nationalist discourse. The Communist Party built its legitimacy in part on its self-proclaimed role as liberator of Chinese women. In other words, maintaining the image of the liberator of women has been a pillar in maintaining the legitimacy of party rule. Just as the Party could not openly abandon Marxism, it was hardly free to abandon the powerful signifier of modernity and socialism – gender equality. Indeed, in the half century history of the People's Republic, equality between men and women is one major constitutional principle that has remained unchanged through social turmoil, constitutional revision, and economic reform. At the same time, while the Party has loudly proclaimed equality, deeply entrenched patterns of gender inequality in social institutions and law have been neglected. As one contemporary Chinese scholar observed, 'Constitutional 'equality between men and women' seems to be an untouchable cultural taboo.' Contemporary attempts explicitly to detach gender equality from the goal of modernization could be seen as illegitimate in this dominant discourse.

Moreover, as the institutional centerpiece of gender discourse, the Women's Federation has continued to serve as both spokesperson for and symbol of gender equality in the reform era. A new term, 'the Marxist theory of women', was created in this period to suggest detachment from a stigmatized political era and to confirm a strong affinity to the party's continued claim to uphold Marxism. Although this stance was awkward in a political era in which upholding Marxism was seen by the public as a project of die-hard conservatives, promotion of the Marxist theory of women served both to remind the party of its commitment to gender equality and to consolidate the power of the official women's organization. Using the Marxist theory of women as leverage, the Women's Federation, and other women in the state apparatus, skillfully negotiated with the party on behalf of women.

Women in and outside the state system have sought with some success to influence public policy, law, and discourse in order to protect women's equal employment rights. A series of policies and laws have been issued countering gender discrimination in the reform era. These include forbidding setting enrollment or recruitment requirements higher for women than for men; stipulating the same retirement age (60) for both male and female senior level professionals; and forbidding laying off women during pregnancy, labor, or breastfeeding. In 1992, the Law on the Protection of Rights and Interests of Women was passed, which reiterated women's comprehensive equal rights in all aspects of social, economic, political and domestic life. Again, the 1994 Labor Law specified women's equal employment rights. However, these gender equality laws and policies lack legal power and are difficult to enforce in a market economy in the absence of a sound legal system. Violations of gender equality laws or policies have often been reported in journals and newspapers run by the Women's Federation system and the Trade Union, but few perpetrators have been punished. Not only does the private sector evade the laws with impunity, even government branches sometimes ignore them. Finding ways to enforce gender equality laws, rather than pushing for their passage, is among the most challenging tasks confronting women cadres and activists inside and outside government.

Unable to stem the tide of layoffs in the late 1990s, the Women's Federation and the Women Workers Department of the Trade Union have devoted much effort to retraining, referral, and reemployment. Vocational training centers and job referral services were established by the two organizations at local levels. Many surveys and reports on laid-off workers have been published by the two organizations to call public attention to the plight of laid-off women, to press for government action to guarantee women's employment rights, and to establish social security and unemployment benefits to buffer the impact of institutional and industrial transformations.

After the Fourth UN Conference on Women held in Beijing in 1995, activists and researchers on women's issues found both reinforced legitimacy and new analytical frameworks to fight for gender equity. Since the Chinese government sponsored the Conference and signed the UN documents pledging gender equality, official women's organizations and women activists sought to hold the government accountable. On March 8, 1996, *The Chinese Women's News* reprinted Jiang Zemin's welcome speech at the Fourth UN Conference on Women. One sentence from Jiang's speech was selected as the title, 'Equality Between Men and Women is the Fundamental State Policy in Promoting Social Development in Our Country.' Following this reprint, presented as a new official document from the top leadership, newspaper reporters interviewed officials around the country asking what concrete measures they had taken to implement the 'fundamental state policy.' The Women's Federation also campaigned to popularize the *Platform for Action*. Feminist scholars in academia utilized the congenial atmosphere to circulate through the official media feminist issues and concepts. In all these discursive maneuvers, the central strategy has been to consolidate the connection between gender equality and modernity. The principles in the feminist documents passed by the UN Conference are presented as standard practice in 'modern civilizations' that China must adopt in the process of modernization.

Preparing and hosting the UN Conference enabled frequent interaction and communication between Chinese women activists and global feminists. A direct consequence of all these activities is that the feminist concept 'gender' (*shehui xingbie*), a term unfamiliar just a few years ago, has been adopted by many Chinese feminists in their analyses of the contemporary situation. The new conceptual tool borrowed from global feminism helped Chinese feminists to break out of their previous dilemma. Pursuing gender justice in the framework of Maoist gender ideology had not only limited their analytical power, but also made them look 'conservative' in the social context of deconstructing Maoism. In the 1980s, with the discourse of femininity on the rise, few women opposed the suggestion of gender differentiation in occupations because it sounded 'progressive' in its attempt to reverse Maoist 'unnatural' gender sameness. In the late 1990s, women researchers began gender critiques of the fad to 'feminize' women and encouraged women to cross gender boundaries to compete for high-tech, managerial and entrepreneurial jobs. Using gender together with other newly learned concepts such as 'sustainable development' and 'human-centered development,' Chinese feminists are calling for a development agenda that prioritizes social justice and gender equity. Activists in and outside the Women's

Federation and scholars from academia have organized many training sessions and workshops to promote gender consciousness. Many of these workshops aim at changing consciousness of decision makers and power holders in different administrative positions and actively intervening in the process of reform. Never openly confrontational to the state, but ever ready to stretch boundaries in their own innovative ways, Chinese feminists have become a significant social force in China's development. In contrast with many other critical voices in contemporary China, this feminist voice has gained some legitimacy in the dominant political discourse.

The growing discursive power of a feminist force is indicative of profound social and political changes. But thus far feminist voices have for the most part been restricted to women's journals and the Women's Federation newspaper. Academic feminists have also organized conferences and publication of research projects, often sponsored by international donors, yet despite recent growth, women's programs and other resources remain few. Women activists and researchers for the most part remain outside the state system and at the margins of the education system, and they have yet to establish a regular forum and institutional base of their own. How to create an influential and constant presence in mainstream society and the mass media remains a great challenge to Chinese feminists. As illustrated in this section, women activists within and outside the state system have devoted much attention and energy to negotiation with the state. However, the rapidly growing market economy has rendered the state impotent in many realms and has generated its own discursive space. Rampant discriminatory practices in the job market and commercially popularized sexism are powerful forces competing with the discourse of gender equality. This new social environment has prepared fertile soil for the growth of feminism in China as well as presented serious obstacles to women activists.

Women's employment and 'modernity'

Despite efforts to send women back home in response to the urban employment crisis of the late 1970s and early 1980s, China's 'modernization' did not produce a large number of professional homemakers or women's withdrawal from the workplace. Quite the contrary, the number of women employees in cities (excluding township and village industries) increased from 31.28 million in 1978 to 57.45 million in 1997. Numerous factors contributed to this growth in women's gainful employment, including women's strong resistance to their domestication.[3]

Fundamentally, almost two decades of economic boom involving privatization, commodification, and expansion of the service sector have created a large number and wide range of jobs in cities as well as in dynamic rural regions. Many new occupations emerged with a distinctive gender label and an image of 'modernity.' The new job market is even more highly gendered than its predecessor with women channeled primarily to the service sector and secretarial jobs while men are recruited for technical and managerial positions. However, gender dynamics intersecting with other social forces have led to certain un-expected consequences.

Changes in employment in the reform era are not limited to industrial restructuring. They reflect the rise of new industries and trades and diversification of ownership forms. While state enterprise workers face mounting insecurity, numerous others have long been immersed in the volatile and risky private sector. According to 1998 statistics by the State Industry and Commerce Bureau, 18.35 million registered private enterprise owners are female, constituting 40.16 percent of the total. Clearly many women have opted to become their own bosses.

The Women's Federation has appealed to the Women Entrepreneurs Friendship Association (*Nüqiyejia lianyihui*) for assistance for laid-off women workers from state enterprises. The Women's Federation proposed a slogan to span different forms of ownership, 'Hand in hand, sisters walk together on the road of career building.' The Women Entrepreneurs Friendship Association responded by calling on entrepreneurs to 'actively share the worries of the state.' It called on its members to absorb laid-off workers or help retrain them. Enterprises were also encouraged to 'actively participate in state enterprise reform, through purchase, merger, and lease to help state enterprises out of their predicament.' The proposal could be interpreted as a discursive maneuver by women entrepreneurs to enhance their social status.

The confidence expressed by women entrepreneurs in this proposal is unmistakable. They are in a position to help the state, rather than to be dominated by the state. A close look at some of their achievements may clarify the source of their confidence. Zhai Meiqing, 34, vice president of the Women Entrepreneurs Friendship Association, is the chief executive officer (CEO) of the multi-billion-yuan Xiangjiang Gold Seahorse Conglomerate in Guangdong province. Its 100-plus enterprises with over 10,000 employees, involve furniture, real estate, and finance among other businesses. Zhai has been credited with donating 60 million yuan to public welfare, helping 9,000 laid-off workers with subsidies and re-employing over 1,000 laid-off workers. Liu Yufen, 46, CEO of the East Xingtai Conglomerate in Hebei, has 26 enterprises with 230 million yuan in assets. She hired 740 laid-off workers and donated 860,000 yuan to build a school for orphans. These entrepreneurs are hailed as models by the Women's Federation and the government for both their business success and their social contributions.

In contrast with women entrepreneurs who have risen in status through their business acumen and public profile, another group of women has achieved upward mobility drawing on human capital, specifically their youth and beauty. Replacing the 'iron rice bowl' of job security in urban China in the 1990s is the craze of creating the 'rice bowl of youth' (*qingchunfan*). Everywhere attractive young women have been sought to represent the shining image of 'modernity.' Booming service, commercial and entertainment industries post numerous age, gender, and, often, height specific advertisements seeking women under age 25 and above 165 centimeters in height. Stylish, elegant, or sexy, young 'Misses' (*xiaojie*) are displayed in remodeled or newly built 'modern' hotels, restaurants, department stores, travel services, night clubs, dance halls, and so on. As older state industries lay off women workers over 35, these 'modern' young Misses, many with no particular education or technical skills, are entering the rising industries (mostly in the private sector, some with foreign investment) where their youth and beauty provide a ticket to incomes several times higher than those of their older sisters. Rather than clinging to a stable job, competitive young women in the fast lane often 'fire' their bosses in search of rapid upward mobility with their time limited human capital.

In a sophisticated study of the 'rice bowl of youth' phenomenon, Zhang Zhen delves deeply into its social psychology and cultural meaning. 'The aura of their youth and beauty, coupled with a trained mellow voice which air-pumps the value of any plain object, magically touches the product and turns it into a commodity.' Zhang points out that:

> The vivacious image of young female eaters of the 'rice bowl of youth' has served in the fast-moving transition to a market economy as a novel energetic labor force, a model of social mobility, and above all, consumption as endorsed by the current official ideology, which intentionally promotes a form of 'democracy of consumption.'

But there is more beneath the dazzling urban scene accentuated with commodified feminine beauty. Seeing the issue as 'a product or, in fact, a symptomatic form, of an urban mass culture that is imbued with sexual and commodity desires,' Zhang finds 'an underlying structural anxiety of historical consciousness in which feminine youth and ephemeral beauty are paradoxically refashioned as a 'timeless' object of male desire and as a rhetorical trope in modernist discourse.'[4]

The creation of the 'rice bowl of youth' is a 'joint venture' of consumerism and sexism that commodifies and objectifies women. Its contradictory aspects should not, however, be overlooked. Many a Miss Public Relations, Miss Shopping-guide, and Miss Travel-guide is far from being a passively constructed 'decorative' object for the fulfillment of her bosses' utility needs and their male clients' sexual fantasies. Rather, many are active players in the melodrama of 'modernity' who consciously maximize their 'profits' by a range of strategies, including frequent job changes to advance their position, and investing in various adult education programs to acquire new qualifications and skills. Seizing the 'rice bowl of youth,' many young women catapult themselves toward lasting careers. The inherent 'modern' values in this position, such as assertiveness and competitiveness, have been expressed prominently in young Misses' pursuit of career development in a competitive job market. This gendered employment pattern with its inherent contradictions, in short, provides opportunities for young women's social and economic advancement, even as it blocks employment access of older laid-off women workers and reinforces gender stereotypes.

At one end of the 'rice bowl of youth,' and far from the lowest paid, is the controversial occupation *sanpeinü* – literally, 'tri-service escorting girls.' These escorts, many working without a boss, accompany their clients in drinking, dancing, and singing, and may provide other services that fall in the murky area that attracts both male clients and public security personnel. A report from Jinan alleges that 70 percent of the arrested prostitutes in that city were *sanpeinü*. But while prostitution, though widespread, remains illegal in China, escorting has increasingly become a legitimate occupation. In recent years, some local governments have begun to levy income taxes on these 'temporary service personnel in the entertainment industry.' The trade has become a target of local revenue bureaus because of its high income and its large size. It is estimated that a *sanpeinü* in booming Shenyang may earn at least 4,000 yuan a month, and that 80 percent of the 20,000 'temporary service personnel' in the city are female. Most *sanpeinü* are migrants, either from other cities or rural areas, as few would like their families to know the nature of their high paid jobs.

Unlike other glittering Misses who have become symbols of modernity, *sanpeinü*, though sometimes indistinguishable from other Misses, are for many the symbol of moral degeneration. Public moral condemnation has mixed messages. Many accuse young women of being 'decadent and hedonistic.' Others are indignant at male clients' decadence and corruption. The prosperous entertainment industry, including the escorting service, is partly sustained by public funds as many male clients are cadres who can easily get their entertainment expenses reimbursed by their work units. By matching wealthy or powerful male customers with young women 'temporary service personnel' – migrants of few means – escorting presents the starkest image of gender disparity in Chinese society. Many young women in this borderline trade earn a high income that they could never make in other occupations. Success stories in the popular literature tell of young women who launched private businesses after a few years of work in the trade. Cautionary tales, however, emphasize violence and abuse encountered by *sanpeinü*. Because of the ambiguous nature of the trade, few *sanpainü* seek protection from the state. Rather, evading state interference and taxation is as much a part of their business as skillful handling of their male clients. 'Resistance' may be a common experience in their daily life, but it involves very different strategies from those adopted by feminist activists.

In metropolises where foreign investment has underwritten acres of new high-rise buildings, another new social group is emerging along with the changed urban landscape. Young college-educated women have found clerical and managerial positions in foreign and joint venture companies. Many from inland cities have secured jobs in foreign companies by migrating to the special economic zone in the south. 'Miss Office,' or 'White Collar Beauty' (*bailing liren*), terms addressing this group of professional women, share an affinity with the 'rice bowl of youth' by accentuating their femininity. However, distinct from the 'rice bowl of youth,' these terms connote a much higher status which is typically bought by a college degree and, more importantly, a high salary, often in a foreign company or joint venture. Most began with a clerical job, considered appealingly 'feminine' and suitable for young women. By the late 1990s, many of these educated young women had moved up to management, which is an 'unfeminine' sphere in popular discourse. A recent report finds that almost half of the personnel departments in foreign enterprises in Shanghai are run by women, and women constitute 63 percent of the employees sent to foreign companies in Shanghai by the Shanghai Foreign Service Company. Of about 7,000 women employees, over 2,000 are at the senior managerial level in these foreign companies. One-third of the representatives, the top position for Chinese in foreign companies in Shanghai, are women. Within a decade the number of women in this position has increased dramatically from a few to over 100.

White collar and managerial positions in foreign companies combined with occupations associated with the 'rice bowl of youth' have given rise to the emergence of an urban young female group with high income earnings. While most studies (by sampling married couples' income) show that the development of market economy raises living standards generally as well as enlarging gender disparity in income in many cities, some researchers in Shanghai have found that the income of unmarried young women exceeds that of unmarried young men. Reportedly, a major reason for the reversed gender disparity in earning, besides the 'rice bowl of youth,' is that more young women than men are white collar workers in foreign companies and joint ventures. Although the reliability of this finding needs to be tested with more systematic and larger scale research, it shows that the job market not only practices gender, but also age, discrimination. It thus calls our attention to other variables that affect women's employment opportunity.

The young urban professional women in foreign companies are a new élite group that has emerged in the reform era. Ironically, certain gender norms unexpectedly worked in favor of women. If we look for factors that contribute to the high percentage of women in foreign companies at a time when even the Chinese government discriminates against female college graduates, gender difference in specialties appears significant. The first requirement for working in foreign companies is a good command of a foreign language, particularly English. Foreign language departments in universities have historically been among the few with more female than male students because foreign language mastery has long been portrayed as an innate female strength. When both male and female foreign language graduates enter the job market, more women than men seek 'feminine' clerical jobs in the private sector, jobs portrayed as glamorous, feminine and modern. The gender term 'White Collar Beauty' shapes young women's career choices. In the late 1990s the term acquired new connotations of ability, high income, and high consumption.

My interviews with young urban professional couples in Shanghai reveal a common pattern in which the wife works in a foreign company and the husband in a government or academic job with less income but (until recently) higher prestige and lifetime security. A young male English professor whose wife works in a foreign company commented, 'It seems that women are more daring in entering the private sector. Or rather, they have fewer qualms.' This pattern may, however, change quickly as privatization speeds up and state enterprises lose what remains of their aura of security and prestige.

The rise of young urban women in the 1990s is also a demographic phenomenon. The state has strictly controlled births since the late 1970s. However, many one-child families emerged in urban areas, especially metropolises, well before state enforcement of the one child policy. With reduced family size and improved living standards, and with education heavily subsidized (until the nineties), even two-child urban families often invested in the education of both sons and daughters. The percentage of women students in colleges has steadily increased from 24.2 in 1978 to 36.4 in 1996 and the number of women college students more than quadrupled in these years from 207,000 to 1.1 million. Women students have also gained recognition for academic excellence. In recent years the top candidates in the national college entrance exams have consistently been women. The phenomenon has caused a panic in a culture anxious to sustain the male sense of superiority. The media swiftly popularized an authoritative interpretation: female candidates' high performance is the product of the poor design of examination questions which fit in well with rigid female minds but fail to test the capacity of flexible male minds. So far no one has suggested that different socialization of a whole generation of only daughters may be the major reason for the rise of confident, assertive, and competitive young women.

The arrival in the 1990s of a cohort of well-educated and strong-willed only daughters on the job market will give rise to new dynamics in gender discourse. Having been brought up with high expectations from their families, many female college graduates will experience frustrations once they try to locate a job that meets their standards. Top female graduates find that male classmates with inferior academic records are recruited for good jobs that are denied them. Gender discrimination is not subtle. Many advertisements of desirable jobs state clearly that only men need apply. A young professional woman related her sad experience: 'In college, I was always admired for my outstanding academic performance. I never experienced gender discrimination. But once I graduated, I was denied the job I sought simply because I was a woman.' Her superb academic record counted for naught. The painful experience strengthened her determination to fight for gender equality. The huge gap between young women graduates' expectations and social reality can be expected to give rise to growing feminist activism at a time when a feminist discourse is gaining increasing influence. This cohort of women may pose serious challenges to gender boundaries in employment and society.

Women and unemployment

In the 1990s, the magnitude of laid-off workers has threatened social stability, prompting action by central and local governments. (See the chapter in this volume by Ching Kwan Lee.) In 1994, the Labor Department began the pilot 'Re-employment Project' in 30 selected cities and in 1995 took it nationwide. The 'Re-employment Project' mobilizes public resources to provide reemployment for laid-off workers with government support and facilities. At best, it is a stopgap measure that mitigates laid-off workers' deep resentment at being abandoned by the state. It does not change the reality that the state has discarded them after many years of service.

The state policy stipulates that laid-off workers retain a relationship with their work units unless they officially terminate it and take a job with another enterprise. Laid-off workers retain entitlement to medical coverage, pensions, and housing unless their work units go bankrupt. Even in rare cases in which laid-off workers succeed in finding a higher paying job, most experience downward mobility. Leaving state enterprises is still seen by many state workers as involving a loss of status. Re-employment, especially for older workers, involves reconstituting one's identity from a previously positively defined state worker to various ambiguous, uncertain, or demeaning categories.

Re-employment options for laid-off women are generally limited and nearly all point to sharp downward mobility both in status and income.[5] In many big cities, laid-off women state-sector workers are being encouraged to work in community services. Shanghai, with large numbers of laid-off women textile workers, has pioneered this structural readjustment by providing low-paid neighborhood jobs caring for the old, the young, and the sick as domestic helpers, or encouraging private or collective service businesses such as laundries, tailors, hairdressers, cleaning and food services. None of these jobs provides benefits or prestige comparable to that enjoyed by a state worker. Aware of the downward mobility in this re-employment, official women's organizations sought both to provide training and to upgrade the social status of domestic and service workers. The Shanghai Women's Federation and the Women Workers Committee in the Trade Union Federation have run training sessions in 'home economics' for laid-off women and issued certificates to graduates. They changed the name 'Maids Referral' to 'Home Economics Referral.' Equipping laid-off women with a certificate in home economics, official women's organizations tried to overcome the scornful image of 'maids,' long associated with rural women, with a respectable location in urban 'modernity.' They also worked to secure state recognition of this 'new' occupation. In 1995, the Labor Department classified 'family service personnel' in the category of technical jobs. Although the state classification does not entail better pay and benefits in the private sector, some women have since officially obtained this credential as a technical worker in the hope that it may help them secure a job. Shanghai's experience has been propagandized nationally as a model.

This gendered re-employment solution promoted by official women's organizations has the negative implication of reinforcing a gender division of labor. However, the propaganda portraying home and community as the arena for women can also be interpreted as women's strategy to meet immediate practical needs, even survival needs at a time of rampant unemployment. The majority of laid-off women are middle-aged with few resources to compete in the new job market. Laid-off women with scant special skills and a family to support have limited choices. Community service provides many new and useful jobs that require minimal training.

Some widely circulated success stories indicate achievements of laid-off women in creating new businesses in community services. A famous 'Mama Zhuang Vegetable Service' was created by a laid-off woman in Shanghai named Zhuang Weihong. She and her husband were both laid-off in 1992 when she was in her mid-twenties. In 1996 she got an idea from a re-employment training school. Renting a room with borrowed money, she began a vegetable cleaning service with her family members. They shopped for vegetables, picked, cleaned and prepared them for ready cooking, then delivered them to clients' homes with a 10 percent surcharge for processing. In 8 months, their clients grew from their six neighbors to 300 families. Zhuang hired 140 employees (120 were laid-off workers) and installed a computer to track customer orders. Asked why a young woman would name the business 'Mama Zhuang' (which suggests an image of a woman at least over 50), Zhuang explained: 'Mama is the warmest person. Mama will never cheat you. Using this name means we will succeed with high quality of service and credentials.' Here women's role as mother is deployed skillfully and positively by a woman innovator tapping a market that had not previously existed while building on maternal images of service. The strength of 'female' roles and 'female' qualities in the service sector is a theme in many of the success stories about laid-off women's re-employment.

The mounting crisis of unemployment and various 'upgrading' efforts including propaganda seem, at least in Shanghai, to have changed the attitudes toward such re-employment of many laid-off women from resistance to acceptance. In 1997 Shanghai trained 3,000 laid-off women in a 'family services' training program. More than 90 percent of them found jobs.

The increasing supply of laid-off women as domestic helpers is shown clearly in the drastic change in the nature of 'Maids Referral' services run by neighborhood residents committees. Until recently, they referred rural women seeking a job in Shanghai to families seeking domestic help. But since early 1998, jobs for rural women are drying up as many of these jobs are being taken by laid-off women. A State Statistical Bureau survey in 1998 shows that in seven large cities, over 90 percent of urban residents prefer local to rural women for domestic and community service. The employers do not have to provide room and board for local employees. They share the same dialect and have 'more harmonious interaction.' Moreover, middle-aged laid-off women come with rich experience in housework and childcare, and 'modern' training in home economics. Urban employment restructuring, therefore, directly affects employment opportunities of migrating rural young women.

'Peasant workers' in the city

Two decades of rapid industrialization and urbanization have resulted in a growing 'rural population' in urban areas. Millions of people with rural residence certificates who now work in cities are called 'peasants' or 'peasant workers' (*nongmingong*) and are subject to discriminatory state and business practices. Policies such as the requirement that families lacking urban residence permits have to pay for their children's education in public schools not only deter rural migrant workers from settling in cities, they also delineate second class citizenship. The urban/rural divide follows migrants who settle in the urban areas as Hein Mallee's chapter in this volume shows.

Most rural workers have low paid, low skilled, low-status, and frequently insecure jobs, many of which are, or at least until recently, were scorned by urban dwellers. Domestic service has long been the entry job for rural women coming to large cities. A 1988 study estimated that 40,000 rural women sought domestic work that year in Beijing alone. 'Little maid' (*xiao baomu*) became a trade associated with rural young women. Many rural women since the 1980s have also secured employment as waitresses and shop assistants. Some state and collective enterprises recruit rural women as contract workers to lower labor and benefit costs.

The majority of rural women work in the private sector where state labor protection and worker benefits are difficult to enforce. Long hours, low pay, and hazardous work environment are common phenomena among private enterprises that employ young rural women. Ching Kwan Lee's study of management strategies in private industry in the booming southern city of Shenzhen, near Hong Kong, finds a pattern of gendered localistic authority that disguises class domination. Young rural women are introduced to factories by male relatives or acquaintances from their hometowns. These male locals exercise paternalistic authority over women on the shop floors. As Lee points out, 'Localism and genderism not only organize the labor market and channel labor from all over China to Shenzhen, they are also incorporated into the factory to facilitate and legitimate managerial control.'

Gender is also embodied in young women's praxis as migrant workers. In a study based on 109 letters between young women migrant workers and their families, Tan Shen notices while many send money home to help their poor families, some young women specifically shoulder the responsibility of paying for their brothers' college education. Sometimes two sisters labor to support one brother. Tan tells a tragic story in which two Sichuan sisters worked extremely hard in a Shenzhen sweatshop for several years to put their older brother through college. Four months after his graduation, both sisters died in a fire caused by managerial violation of labor safety. Tan's study forcefully demonstrates that in such instances migration is not taken as a route for personal advance.

The widely circulated new term 'maiden workers' (*dagong mei*) for young rural women workers connotes the lowest rank of the urban work force. Being young and female in the context of Chinese traditional generation and gender hierarchy automatically places them in a subordinate position to senior males. Being 'rural,' seen in urbanites' eyes in the context of urban craving for 'modernity,' not only means that they lack a permanent urban residence, but also suggests their distance from the 'modern.' The social and cultural meanings of this element in their identity are new to many women who had never left their villages. The worst pain experienced by many is bearing the stigma of being 'rural.' At a meeting in Beijing organized by a women's journal, *Rural Women Knowing All*, to hear about migrant workers' experiences, some 'maiden workers' from Xiamen were invited to speak about their success stories. These 'maiden workers' had recently obtained Xiamen residence because of their excellent performance at work and also because the Women's Federation in Xiamen struggled hard to obtain a quota of twenty urban residences for 'maiden workers.' Contrary to the expectations of the meeting organizers, however, what they heard was a litany of sweat and tears. One after another these model 'maiden workers' recounted painful experiences of prejudice and discrimination based on their rural identity. In work, love, marriage, children's education, housing, and all other aspects of their lives, they encountered adversity – constantly reminding them that they are the 'other' to urbanites.

Despite discrimination, rural women workers generally regard working in cities as an opportunity. Many young unmarried women use migration as an effective means to resist undesirable arranged marriages. Freedom of mobility, in fact, also enables them to quit and change jobs frequently, the most common form of their resistance to abusive bosses and intolerable working conditions. In order to leave options open for a better job, Tan Shen finds that many young women workers opt not to sign a contract. Many young women from families that do not rely on their income come to big cities with a dream of personal development. Metropolises provide them with educational facilities and opportunities and many have enrolled in secondary vocational schools or even colleges. As one 20-year-old woman from Shaanxi said, 'The best thing in Beijing is that there are so many schools. You can learn whatever you want to. You can also go to evening college. Our hometown does not have these. There is nothing there.' Arriving in Beijing with 800 yuan in savings from her family, she paid 400 yuan to enroll in a hairdressing school. Her dream is to open the first hairdressing salon in her hometown after 5 years of work and study in Beijing. The freedom to migrate has enabled this young woman to make a career choice likely to lead to upward mobility.

The deepening crisis of urban unemployment threatens such opportunities for rural as well as urban women. Since the mid-1990s, many big cities have restricted employment of rural workers. Many of the most desirable jobs always required urban residence. But now even many humble jobs are reserved for laid-off workers. For example, a 1996 Shanghai government document stipulated that any enterprise with 10 percent laid-off workers cannot hire outside labor freely, and commercial and service enterprises must hire 50 percent laid-off workers in their new recruitment of non-technical workers. Although some intellectuals criticize state regulations for blocking the free flow of labor and restricting competition, the state can be expected to adopt measures to limit the influx of rural migrants in order to maintain urban social stability.

Conclusion

A widely circulated cliché in contemporary Chinese society is that 'reform gives women both opportunities and challenges.' Sounding inclusive, it glosses over tremendous differences among women, ranging from those who have ample opportunities and resources to those who face monumental challenges. This chapter illustrates a process of differentiation and diversification among women in the reform era. Women as a social category has to be complicated and concretized to provide explanatory utility. Age, education, geographic location, residence (rural or urban), ownership of enterprises, type of industry, skills and resources are all important variables that intersect with gender in placing women in different categories in the turbulent social and economic transformations that are reshaping China.

Differentiation and diversification among women, however, does not blur the salience of gender. Rather, the reform era has brought accelerated gender discrimination and gender conflicts. Conflicting gender interests are prominently expressed over women's employment. Gendered layoffs expose women's disadvantaged and subordinate status. Masculinist usage of young women as a trope for 'modernity,' both in jobs and in advertisements, demonstrates not only men's dominance in economic enterprises but also their dominance in reproducing gendered cultural norms. Yet we have also noted the ability of women to seize diverse opportunities to rise in important sectors of the economy. In all of these contradictory sites 'women' retains its usefulness as a collective category. In contesting and manipulating gendered categories, we see multiple strategies of resistance ranging from those pursued by the Women's Federation and women's labor organizations, to the individual strategies advanced by women of older and younger generations.

Although most rural and urban women retain their subaltern positions in the reform era, increasingly articulate voices of urban, educated women have declared the end of both male and state monopoly on defining and representing women. One of the most significant political changes in the reform era is that women activists, intellectuals, and cadres have successfully made gender a legitimate category in the dominant political discourse. Building on that achievement, the growing feminist force further demands not only a fair place for women in economic development, but also the right to share in the redefinition of that elusive 'socialist market economy.'

Notes

1 Many surveys, however, reveal situations contrary to this stereotype. They report 'extreme actions' taken by some laid-off women workers. 'Extreme actions' include destroying public property and factory equipment, and stealing enterprise property.
2 The CCP myth of liberated Chinese women was most heartily embraced by these male advocates even when many cases of violence and discrimination against women were widely reported. For a discussion of Chinese women's critique of Maoist gender equality, see Wang Zheng, 'Research on Women in Contemporary China,' in Gail Hershatter *et al.* (eds), *Guide to Women's Studies in China* (Berkeley: Center for East Asian Studies, 1998).
3 As I was about to complete this chapter, a friend wrote to me from China saying that a famous economist was harping on the old tune of 'sending women home' again. She and other women scholars were preparing for a TV debate with him.

4   Zhang Zhen, 'Mediating Time: Or, How to Eat the "Rice Bowl of Youth" and Figure the Value of Beauty in *Fin-de-siècle* Chinese Urban Scenes,' paper presented at the annual conference of the Association of Asian Studies, Washington DC, 1995.

5   Some surveys reveal, however, that in special economic zones in Guangdong laid-off women have more opportunities to go into the private sector using family resources. They are less inclined to insist on a job in state owned enterprises as a longer history of privatization has reduced the prestige of such jobs and increased the desirability of working in the private sector.

Suggested reading

Chinese Sociology and Anthropology, Spring 1997, Vol. 29, No. 3; and Spring 1998.

Emily Honig and Gail Hershatter, *Personal Voices: Chinese Women in the 1980s* (Stanford: Stanford University Press, 1988).

Gail Hershatter, Emily Honig, Lisa Rofel and Susan Mann (eds), *Guide to Women's Studies in China* (Berkeley: Center for East Asian Studies, 1998).

Ching Kwan Lee, *Gender and the South China Miracle. Two Worlds of Factory Women* (Berkeley: University of California Press, 1998).

Ching Kwan Lee, 'The Labor Politics of Market Socialism,' *Modern China*, 24, No.1, (January, 1998).

Lisa Rofel, *Other Modernities: Gendered Yearnings in China after Socialism* (Berkeley: University of California Press, 1998).

Tamara Jacka, *Women's Work in Rural China: Change and Opportunity in an Era of Reform* (Cambridge: Cambridge University Press, 1997).

4 Migration, hukou and resistance in reform China

Hein Mallee

For about two decades, China was characterized by very low levels of rural–urban migration. This was in the first place due to a strict system of residential regulations, propped up by central control over employment and housing, and by state-dominated marketing of daily necessities. During the reform era, this changed at a rapid pace and by the late 1980s rural–urban labour migration had assumed huge proportions. While not denying the role of the state in these processes, this chapter emphasizes the role of millions of migrants in bringing about change. After the restoration of production management to the farm households and the revival of retail marketing, which coincided with the emergence of acute urban labour shortages, the active resistance of these enterprising rural migrants gradually eroded many of the control mechanisms. More often than not, local authorities could barely stay ahead of developments and reacted relatively passively by adjusting the regulations affecting migration. Still, while the registration system can no longer prevent migration, it has not fundamentally changed, and it remains crucial in determining people's life chances.

Introduction

One of the most conspicuous changes in the reform era in China is the rapid growth of rural labour migration and the formation of large migrant populations in the cities and throughout the coastal regions. This change is all the more spectacular for the fact that, up to the late 1970s, the Chinese state exerted tight control over population mobility. This control mechanism did not disappear overnight; indeed, essential parts of it are still in place today. Therefore, the story of rural labour migration in the reform period is the story of how control was gradually eroded, and how the system coped with a continually changing and volatile situation. It is the story of how the state attempted to continue its domination over migrants and of how migrants resisted these attempts.

One of the critical dimensions of friction is rural–urban. Migrants are villagers in the city. This chapter is about migrants *as migrants*. From the point of view of power and domination, migrants have two important characteristics. First, they are outsiders. As newcomers, and especially because their legal position is at best ambiguous, they are easily exploited. They have little leverage to make claims on public resources. Indeed, their position is precarious in ways analogous to the plight of illegal aliens in many other countries. Second, migrants are members of two worlds. They work and live in one (urban) world, but socially and economically they retain important ties with their home community. The structure of this chapter largely follows from these two points. First is a roughly chronological account of the development of migration. The core theme here is how state regulations attempted to maintain the outsider status of migrants and how this has become increasingly difficult. Second is a description of those aspects of migrants' daily lives that are most susceptible to state intervention. Here I analyse how they resist such intervention, in particular by means of self-organization.

Migration control on the eve of reform

In the decades prior to reform, China maintained a rigorous system controlling rural–urban and intra-urban migration. Since the late 1970s, this system has gradually eroded and adjusted. There are two factors that explain the situation in the late 1970s. The first has received considerable attention in the literature: the development strategy, predicated on restricted urbanization, followed since the 1950s. It is less often recognised that a strong cultural–political preoccupation with preventing 'chaos' (*luan*) also lay behind migration policies. That is, the state viewed rural–urban migration as a public order issue.

During the 1950s, China adopted a heavy-industry led development strategy. In a situation of relative international isolation (even allowing for substantial assistance from the Soviet Union) and a weakly developed industrial base, the investment funds needed for this costly industrialization programme could only be found in the agricultural sector. The rural surplus was channelled into industry by means of a state-controlled distribution system, differential pricing of agricultural and industrial products, and collectivised agricultural production.

During the 1950s China witnessed rapid urban growth as a result of high levels of migration from the countryside. Confronted with economic crisis and famine in 1960 as a result of the failure of the Great Leap Forward, the Chinese state opted to sharply restrict entrance into the cities, implementing the *hukou* system (usually translated as household registration system, HRS). In addition, the state presided over forced rural migration of 20 million workers in the years 1961–62, and a program of sent-down urban youth numbering some 17 million, in the years 1964–78. China thus entered a period of low net urban migration, brought about by the strictly enforced HRS (forcefully propped up by central control over employment and housing and especially by rationing of basic necessities including food) and rustication of large groups of urban residents.

Under the HRS, every citizen was required to register at his or her place of permanent residence. Transfer of this registration required official approval, and this was rarely forthcoming in cases involving moves from the countryside to urban areas, or from smaller to larger urban places. Apart from restricting changes of permanent residence, the regulations also strictly limited temporary stays in cities. While initially conceived as an instrument for migration control, the HRS soon developed into a social institution which divided Chinese society into spatial hierarchies whose sharpest division was between 'agricultural' and 'non-agricultural' *hukou* status. This status defined the claims that citizens could make on state resources, creating a fundamental cleavage between people 'eating state grain' and those growing their own grain. The essential difference between these two groups was their different relation to the state: the peasants basically depended for their livelihood on their own labour and the fluctuating harvests, while the state cared for almost every aspect of the welfare of holders of urban registrations. The state provided the latter with lifetime employment, subsidized housing, inexpensive food, education, medical care, and pensions. The high cost of this benefit package explains why the state tightly controlled access to urban *hukou*. *Hukou* status was inherited from one's mother, and it was virtually impossible to change an 'agricultural' *hukou* to a 'non-agricultural' one in the years 1960–78.

Although generally speaking, people with a 'non-agricultural' *hukou* were far better off, the HRS also inconvenienced many urban people. Urban places were divided into different size categories and movement from smaller to larger cities was rarely sanctioned. Combined with the rigidity of the labour system, which assigned people to jobs regardless of their family situation and made transfers difficult, this policy forced millions of married couples to live permanently apart in different cities, often only able to meet once or twice a year. Another problem occurred when members of a family had different types of *hukou*. A rural woman who married an urban worker or whose husband changed from 'agricultural' to 'non-agricultural' status did not qualify for an urban registration and would not be allowed to live with him in the city. The same was true for their children.

The second heritage of the pre-reform period concerns maintenance of public order. City dwellers also pose a potentially powerful political threat to state power. For this reason, urban life was rigidly controlled with work units and neighbourhood committees dominating most aspects of city life. Migrants did not fit neatly into this system. Security officials viewed them as 'rootless' people who, lacking the constraints of government and community, were prone to behave in 'antisocial' or criminal ways. Labour migration, posing a potential threat to social and political stability, was conceptualized primarily as a public order issue. But whether viewed as a fiscal or as a public security issue, the state found powerful reason to exercise tight control.

From the mid-1950s onwards, migrants were dealt with by the Public Security Departments. Already during the 1950s, the increasing unease of the authorities with the rural-to-urban migration flows triggered by industrialization was expressed in repeated calls to halt the 'blind' townward migration. State action and regulations were directed towards preventing 'spontaneous' (*zifa*), 'disorderly' (*wuxu*), or even 'chaotic' (*luan*) mobility, and towards turning these into 'organized' (*you zuzhide*) channels. Just as the Chinese state would not tolerate autonomous organizations (unregistered religious groups, unofficial labour unions, opposition political parties), and either destroyed or co-opted them, it would not tolerate autonomous 'movements' and 'crowds'. From the state's point of view, people without, or far removed from, their organization or village are 'anonymous', in the sense of unaccountable, untraceable, hard to control. Although the more extreme strand of this type of thinking gradually lost ground during the reform period, the basic tenet that migrants pose a potential threat to public order continues to be a powerful undercurrent in the official discourse about labour mobility (see Box 4.1). Many of the adaptations and alterations of the *hukou* system during the 1980s and 1990s were attempts to bring aspects of migration back into the scope of state control.

At the end of the 1970s, the *hukou* system divided Chinese society into two large segments: about 16 per cent, labelled as 'non-agricultural', was eligible for state benefits, while the great majority of Chinese fell in the other category. People were born into either of these segments, and there was minimal mobility between them. Individuals obtained 'non-agricultural' *hukou* by entering government jobs at commune or higher levels, or by gaining entrance to a university. But such cases were rare: in one village in Guangdong, on average out of every

---

Box 4.1 The battle of words

The public discourse about migrants and migration has been dominated by an urban/state perspective. This highly political labelling game serves to identify migrants as outsiders, as a problem, *to put them in their proper place.* James Scott (1990) points out that acts of description are politically loaded and draws attention to euphemisms. In this vein, the 1958 *hukou* regulations demand that migrants have a 'proper reason' for staying in the cities. Those who are unable to do so end up in 'detention stations' to be 'mobilized', 'persuaded', or 'educated' to return to the countryside.

The term *mingong*, today the most common designation for rural labour migrants, can be found as early as the regulations of the 1950s. *Mingong* are not 'full' workers, *gongren* (with all its ideological implications), because the *gong* is qualified by *min*, which may come either from *nongmin*, peasants, or from *renmin* (the People *at large*, but not part of the inner circle). In either case, it is clear that these people work, but that they cannot claim the superior 'worker' status. During the 1980s, this term, with all its implications, naturally fitted the newly emerging migrant population in the cities.

Other labels are simply demeaning. Migrants are 'blind vagrants' (*mangliu*), because they are 'chaotic' or 'disorderly' *(wuxu)*. When there are many of them, migrants become an irresistible 'wave' or 'tide' *(mingongchao)*. Once they have children, they become 'excess birth guerrillas' (*chaosheng youjidui*). The foundation of this discourse is the dichotomy contained in the *hukou* system. No matter how long migrants stay in the cities, they remain a distinct legal category. This leads to the migrants' identification as 'floating population' (*liudong renkou*) in surveys, and as *mingong* in daily speech.

thousand men, only 0.228 changed *hukou* status per year, that is, one person every 5 years. Among women, this was only 0.028 per thousand or one person every 50 years (Potter 1983).

Migration in general was rare and was tightly controlled by the state. Officially approved movement mainly concerned people who were assigned new jobs, who were transferred to other places, and, in some instances, the family members of such people. In the countryside, the only largescale legally sanctioned migration involved young women who moved to the villages of their husband, transferring household registration to his village upon marriage.

Yet even in these years inventive farmers skirted restrictions and moved around both the countryside and cities, earning income at the margins of legality but almost always retaining rural registrations. Xiang Biao (1998) recounts how farmers from Wenzhou used the chaos of the Cultural Revolution to move in small bands to other places to work as carpenters or shoe menders. They avoided the larger cities and the eastern part of the country, where controls were stricter. Travelling to county seats and suburban areas in Inner Mongolia and other provinces in the northwest, they went from house to house offering their carpentry skills, constructing furniture and making repairs. Sometimes they had to hide in pigsties and cowsheds to avoid detection. When arrested and sent back to Wenzhou, many simply set out again. By the second half of the 1970s, they had begun to draw on personal connections to set up businesses in larger urban centres.

Migration and control in the reform era

If migration on the eve of reform was negligible, by the second half of the 1980s dramatic change had occurred. Scores of millions of rural migrants were then working in China's major cities and rural industrial zones. It is common to describe this process of change as a sort of 'cork out of the bottle' phenomenon. In this view, decades of migration control had led to enormous pent-up urbanization pressure. As soon as the authorities relaxed some of the controls over population mobility (the 'cork'), enormous migration currents were unleashed. The term 'migrant flood' (*mingongchao*), which gained currency in the 1990s to describe rural labour migration, fits in well with this type of explanation. While it is true that a number of milestones in the recent history of Chinese migration are marked by liberalizations of the *hukou* system, it is wrong to depict the government as the main initiator of events. In many cases, it is probably more accurate to describe the changes in regulations as adaptations to a situation that was already changing rapidly on the ground. The initiative of migrants, their ingenuity in finding loopholes, in evading, bribing, and stretching the limits, were at least as important in bringing about change as was government action. Perhaps, rather than migrants reacting to changes in official regulations, it was the various government agencies that trailed behind the facts and could only passively adapt and adjust. (Relative) freedom of movement was not granted, it had to be conceded. It was won. However, while changes in regulations are published in the State Council Gazette and further spread by the media, the countless minor acts of migrant resistance that were instrumental in bringing about the change by their very nature go largely unrecorded. The account of the main developments of the reform period that follows in this section, must draw on material which inevitably is biased towards the official 'transcript'. It is therefore important to keep in mind that the best evidence of active migrant resistance is the fact that migration took place on a vast scale.

The reform period can be loosely divided into four subperiods: (1) 1978–84, when the rural reforms rapidly spread and labour mobility was still limited; (2) 1985–88, during which rural industry grew rapidly and migration began to assume massive proportions; (3) 1989–91, a period of financial retrenchment and economic downturn during which rural labour mobility continued to increase and came to be regarded as a major social problem; and (4) the years from Deng Xiaoping's southern tour in 1992 to the present, which saw parts of the economy once again booming, but with some groups increasingly being unable to share in the benefits. During the last few years, economic performance has declined, with a sharp reduction in job creation coinciding with largescale layoffs in urban areas. Migration continued at a slower pace.

1978–84

The period from the Third Plenum in late 1978 to 1984 is mainly remembered as one during which fundamental institutional changes in rural areas went hand-in-hand with rapid growth in agriculture. In late 1978 and early 1979, however, foundations were also laid for changes in rural–urban relations and migration. During the 1960s and 1970s, especially after Mao's personal 1968 call, some 17 million young large-city dwellers had been sent 'up to the mountains and down to the villages'. The permanence of the move was powerfully expressed by the fact that the youths were stripped of their urban registrations. This rustication movement was deeply resented by many of the youths and their families. The political changes that followed the death of Mao and the fall of the 'Gang of Four' fuelled expectations that they might after all be allowed to return. Many returned home illegally on their own initiative. After the Party's Third Plenum of 1978, the returned youths petitioned the authorities, putting up posters, organizing demonstrations and sit-ins, and disrupting rail traffic. In 1979 the policy towards the sent-down youths was reversed, and the great majority were allowed to return to their home cities or at least restored to 'non-agricultural' status in local towns in a brilliant example of successful resistance to the state.

The actions of the youths show that the strict state control over citizens' movement had only been achieved at a high social cost and that people were willing to go to enormous lengths to redress this situation. The return of millions of (no-longer young) city dwellers put pressure on urban employment and welfare systems. A number of early reform measures, such as the encouragement of small-scale private entrepreneurship and the *dingti* system that allowed a parent working in a state enterprise to retire, transferring his or her job to a child, were primarily aimed at solving the returnees' problems. Enterprising farmers and rural entrepreneurs were quick to grasp new opportunities opened by the weakening of social and political control.

In the early years of the reform other changes took place that would influence migration. With dramatic increases in agricultural production and more income flowing from higher state purchasing prices, newly available capital would finance booming rural sideline and industrial activities. The dismantling of collective farms and the contracting of land to households paved the way for largescale mobility by villagers now free to pursue off-farm economic activities.

Increasing numbers of farmers began to sell their products in the cities, at first stealthily and illegally, trying to stay one step ahead of public security forces. This quickly changed. In Beijing, official farmers' markets were established in the suburbs in April 1979 and extended to the city districts the next year. Migrants also began to run other businesses, selling clothes, for example. The ban on long-distance trading, before 1980 still regarded as 'opportunistic profiteering', was also lifted. Within a few years, this revival of marketing not only improved urban consumption levels, but also enabled farmers to stay in the cities for longer periods without rationing coupons for daily necessities.

Already in 1981, the State Council was exhorting urban enterprises strictly to enforce the regulations barring employing people with 'agricultural' status. The reasons for this are clear. Excluding permanent workers, at the end of 1980, some 9.31 million peasants were employed in state enterprises. Obviously, employing low-wage rural workers was an attractive proposition both to the workers themselves and to the enterprises, whatever the rules. In some sectors, such as mining, logging, construction and salt works, it had always been difficult to find sufficient workers from urban areas, and farmers were sometimes taken on as temporary labourers. Now industry was rapidly expanding and the labour surplus of the late 1970s began to give way to labour shortage. Due to changes in the age structure of the urban population (with more young people entering the labour market) and to changing expectations towards work (as a result of better schooling), this trend was to become increasingly clear during the following years. Rural migrants were also much cheaper to employ, because they received lower wages and did not enjoy the comprehensive welfare package of official state workers. Faced with increasing numbers of enterprises which preferred to hire migrant workers and were adept at evading the restrictions, the government's attitude towards migrant labour gradually changed. By October 1984, enterprises were encouraged to hire rural contract workers and to reduce the number of permanent workers in order to 'increase productivity and economic efficiency'. Thus, during the first years of the reform period, the authorities gradually came to see 'temporary' labour as a way to reconcile the urban need for (cheap) labour with the state's need to reduce the financial burden of urban entitlements.

While the number of rural migrants was still limited during this period, the roots of later labour mobility were created at this time. Throughout the Third World, rural–urban mobility mainly takes place in the form of chain migration.

China is no exception. Earlier migrants provide information and assistance with moving, finding jobs and accommodation to later migrants from their own villages, thus linking specific origins with specific destinations. The networks that facilitated later mobility began to emerge in these years. In this period, for example, the small bands of migrants arrived in the capital and began to settle in what later became known as 'Zhejiang Village'. However, most labour migrants in the major cities during these years probably came from the suburbs and adjacent counties. The later increase of labour migration, then, rested on mobility networks that spread gradually over the countryside and linked up more and more villages with the cities.

1985–88

Encouraged by the success of the rural reforms, from 1984 onwards the leadership shifted the focus of reform towards the urban areas. At the same time, rural development also changed character. Now, earlier growth in rural industry and services began to assume massive proportions. Grain production, however, stagnated after 1984. As prices of agricultural inputs grew, this led to deterioration of farmer incomes in comparison with urban dwellers, after significant earlier gains.

Facing the spectre of massive migration to the largest cities, the state called on villagers to *litu bulixiang*, 'leave the land but not the countryside.' Farmers were urged to take up and invest in non-agricultural occupations but to do so in the villages or in small rural towns. To this end, small town migration was liberalised in late 1984. Peasants who had obtained jobs and accommodation in towns were to be allowed to settle there officially, and enjoy the same rights as the original town dwellers, on condition that they provide their own grain. They would be registered as holding an 'urban registration with self-supplied grain' (*zili kouliang chengzhen hukou*). The new policy premise was that these farmers would solve their employment, housing and food problems themselves. Only then would the state register the successful migrants as urban residents. As welfare entitlements of small town residents are far less generous than those in large cities, the costs to the state of such formal registration were low. Moreover, the provision that these townward moving farmers provide their own grain marked the first time since the famines of the early 1960s that the link between grain supply and urban registration was broken. Although five to six million peasants used this opportunity to settle in towns, by the late 1980s the experiment died a quiet death. Apart from implementation problems, perhaps most important was the fact that grain harvests had been disappointing since the start of the programme, which followed the bumper harvest of 1984. It appears that, in spite of the many changes, the grain constraint on urbanization still prevailed during the late 1980s (Mallee 1994).

In this context, it is interesting to see how such new state initiatives were immediately highjacked and used for other purposes. A study of the implementation of the policy in towns near Shanghai indicates that, at least in the beginning, the new registration was used to solve the problems of mixed *hukou* families by giving the 'agricultural' members (mostly women) official urban status. Over half of the people who received the new registration were already living in these towns at the time it was introduced, and 35 per cent had lived there since before 1981. Women constituted up to 80 per cent of the beneficiaries in the first year of the scheme and 84 per cent had relatives in the towns, in most cases including a spouse (Mallee 1994). In Zhejiang, cases have been documented where the registrations mainly went to the 'agricultural' spouses of rusticated youths who had settled in local towns (Middelhoek 1989). Thus, rather than attracting new migrants to towns, the urban-registration-with-self-supplied-grain recognized a fait accompli and helped alleviate the family plight of some who suffered most from the rigidities of the HRS.

At the same time migrant labour began to be seen as a way to solve urban labour shortages, as long as migrants retained their 'agricultural' *hukou*. Urban enterprises faced mounting labor shortages in textile and machine-building industry, in construction, in urban sanitation and others. In 1985, Beijing construction firms only managed to find 37 per cent of the labour needed (Liu and Wang 1988). A large textile mill in Wuhan planned to hire 500 new workers in 1987, but was only able to recruit five. The state's response was to ease provisions for temporary residence which enabled labor shortages to be overcome without committing the state to the costs of providing costly services for a growing urban population. This solution also gave enterprises much greater flexibility, as temporary workers are easy to dismiss in times of economic slump.

1989–91

During the second half of the 1980s, inflation soared and in late 1988 the government launched an austerity drive to quell it, touching off a contraction in growth with cancellation of construction projects and closure of rural enterprises. Rural migrant workers bore the brunt of the retrenchment. Still, that rural labour migration is not simply a function of urban demand becomes clear from the fact that during these years migration increased rapidly. Zhao Shukai (1996) estimates that the annual increase from 1989 to 1993 was about 25 percent. Surveys indicate that by the early 1990s between 50 and 60 million rural migrants were working outside of their townships.

It was in 1989 that the large-scale population movements around the Chinese New Year Festival began to receive widespread attention and that reporting on migrants began to assume a sensationalist and almost panicky tone. Throughout the country, people returning to their place of work after visiting their families turned up in such massive numbers that the public transportation system could not cope with them. Although quite soon the problem largely solved itself, the 'migrant worker wave' as the phenomenon would become known, had at least two longer-term consequences. First, it confirmed and strengthened the stereotype of rural migrants as 'blind' drifters who, propelled by enormous rural employment pressure ('surplus labourers'), 'flocked' to the cities or 'roamed' around the country in search of work. Few commentators pointed to the underdeveloped transportation system or to the fact that not only rural migrants but also tens of millions of students, state employees, and others were returning home at New Year, as causes of the dislocations. Second, this stereotype fits closely with the conception of migration as a public order issue, causing local governments to step up their interventions in labour mobility.

In spite of the fact that migrants were denied local 'non-agricultural' registrations and had to remain 'temporary' residents, throughout the reform period the 'non-agricultural population' (NAP) had been rising. From 1968 to 1978, the NAP had never exceeded 16 percent of the total population, but by 1989 it topped 21 percent. This increase of over five percentage points in just over a decade greatly worried the authorities, as it considerably exacerbated the financial burden of the state subsidies to the urban population. Theoretically, change from 'agricultural' to 'non-agricultural' registration status (*nongzhuanfei*) was controlled by rigid procedures, but in practice many loopholes existed. In fact, the state manipulated access to 'non-agricultural' status. At different times, special regulations on *nongzhuanfei* were issued for miners, highly qualified intellectuals, military officials, relatives of overseas investors, and the like (Mallee 1995). It is significant that the problems were not only the result of ingenious individuals finding their way to 'non-agricultural' status, but also of the institutional interests of various bureaucracies.

In 1989, the central government cracked down on *hukou* transfer. The State Planning Commission took charge of *nongzhuanfei* policy. The NAP decreased by almost 5 percent to under 20 percent of the total population, the first real decrease since 1977. It was also during this period that the 'urban-registration-with-self-supplied-grain' disappeared from the stage. During the late 1980s, the HRS had undergone a steady 'commodification': 'non-agricultural' registration status gradually became a commodity that could be bought with money. *Hukou* sales started to gain momentum in 1991 when the region around Dezhou in Shandong publicly announced the prices for urban residence. The next year, *hukou* 'auctions' spread over most of the country, and received considerable media attention.

> [A]t places where the transaction 'to change agricultural household registration to non-agricultural household registration' [took place], long lines formed, traffic was blocked, there was a hubbub of voices, and bends occurred in the lines. Peasants in surrounding villages and townships filled satchels and flour bags with money they had earned by their blood and sweat and had saved for several years to conduct a transaction in which 'agricultural household registration was changed to non-agricultural registration.'
>
> (JPRS-CAR-94-050: 56)

The wave of registration sales prompted the Ministry of Public Security in May 1992 to issue an order strictly prohibiting the practice. That October a county secretary and 30 other officials were dismissed and brought to trial for 'arbitrarily changing registrations from agricultural to non-agricultural.' The *Sichuan Yearbook 1993*, on the other hand, candidly reports that the non-'agricultural population' in 1992 had grown relatively rapidly, and that half of this was due to the practice of 'economic registrations' (*jīngji hukou*). Whatever the central government's stance, the temptation for local governments to raise money in this fashion is large.

1992–97

From about 1992, the reforms gained new momentum with Deng Xiaoping's southern tour early in the year, and later the Fourteenth Party Congress, where the term 'socialist market economy' was coined. Economic growth rose to double-digit levels, and the southeastern coastal provinces in particular boomed. The agricultural picture, however, was mixed. While grain harvests improved, the worsening price-scissors eroded agricultural incomes. In many areas local governments, claiming that they lacked the funds to pay for the (again compulsory) grain deliveries, issued IOUs rather than cash to pay for procured farm products. At the same time, a host of taxes, levies and extortions had proliferated. Newspapers widely reported cases of suicide and rural unrest. While the economy as a whole grew at a dazzling pace, the differences between the richer and poorer parts of the population became more pronounced.

Rural labour migration continued to grow, but at a more modest rate. By the mid-1990s, the total migrant population was probably about 80 million people. In most major cities and rapidly developing rural industrial belts, sizeable migrant populations had developed, often accounting for 10–20 percent or more of the total population.

Some of the more sophisticated studies of interaction between migrants and the state (e.g. Zhao Shukai 1997) link the tendency towards stabilization of migration volume to more effective measures taken by local authorities. Nevertheless, the realism of local authorities in regulating migration was periodically punctuated by draconian measures such as the demolishing of the Zhejiang Village (see Box 4.2) and by the formal exclusion of migrants from a large number of specified occupations in cities such as Beijing and Shanghai.

Encouraged by good grain harvests in the early 1990s, the government first raised retail prices of grain and finally abolished the rationing system. The simultaneous elimination of grain subsidies to urban residents reduced pressure on state budgets. After grain coupons were abolished, calls for reform of the HRS became louder. Many began to see the system as unfair, inefficient, or simply outdated. In fact, during the 1990s, numerous alterations were aimed at alleviating some of the worst inconveniences and providing special treatment for specific groups. The exceptions, special treatments, and disguised sale of 'blue seal registrations' made the HRS ever more susceptible to corruption. For those with money, urban citizenship was within reach. The total 'non-agricultural' population continued to grow during the 1990s, reaching 23.8 percent of the

---

Box 4.2 'Seesaw warfare': the turbulent history of 'Zhejiang Village'

In 1983, small bands of migrants from Zhejiang Province began to arrive in Fengtai District, on the fringes of Beijing. Many of them had already spent years away from home, earning a living by making clothes or furniture, and had gradually ventured into the larger cities. They came from Wenzhou, an area with a long history of emigration to Europe and a tradition of small-scale entrepreneurship. They set up small businesses in the capital as they had in other places. By 1986, several thousand Wenzhouese lived in the area, which began to be known as 'Zhejiang Village'. The Village began to play an important role in the north China textile market, especially after the introduction of leather jackets in 1989. From that time, the flow of people from Wenzhou assumed a mass character. Gradually a bipolar community (Wenzhou–Beijing) took shape, as factor markets (labour, cloth) developed in Wenzhou, serving the Village. By 1994, Zhejiang Village covered twenty-six natural villages in Fengtai District, with about 14,000 local residents and 96,000 migrants. Of the migrants, about 50,000 were from Zhejiang. Most others worked in the workshops of the Wenzhou entrepreneurs, coming from Hebei, Anhui, Sichuan, Hubei and elsewhere.

While the Wenzhou migrants at first mainly engaged in dispersed 'guerrilla warfare', from the mid-1980s 'seesaw warfare' became the main mode of conflict with the state. Local authorities resorted to periodic cleanup campaigns in 1986, 1989, and 1990, but each time the migrants retreated to the outer suburbs of Beijing or neighbouring Hebei, where they weathered the storm. In November 1995, after a particularly harsh newspaper report drew the attention of the central government, the authorities made a concerted effort to permanently uproot and destroy the village. A special 'headquarters' was formed, and a 'battle campaign' launched. About 80,000 migrants were forced to leave and forty-six large residential compounds (*dayuan*) were torn down. However, by March 1996, the first migrants had begun to trickle back into the area and began to set up stalls on the rubble where once the vegetable market had stood. A year after the 'campaign', two *dayuan* began to arise again. The seesaw war had come full circle.

Sources: The work of Xiang Biao (1998, 1999) provides a full record of the village. (See also Ma and Xiang (1998).)

---

total population in 1995. Despite increasing calls for fundamental reform, the essence of the HRS – entitlements based on ascriptive status – remained intact.

Summing up the changes of the reform era, a number of observations can be made. First, rural labour migration greatly increased and 'floating populations' came to account for one-fourth to one-third of the total population in most cities.

Second, without the migrants, the economic boom of this period would not have been possible. Third, the migrant population in the cities came to be more and more dominated by rural labour migrants rather than by relatives of official urban residents. Fourth, the *hukou* system changed, for example with the increasing availability of purchased *hukou*, but not in essentials. While no longer capable of preventing migration, it still plays an important role in determining claims to public resources and thus continues to shape life chances across the urban-rural divide.

The effectiveness of the HRS (and associated mechanisms), was gradually eroded by the evasion, non-co-operation, resistance, and bribery of millions of migrants. The situation is aptly summarized in the often quoted saying *shang you zhengce, xia you duice* ('There are policies on high but those below have counter-measures'). At the same time, increased migration was sometimes also in the interest of specific local government organs and officials, either because it made cheap labour and services available, or simply because it increased the opportunities for institutional revenue raising and personal corruption. The more adaptations and exceptions were made, the harder it was to enforce the system, the more corrupt it grew, and the easier it became to evade it. We observe a dialectical relationship between migrants' resistance and migration control. Over the course of the reform period, migration increased, thereby eroding the controls, which in turn made migrating easier.

Migrants and the state

Rural labour migrants are not a uniform entity. Three main groups can be distinguished by occupation. In the major cities, the largest group consists of construction workers. Virtually all unskilled and semi-skilled construction is done by rural migrants, mostly young males, organized in teams along native-place lines. Many teams are run by or associated with the authorities at origin. The construction workers work long days and usually eat and sleep at the construction site. Their daily lives are often highly regimented, with strict rules about leaving the site (Victor Yuan 1999). A second major group consists of industrial workers, not only in the large cities, but also in industrialized parts of the countryside. In some industries, such as textiles and electronics, young migrant women predominate. Larger factories usually offer accommodation and food; and most industrial workers lead disciplined and isolated lives. The third main group consists of self-employed migrants and those working in small enterprises and households. This includes peddlers, traders operating market stalls or counters in shops, garbage collectors, and waitresses as well as domestic workers and sub-contractors of agricultural land on the outskirts of the cities. In comparison to the first two groups, these migrants are in much more frequent interaction with the local population and many come into direct contact with the authorities.

When migrants face the representatives of the state and the established population, they usually rely on 'invisible' resistance, yield, or attempt to take refuge elsewhere and weather the storm. A number of incidents, however, suggest the pent up frustration beneath the surface. In 1986, 400 migrant traders in Tianjin's Hexi District surrounded and beat up tax officials and public security officers. In March 1994, fed up with paying one fee after another, migrant traders in the Muxiyuan Light Industrial Wholesale Market (inside Beijing's Zhejiang Village) went on strike. They sustained the strike for a week until the authorities met their demands. Such open conflicts are relatively rare, however. We will look at residence permits, work permits, housing, and forced repatriation, from the angle of conflict and resistance.

Residence permits

By the mid-1990s, the temporary residence permits (*zhanzhuzheng*) introduced in 1985 had become fairly well-established. Over two-thirds of migrant workers hold one, preferring registration to the semi-illegal status associated with non-registration. Among dependents, however, non-registration is much more common. The main reason for evading registration is the cost: typically, applying for a permit costs 1–5 yuan, and a monthly management fee of 10–20 yuan is levied. Some localities demand additional fees for health care (Zhao Shukai 1997).

Work permits

In early 1990, the authorities began to consider using work permits to control rural out-migration. Initially, this took the form of a 'labour migration permit' to be obtained at place of origin and a 'work permit' at place of destination. After 1994, the Ministry of Labour unified this procedure for inter-provincial migration. Both at origin and destination procedures need to be followed to obtain a legal work permit. In practice, only a fraction of the migrants (less than one-quarter in one study) actually obtain these papers and two-thirds do not even know about the most recent rules (Research Group 1997). One study found that migrants on average paid over 60 yuan both at origin and at destination; in extreme cases, the amount was several hundred. Thus, rather than giving labour migrants a well-defined legal status, the work permits merely expose them to additional fees. Most migrants apparently find employment without cards and permits.

Housing

Migrants have made quite diverse housing arrangements. Construction workers usually live on the work sites, while industrial workers live in dormitories provided by the factories. A 1994 Beijing study found 470,000 people living at construction sites and 430,000 on the premises of work units. Domestic workers, on the other hand, often live in the homes of their employers. Where weather conditions permit, small traders and peddlers not infrequently spend the night on the streets and in market places next to their wares. Similarly people working in shops, restaurants, and service workshops simply spread their mattress on the floor once the customers are gone and the doors closed.

In 1985, as part of the loosening of the control over temporary residence in cities, renting accommodation by migrants was officially sanctioned for the first time. The largest concentration of labour migrants in most cities is on the fringes of the central city districts. In these zones, where city gradually merges into countryside, finding accommodation is usually easier, official control less strict, and commuting distances to the downtown areas not too prohibitive. Local farmers soon discovered that their land yielded much more income when it was occupied with rented-out rooms than when it was cultivated with crops. By the late 1980s, migrant enclaves had emerged on the periphery of most large Chinese cities. And even when there are no clearly unidentifiable settlements or (sub-) ethnic concentrations, on the rural–urban fringe migrants often account for a considerable proportion of the *de facto* population, sometimes even equalling or surpassing the number of original residents. In Shanghai, for example, most migrants live in the 'remote wards'; i.e. the outskirts of the city proper: 41 percent in 1986 and 65 percent by 1993 (Wang Wuding 1995: 52).

Detention and deportation

All Chinese cities have 'detention stations' (*shourongzhan*), where a variety of people unwanted in the city are kept before being sent 'back' to the countryside. The definition of 'unwanted' has varied considerably since the 1950s, but in 1986, the detention station in Guiyang City reportedly contained the following people: 1,972 'blind vagrants' (*mangliu*), seventy-four beggars, twenty-seven swindlers, eighty-six thieves, eighty-two pick pockets, 111 people who had been cheated, fourteen people who had come in contact with the authorities, five people engaged in chaotic sexual relations, eight prostitutes, two gamblers, three woman traffickers, seven fortune tellers, eight people released from reform through labour, twenty-three mentally ill, and eighty-four retarded and handicapped people.

Detention and deportation of people lacking the necessary papers (the 'three without' population, *sanwu renkou*) is still fairly common. Usually it takes the form of sweeping 'clean-up' campaigns, in particular when a large public event is about to take place. Changning District in Shanghai deported over 1,000 people in 1994 and Wuxi County over 2,000 in 1993. In some cases, deportation means that the people are actually taken back to their place of origin, in others, they are simply dropped outside the city or provincial borders. It is an expensive and largely ineffective measure. Sometimes the deportees manage to get back in town before the officials who accompanied them return! (Zhao Shukai 1997) A professional beggar woman in Beijing said: 'We usually know beforehand when a campaign is coming and then we stay inside for a while' (Horizon 1995:11).

Migrant organizations

The main organizing principle of migration chains is the reliance on kinship and native place ties. An investigation of 500 labour migrants at the Beijing railway station in 1989 showed that 95.4 percent had fellow village migrants who had provided information (Mallee 1996). One study (Research Group 1997), categorizes 75.6 per cent of moves as being facilitated by various forms of self-organization.

Organization does not cease once migrants reach their destination. Facing discrimination and official harassment, many migrants seek comfort and protection in groups. Research Group (1997) reports that most migrants band together when going out on a stroll, shopping, or watching videos 'because going out alone is not convenient, you easily get bullied (*shou qifu*)'. Informal groups also are important in providing migrants with mental comfort, through contacts with *tongxiang* (people from the same home area). A 1993 Beijing survey found that 76 percent of the migrants interviewed had regular contacts with more than two *tongxiang* other than their family and over half had contacts with over five *tongxiang*. A 1994 survey found that almost three-quarters of the migrants received help from *tongxiang* when they fell ill or met other problems (Horizon 1995). In factories in the south, migrant workers form small mutual help groups. They stand in for sick fellow workers, lend each other money, and fight (in the streets or with the boss) if necessary (Mobo C. F. Gao 1994).

Organization helps migrants to defend their turf and to cultivate relations with the authorities. Beggars, for example, are often led by a boss who protects their interests (as well as his own) (Horizon 1995: 9–11). In Wuxi County, in 1993 a full-scale battle ensued between two competing groups of Anhui loaders, involving close to a hundred people and leaving one dead and five seriously wounded (Research Group 1997).

The form and degree of internal organization of migrant groups differs greatly. Some are small, loosely structured and lack clear leaders. At the other extreme are groups, such as a large organization of transport workers in Wuxi, which was tightly organized, with strict rules governing work and leisure, with advanced division of labour and equipment, under the strong leadership of one person. However, regardless of their functions and internal structures, all are organized by native place, kinship, and occupation.

In a number of cases, co-ordinated action by migrants have given rise to new institutions. These include a variety of markets, some of which supply migrants with daily necessities, and others of which buy goods produced or collected by migrants. In most cities, specific migrant labour markets have emerged. Such markets are subject to continual monitoring and periodic suppression by the authorities. An even more tangible example of migrant institutions are the migrant 'work shed' schools (*gongpeng xuexiao*). Children of migrant workers are usually refused access to regular local school, or required to pay extra fees. In reaction to this, in many places migrants set up their own schools, inviting teachers from their home areas. Like the labour markets, most of these schools are periodically closed down by the authorities because they cannot meet the standards of urban planning, hygiene, safety, and educational requirements.

The attitude of the authorities towards migrants' self-organization is ambiguous. On the one hand, informal organizations can be used to control migrants. This is the case in many larger work units, where migrant leaders are asked to shoulder responsibility for the behaviour of a whole group. Sometimes local authorities cultivate personal relationships with individual migrant leaders as in Wuxi, where one powerful migrant headed an organization of several hundred transport workers and monopolized most work in the harbour (Research Group 1997). On the other hand, there are many instances in which migrant organizations are suppressed. Analogous to the semi-legal status of their members, migrant organizations are engaged in a continuous balancing act, midway between interest representation and breaking the (unclear) limits set by the authorities.

Conclusion and prospects

Among the most striking and important developments of the two decades of reform is the emergence of large-scale labour migration. On the eve of reform, there was very little mobility except for state-arranged moves. By the mid-1990s, 80–100 million people were working or living far away from their place of permanent registration. Like many other changes in post-Mao China, the story of this mobility is often told in terms of state-initiated changes. Such an account is not entirely implausible, as the Chinese state did dismantle many controls on population mobility. Such changes, in particular in the mid-1980s, were in line with the general policy reorientation going on at the time. This chapter has shown, however, that the relation between institutional reform and social change is complex, and it has emphasized the creative initiatives of migrants in shaping outcomes.

During the initial reform years, a number of structural changes took place which provided the conditions for increased mobility. The most important of these were the restoration of production management to the farm households, an acute urban labour shortage, and the growing role of markets in supplying daily necessities. In this situation, inventive and entrepreneurial rural migrants gradually stretched the limits of the possible. The foundations were laid for the mobility networks which over the years would become the main channel for large-scale rural labour migration. Faced with increasing mobility, the authorities were impelled to reconsider basic aspects of rural development and urbanization policies and to adjust the *hukou* system and associated controls to the changing situation. Sometimes, such changes were also in line with the particular interests of local government organizations and officials. In this way, the limits were widened and growing numbers of migrants gained new space to further test these limits. Thus mobility gradually eroded the controls, making possible yet more mobility. The proliferation of new regulations – exceptions, special cases, and exemptions – made the system more and more liable to corruption.

Despite all the changes, the core of the *hukou* system has not changed. The division along rural–urban residence lines is no longer clearcut, but Chinese society by and large can still be divided into an 'agricultural' segment and a 'non-agricultural' one, and glaring differences remain in entitlements between the two.

The worst excesses have been trimmed away and in rural towns, where the entitlement gap was never very large, experiments with easier access to urban registration have been resumed. Still, the large majority of migrants is denied urban citizenship. The HRS has become less transparent and more open to corruption as personal connections and money play decisive roles in determining people's chances in life. Rural people continue to suffer severe disadvantages.

Prospects for the future are mixed at best. On the one hand, while bringing no revolutionary change, if the recent changes in the HRS are implemented well, they will benefit migrants, particularly the more successful ones. On the other hand, the employment prospects in the late 1990s are very bleak. For the first time in more than a decade, Township and Village Enterprises (TVEs) are no longer absorbing workers and major layoffs have been experienced in many cities. The austerity measures introduced in 1995 dampened activity in some sectors, including construction, which is one of the main employers of rural migrants. Moreover, since the Fifteenth Party Congress of 1998, the Chinese government has embarked on the restructuring of industrial enterprises involving large-scale dismissal of workers. These workers inevitably compete for jobs that have been the preserve of rural migrants. Moreover, migrants are more likely to be seen as a threat to urban dwellers' livelihoods. Finally, positive adjustments of the *hukou* system have been accompanied by exclusionary measures. In recent years, the largest cities have banned migrants from a large number of jobs. And in 1998 it was rumoured that Beijing and Shanghai were planning to send home up to a million rural workers (Becker 1998). After two decades of reform, the authorities are still trying to come to grips with rural labour migration.

Notes

1   James Scott's analysis (1990) of parades and mobs, of anonymity and of spontaneity, is illuminating in this context.
2   We will use the term 'official migration' to indicate moves like these, which are accompanied by a transfer of registration to the new place of residence.
3   'Temporary' as used in the official jargon, means that the people involved do not get a permanent local *hukou*, but remain registered as 'agricultural' in their place of origin. In later years, many of these so-called temporary workers had been in the cities for many years. Thus, the term 'temporary migrants' in the Chinese context is an expression of wishful thinking, rather than an accurate description of reality.
4   Note that throughout, 'non-agricultural' (in quotation marks) refers to *hukou* status, not to actual occupation. There was also a strong increase in people engaged in non-agricultural occupations due to the growth of rural enterprises and labour migration, but this is only very partially reflected in the *hukou* figures.
5   Surveys invariably refer to the 'floating population', which includes all people in a place who are not registered locally. Thus, in addition to the rural labour migrants, the figures also include tourists, people attending training courses or conferences, medical patients, business people, etc. Furthermore, some studies (in particular those undertaken by the Public Security Bureaux) also include the daily population flow. Therefore, many of the figures are inflated.

References

Becker, J. (1998) 'A collapse of the working class', *South China Morning Post*, 8 August, 15.

Mobo C.F. Gao, 'On their own, the plight of migrant workers in South China', *China Rights Forum*, Fall 1994, 4–7, 28.

Horizon (1995) (Horizon Market Research Inc.) *Luoren, Beijing Liumin de Zuzhihua Zhuangkuang Yanjiu Baogao* (The naked, research report on the organizational situation of Beijing migrants), Beijing: Mimeo.

Liu Dawei and Wang Qiang (1988) 'Survey report on the 'difficulty in recruiting labour' in Beijing municipality', *Chinese Economic Studies*, 21 (4), 45–63.

Ma, L. J. C. and Xiang Biao (1998) 'Native place, migration, and the emergence of peasant enclaves in Beijing', *The China Quarterly*, 155, 546–81.

Mallee, H. (1994) 'Reforming the *Hukou* system: the experiment with the "urban registration with self-supplied grain"', in Dong Lisheng (ed.) *Administrative Reform in the People's Republic of China since 1978* (Leiden: International Institute for Asian Studies), pp. 100–20.

Mallee, H. (1995) 'China's household registration system under reform', *Development and Change*, 26 (1), 1–29.

Mallee, H. (1996) 'In defence of migration: recent Chinese studies of rural population mobility', *China Information*, 10 (3–4), 108–40.

Middelhoek, J. (1989) 'Spatial aspects of China's rural labour surplus, policy outlines and a case study', *China Information*, 3 (4), 36–55.

Potter, S. H. (1983) 'The position of peasants in modern China's social order', *Modern China*, 9 (4), 465–99.

Research Group (1997) (Research Group on organizational characteristics of rural labour mobility) *Nongcun laodongli liudong de zuzhihua tezheng* (The organizational characteristics of rural labour mobility), *Shehuixue Yanjiu*, 1, 15–24.

Scott, J. C. (1990) *Domination and the Arts of Resistance: Hidden Transcripts* (New Haven and London: Yale University Press).

Wang Wuding (ed.) (1995) *90 Niandai Shanghai Liudong Renkou* (The floating population of Shanghai in the 1990s), (Shanghai: Huadong Shifan Daxue Chubanshe).

Xiang Biao (1998) 'Taobi, lianhe yu biaoda: 'Zhejiangcun' de gushi' (Escape, alliance and expression: the story of "Zhejiang village"' *Chinese Social Sciences Quarterly* (HK), 22, 91–111.

Xiang Biao (1999) 'Zhejiang village in Beijing: creating a visible non-state space through migration and marketised networks' in F. N. Pieke and H. Mallee (eds) *Internal and International Migration, Chinese Perspectives* (Richmond: Curzon).

Victor Yuan (1999) 'Contract worker teams in Beijing' in F. N. Pieke and H. Mallee (eds) *Internal and International Migration, Chinese Perspectives* (Richmond: Curzon).

Zhao Shukai, (1996) '1995 nian nongming liudong: taishi he jiaodian' (Peasant mobility in 1995: trends and focus), in Jiang Liu, Lu Xueyi, Dan Tianlun (eds) *Shehui lanpishu, 1995–1996 nian Zhongguo shehui xingshi fenxi yu yuce* (Social Blue Book, Analysis and prediction of the Chinese social situation in 1995–1996), pp. 78–96.

Zhao Shukai (1997) 'Liudong jiuye renkou de guanli xianzhuang he zhengce yijian' (The present state of and policy recommendations with regard to management of the working floating population), in Ma Hong and Liu Zhongyi (eds) *97 Ban Zhongguo fazhan yanjiu, Guowuyuan fazhan yanjiu zhongxin yanjiu baogao xuan* (*97 Edition of Studies of China's development, A selection of research reports of the State Council Development Research Centre*) (Beijing: Fazhan Chubanshe), pp. 121–33.

5   Domination, resistance and accommodation in China's one-child campaign

Tyrene White

China's one-child policy, launched in 1979, was one of the most radical acts of social engineering attempted by any state in the twentieth century. In urban areas, social and economic conditions, combined with tight administrative control, kept resistance to a minimum. In rural China, by contrast, resistance was widespread and difficult to contain. As in other agricultural societies, offspring were valued for their contribution to the family economy, and males were especially valued both for their economic contribution and for their role in preserving the family line.

Resistance to the one-child policy took three forms: direct confrontation between policy enforcers and targets; evasion of enforcement, either through deceiving rural cadres or colluding with sympathetic ones; and the middle ground of accommodation. By accommodation, I mean those acts of resistance that appear to signal compliance with state power, but on terms that simultaneously defy state power. When couples accede to state pressures to limit themselves to only one child, despite a desire for more children, the state succeeds in its attempt at material domination, i.e., domination of their fertility. When they resort to female infanticide, however, or much more commonly, infant abandonment or sex-selective abortion, those same couples reveal the influence of a counter-discourse that challenges the state's ideological claim to dominate child-bearing. Mediating these two discourses is ultrasound technology, which has made it progressively easier for determined individuals, rural or urban, to engineer the sex of their child.

In 1949, as the Chinese Communist Party was poised to establish its new regime, China's population numbered nearly half a billion, a staggering figure that many believed would prove an unbearable drag on China's attempts to develop. It was only after two decades, however, that China began to make population control a state priority. In the early 1970s, birth limits were set at two or three children. By 1979, however, China's post-Mao leaders were so disturbed about the likely impact of population growth on their new development plans that they took the extreme step of launching a one-child-per-couple policy – the most extensive, aggressive, and effective attempt ever made to subject child-bearing to direct state control and regulation.

Looking back, China's leaders and demographers argue that the two-decade delay after 1949 was a fateful mistake. By the time the state began to encourage fertility control, a huge new generation of young people had already been born – young people who had yet to move through their child-bearing years. As a result, even with declining fertility levels (i.e., the average number of children born to a woman during her reproductive years), demographic momentum meant continued growth of total population size. By 1979, China's population hit the one billion mark. Twenty years later it was approaching 1.3 billion, and by the mid-twenty-first century, it is predicted to increase by another 300 million. This expansion will continue to occur even though China's demographic transition from a high fertility, high mortality society to a low-fertility, low-mortality society is largely complete.[1]

No demographic transition can be explained by a single variable, and China's transition is no exception. The sudden and rapid decline in fertility which occurred after 1970 in both urban and rural areas suggests the strong influence of population control policies enacted at that time. Other factors were also at work, however. By the 1970s, improvements in levels of socioeconomic development, education, and communications networks meant that more people were aware of the option of birth control. As young men and women born after 1949 entered into their child-bearing years in the 1970s, attitudes and preferences began to shift. Infant mortality had declined, while the cost of child-rearing had gone up. In urban areas, living space was cramped and scarce, and the 'iron rice bowl' of state employment meant secure, if modest, retirement pensions and health benefits. A growing proportion of women worked full-time, only to pull a second shift of housework, cooking, and child care at home. Although data on this period remains very scarce, there can be little doubt that these changes, particularly in urban areas, began to affect individual calculations about how many children were desirable. As demographers have seen elsewhere, once the idea of smaller family size begins to take hold, it can spread within a particular cultural and social context very rapidly.

With 80 percent of the population living in the countryside, however, it took more than socioeconomic development and attitudinal changes to bring fertility rates down so rapidly. After 1970, six forms of state intervention were used: (1) free access to contraceptives, abortion and sterilization; (2) enforcement of late marriage guidelines, raising the average age at marriage from 22 in 1970 to 25 by 1979 (Bannister 1987); (3) use of material incentives and penalties to encourage compliance with birth limits; (4) a mass mobilization campaign to promote smaller families and enforce birth limits; (5) the creation of a large family planning bureaucracy to implement birth control guidelines; and 6) the inclusion of population targets into the national economic planning process.

Making population targets a part of the central planning process in 1971 marked the culmination of a long internal political battle over how to view China's large and growing population. In 1949, Mao Zedong was inclined to see population as an asset. Like Marx, he believed that capitalism, not overpopulation, was the cause of poverty, disease, and unemployment. By the mid–1950s, however, the shock of China's first census results, combined with lagging levels of agricultural output, led other CCP leaders (including Zhou Enlai and Deng Xiaoping) to urge the abandonment of China's pro-natalist policy and the promotion of voluntary birth control. Just as a public birth control campaign got underway, however, the program became the victim of the political and policy disputes that eventually led to the Great Leap Forward.

Paradoxically, it was during this period of mobilization prior to the Great Leap that the core idea behind China's approach to population control took shape. Though Mao remained suspicious of the arguments for birth control and had a direct hand in preempting the fledgling campaign, it was he who suggested in 1957 that China should attempt to plan reproduction in the same way it aspired to plan material production. At the time, birth planning (*jihua shengyu*), i.e., the attempt to regulate population growth so as to keep it in balance with levels of economic production and growth, was a goal to be reached only at some more advanced stage of socialist development. As China's population continued to grow, however, key leaders such as Premier Zhou Enlai came to believe that birth planning could not be postponed. In the early 1960s, after the disastrous Great Leap Forward, Liu Shaoqi and Zhou Enlai attempted to revive the birth control campaign, and in 1965 Zhou Enlai proposed the first national population control target – reducing the annual rate of population growth to one percent by the end of the century. This second campaign, like the first, was aborted by the Cultural Revolution, but Zhou revived and accelerated it in the early 1970s, introducing specific population targets into the annual and 5-year economic plans. Socialist planning thus came to embrace human reproduction in much the same way that it embraced agricultural and industrial production. Local officials who were responsible for meeting grain and steel production quotas now began to receive quotas for babies.

In the early and mid-1970s, the campaign focus was 'later, longer, fewer,' i.e., promoting late marriage, longer spacing between births (3–5 years), and fewer births (a two-child ideal and a three-child limit). By mid-decade, however, the child-bearing norm began to tighten; the new slogan became 'one is not too few, two is enough, three is too many.' Even that policy was judged too lenient by the new Deng regime. In 1979, Deng commissioned some of China's top demographers and scientists to announce the bad news: if China was to achieve its economic goals by the year 2000, population had to be contained within 1.2 billion. To attain that goal, the official birth limit was lowered to one-child-per-couple (with some exceptions for special circumstances), and all child-bearing age couples, urban and rural, had to receive official birth permits from the state in order to give birth legally.

In China's cities and towns, growing acceptance of the small-family norm, reinforced by the late marriage policy and tight administrative control in workplaces and neighborhoods, had brought the total fertility rate down to about 1.5 by 1979, a remarkably low level for a developing country. With a large cohort of women about to enter their peak child-bearing age years, however, even this low level was deemed inadequate. To further suppress fertility and prevent more second births, state monitoring intensified in workplaces and neighborhoods.¹ Monthly gynecological examinations for child-bearing age women, plus a system of marriage and birth permits provided by the work unit, ensured that anyone who desired to have a second child was caught in a tight surveillance net. Anyone who escaped the net faced severe economic penalties, including fines, loss of employment, and perhaps even one's coveted urban household registration.

If changing child-bearing preferences and state control worked together to induce compliance with the one-child policy in urban China, rural China was altogether different. Like rural populations in other places and times, life in the countryside encouraged higher levels of fertility. Agricultural work requires household labor, and unlike their urban counterparts, even very young children can be put to work in service of family income. Moreover, while urban retirees could depend on a pension for retirement support, rural families had no such guarantees. Children were the only guarantee of old-age support, and the most poor and pitied villagers were inevitably those who were alone and childless. Only a son could assure a couple that they would be spared such a fate. Daughters usually married out of the village, transportation links were often poor, and upon marriage a daughter's first obligation transferred to her husband's family. Even the most devoted daughter could not be counted on to provide either income or assistance. In urban areas, in contrast, nearby residency and convenient transportation allowed married daughters to be valuable assets to aging parents.

In addition to these practical considerations, the traditional emphasis on bearing sons to carry on the ancestral line remained deeply entrenched in the countryside. As a result, although fertility levels were cut in half between 1971 and 1979 (declining from approximately six to three), much of rural China remained hostile to a two- or one-child limit, including the rural cadres who would have to enforce the policy.² When the rural reforms implemented after 1978 began to relax the state's administrative grip on the peasantry just as the one-child policy was launched, therefore, it set the stage for a prolonged and intense struggle over the control of childbearing.

To date, most of the scholarship on China's birth planning program has examined the process of policy evolution and implementation at the national or local level, and the means by which the state has succeeded in meeting its fertility goals and overriding resistance (Greenhalgh 1990, 1994; Greenhalgh, Zhu, and Li 1994; Li 1995; White 1987, 1990, 1991, 1994). Societal resistance, though pervasive and widespread, especially in the countryside, has received less systematic attention.³ Even less attention has been given to the question of whether, and to what degree, societal resistance has shaped or influenced the evolution of policy.

Given the overwhelming evidence of grassroots resistance to China's population policy, this lacuna in the literature is odd. After all, rarely has there been a case where the evidence of resistance is so easily detected and measured. Though violations of the birth plan are by no means the only form of resistance, the tens of millions of such births that have occurred over the past two decades are a living testament to just how widespread and sustained the resistance has been. Yet by the mid-1990s the state had nevertheless succeeded in pushing the total fertility rate down to the remarkably low level of 1.8. The case of birth planning in China thus confronts us with the apparent paradox of what appears to be a strong state *and* a strong society.

How can that be? Models of state–society relations generally assume that the distribution of power between state and society is zero sum; as the state gains in power, society loses, and vice versa. In China, however, the large overlap and vague boundaries between 'state' and 'society' have led many scholars to challenge that model.[4] In this case, tight fertility control applied to all child-bearing age couples, whether they were state officials in Beijing or poor peasants in a remote village. Moreover, party members, family planning officials, and rural cadres were asked to set an example by taking the lead in embracing the one-child limit. If they were past their child-bearing years, they were pressed to see that their children and relatives complied. The significance of this – that no one was left untouched by the policy – cannot be overstated. It meant that the state was at least as vulnerable to resistance from within its own ranks as it was to societal resistance. The struggle over childbearing, then, has been more than a struggle by the state to dominate society's child-bearing. It has also been a prolonged struggle to contain and eliminate resistance at every level of state administration, particularly the local level.

The limitations of a zero-sum, state–society model of power relations are also revealed by the pattern of resistance that has emerged in this case. Not only has resistance taken on the traditional forms of open confrontation or more disguised evasion, it has also taken the form of accommodation. Caught between state demands to limit childbearing to only one or two children, and cultural and social pressures to have a son, many couples have attempted to resolve the conflict by resorting to female infanticide, or more commonly, female infant abandonment and sex-selective abortion. Can strategies of accommodation such as these, poignant and tragic as they are, constitute a form of resistance? I will argue here that they can, for it is precisely in these places that we get to the heart and extremity of the struggle. Though strategies of accommodation reveal the extent of state domination and power, they also reveal vividly the extent to which the right to engineer fertility remains contested political terrain.

Patterns of resistance

However successful the state's policy may appear to be in the aggregate, success has been achieved in the face of widespread resistance that has taken three basic forms: confrontation, evasion, and accommodation. Changing socioeconomic and political conditions in the 1980s and 1990s have created opportunities for new elaborations on existing approaches and techniques, but the three basic strategies have persisted.

Strategies of confrontation

The one-child policy posed a profound threat to Chinese cultural traditions that emphasized the importance of a male offspring. Only sons could carry on the family's ancestral line, and only sons could reliably be counted on to care for parents in their old age (daughters married, moved away, and undertook duties to their husband's household). More broadly, the new determination of the state after 1979 to prevent any 'unplanned' birth, but especially third or higher parity births (*duotai*), by pressing hard for abortion, sterilization, or intrauterine device (IUD) insertion, confronted millions of households with the reality of state intrusion into the heart of family life. Families who saw childbearing as their best long-term guarantee of strength, respect and stature in the village (and their best defense against weakness, bullying and abuse by powerful families or clans), believed that birth limits represented a profound threat to their future security. Little wonder, then, that attempts to round up pregnant women could provoke direct, and often violent confrontation.

Violence and the threat of violence against birth planning officials began to occur in the early 1980s, as pressures to limit childbirth increased dramatically. Irate husbands attacked birth planning officials who pressured their wives or relatives to have abortions. Others were assaulted out of anger over botched abortions, sterilizations, or IUD insertions, and the failure of local officials to provide sufficient follow-up health care. The attacks were often directed against female cadres or doctors, who were frequently on the front lines of implementation. In some cases, they were attacked by family members and killed. In one case, reported in *Hubei Daily* in April 1982, a doctor who reported a woman with a third pregnancy to the commune authorities was attacked by the woman's husband after he was fired from his job. Eight family members joined him in the beating, one of whom was the brigade party secretary.[5]

In the second half of the 1980s and the 1990s, as the reform process loosened the choke-hold of rural cadres on peasant livelihood, the pattern of rural conflict escalated. In Suining county of Jiangsu province, for example, there were a reported 381 'incidents of revenge' between January 1987 and May 1988, one-third of them directly related to birth planning.[6] All of these incidents involved physical attacks on cadres by angry peasants, but attacks on property were also frequent. Since cadres sometimes seized or destroyed peasant property in order to deter or punish birth planning offenses, peasants retaliated in kind, destroying crops on cadres' land, killing their chickens or pigs, and damaging their homes and furnishings. These attacks became so frequent that one Henan county passed a law explicitly banning such acts of retaliation. Such measures were hardly effective, however. As the number of strikes, protests and demonstrations by peasants escalated in the 1990s, strict enforcement of the birth-control policy ranked high on the list of villagers' complaints. When local officials were pressed by their superiors to tighten implementation and crack down on 'unplanned' births, villagers sometimes struck back by attacking township authorities *en masse*.[8]

Strategies of evasion

The most common strategy employed in resisting the one-child policy was that of avoiding the detection of an 'extra-plan' pregnancy until the child has been born. Within this category, there were two further subtypes – the independent evader, and the dependent one. Independent evaders attempted to circumvent the birth limits without relying on the silent acquiescence or active assistance of local officials. Dependent evaders, in contrast, relied precisely on such forms of cadre collusion in order to succeed.

The simplest approach to avoiding detection was the attempt to time a pregnancy for the autumn. As women bundled themselves in several layers of clothing, or padded jackets, to protect against the winter cold, they were able to hide the pregnancy for several months. Assuming no one in the village betrayed their secret, they might succeed in avoiding detection until very late in the term or until childbirth. Keeping the secret was difficult, however, and women's leaders counted on village gossip to help with their work. Pregnant women usually told at least one person about the pregnancy, often their mother-in-law. Once she knew, however, she could not resist telling a friend. As the word began to spread, the women's leader discovered the pregnancy very quickly. How much pressure was brought to bear upon the pregnant woman, however, depended on how quickly the women's leader reported the problem to higher-level authorities. A small delay could mean the difference between getting caught or getting away, i.e., leaving the village until it was safe to return, or until the baby was born.

In other cases, women evaded detection by leaving the village altogether until after the child was born. In the 1970s and early 1980s, this strategy generally depended on having a relative or acquaintance outside one's village or town (ideally in a large county town or a city) with whom one could board for the duration of the pregnancy. By the mid-1980s, however, relaxations on travel and population movement led to the emergence of a burgeoning army of temporary migrants that came to be known as the 'floating population.' Numbering some-where between 50–100 million by the mid-1990s, this migrant population defied even the best efforts of birth control officials to keep track of their childbearing. Those who were determined to have another child, therefore, often joined the ranks of the migrants and became part of the 'guerrilla birth corps.' The sound logic behind this strategy was spelled out by a Yunnan peasant:

> Since I am from another locality and my residence is not registered here, nobody here will interfere with how many children I am going to have . . . [When I go home] I will simply say that I have picked up and adopted an abandoned child here. Even if the residence of the child is not allowed to be registered, it will not matter because the child will then already be two or three years old. Somehow he will be recognized as my son.[9]

Notice that for this plan to work, his story does not have to be believed. All he is counting on is that village cadres will eventually accept the presence of this additional child, since they will not be held directly responsible for births outside their own village or township.

A third strategy was to bribe medical personnel to remove IUDs, normally implanted after the first birth. Some doctors began to provide such services on a regular basis, while others faked the quarterly or monthly gynecological examination results, allowing 'illegally' pregnant women to go undetected. Still others could be paid to tie only one fallopian tube during sterilization, or to provide false certification of having undergone sterilization (normally required after a second birth). In 1994, a former vice-president of a county hospital in Hunan was executed for taking nearly 200,000 yuan in bribes between 1986 and 1991 in exchange for falsifying 448 sterilization certificates.[10] Medical personnel were also implicated in phony certification schemes. Under China's rules, a couple was allowed to have a second child if the first was born with physical or mental disabilities that would prevent the child from being a full-time laborer as an adult. This gave doctors another opportunity for fraud, since they could certify a healthy child as a defective one.[11] Similarly, official birth permits were controlled and issued by birth planning cadres. Peasants who could not find other ways around the birth limit sometimes discovered that local officials were willing to sell the permits for the right price. In 1988, officials in some localities were charging 1600 yuan for a permit.[12]

Another evasive strategy was to marry or cohabit unofficially, without receiving an official marriage permit or registering with the Civil Affairs Bureau. This was a strategy frequently employed by rural families anxious to arrange marriages before their children had reached the legal ages of 20 for women and 22 for men. Since family planning officials concentrated their efforts on married women, those who were secretly married and sheltered by their families were often able to become pregnant and give birth without detection. Nationwide, 6.1 million people had married under the legal age by 1988. That figure translated into about 15 percent of all marriages, and those marriages contributed about ten percent of all births annually.[13] By 1994, under-age marriages numbered 1.6 million annually, representing 16 percent of all marriages.[14] This large number of illegal marriages could not occur without the help and collusion of local officials, especially village and township cadres. In some cases, evading the one-child policy was the primary motive; in other cases, profit was the primary motive, and peasants paid hefty bribes to acquire false certifications of age by village cadres or marriage certificates by township officials. From the perspective of rural cadres, the two motives, resistance and profit, were hardly incompatible.

One of the most pervasive strategies used by cadres to cope with enforcement pressures from above and resistance from below was the cover-up – engaging in statistical fraud to hide excess births. Village leaders used any pretext to under-report the number of local births. Women known to have given birth, but who did so outside the village, were left off local birth rolls. Even those who gave birth in the village were sometimes omitted, and the omission was covered up by refusing to issue a household registration for the infant. Sending township officials into a village did not necessarily increase the likelihood of full disclosure. One former township cadre complained that village leaders did everything they could to obstruct the work of such teams. Village leaders warned peasants about the impending visit by the team, giving offending couples a chance to flee or hide. Village leaders sometimes hid themselves so as to avoid a confrontation. Other cadres welcomed the team and accompanied it into the village, but their 'assistance' was actually resistance, their actions designed to minimize the team's access to accurate data and move them quickly out of the village. These tactics were so effective that one former township official concluded that it was impossible for outsiders to know the true state of affairs in a village.[15]

Township officials did not always want to know the truth, however, since exceeding the local birth quota would have a negative impact on the leaders' work evaluations, salaries, and bonuses. Family planning officials learned quickly that the local party secretary did not want to receive reports that would reflect badly on the township or threaten its privileged standing as an 'advanced unit.' And zealous cadres who sought out fraud learned that they would not be rewarded for 'rectifying' a fraudulent statistical report. As one former township cadre put it, an honest report would accomplish nothing but the destruction of one's own career, since higher-level political leaders would be embarrassed and angered by the revelation.[16] He admitted that he had knowingly submitted false reports rather than face the censure that would come with accurate accounting.

Another form of cadre–peasant collusion was to levy fines for unplanned births rather than expend extra effort attempting to prevent them. If grassroots women's leaders were unsuccessful in persuading a couple to abort an unauthorized pregnancy, village leaders sometimes did little or nothing to reinforce their efforts. This strategy allowed cadres to fulfill the letter of the law without provoking major confrontations with villagers. They could make it clear that heavy penalties would be levied after the child was born, but if that threat was not a sufficient deterrent, no further deterrence efforts were made. Leaders in some localities went further, implementing fines that were lower than those authorized by county or township regulations.

Cadres were particularly lenient with 'single-daughter households' (*dunühu*), or couples with two or more daughters but no sons. Sympathetic to their plight, village cadres often made no effort at enforcement, even refusing to impose fines if they gave birth to another girl. If couples violated the policy and had a son, however, payment of fines was transformed into a near-ritual performance. Cadres sent to collect the fines were received happily, and couples paid the fine as a part of the celebration over the birth. As one brigade women's leader said: 'They [rural couples] want to have a son. What can we do?'[17]

The same pattern prevailed with respect to sterilization. Pressed to meet sterilization quotas for couples with two or more children, cadres made every effort to avoid couples who had no sons. Even during major mobilizations like that of 1983, cadres worked to shield couples with no sons from the campaign. Because of the extreme pressures to meet sterilization quotas, they were not always successful in this effort, but during less intense periods they had no difficulty bypassing them. In Xinyu city of Jiangxi province, for example, more than 82 percent of *duotai* births in 1985 were born to couples with two or more daughters, including those with six or seven daughters. These births occurred despite a major sterilization mobilization during 1983 and 1984, because cadres had been unwilling to impose permanent birth control measures on couples without a son. Rather than resent the exceptions, other couples, even those with sons who had been mobilized for sterilization, tended to be sympathetic with this discriminating use of power.[18] So severe was the problem of official collusion that provinces and localities drafted administrative regulations laying out punishments for various kinds of policy violations. In 1998, for example, Hainan Province drafted provisions for punishing eight specific forms of collusion to violate the birth planning rules, including all of those discussed above.[19]

Strategies of accommodation

Situated between the confrontational (public) and evasive (hidden or disguised) forms of resistance was a third pattern of response. Those desperate to have a son sometimes resorted to female infanticide, female infant abandonment, or, as the technology became available, sex-selective abortion. In one sense, this pattern of accommodating state controls on childbearing may seem to be the ultimate evidence of state domination, an indicator of defeat and subordination rather than resistance. As James Scott argues, however, material domination – in this case, control over the number of children one has – is only one form of state domination. Transformative states also seek ideological and status domination, or control over the realm of legitimate ideas and the distribution of status and prestige within society (Scott 1990; Migdal 1995). Despite the CCP's massive and prolonged effort to justify its claim to control childbearing by emphasizing the public and social costs of childrearing and insisting that population growth is an impediment to modernization, it has been unable to overcome the influence of traditional patriarchal culture. This competing world view, which continues to hold sway across rural China, places family loyalty and filial obligation, not socialist ethics, at the center of the childbearing calculus. The duty to produce a son and male heir supersedes any duty to the motherland, a conviction reinforced by the realignment of status and power since 1979. In the new rural world of money, markets, corruption, and clans, the weak can be bullied and preyed upon by the strong. Having a son can help a family avoid the miserable fate of being among the weak.

Ironically, and tragically, the state's own policy has helped to further inscribe and reproduce this traditional world view (Greenhalgh and Li 1995; Anagnost 1995). After the extreme and ill-advised sterilization campaign in 1983, and in the wake of growing evidence of female infanticide, the state responded by simply reversing itself on the crucial issue of the value of female offspring. In the early 1980s, the thrust of the education campaign had been on repudiating the feudal idea that males (traditionally called a 'big happiness') were superior to females (a 'little happiness'), and insisting on the equal value of a boy or girl. In

1984, however, it effectively conceded the issue by modifying rural policy to allow single-daughter couples to try again – for a boy. Though the state did not condone the cultural preference for males, it did concede the economic and social realities that made sons more valuable. With the abandonment of collective agriculture and welfare, and with men privileged in the process of distributing collective goods (e.g., land, contracts, equipment), the importance of a son for prosperity and security was only reinforced. Rather than challenge that reality and risk further peasant unrest, the state chose to concede the issue. Single-daughter households were given special dispensation to have a second child – to try again for a son.

Although the intent of the 1984 policy change was merely to legitimize what was already the *de facto* rural policy in many areas, its effect was to split the state's ideological hegemony into two conflicting spheres: one sphere that applied to all urban residents, state cadres and administrative personnel, and another that applied to the peasantry. Rural women were thus left in the tragic situation of being caught in the crosshairs of two mutually exclusive modes of discourse. With no means of escaping this dual subjugation, many chose, or were forced by family members to choose, a strategy of accommodation that guaranteed the birth of a son. Those who could not achieve this result were vulnerable to a lifetime of pity, social ridicule, and self-blame.[20]

In the early 1980s, when collective life, limited cash income, and restrictions on travel severely constrained the options of rural families, some took the desperate course of female infanticide to preserve the chance to have a son. As the 1980s progressed, however, two alternative strategies of accommodation became very common. The first was infant abandonment, which increased in the late 1980s and 1990s in response to a tightening of the birth control policies (Johnson, Huang, and Wang 1998). Civil affairs officials, who have primary responsibility for social welfare, estimate that about 160,000 children were abandoned annually in the early 1990s, the vast majority of whom are girls. As Kay Johnson has argued, however, this figure likely underestimates the size of the problem, since many abandoned girls may never enter state institutions such as those managed by the civil affairs bureaucracy (Johnson 1996). Instead, birth parents often try to identify likely prospects for adopting the child, e.g., couples with a son but without a daughter.

Even more disturbing is the escalating incidence of sex-selective abortion and its impact on China's sex ratio. In 1979, China produced its first ultrasound B machine, designed for a variety of diagnostic purposes, including pregnancy monitoring. By 1982, mass production of ultrasound equipment had begun, and imports added to the number in use. Thirteen thousand ultrasound machines were in use in hospitals and clinics by 1987, or roughly six machines for each county. By the early 1990s, all county hospitals and clinics, and most township clinics and family planning stations had ultrasound equipment capable of fetal sex determination.[21] Henan Province, for example, spent four million yuan during the 1991–95 plan period to equip its 2,300-plus township technical service centers with ultrasound scanners.

Despite attempts by the state to outlaw the use of ultrasound technology to determine the sex of a fetus, easy access to the technology, combined with the lure of lucrative bribes and consultation fees, made ultrasound use vastly popular. This was especially true in newly prosperous county towns and rural townships, where prosperity and proximity made ultrasound diagnosis possible, but where modest degrees of upward mobility had done nothing to undermine the cultural prejudice and practical logic that favored male offspring. Young couples raised as peasants in a village but now employed in township factories and living in the township seat may have been far more willing than their peers a decade earlier to have only two children. If the first were a girl, however, it remained vital to many that the second be a boy. They may have been modern in their preference for a small family in order to hold on to their newfound prosperity, but when it came to desiring a son, tradition and contemporary social realities conspired. Because township and village cadres tacitly agreed with them, they could count on them to look the other way when they made their payoff to the medical technician. The cadres, after all, would much prefer to see couples resort to induced abortion of females to guarantee having a son, rather than have a second daughter and be tempted to try again, as many two-daughter households did. If the couple kept trying for a son, the local birth plan was threatened. If the couple used available technology to guarantee the birth of a son, the couple was happy and the cadres' problem was solved.

The impact of sex-selective abortion on China's sex ratio became increasingly clear in the 1990s. In 1982 the Chinese sex ratio at birth, 107.2 males for every 100 females, was already slightly in excess of the norm of 105–06 males for every 100 females. Though this figure raised questions about female infanticide and 'missing girls,' those questions were dismissed by Chinese spokesmen, who argued that the sex ratio was well within normal bounds and in keeping with China's own population history. Over the next ten years, however, the sex ratio at birth rose dramatically, to 111.2 in 1985, 113.8 in 1989, 116 in 1992, and 117.4 in 1995. Some of this increase was evident in first births, but sex ratios in second and higher-order births reflected a very strong male bias. By 1989, for example, the sex ratio for second-order births was 120.9; for third- and fourth-order births, it was 124.6 and 131.7, respectively.

Some of this gap can be accounted for by the underreporting of female births. Underreporting is suggested both by surveys of rural areas that reveal 'hidden' births not reported in official statistical reports, and by the lessening of the sex ratio imbalance for school-age children. In the 1992 sample survey, the sex ratio for the age 0–4 cohort was a very skewed 113.9. For the age 5–9 cohort, however, the ratio dropped to 107.81. This decline is what would be expected if previously unreported females were registered for school and then placed on local population rolls. Such children might never have appeared in vital statistics on births and deaths, sparing local officials the embarrassment of exceeding their local birth targets. Once older, however, they may be registered as migrants or adoptees, and the degree of male bias in the sex ratio declines accordingly.

Chinese demographer Zeng Yi, along with several colleagues, has argued that such underreporting accounts for anywhere from 43 to 75 percent of the skew in the sex ratio at birth (Zeng *et al.* 1993). However, since incentives and pressures to undercount all unplanned births have been relatively constant over the past decade, underreporting alone cannot explain the steady rise in the sex ratio at birth. Moreover, the results of a 1995 sample survey revealed that urban areas were also experiencing skewed sex ratios. Beijing, for example, registered an overall sex ratio at birth of 122.6, and 148.8 for second and higher parity births. This high sex ratio at birth placed Beijing on a par with such provinces as Jiangsu (125.1), Fujian (126.2), Jiangxi (129.1), Henan (128.0), Hubei (134.6), Guangdong (125.2), and Shaanxi (125.4). Tianjin also came in high, with an overall sex ratio at birth of 110.6 and a rate of 142.9 for second and higher parity births. And while Shanghai's overall rate was within a normal range, the rate for second and higher parity births was an exceptionally high 175.0 (Gao, Liu and Xia 1997). These data have led US Census Bureau experts to conclude that China's 1995 sex ratio was about 116 males to 100 females, only slightly less skewed than China's officially reported rate of 117.4 (Eberstadt 1998).

Although the one-child policy is no doubt a contributing factor in producing these alarming figures, they are consistent with trends elsewhere in East Asia. South Korea, Taiwan and India have all registered increases in the male to female sex ratio as ultrasound technology has become widely available (Park and Cho 1995; Das Gupta and Bhat 1997; Eberstadt 1998). Outside of China, the problem is most severe in South Korea, where the sex ratio at birth in 1993 was 116. This figure, which is roughly equivalent to the Chinese case, demonstrates clearly that the problem is not limited to China, nor is it merely the result of the one-child policy. Rather, it is a cultural and structural problem, one that cannot be explained away (as the CCP has sought to do) as the product of rural backwardness.

Still, the Chinese case, which pits state control over childbearing against deeply imbedded cultural prejudices and childbearing preferences, remains unique. China's relentless emphasis over the past thirty years on sheer numbers of births – on targets, quotas, and per capita accounting – combined with its conscious neglect of women's issues and its gendered politics of reproduction, has opened up the space within which an accommodative style of resistance can grow. Just as new birth-control technologies and surgical advances facilitated the state's move to engineer childbearing, so too has technology become the medium through which couples struggle to engineer the sex composition of their offspring. They may accommodate the state's birth limitation policy, but they seek to do it on their own terms, rejecting in the process the state's claim of ideological hegemony.

Resistance and the prospects for policy change

The struggle for dominion over childbearing in China has led to paradox, tragedy, and irony. The paradox we are confronted with by China's experience with the one-child policy is the simultaneous existence of massive evidence demonstrating the state's capacity to engineer childbearing, *and* massive evidence of resistance, including successful resistance. The tragedy of the policy is that it has forced a large portion of the population to choose between two types of hegemonic discourse – a modern 'socialist' one that emphasizes duty to the collective society, and a traditional patriarchal one that emphasizes duty to family and ancestors – both of which have been legitimated by the state, though one was intended to be subordinate to the other.

The sad irony of this case is that if policy change is going to occur, it will not be due to the combined effects of acts of unambiguous resistance so much as it will be the result of countless acts of accommodation, a pattern of action that has been made possible by the potent combination of technology and prosperity. The ultrasound technology that allows couples to discover the sex of the fetus, combined with the prosperity that has led to its widespread distribution, has made it possible for those caught between the state's discourse linking modernization and prosperity to birth planning and a secondary, state-complicit, cultural discourse linking status and dignity to male offspring, to attempt to accommodate both. The consequences, however, have been alarming enough to produce a type of 'voice' that is increasingly urgent in content, but corporate in structure, and non-confrontational in tone.[23] The core constituencies behind this 'voice' are demographers, family planning officials, and Women's Federation officials who are alarmed about the implications of current trends with sex ratios and rapid population aging. The skewed sex ratios mean an impending shortage of wives for as many as fifty million men, which the Women's Federation rightly describes as an 'army of bachelors.' Since the marriage market will place poor men at the greatest disadvantage in competing for a wife, this shortfall of brides could have explosive social consequences. And rapid fertility decline, coupled with increasing life expectancy, means that over the next several decades China's population will age almost as rapidly as the populations of western Europe, North America and Japan. In these countries, which enjoy wealth and stable systems of welfare, anxieties about rapid population aging are already monopolizing leadership attention. China will face similar levels of elderly dependence without either of those advantages, and with the disadvantage of a demographic structure in which a shrinking proportion of the population will have to support a very large population of both old and young.

Some of those who stress these negative side-effects of the one-child policy have been advocating a modified and less coercive approach to population control since the early 1980s. As insiders within the system of population institutes, think tanks, and academic departments, they have had to be very cautious in how, and to what degree, they challenge the reigning orthodoxy. By 1998, however, they had succeeded in getting the post-Deng leadership to launch an experiment in several counties implementing what is described as a genuinely voluntary family planning program, one that stresses positive incentives to limit childbirth rather than mandatory control. This project, which is supported by the United Nations Fund for Population Activities (UNFPA), is the first sign that these corporate appeals may have begun to have an impact, and that China may finally be shedding its crude and mechanical approach to population control. It will no doubt be watched very closely by those who fear relaxing the strict controls, and by those who worry that genuine voluntarism cannot live in the midst of China's regulatory and punitive administrative culture.

If the advocates of a more flexible policy succeed in bringing about a change in policy, they will be aided by conditions that were not present when the one-child policy was adopted in 1979. First, those entering their childbearing years in the late 1990s have grown up against the backdrop of rapid development, increased prosperity, and the one-child policy. Their hopes and dreams often center on leaving the village, or alternatively, leaving agricultural work. The images brought to them from the vastly expanded communications networks and opportunities for travel reinforce the idea of the urban, one-child family as the symbol of modernity. As a result, many of today's young rural couples may simply take for granted the message that had to be drilled into the generation before them – that their lives will be more prosperous and secure if they choose to have fewer children. If this last is true, if the new world they have grown up in has instilled a genuine desire for a one- or two-child family, then moving toward a more voluntary approach to birth planning without risking a significant fertility rebound should be feasible.

The second condition that may foster a transition to a less coercive policy is a change in the international environment over the past decade – a shift of focus in the global discourse on population growth in the 1990s. When China began to implement its one-child policy in 1979, it was widely lauded by those in the population community who subscribed to the dominant theory that population growth was a primary, if not *the* primary, impediment to economic growth. For that portion of the international family planning community, China's acceptance of this position, and its determination to place tight curbs on population growth, was so important that the very disturbing methods by which China sought to achieve its aims were often overlooked. By the mid-1990s, another school of thought began to dominate the discourse on population and development. This alternative approach, which was crystallized at the 1994 United Nations International Conference on Population and Development, emphasizes the importance of alleviating poverty, improving the status of women, and protecting women's rights (including reproductive rights), as the more just and effective approach to population issues.

Those in China in a position to argue safely and persuasively for a shift in China's methods and goals were aided by this shift in the global discourse and agenda. In the 1970s, China's leaders had quietly but radically embraced the dominant Western demographic theory of the time – that reducing population growth was necessary to socioeconomic development, and that the over-populated nations of the developing world could not afford to wait for a development-induced demographic transition like that which had occurred in Europe. In the post-Mao era, this theory has been used to legitimate the regime's insistence that population control is the linchpin of the modernization strategy, even as it has come under increased scrutiny and criticism in the west as a simplistic and flawed theory. With that theory now subjected to a serious international critique and modification, perhaps it can be deployed by influential voices within China to help buttress their arguments for the necessity to modify current policy. Let us hope that their arguments will lead to change sooner rather than later, remedying the most appalling side-effects of the one-child policy and releasing China's childbearing-age couples from the hard choices and temptations that now confront them. It is the state that has taught the population that the social engineering of childbearing is a legitimate and virtuous course. Now that individual couples have a modern, efficient, and hi-tech method by which to engineer the sex composition of their own households, the dangers that have always been inherent in such a course are revealing themselves. Ideological exhortation alone will not solve this contradiction. To remove it, the state will also have to alter the structural conditions and policies that encourage the continued cultural and social subordination of women.

Notes

1 Even in the absence of China's one-child policy, surveys suggest that most couples would prefer no more than two or three children, while many would continue to choose to have only one, particularly in urban areas. This suggests that, while China's demographic transition may not yet be fully complete in the countryside, its overall fertility levels would remain relatively low even if couples were left to exercise their individual choice.

2 The total fertility rate refers to the average number of children that would be born to a woman during her lifetime if she conformed to the actual fertility rates of women at all ages during a specific year. In other words, this figure is reached by adding up all of the age-specific fertility rates for a given year (e.g., the number of births per 1000 women at age 15, 16, 17 . . . 48, 49, and so on until childbearing ceases).

3 Two exceptions are Wasserstrom (1984) and Greenhalgh and Li (1995).

4 For a discussion of recent scholarship on state-society relations in China, see Elizabeth J. Perry, 'Trends in the Study of Chinese Politics: State-Society Relations,' *China Quarterly* (1994): 704–13.

5 Wan Simei, '*Ouda jihua shengyu gongzuo renyuan faji burong*' (Beating birth planning work personnel in violation of law and discipline will not be tolerated), *Hubei ribao*, 12 April, 1982, p. 2.

6 Su Suining, 'There are many causes of strained relations between cadres and masses in the rural areas,' *Nongmin Ribao*, 26 September 1988, p. 1., in *FBIS-China*, 7 October 1988, p. 13.

7 '*Zhizhi silei pohuai jihua shengyu gongzuode xingwei*' (Stop four kinds of behavior that wreck birth planning work), *Jiankang bao, jihua shengyu ban* (*Health Gazette, Birth Planning Edition*), 1 March, 1985.

8 See, for example, the report of a riot in Caojiang township, Guangdong Province, after officials tried to impose severe fines on offending couples. Daniel Kwan, 'Caojiang official denies riot over family planning policy', *South China Morning Post*, 8 September 1997, p. 8, in *FBIS-China*, 8 September 1997.

9 Xu Yaping, 'Plug up a loophole in planned parenthood work,' *Renmin ribao* 4 June 1985, translated in *FBIS-China*, 5 June 1985, p. K3.

10 Du Xin and Yu Changhong, '*Zhongguo nongcunde shengyu dachao*' (The great tide of rural child-bearing in China), *Liaowang zhoukan haiwaiban* (*Outlook Weekly Magazine, Overseas Edition*) 43 (23 October, 1989), p. 19; *Xinhua*, 'Henan Province executes hospital official,' in *FBIS-China*, 24 October 1994, p. 79.

11 Henan Province Rural Survey Team, Rural Economy Bureau, '*Yao duzhu chao jihua shengyude loudong*' (Loopholes for extra-plan births must be stopped up), *Nongcun gongzuo tongxun* 5 (1988), p. 46.

12 Zhong Cheng 'Delegates and members show concern for birth planning,' *Zhongguo xinwen she*, April 11, 1988, in *FBIS-China*, 13 April, 1988, p. 33.

13 *China Daily*, 9 January, 1988, p. 1; Zhu Baoxia, 'Birth control planned for transient population,' *China Daily*, 27 February, 1991, in *FBIS-China*, 27 February, 1991, p. 35.

14 *Xinhua*, 'Government to curb illegal marriages,' in *FBIS-China*, 1 March 1994, p. 23.

15 Interview File 900307.

16 Interview File 900722.

17 Interview Files 821012 and 900307.

18 Wang Peishu, '*Wanshan shengyu zhengce, kaihao 'xiao kouzi'de guanjian shi duzhu 'da kouzi'*' (The key to perfecting birth policy and 'opening a small hole' is stopping up the 'big hole'), *Xibei renkou* 3 (1987), pp. 20–21.

19 *Hainan Ribao*, 20 December 1997, p. 5, in *FBIS-China*, 14 January 1998.

20 The agony of being caught in this double bind is rendered very poignantly in Mo Yan's short story, 'Explosions.' Mo Yan, *Explosions and Other Stories* (Hong Kong, Renditions Paperbacks, 1991).

21 Zeng *et al.*, 'Causes and implications,' p. 291; Su Ping, '*Wo guo chusheng yinger xingbie wenti tanlun*' (Investigation into the question of our country's birth and infant sex ratio) *Renkou Yanjiu* 1 (1993); Mu Guangsong, '*Jinnian lai Zhongguo chusheng xingbie bi shanggao pian gao xianxiangde lilun jieshi*' (A theoretical explanation of the elevation and deviation in recent years of the sex ratio at birth), *Renkou yu jingji* 88, No. 1 (1995): 48–51.

22 Henan Provincial Family Planning Commission, 'Strengthen leadership, put an end to the backward state in family planning work,' *Nongmin Ribao*, 27 March 1996, p. 2, in *FBIS-China*, 27 March 1996.

23 The concept of 'voice' as a type of response to institutional pressures is drawn from Albert Hirschman, *Exit, Voice, and Loyalty: Responses to Decline in Firms, Organizations, and States* (Cambridge, MA: Harvard University Press, 1970).

References

On resistance to the one-child policy

Greenhalgh, S. and Jiali Li (1995) 'Engendering reproductive policy and practice in peasant China: for a feminist demography of reproduction,' *Signs: Journal of Women in Culture and Society*, 20, 601–41.

Wasserstrom, J. (1984) 'Resistance to the one-child family, *Modern China* 10, 345–74

On policy evolution and implementation

Greenhalgh, S. (1990) 'The evolution of the one-child policy in Shaanxi,' *The China Quarterly* 122, 191–229.

Greenhalgh, S. (1994) 'Controlling births and bodies in village China,' *American Ethnologist*, 21 (1994), 3–30.

Greenhalgh, S., Zhu Chuzhu and Li Nan (1994) 'Restraining population growth in three Chinese villages,' *Population and Development Review* 20, 365–93.

Jiali Li (1995) 'China's one-child policy: a case study of Hebei Province, 1979–1988,' *Population and Development Review*, 21, 563–85.

White, T. (1990) 'Implementing the "one-child-per-couple" population program in rural

China: national goals and local politics, in D. M. Lampton (ed.), *Policy Implementation in Post-Mao China* (Berkeley: University of California Press).

White, T. (1990) 'Postrevolutionary mobilization in China: the one-child policy revisited,' *World Politics* 43, 53–76.

White, T. (1991) 'Birth planning between plan and market: the impact of reform on China's one-child policy,' in Joint Economic Committee, US Congress, *China's Economic Dilemmas in the 1990s: The Problems of Reform, Modernization, and Interdependence*, volume 1, pp. 252–69.

White, T. (1994) 'The origins of China's birth planning policy,' in C. K. Gilmartin *et al.* (eds), *Engendering China: Women, Culture, and the State* (Cambridge and London: Harvard University Press), pp. 250–78.

On gender and birth control in China

Anagnost, A. (1995) 'A surfeit of bodies: population and the rationality of the state in post-Mao China,' in F. D. Ginsberg and R. Rapp (eds), *Conceiving the New World Order: The Global Politics of Reproduction* (Berkeley: University of California Press), pp. 22–41.

Greenhalgh and Li (1995), cited above.

On infant abandonment

Johnson, K. (1996) 'The politics of the revival of infant abandonment in China, with special reference to Hunan,' *Population and Development Review*, 22, 77–98.

Johnson, K., Huang Banghan, and Wang Liyao (1998) 'Infant abandonment and adoption in China,' *Population and Development Review*, 24, 469–510.

On the sex ratio of the Chinese population

Gao Lin, Liu Xiaolan and Xia Ping (1997) *'Beijing shi renkou chusheng xingbiebi fenxi'* (An analysis of the sex ratio at birth in Beijing), *Renkou yanjiu* (Population Research), 21, 25–33.

Zeng Yi *et. al.* (1993) 'Causes and implications of the recent increase in the reported sex ratio at birth in China,' *Population and Development Review*, 19, 283–302.

On skewed sex ratios elsewhere in Asia

Chai Bin Park and Nam-Hoon Cho (1995) 'Consequences of son preference in a low-fertility society: imbalance of the sex ratio at birth in Korea, *Population and Development Review*, 21, 59–84.

Monica Das Gupta and Mari Bhat, P. N. (1997) 'Fertility decline and increased manifestation of sex bias in India,' *Population Studies* 51, 307–15.

Eberstadt, N. (1998) 'Asia tomorrow, gray and male,' *The National Interest*, 53, 56–65.

On state–society relations and patterns of resistance

Migdal, J. S. (1995) 'The state in society: an approach to struggles for domination,' in J. S. Migdal, Atul Kohli, and V. Shue (eds), *State Power and Social Forces: Domination and Transformation in the Third World* (Cambridge: Cambridge University Press), pp. 7–34.

Scott, J. C. (1990) *Domination and the Arts of Resistance: Hidden Transcripts* (New Haven: Yale University Press).

6 The 'externalities of development'

Can new political institutions manage rural conflict?

David Zweig

Can China's current political and legal institutions manage the rapid economic development underway today? Using data drawn from 10 years of the Chinese journal, *Minzhu yu fazhi* (Democracy and Law), as well as several case studies based on field research in China, this paper puts forward several propositions. First, the scale of development projects in China and the externalities created by them have given rise to largescale social protests. Urbanization, marketization, industrialization and deforestation, all eat up suburban rural land, encourage cadres to impose onerous taxes on villagers, and cause pollution and flooding. As a result, the number of citizens affected by these 'externalities of development' are quite large. Second, the increasing scale of protest – what I call 'political externalities' – sorely tests China's political and legal institutions. This chapter looks at villagers' use of courts, the Administrative Litigation Law, the role of local elections, and the writing of petitions to higher level officials, and finds that in most cases the state's political institutions do not respond quickly or effectively to these protestations. Villagers, recognizing the weaknesses of the courts, the petitioning process, elections and the administrative legal system, combine legal recourse with collective acts of civil disobedience to seek solutions to their grievances.

Introduction[1]

Rapid economic development is highly destabilizing, and in China today 'externalities' associated with accelerated economic growth are generating widespread protests. Thus the pages of newspapers worldwide – in Hong Kong, New York and even China – are replete with stories of villagers joining together in protest marches. But as Huntington warned, if political demands overwhelm weak political institutions, political participation can trigger 'political decay'.[2] What is the current situation in rural China? Why do protests occur so frequently? What are the political and legal institutions that the leadership hopes will manage this increased demand for conflict resolution?

First, why are protests so ubiquitous? Intensified commercialization and commodification of land, labour, and agricultural products, rapid urbanization, enormous capital construction and public works projects, and rural industrialization, are all occurring within the context of weak market norms, a nascent legal and tax regime, a pliant environmental monitoring system, and a political system that often ignores or suppresses, rather than responds to, grievances emerging from society. As a result, economic development generates enormous 'externalities', defined as costs imposed on society that are not paid for by those carrying out development projects. In turn, these phenomena, such as environmental degradation and the economic and health costs it entails, excessive and at times illegal taxes imposed by local cadres, widespread official corruption, failures to fulfill business or contract obligations, and the widespread confiscation of collective rural land which is then resold by governments and developers at astronomical profits, all impose 'political and social externalities' on the system, leading large numbers of citizens to take collective action. As with economic externalities, these political and social externalities are the inadvertent repercussions of rapid economic development under weak institutional norms. Widespread demands by citizens for social justice and conflict resolution challenge the capacity of state institutions that remain rather ill-equipped to manage (rather than simply suppress) these higher levels of popular political participation. Therefore we must ask: Can China's new, yet still weak, political institutions manage this burgeoning demand for political and legal action and can the regime at the same time build strong and legitimate political and legal institutions to contain it? Or will rural residents be forced to resort to extra-legal forms of collective action and civil disobedience? Can China's institutions handle the stress, or will rural China fall prey to massive social unrest, maybe even a large-scale social movement, that could imperil the political system? In essence, will economic development lead to political modernization or political decay?

The emergence of new political institutions

Since 1978, a new set of political and legal institutions have developed to manage some of this burgeoning demand for political involvement. Elections for village leaders, the introduction of contract law and an increased role for the courts in solving villager–cadre conflicts under the Administrative Litigation Law, petitions to higher level officials (*shang fang gao zhuang*), as well as a much more aggressive role for journalists and television, have helped villagers express their grievances, influence local economic decisions, and seek redress for unfair cadre behaviour. Some of these institutions emerged autonomously from society and were then borrowed by the state, while others were introduced by a state deeply concerned that rural demands for change and the rapaciousness of local cadres could trigger massive rebellions.

The current effort to establish Villagers' Committees, based on direct elections of popular representatives, first emerged from rural Guangxi Province to fill the yawning power vacuum that had emerged there in rural China after decollectivization. By 1988, following several years of heated debate, leaders of the Chinese Communist Party (CCP) became convinced that direct elections for Villagers'

Committees and particularly for the director of these committees, as well as the shift of economic authority to the committees, would strengthen the state's political power, placate villagers' concerns that local taxes were being mis-appropriated, and stabilize the basic level of China's rural society. Clearly, the CCP still sees the local CCP secretary and the local party branch as the core organization for controlling village politics, but by allowing the villagers' own elected representatives to manage village finances, the state hoped to increase its legitimacy in the countryside.

Second, 'public petitioning' has emerged as a new norm, supported by central élites, through which citizens can challenge local bureaucratic decisions and cadre corruption.[3] Under this procedure, higher level officials are informed of corrupt behaviour by local officials so that festering issues can be resolved without moving into the formal realm of the courts. By righting wrongs on their own, cadres need not lose their positions thereby preserving rural order. Such actions also conform with the Chinese traditional preference for mediation over litigation, as rural litigants in China often live in close proximity to each other and a final, clear-cut legal decision in favor of one claimant could have long term influence on intra-village relationships.

Third, since the mid-1980s, the Chinese government has tried with some success to introduce 'rule *by* law', if not the 'rule *of* law', by encouraging Chinese citizens, including villagers, to take their grievances against cadres to court. Initially, as rural China shifted from plan to market and many goods and services previously allocated by the bureaucracy moved onto the market, villagers and cadres often broke their agreements in response to sudden changes in market prices or supplies. To prevent social unrest within villages, the state introduced the idea of rural contract law and offered citizens the chance to take their disputes to court for mediation or resolution.[4] In 1990, the state also introduced the Administrative Litigation Law which institutionalized the process by which individuals and collectivities sought legal redress for a wide array of issues, including abuses by public security officials and other zoning, land and real estate related abuses.[5]

Can these new institutions manage the enormous social and political conflicts generated by the externalities of rapid economic development? Public partici-pation and political demands in changing times can tax any political regime; how much greater is the pressure on China's system since local cadres see the emergence of new legal and political institutions as a challenge to their ability to manipulate the system to their advantage.

Moreover, these 'externalities of development' affect large groups of citizens, triggering widespread collective action. Rivers that are polluted by rural industry affect the lives of hundreds, if not thousands, of people. As became apparent in the summer of 1998, because cadres allocated investment funds to rural industry, coastal regions, or excessive wining and dining, and not to building dykes, floods inundated millions of acres of land and homes. As urbanization expropriates the land of villages around major cities or along new highways, villagers in nearby communities have common cause to unite to protect their land and livelihoods.

The fragile nature of the Chinese market and legal system, as well as a remarkably weak sense of legality among most rural actors, also invites much unscrupulous business activity which can have largescale political or legal ramifications. For example, when a vegetable seed company in Shandong Province was unable to meet its payments, 4,200 producer households in thirty-six townships across sixteen counties joined together and petitioned the county government where the company was located.[6]

Central leaders know that economic modernization, in the absence of new political and legal institutions, could bring on the regime's collapse. But how effective are these institutions? Do they resolve villager–cadre problems and mitigate social unrest and the need for collective political action? Or are villagers still forced to adopt more informal, extra-legal forms of collective action?

This chapter uses two different sources of data to demonstrate the relationship between economic development and political change. First, it analyzes a series of articles about rural petitioning and protests that appeared in the journal *Minzhu yu fazhi* (Democracy and Law; hereafter, *MZYFZ*). Second, it presents two related cases of villager resistance in a city in coastal China. While these cases are in no way statistically representative of the conditions in China, the articles in *MZYFZ* reflect most of the externalities generated by economic development in rural China, while the suburban cases are telling examples of the crisis gripping much of suburban China as villagers resist the externalities of rapid urbanization.

Data from *Minzhu yu fazhi*

In the absence of systematic data on protest activity across rural China, I collected all the examples of political or legal action by individuals and collectivities against state and local officials as reported in *MZYFZ* between 1988 and 1997. Of the thirty cases collected, twenty-six appeared in the journal between 1993 and 1997, two in 1991, one in 1990 and one in 1989.[7]

I subdivided the main issues that triggered these protests into five categories: land related cases, unofficial taxation (*luan shou fei*), administrative or business related problems, cadre abuse of power, including administrative power and election fraud, and wrongful attacks on cadres or resistance to what seems to be fair state policies.

Land problems reflect the dilemma of the commercialization of formerly state-controlled resources. Of the thirty cases, six (20 percent) related to land issues. In three cases, cadres illegally requisitioned and sold off collective land and then kept a large amount of the proceeds for themselves. Here the incredible value of land becomes apparent, as in one case where 1,738 *mu* (1 mu = 1/6 acre or 1/15 ha) of land was sold to the state for 40 million *RMB* (*ren min bi* also known as yuan).[8] With so much money involved, the stakes are very high, so it is no surprise that cadres threaten villagers (and their representatives) who bring illegal cadre behaviour to the attention of the courts. Also, with land perceived as a collective asset that was being privatized and plundered by cadres, villagers turned to collective action.

A case from Shantou, Guangdong Province, where cadres stole over 24 million *RMB*, is particularly interesting. Although villagers petitioned over 1,000 times over many years because they had received very little personal compensation for land requisitioned by the state, they were constantly thwarted by township, district, and municipal level officials who protected the local cadres. When letters to the provincial government did not bring results, villagers went to Beijing. This case involved many new political and legal institutions: villagers hired lawyers who were beaten by thugs hired by the village cadres; village cadres manipulated village elections to protect their positions while villager protests over electoral fraud, backed up by their team of lawyers, triggered no response; and, villagers contacted the media – in this case, *Minzhu yu fazhi* – whose investigating journalist was threatened with physical violence.

A second source of protests, the imposition on villagers of local taxes (*luan shou fei*), comprised seven of thirty cases (23 percent). For Bernstein, excessive taxation is the core of rural unrest.[9] The scale of these burdens is quite high, reaching over 20 percent of per capita income in one case.[10] Some burdens arise because cadres want to develop the local economy – build a road, a power plant, or some other modern facility – but, with the level of legal taxation set by the state at only five percent of villagers' per capita income, the local government lacks the tax base for such public works. So they force villagers to contribute more of their income to the local state. Thus in one case, county cadres who wanted to build an electric power plant 'to promote the development of the county', demanded that each male villager donate 20 days of labour while women give 10 days.[11] Or instead villagers could give three *RMB*/day – reaching 90 *RMB*/household – which would have brought the county 12 million *RMB*.

On the other hand, some cadres simply stole the funds or freely used force to gain them. In one case, cadres broke into villagers' homes and threatened them,[12] while in another they contracted out tax collection to collection agencies. While cadres often extort funds through these tax schemes for their own benefit, there are many areas of rural China where cadres cannot promote development because tax levels are simply too low.

A third set of cases reflects the type of economic or business problems that emerge during an incipient period of market development. These five cases included the selling of fraudulent products, the mistreatment of migrant workers, and one instance where villagers who had been compelled to raise seed for the township seed company were paid in IOUs when China's economy slowed dramatically in 1990.[13] The villagers, however, having been forced to grow the seeds, felt that they should not bear the burden of a downturn in the macro-economy, so they sued the township company, its parent at the county, and the village government that had made them turn over their seed. Despite efforts at reconciliation, the villagers insisted on full repayment, and in the end won their case.

Not all examples in these thirty cases result from the 'externalities of development'. Ten cases (30 percent) involved cadres or police who beat villagers, stole money, or used their political authority in unethical ways unrelated to business, taxes, or land. Several cases involved election fraud. Still, these abuses led villagers to file petitions or sue officials themselves, or turn to other citizens or relatives to file petitions on their behalf. Finally, three cases involved what the journal presented as unfair attacks on good cadres by citizens who either resisted state policies – in this case the one-child policy – or who suspected (incorrectly) that cadres had been stealing money when the collective's income increased but the villagers' income did not.

Several common characteristics emerge from these stories (Table 6.1). Externalities of development do trigger collective action. Of twenty-four cases that specify the actor, eighteen involved collective action, while six involved individual actions. Despite the emergence of household farming and contrary to rational choice arguments that private farmers are generally incapable of collective action,[14] most cases described in *MZYFZ* involved collective action. Why? First, many of these 'externalities' had an impact on dozens of families within a single village or on villagers in more than one locality, leading to a united response. Second, the cost of filing petitions, in terms of capital and time, may lead villagers to pool monies quickly in order to begin a formal process to seek redress. Third, there is probably greater security in large numbers, given the political risks of challenging the state and the potential for revenge by state cadres.

Second, despite the state's effort to promote petitioning as a peaceful, system-supportive means of conflict resolution, many petitions are initially rejected by higher level authorities, forcing villagers to include civil disobedience as part of their repertoire of protest activity. In nine of twenty-five cases, the initial petition was rejected or delayed for a long time by upper level authorities, while in twelve cases local officials resisted the decisions taken by their administrative superiors and the courts, and sometimes continued to do so even as the story was being written. For example, in one case where villagers approached a semi-government organization (called the Democratic Progressive Association – *Minzhu cujin hui*) in 1988, which then published reports of this case in its newspaper, the problem remained, triggering another investigation in 1994. Similarly, many local cadres resist villagers' claims, threaten them, or simply ignore the court's decision. By dragging out these affairs or threatening villagers, the state and its agents increase villager anger and frustration and encourage the violence that has become part of the process by which peasants seek redress.

In fact, winning a case is not always the best solution if cadres take revenge.[15] According to one article, family members were quoted as saying: 'No matter whether you win or lose, you lose. You still have to live here and the township government won't forgive you'. Little wonder that China advocates mediation or more conciliatory solutions, seen to be in line with traditional cultural preferences, because people, even after a court decision, often live in face-to-face proximity.

The cases show the aggressive role the media plays in bringing cases of cadre abuse to light. In some cases, villagers wrote letters to newspapers or magazines – other than *MZYFZ* – seeking help; the media then investigated the story. Particularly if the case stalled – either because higher level officials were protecting their underlings or because officials passed the case back down for resolution to

Table 6.1 Content of 30 cases of protest activity, 1989–1997

(1) Nature of political action*		(2) No. of cases involving public media	(3) No. of cases with petitions to higher level officials	(4) No. of cases that went to court	(5) No. of cases involving lawyers	(6) No. of cases already resolved as of 1997	(7) No. of villagers favored in resolved cases	(8) No. of government cadres favored in resolved cases	(9) No. of cases unclear in resolved cases	(10) Actors favored by article*	
										Villagers	Government cadres
Collective	Individual										
22	7	14	23	13	8	20	14	4	2	19	8

*Source: Cases reported in *Minzhu yu Fazhi*, 1989–1997.

Note: When number of cases in columns 1, 5 and 6 does not total 30, the missing values are either not applicable or not clear.

the very lower level officials who had perpetrated the abuse in the first place – gaining the attention of national newspapers was critical to triggering a serious investigation by higher level officials. Newspapers, as well as *MZYFZ* itself, apparently follow up on old stories to see if problems reported previously remained solved or emerged anew.[16] The media appeared to be an effective weapon of protest because middle level officials fear adverse publicity. Nevertheless, some journalists put their lives at risk, as abusive cadres and public security officials were not averse to using physical threats to warn the journalists off.[17] The large amounts of money involved in some of these cases give cadres strong incentives to resort to violence if it becomes necessary to protect their interests.

A reading of these cases and additional scholarly literature suggest that villagers are developing a strong 'rights consciousness' and using the law to their own advantage. Admittedly, this journal is likely to promote the use of the courts as a mode of conflict resolution. Nevertheless, of the total cases reported, thirteen of thirty (43 percent) made it to court and in eight of those cases (61 percent) villagers hired either a lawyer or some kind of legal worker. In several cases villagers studied national laws before presenting their case. In one case, a villager testified that according to the province's regulation he should have only paid 12 *RMB* in local taxes, but the township demanded over 75 *RMB*. These findings, therefore, support Li and O'Brien's contention that many villagers now carry out 'policy based resistance'.[18] Also, in two of the cases newly emerging democratic institutions play important roles in resolving these problems. In one case, overtaxed villagers protested to the city people's congress, which voted to dismiss the party secretary from his position as a people's representative.[19] In another case, villagers took their concerns to the branch of the Democratic Progressive Association, which intervened on their behalf. Villagers also turn to the media, asking them to help bring these court cases to light.[20] By reporting such successful cases, *MZYFZ* is encouraging villagers to turn to such organizations.

The state did not, of course, always take the villagers' side. While the state favored the villagers in nineteen cases, they supported government cadres in another eight cases. Interestingly, when one looks at the cases that were resolved, fourteen of the twenty occurred in cases where the article clearly favored the villagers, while only four of the cases were resolved in favor of government cadres. One dilemma with a 'rights conscious' peasantry is that many of them may not really understand or even support the rule of law because they are uncomfortable with its impartiality. In some of the business cases, villagers were unfamiliar with and often disregarded contracts and the role of contract law, even though other villagers successfully used law to protect their interests. Also, cadres' reputations may easily be destroyed by peasants who bring wrongful cases against them.

Urbanization, land markets and the politics of protest

One component of China's modernization – urbanization and the attendant marketization or commercialization of suburban land – has generated enormous

levels of conflict over the past few years. As cities modernize, they eat up
suburban land; since the mid-1980s, cities have expanded at a furious pace.
Moreover, following Deng's southern trip in 1992, the 'zone fever' that swept
China accelerated the pace with which cities have swallowed up their suburban
rural land.[21] Also, city mayors who in the 1990s are trying to improve the lives of
urban residents need to turn suburban land, formerly owned by rural collectives
and managed by individual households, into bedroom communities. However,
commercialization of the rural land needed to facilitate urban growth is one of the
most incendiary issues in Chinese society today. Among 236 cases filed under
the Administrative Litigation Law collected by Pei, fifty (or 21 percent) were
over land use, urban zoning, and real estate.[22] Why?

First, the process of urbanization mirrors the reforms in general, where economic changes, commercialization, new opportunities, and the generation of
wealth occurs before the establishment of new economic and legal institutions
which would regularize the creation and distribution of these new market opportunities. Thus the formal legal framework needed to manage the emergence of a
land and suburban housing market, as well as the informal norms that could
moderate political and economic confrontations, are only beginning to develop.
Land laws are easily ignored and much of the confiscated land is simply used as
collateral for getting loans from the bank; after that, the land is left to lie fallow.[23]
But because the market has outpaced the growth of legal institutions – land laws,
real estate laws – enormous political problems have emerged that themselves are
difficult to manage because the mobilization of interests generated by new
markets and economic opportunities far outweigh the political institutions that
would otherwise handle political demand. Huntington's conundrum, where
demands for participation are greater than political institutionalization, is clearly
at work.

Second, the financial stakes are enormous as the real property value of land at
the time it is taken over by the local government is unknown: its value material-
izes only after it is zoned for suburban housing, or as the surrounding infrastructure, such as new roads and housing units, is developed. Yesterday's patch
of tomato fields is tomorrow's three-story townhouse or modern sixty-story high
rise tower. According to the 1986 Land Management Law, the price to be paid
for land could not exceed twenty times the average annual output value of the
land.[24] According to *MZYFZ*, this growth in the value of suburban land attracts
much corrupt activity.[25] In one case reported in *Ming bao* (Hong Kong), cadres
earned 2.8 million *RMB* by renting out 240 *mu* of land of which only 350,000
RMB (12.5 percent) was distributed to the villagers.[26] Rapaciousness mounts as
city officials see land sales as the last source of capital to shore up their shrinking
tax bases,[27] while managers of development companies (and their supporters in
the city or district governments) make millions selling housing units that had cost
them perhaps 5–7 percent of the land's ultimate market value. Thus, powerful
urban interests in China's opaque political system are scurrying to extract their
share of wealth before a more stable, transparent system emerges.

Unlike other aspects of development, however, urbanization has both positive and negative impacts on society. For some rural residents, urbanization means the shift from rural to urban household registration; this rise in status has psychological, educational, social, political, and financial benefits.[28] Cadres, too, benefit as their locality's status rises within China's administrative hierarchy due to the shift from rural to urban space. For example, rural cadres can become state officials with retirement pensions and much higher salaries. Also, if cadres behave fairly, the entire village can benefit. For example, a village in Wuhan's suburbs has grown wealthy by developing its own land and distributing that wealth to all members of the collective.[29]

But for many other suburban villagers, the disappearance of their land causes their world to spin out of control. Nationwide reports tell of frequent confrontations between villagers and the police or the army. Major protests occurred in October 1998 in Guiyang, capital of Guizhou Province, as villagers from Tongzi County marched on the provincial capital to protest against the low level of compensation they received after being forced off their land to make room for new urban housing.[30] When a well-connected developer failed to pay villagers for land he had acquired, they blocked the construction site and put up huts to stop the work. After police arrested four villagers, 300 peasants marched into Changsha and surrounded the provincial government buildings.[31] Even Star TV, viewed in Wuhan on Saturday 5 December 1998, showed violent clashes between villagers and the army over land confiscation.

In the section that follows we will look at the political and legal externalities of urbanization that emerged in a suburban community in a city in central China.

The case study

Sitting in the home of a former brigade cadre, now an official in a newly established street committee (hereafter *jiedao*), the widespread impact of urbanization became clear. While he spoke of the court case he had just completed to win back land transferred by the city government to a neighbouring township, land whose value had increased fifteen times in 2 years, his best friend piped in with his story. He and fifty-two other families in August 1998 had battled the director of the district's urban planning and construction bureau (*chengjian ju*) who, after knocking down their homes, tried to resettle them in apartment units built in a renovated factory. But without sunlight and adequate facilities, he and his neighbors revolted. I then discovered that the former brigade official's 72-year-old father had been a leader of a group of 108 rural retirees who had fought to save their pensions and their health care benefits which were cut off because of the simultaneous occurrence of land transfers and the redistricting of the suburban boundaries. Their strategies involved both formal, legal activity and various degrees of civil disobedience.

In the following section, I will tell the story of two separate but related cases of villager resistance over land, while in an analytical section I will relate these events to the patterns discovered in *MZYFZ*.

The facts of the case

The case began in 1992, when Nanjing's government having decided to widen the streets within the city core, needed to build new housing for urban residents. With the approval of the province, the city took over some rural land. At the same time, the city formally terminated two administrative villages, Village A and Village B (both former production brigades), and incorporated them into District No. 1 under the city government. In June 1993, both brigades' long lives as rural units became history.

With the district becoming a bedroom community and the two brigades' administrative status in limbo, their farm land was transferred to the city Land Bureau, which paid the two brigades' superior administrative unit, the Township, 33 million *RMB* for the land. Also, nine *mu* of land belonging to Brigade A was transferred to the Township. Several brigade factories built since the mid–1970s were knocked down, but one clothing factory and a department store, formerly the property of Brigade A, were given to the Township, while District Government No. 2, above the Township, kept a restaurant. The Township, however, was expected to use part of that 33 million *RMB* to care for the residents of Village A because, unlike all but a small number of very prosperous rural communities, Village A had given all its retired commune members retirement and health care benefits. Thereafter, with the brigades' territory now incorporated into the city, the Land Bureau sold the land to several development companies under District No. 1's urban construction bureau. Finally, to make room for the new apartments and town houses that would line the streets of this new urban district, villagers' homes were to be leveled and the villagers relocated into new apartments nearby.

Incorporation into the urban sector brought villagers some benefits. First, their rural residence permits (*hukou*) were turned into urban residence permits, a lifelong goal for many rural residents. Second, based on the square footage of their homes – including the area of the second and third stories – villagers received an equal amount of square footage in new apartments. Most villagers got three to four apartments, while some got as many as seven flats. Most villagers moved into one or two flats, sold a couple and rented the rest, allowing them a life of leisure as rentiers. Without land to tend, however, older villagers were expected to retire or find jobs in the private sector, while their children – teenagers and young adults – were all offered jobs in state-owned firms or a one-time pay out of 10,000 *RMB*.

Around 1994 or 1995, urban boundaries were redrawn. While Village A became an urban Street Committee (*jiedao*) under District No. 1, the Township remained in the countryside under District No. 2. Suddenly the Township announced that it no longer had the obligation to pay the retirement benefits of the 108 villagers of Village A, although it had received 33 million *RMB* for the land formerly held by Villages A and B, as well as some of Village A's property. The old villagers of Village A then sued the Township and took their case to the civil court (*minjian ting*) in the city's Middle Court. Although eventually they lost the case, the city government pressured the Township to turn over 300,000 *RMB* to help cover their retirement costs.

Several years later, after Village A became part of a larger Street Committee, it, with the support of District No. 1, sued the Township in the city's Administrative Court (*xingfa ting*). The court, however, while publicly recognizing that 'the living standards of the villagers in Village A had gone down since they had lost their land,'[32] refused formally to accept the case and passed it back down to the three districts, with a copy to the city government, insisting that they settle out of court. The terms of the final mediated settlement (*minshi tiaojie shu*) were as follows:

- The Township, in two installments over three months, had to pay the Street Office 300,000 *RMB*, with 200,000 going to Village A and another 100,000 *RMB* going to Village B.
- The Township had to return the factory and the department store to the Street Office (Village A).
- Of the 36,760 *RMB* in legal fees accrued by the Street Office, the Township had to pay 30,000 *RMB*. Village A had to pay 3,380 *RMB*.
- The Street Office received the nine *mu* of land that had been taken from Village A.
- Village A had to persuade villagers to give up their remaining claims to small plots of land and let the developer knock down the final set of homes in Village A, facilitating the area's continued development.

Though some people in Village A were dissatisfied, the Middle Level Court which had refused to hear the case told officials in the Street Office that if they did not sign the mediated settlement and end all claims once and for all, they would get nothing.

Listening to the participants

While the articles in *MZYFZ* help us understand the broader macro-issues involved in these cases, we need to hear the stories of the participants themselves to see how urbanization affected their lives and how they viewed the process of resistance in which they engaged. As we will see, the views of the actors in this drama differ dramatically, based upon their own interests. What may be one person's calamity is another's opportunity. For officials, development, modernization and urbanization are buzz words connoting new sources of revenue and capital, new opportunities, and new forms of prestige. For villagers, whose homes are taken away and who find the state's compensation insufficient and its behaviour exploitative, urbanization is an unwelcome intrusion that forces them onto the road of passive resistance to get fair compensation for their homes.

The 108 retirees[33]

At risk was their long-term security, particularly their retirement and health care benefits. Since 1958 these commune residents had contributed their labour, energy, and intelligence to turning Village A into a wealthy suburban brigade. Their reward? In the 1980s, due to its industrialization, Village A had been one of a handful of rural collectives in China that awarded its members with retirement certificates (*tuixiu zheng*), promising them retirement payments (*yang lao jin*) until death did them part. For some, these payments were high: while former employees of the brigade administration received 150 *RMB*/month, retirement benefits for simple field hands were 30–40 *RMB*/month. More important, argued one retiree, with most of them close to 70, their great fear was that the high cost of long-term medical care brought on by disease or infirmity would bankrupt their families. While the collective's health program had not covered all costs, villagers had felt protected by the collective: 'we were reimbursed for the majority of costs, and if you had a really big illness, most of it would be paid.' Now, by a sleight of administrative hand, the collective wealth that should have sustained those benefits was transferred to the Township, only to be whisked away entirely when Village A joined urban District No. 1, leaving the Township in the countryside. In the words of one informant, 'when they redrew the boundaries, we lost our benefits.'

But these older villagers, who had fought the party's 'class enemies' in the 1950s and 1960s, were ready to defend their own interests in the face of injustice. They built a war chest, with each retiree contributing 30–40 *RMB*. They elected ten representatives, composed of 'older people who could talk well.' While each representative had the right to speak, the group had an informal leader who, through personal ties, found a lawyer who sued the Township in the city's Middle Court.

In retrospect, the group's lawyer erred in filing the case with the civil tribunal (*minjian ting*), rather than the administrative court (*xingfa ting*), since they were suing a government office, not other citizens. But in China it remains extremely difficult for civilians to win cases against officials, what many call '*min gao gong.*' According to Pei, the government wins twice as often as civilians, and the citizen's likelihood of success decreases if the case is brought against a local government.[34] Also, while the resources they lost were collective property, they were demanding individual compensation. In the eyes of local residents and officials, their strategy from the start was doomed to fail. Nevertheless, although it refused to hear the case, the court's '*opinion*' (*sifa jianyi shu*) was that the income of the rural residents bringing the suit 'had really dropped.' It referred the report to the three suburban district governments and the city government to be resolved out of court.[35]

Buoyed by a somewhat favorable decision – 'we felt good because the opinion showed the government's concern' – the representatives set off on a deeply frustrating effort to find some government bureau or official who would respond to the court's 'opinion' and solve the case. Everywhere they confronted 'buck passing' (*ti pi qiu*), not solutions. The city government's General Office would not solve the problem, but stamped a letter approving their visit to the city's Land Bureau, which after hearing their plight 'put off our case again and again'. Several weeks later, in the winter, the representatives went and, in classically traditional form, bowed outside the door of the Administrative Litigation Bureau of the city government, pleading for assistance. Members of both the city's and Village A's police force brought the aged supplicants home. Frustrated by continued government inaction, the 108 retirees fanned out all over the city, visiting various district governments; but since the Township had been allocated the property, the land, and the money by a government decision, other levels of government refused to intervene.

Civil disobedience became their only option. Organizing a month long sit-in at a restaurant that had been taken from Village A, they dug in for a long struggle. Were they afraid? 'No! Old people are not afraid to resist. You want to arrest us, well it's not easy; you want to control us, well that's not easy either' (*zhua, ye zhua bu zhu; guan, ye guan bu zhu*). Emboldened by the original court opinion which showed the city's moral support for their cause, they carefully avoided giving the Public Security Bureau any pretext for arresting them. 'We behaved well when we went to the city government. We knew that we were making a fair (*heli*) request, so we told everyone not to curse in public.' But as each government office sent them off with no resolution, their anger grew. 'Eventually we made trouble (*nao shi*). Without making a little trouble, we would have had no results. We had no choice.'

As the strike dragged on some retirees slept in the restaurant all night, making it impossible to open for business – the city government was forced to respond, instructing the Township to make a one-time payment of 300,000 *RMB* to the villagers. And in an effort to put the case behind them, and without mentioning the 108 veteran commune members, the city government, echoing the court's finding, announced that 'the remaining problem of a shortfall in people's livelihood' (*shenghuo bu zu de yiliu wenti*) was now solved. The 108 veterans accepted the decision and quickly abandoned their collective action, even though they did not get their long-term health benefits. Why? 'We got the money, so there was no need to continue to make trouble'. The funds were then transferred to the government of District No. 1 to be managed by the Street Office.

In some ways it was surprising to see how quickly the 108 retirees gave up the struggle, as the 300,000 *RMB* would not go far. By late 1998 almost half had been used up, although ninety-five veterans remained alive and in need of some financial support. Perhaps they felt that this already was a large sum of money; or they knew that since they had lost the legal case, this was the best deal they could get. As a result, several years later the Street Office decided to resurrect the legal challenge and go after the nine *mu* of land, another financial payment, and some of the enterprises awarded to the Township.

The 53 homeowners

It began spontaneously. To turn the lake beside their homes into an amusement park for urban residents moving out to the suburbs, the homes of fifty-three rural families which sat below the city's Western gate were demolished on 1 January 1997. The residents were expected to find temporary housing for 2 years while the development company, under District No. 1's urban planning and construction bureau (*cheng jian ju*), built them new homes. To cut costs, the urban planning bureau tried to push the homeowners into flats constructed in an old renovated factory, but when the homeowners saw this they immediately went en masse to the development company to protest.

> Under law, the company was supposed to sign a contract with us, but they refused. District No. 1's bureau of urban construction was responsible for this situation; they were supposed to set us up and guarantee us standard (*biaozhun*) homes. But this was a terrible place: no air, no sunlight. All fifty-three families refused to move in.

Each family contributed 150 *RMB* to a kitty, selected six representatives, and then drafted a document (*weituo shu*) entrusting the six to represent the group's interests in solving this problem. Every family signed.

> Without the *weituo shu*, it was not legal, and we wanted to do everything as legally as possible (*guo you xing wei*). This way we knew that we could step over the boundaries of what was acceptable behaviour a little bit. . . . We called this group our 'representative small group' (*daibiao xiaozu*), and it was a short-term organization just for this purpose.

The man selected to lead the group was a middle level administrative cadre, a party member who managed an office of six to seven people, 'so he knew how to organize things.'[36] He and his family lived in this village and were directly affected by these events. According to one observer, during confrontations with the party secretary of the bureau of urban construction he demonstrated a strong spirit, standing head to head with him. 'When Party Secretary XXX banged the table and warned us that our behaviour was illegal, this man banged the table back and accused him of not caring about the people'.

The six representatives first petitioned the Administrative Litigation Bureau of the city government, which told them that their complaint was fair (*heli*). The bureau then called District No. 1's Administrative Litigation Office and told them to give the delegation a fair hearing, which they did. In fact, the district's Administrative Law Office sent a car to bring the complainants to their offices. But the villagers had few illusions about receiving any swift response.

> We knew that petitioning was of no use, but we also knew that we had to go through that process or else we could not justify using other tactics. So we

went to the Administrative Litigation Office of the city government. But we knew that we needed to 'grab on and not let go' (*zhua bu fang*) or else they would not give in to us.

Events would prove their that their cynicism was well founded as both the development company and the party secretary of the urban construction bureau refused to meet with them. So they decided that civil disobedience was necessary. Sixty residents, led by their representatives, then descended on the bureau of urban construction and occupied its offices for three days. They had dug in for the long haul, bringing their own food which they prepared in the office's small kitchen, and despite the oppressive summer heat, many passed the night in the offices. In their own words, they 'suffered greatly' (*hen xinku*). But after the bureau's employees went home that first night, leaving only the protesters, they realised that they needed to escalate the confrontation. The next morning, after the office workers returned, the villagers barricaded the door, locking themselves and the office workers inside. They then demanded that the deputy director of the bureau call in the party secretary of the urban planning bureau to negotiate with them. But when he appeared the next morning, he brought along fifteen police officers in a failed attempt to intimidate the protestors. Were they afraid, I asked?

> Not at all! This was a fair request of the masses (*qunzhong de heli yaoqiu*). We told our people – don't swear, don't break public property, and when the police came and told us not to make trouble, we didn't let them take us away. . . . We wouldn't leave because we knew that the party secretary wouldn't come again. We told the police that we had been trying to find the party secretary for days, but he had been ignoring our complaints.

The homeowners, however, carried out a multi-pronged attack. While some occupied the government offices, others went to the provincial television station and persuaded it to send a camera crew to film the sit-in. The province's television station filmed the protest, the renovated factory, and interviewed specialists on these problems. It also filmed the villagers' protest banner whose slogan – 'We trust that the government will return our homes to us' (*xiangxin zhengfu huan wo zhufang*) – was calculated to shame the authorities by showing that the homeowners had faith that the government would do the right thing. And despite efforts by the district government's propaganda department, which is part of the media-related 'system' or *xitong*, to persuade the TV station not to air the report, journalists understood the leverage they brought to the villagers' case. So they insisted that they would air the report, but agreed to give the government time to solve the problem first. In fact, the title of the show – 'After a knot is tied, you still need someone to undo it' – was selected to pressure the city government to solve the case, which it did, allowing the news story to end with a shot of the Party Secretary shaking hands with the homeowners' representatives.

But the struggle was not an easy one. After the party secretary failed to have them arrested, the protestors forced him to telephone the district government which sent a representative who asked for 15 days to study the problem. And to the delight of the homeowners, 15 days later the district government agreed to build them new housing. However, the government asked for a year to prepare that housing, which meant that the villagers would ultimately have waited 2 ½ years for their new homes. Still, all these problems had not harmed the legitimacy of the government in the eyes of this rapporteur.

> Overall I still trust the government. It has been making many new laws and I trust these laws. What I do not trust are many people in the government; in fact, I hate them. . . . People with power don't do things according to law; this is quite prevalent. The law is good, but people don't follow it, and this is particularly a problem in smaller government bureaus where there is no one to check (*jiandu*) on how the laws are being implemented.

The role of local leaders

A key force supporting the 108 Retirees' efforts to regain their economic security was the former deputy party secretary of Village A who became party secretary when the old brigade secretary retired in 1992. As a native son, with relatives dotted all over the village – his father was one of the 108 retirees and his best friend lived in one of the fifty-three homes that were knocked down – he defended the villagers' interests. He also understood the need for a double-barreled attack that combined legal process and civil disobedience.

From his perspective, sit-ins and protests were necessary because the main bottleneck to resolving the case was the fact that the city's Middle Court would never make a legal judgement that challenged, let alone overturned, a formal decision taken by the city government. While some court researchers who investigated the 108 retirees' complaint had apparently believed the village would win its case,

> I doubted it. The original decision to take the land was made by the city government, which had received permission from the provincial govern-ment, so this was a government decision based on official government documents. . . . The courts cannot overturn such government decisions. So the court promulgated a statement that 'the land and property could be used only for development, and no unit or individual could expropriate it' (*bu keyi zhanyong*), but this was really the same as not giving us any result.

But because of the sit-ins and constant harassment by the 108 retirees, the township could not run the factory nor could the district run the restaurant. So 'returning the factory was an easy decision for the township because, although it had sent people to manage the factory, no one listened to them'; in fact the old people had gone and surrounded the officials and screamed at them, asking 'why have you taken over our land?'

Discussing the cases

What do these cases tell us about the nature of rural collective action and even the possibility of the emergence of a mass movement? First, there are clearly two sampling biases here. The cases in *MZYFZ* probably reflect a more civil process of resistance and protest than may exist in some parts of the country. After all, their purpose is to promote a more legalistic conflict-resolution culture. Bernstein's study reports numerous cases of violent protest where villagers burned government and constabulary offices and beat their employees. Reports by human rights groups in Hong Kong tell of two cases of tax resistance and anti-corruption protests that ended in police beating villagers to death.[37]

Second, there are significant differences between the conditions faced by our suburban protagonists and villagers in more distant localities. The former had relatively easy access to higher level government officials, the mass media, and the courts. Nevertheless, in both situations, the externalities of development are creating major conflicts among villagers and the state, increasing the need for protests. Also, the strategies adopted by suburban villagers and their more distant cousins, especially their reliance on modern political and judicial institutions and a willingness to resort to civil disobedience when those institutions fail to deliver justice, seems to be a common pattern in the 1990s.

Both sets of cases support Li and O'Brien who assert that formal petitions to higher level officials have increased dramatically in the past 10 years.[38] In the city suburbs, as well as the journal articles, we see villagers using petitions aggressively to defend their individual and collective interests. In the case of the 108 retirees, they believed strongly that there were good officials in the system who would respond to their just petitions and in the end the courts and city government did respond to their complaints. In fact, the state seems to support petitioning not only because it invites villagers to seek redress within legal bounds, but also because it informs the state of grievances generated by cadres in the countryside, making it an important channel for the upward flow of information. On the other hand, one of the leaders of the fifty-three homeowners was quite cynical about petitioning, seeing it only as a necessary step to protect themselves from recriminations by the police. The only really effective strategy, he believed, was public protest. Clearly, political reforms and the creation of important new political and legal institutions have increased the channels for formally presenting grievances; however, the most effective strategy seems to combine petitions with protests, thereby attracting upper levels' attention while at the same time threatening them with civil disobedience unless they respond to the petition.

Villagers today are far more aware of their legal rights than they were 10 years ago and more willingly assert those rights, in large part because the state encourages them to do so. Increased communication, such as newspapers, word of mouth, and magazines, have informed villagers about official regulations, creating more 'policy-based resistance' whereby villagers use government laws to challenge cadres who misbehave.[39] Journals, such as *MZYFZ*, generally support villagers' claims (nineteen versus eight in the thirty cases), which may encourage them to petition and use the courts more frequently. No doubt, lawyers are beyond the financial means of most villagers, while in the case of the 108 Retirees, hiring a less expensive but less skilled lawyer may have hurt their case. Only the Street Office could afford the 30,000 *RMB* needed to take the case to court properly. Still, in the case study above, villagers cited laws and court decisions to justify continuing their case. For the 108 retirees, the courts' recognition that 'their income had really dropped' made them believe that the government, if pressed, would help. One of the fifty-three homeowners stressed the existence of laws that supported their claims; the trick was to force cadres who were subject to the laws to follow them rather than ignore them.

Interestingly, in neither of the two cases did the Administrative Litigation Bureau or the courts hand down a judgment favorable to the complainants. Initially the courts refused to overrule the city government which had made the original decision to expropriate the land and transfer the village's resources to the township. But that failure simply angered the villagers even as it encouraged them to move on to the next stage – civil disobedience. Changing the political or legal context and opening new channels for pursuing grievances encourages citizens to seek redress. Yet if local governments and cadres persist in the old authoritarian leadership styles, there is greater likelihood of conflict than if villagers' expectations had not been raised or if villagers saw no new opportunities for pursuing their interests.

The mix of strategies adopted by these villagers reflects an ability to integrate modern legalistic 'repertoires of contention' with a more traditional or extra-institutional strategy of protest and resistance.[40] Villagers understood the legal bounds that had to be maintained, knowing that violence would trigger a police response; but if they avoided damaging property or cursing government officials, it would be difficult for the state to use force against them. Therefore, they combined legal procedures with civil disobedience – in both cases sit-ins – or what they called 'making trouble' (*nao shi*).

The Chinese media has emerged as a critical resource in the villagers' struggle for social justice. This role is not completely new. In 1977–79, the reformers orchestrated a series of 'Letters to the Editor' in national and provincial newspapers which attacked 'leftist' cadres who held onto 'agrarian radicalism' and triggered investigations by correspondents or work teams who defrocked recalcitrant Maoists holding sway in the villages and townships.[41] In the 1990s, the media is a more independent collaborator in the struggle against cadre corruption and misdeeds, at times triggering angry responses from the bureaucrats they attack. For example, after it reported how an armed force of cadres and police, demanding funds for education, shot one villager who resisted their extortion, party officials in Luoding City accused the *Guangzhou Daily* of meddling in matters outside its jurisdiction.[42] Similarly, a journalist in Tongzhou County, northern Jiangsu Province, who helped a village party secretary draft a letter to the *People's Daily* protesting excessive tax burdens, was fired for his efforts due to pressure from local party authorities.[43] According to analysts of social movements, media support is critical if a social movement is to remain sustainable.[44]

With most households outside impoverished areas of rural China owning their own television sets, television is becoming an important ally of resistance as well. Suburban villagers understood the potential of this medium, though they were surprised at its real effectiveness. In the words of one activist, 'our general summary of these events was that the television station had a big impact. The government is very afraid of the publicity.' Thus the fifty-three homeowners sent delegates to the provincial TV station which filmed their protest and the poor housing they were being pushed into. And, despite efforts by the district government to stop them from broadcasting their story, outside observers from the TV station felt that once the story was taped, neither the district nor the city government could have killed it. In fact, he argued, 'If district officials had asked them not to run it, they would have been more likely to run it the next day'. The media helped settle the case by informing district officials that the TV station would hold off broadcasting the report until district officials resolved the case.

Local village elections, another institutional innovation that helps manage the externalities of development, did not play a very great role in resolving these cases. Almost half the cases in *MZYFZ* involved problematic activity by cadres at the township level or above, placing them beyond the electoral reach of the villagers.[45] Still, villagers do directly elect representatives to the township people's congresses which today may be playing an enlarged role in supervising township cadres' activities.[46] Second, village cadres who steal public funds or extort taxes from private villagers are clearly not averse to manipulating elections. Finally, if the misconduct was carried out by the branch party secretary, it again was not subject to electoral politics.[47] Nevertheless, protests by villagers following electoral fraud did prompt investigations by higher level officials, and have become one more arrow in the villagers' quiver of rural resistance.

A modern political institution not available to villagers, however, is the independent civic organization, which would probably help them deal with the externalities of development. Despite the image of a powerful party/state, the CCP feels deeply threatened by society and suppresses most forms of permanent independent organization. Some villagers are turning to traditional, not modern, organizational structures, such as lineage groups or religious organizations, as a means of dealing with an intrusive state. But the state's coercive institutions have little patience for such religious-based anti-state behaviour. Also, villagers in our cases recognized that while they could organize to press their petitions, long-term autonomous organizations were not allowed. Both groups dissolved their elected 'representative small group' once the issue was resolved. But if organizing to develop a petition is allowed, and if the petition fails – as they initially often do – villagers have already established an organizational structure, replete with leaders and funds with which they can pursue more anti-state activity.

A final resource available to the 108 retirees in their challenge to the Township was the support of the local urban government, which saw the nine *mu* of land as a critical opportunity for its economic development. Thus the successful case was litigated in the name of the Villagers' Residence Committee by a professional lawyer to whom the Street Office paid 30,000 *RMB*, a sum of money far beyond the capabilities of the villagers. Government to government cases go to a different tribunal in the city court, and resolving them in favor of a formally constituted citizens' organization – in this case the Residents' Committee – may be less threatening to the state than resolving a case in favor of a self-organized group of citizens against a formal level of the government.

Conclusion

As economic development proceeds in China, affecting wider and wider spheres of society, its externalities produce political consequences, or what we may even see as 'political externalities' of economic development. These spillovers of development – such as environmental degradation, breakneck urbanization, massive jumps in the value of suburban land, excessive local taxation, or the movement of capital into short-term rather than long-term projects – move the economy and the sociopolitical system into unchartered waters, where the economy and society meet in an often unregulated space. Within this sphere, and given the opaque nature of the administrative system, winners and losers are often determined by their relative personal and administrative power, not the rule of law, creating remarkable levels of social tension. But society, too, has power, especially if people act collectively. And as we have seen, the arbitrary acts of officialdom do fire up the ire of villagers, sometimes triggering a powerful social backlash.

Herein lies China's current political and social dilemma – the confrontation between an emerging 'rights conscious peasantry' and hungry or entrepreneurial bureaucrats. The state's role then is to respond to these externalities and manage that conflict. But to date, weak laws regulate those interstices between the economy and society, while the political culture conducive to the rule of law is only beginning to resolve conflicts emerging under China's partially reformed economy. If cadres think that they will be punished by the state or successfully challenged by society, these new norms should decrease cadre abuses, and by strengthening villagers' legal consciousness, press them to utilize formal legal means of conflict resolution. Interestingly, the central state has shifted its loyalties somewhat, away from cadres, particularly unethical ones, and to society and villagers, so long as they eschew violent protests. The cases in *MZYFZ* document this shift.

Nevertheless, villagers remain frustrated by the ability of the bureaucracy initially to deflect their claims. The rule of law is still weak; instead rule by law, while strengthening the villagers' resolve and ability to affect cadre misbehavior, remains prey to administrative power which can manipulate (or undermine) the level of justice distributed by a new legalistic system. And to the extent that what are perceived as just verdicts are not forthcoming, villagers will still adopt extra-legal forms of civil disobedience and collective protest, combining them with more modern, legalistic forms of resistance.

With so many villagers in more distant rural regions, as well as the suburbs, facing excessive taxes, land expropriations, environmental degradation, and cadre corruption and abuse of power, widespread but uncoordinated civil disobedience and protests will occur. But if the legal and political system proves too malleable to cadre influence to enforce its own laws and resolve these conflicts in non-violent ways, rural China will remain fertile soil for widespread social unrest that could threaten the stability of the communist regime only 50 years after its establishment.

Notes

1 Funding came from a Direct Allocation Grant, Research Grants Council of Hong Kong. Research assistance was provided by Yiu Keung, Ken and Dr. Mak Hung Fa.
2 Samuel Huntington, *Political Order in Changing Societies* (New Haven: Yale University Press, 1968).
3 Lianjiang J. Li and Kevin J. O'Brien, 'Villager and Popular Resistance in Contemporary China', *Modern China*, 1996, 22, no. 1, pp. 28–61.
4 David Zweig, Kathleen Hartford, James Feinerman, and J. X. Deng (1987) 'Law, Contracts and Economic Modernization: Lessons from the Recent Chinese Rural Reforms', *Stanford Journal of International Law*, vol. 23, pp. 319–64.
5 Minxin Pei (1997) 'Citizens vs. Mandarins: Administrative Litigation in China', *The China Quarterly*, no. 152, p. 840.
6 'Si qian jia nong hu zhuang gao "bai tiao"' (4,000 rural households sue over IOUs*)*, *Zhongguo nongmin* (*China's peasants*), 1995, no. 3, pp. 45–7.
7 Before 1993–4, the journal's articles were more philosophical than concrete; afterwards, the content seems to have changed. Hence the larger number of articles since 1993.
8 *MZYFZ*, 1993, no. 9, pp. 2–6.
9 Thomas Bernstein, 'Instability in Rural China?', in David Shambaugh (ed.*)* *Is China Unstable? Assessing the Factors* (Washington, DC: The Sigur Center for Asian Studies, July 1998), pp. 93–110.
10 *MZYFZ*,1996, no. 11, pp. 18–20.
11 *MZYFZ*, 1991, no. 6, pp. 4–8.
12 *MZYFZ*, 1996, no. 11, pp. 18–20.
13 *MZYFZ*, 1996, no. 14, pp. 10–11.
14 Robert H. Bates, 'Macropolitical Economy in the Field of Development', in John E. Alt and Kenneth A. Shepsle (eds) *Perspectives on Positive Political Economy* (Cambridge: Cambridge University Press, 1990), pp. 31–56.
15 Pei cites one article which quoted a Chinese citizen who said that one could 'win once but lose the rest of his life'. See Pei, 'Citizens vs. Mandarins', p. 841.
16 *MZYFZ*, 1997, no. 1, pp. 22–3.
17 *MZYFZ*, 1993, no. 9, pp. 2–6.
18 Li and O'Brien, 'Villager and Popular Resistance'.
19 *MZYFZ*, 1996, no. 7, p. 13.
20 *MZYFZ*, 1997, no. 1, pp. 22–3.
21 David Zweig, 'Distortions in the Opening: "Segmented Deregulation" and Weak Property as Explanations for China's "Zone Fever" of 1992–93,' *University Services Centre Occasional Papers* (The Chinese University of Hong Kong, 1999).
22 Pei, 'Citizens vs. Mandarins', p. 849.
23 Zweig, 'Distortions in the Opening'.
24 Mark Selden, *The Political Economy of Development* (M. E. Sharpe, Armonk, NY, 1993), p. 198.
25 *MZYFZ*, no. 23, 1996, p. 40.
26 *Ming bao*, 17 May 1998.

27 Interview in Nanjing, October 1998.
28 See Hein Mallee, 'Migration, Hukou, and Resistance in Reform China', in this volume.
29 Ning Lingling's MA thesis at Huazhong Normal University focuses on this village.
30 Kai Peter Yu, '"Cheated" Villagers Take Dispute into Streets', *South China Morning Post*, November 8, 1998, p. 5.
31 'Farmers Abandon Protest over Land after Threats', *South China Morning Post*, 2 October 1998, p. 6.
32 It put out what my informants called a '*sifa jianyi yishu*' or legal opinion.
33 According to Elizabeth Perry, the number 108 may be apocryphal, as this was the number of good bandits/rebels in the classic Chinese novel *Water Margin*. In my conversations with people in Nanjing, however, there was no reference to this novel or traditional protests.
34 Pei, p. 845.
35 Chinese courts commonly dismiss cases without rendering a verdict or pass cases to lower level officials for mediation, resolution through informal means, or other forms of out-of-court settlement. See Pei, pp. 842–3.
36 Some rural protest leaders are cadres who take the interests of the villagers to heart. See Bernstein, 'Instability in Rural China', p. 99.
37 'Chongqing zhenzhang ji gongan da si liang nongmin. Nongmin caigü shewei kangyi' (A town leader and public security forces in Chongqing beat two peasants to death; peasants march in protest), Information Centre of Human Rights and Democratic Movement in China, 17 December 1998 and John Pomfret, 'Beijing's Law and Order Problem', *International Herald Tribune,* 19 January 1999, p. 1.
38 Li and O'Brien, 'Villager and Popular Resistance'.
39 Kevin J. O'Brien and Lianjiang J. Li, 'The Politics of Lodging Complaints in Rural China', *The China Quarterly*, September 1995, no. 143, pp. 756–83.
40 Tilly defines 'repertoires of contention' as 'learned cultural creations that emerge in political struggle'. See C. Tilly, *The Contentious French* (Cambridge, MA: Harvard University Press, 1986), pp. 390–91.
41 David Zweig, *Agrarian Radicalism in China, 1968–1981* (Cambridge, MA: Harvard University Press, 1989).
42 'Chinese Peasants Have a Tough Row to Hoe', *Asia Times*, 16 August 1997.
43 *China Focus*, October 1998, p. 3.
44 Doug McAdam, John D. McCarthy, and Mayer N. Zald, 'Introduction: Opportunities, Mobilizing Structures, and Framing Processes – Towards a Synthetic, Comparative Perspective on Social Movements', in D. McAdam, J. D. McCarthy, and M. N. Zald (eds) *Comparative Perspectives on Social Movements* (Cambridge: Cambridge University Press, 1996), pp. 1–20.
45 Bernstein stressed this factor as a reason why elections could not solve the problem of 'random fees' (*luan shou fei*). See Bernstein, 'Instability in Rural China?'.
46 Personal communication with Elizabeth Perry, January 1999, following her visit to observe township elections in China.
47 This may not hold true in future as experimental elections for party secretary are being carried out in parts of rural China. See Lianjiang Li, 'The Two-ballot System in Shanxi Province: Subjecting Village Party Secretaries to Popular Vote,' unpublished paper.

7 Environmental protests in rural China

Jun Jing

China's environmental artery is bleeding. The problems of air pollution, soil erosion, and fouled water have become so grave that they are reported in the Chinese press practically every day, often accompanied by announcements of government plans to combat one ecological problem after another. What the Chinese news media rarely mention is the question of how ordinary people are reacting to the country's deepening environmental crisis. This question is addressed by looking at environmental protests in rural China, focusing on two specific cases. Environmental protests in the People's Republic are a relatively recent phenomenon. The promulgation of China's first environmental law, in 1979, has not only provided a legal basis for environmental protection but also enhanced the public's sense of basic rights in favor of justifying forceful, sometimes even violent, environmental protests. Such protests also embody a rich, culturally informed repertoire of social movements in Chinese history. Specifically, kinship, popular religion, moral concerns, and ancient tales of justice serve as crucial institutional and symbolic resources in the mobilization of protesters at the grassroots level. The interplay of these issues informs the social and cultural context in which rural environmental protests take place and are organized, usually with emphasis on ecological improvements essential for people's well-being rather than on trying to save the natural environment for its own sake.

Over the last two decades, an upsurge of environmentally related social protests has enabled many Chinese, both urban and rural, to air their grievances over the abuses of air, water, and land by industrial enterprises or development projects. These protests reflect the growing public awareness of a deepening environmental crisis, which is in effect the other side of the coin of China's vaunted rapid development in the post-Mao era. They also reveal the rising consciousness of legal rights in rural communities, partly as a result of China's promulgation of environmental laws since the late 1970s. Of special note is the emphasis in rural environmental protests on protecting people's welfare, not on preserving nature for its own sake. Informed by a historically sanctioned repertoire of popular protest, this people-centered orientation is derived from social concerns over an increasingly endangered ecological environment.

A brief explication: why rural China?

More than 70 percent of China's people live in rural areas, mostly on land that has been intensively farmed for centuries. Over the past 50 years, the precarious ecology of soil and water, already pushed to their limits to sustain a large population, has come under even greater strain with the drive toward industrialization and rapid economic development. Ambitious development projects of the Maoist era and the post-Mao economic reforms have in many ways improved general living standards. But they have also inflicted immense environmental damage in a countryside that could ill afford it. One result has been mounting protests against industrial polluters and ill-conceived projects that jeopardize the livelihood of rural residents. I have chosen to focus on rural-based environmental protests because these have been a rarely studied aspect of rural life in China and also because so much of the environmental movement literature elsewhere has focused urban activists.

In preparation for this chapter, I reviewed official records of 278 environmental disputes dating from the mid-1970s to the early 1990s.[2] Of these, forty-seven involved forceful popular protests in rural China, which ranged from collective lawsuits and petition movements to sabotage and even riots. These official records reveal how a severe conflict between unbridled development and ecological balance has placed many villagers on the front-lines of environmentally related political action in China, both in identifying problems and in seeking to solve them, by influencing government policies, the behavior of enterprises, and even court decisions. To make better sense of the rise of environmental protests in the Chinese countryside, I focus my discussion on two specific cases. Both were encountered in the course of my field research, enabling me to interview the protest organizers. Central to this discussion is an analysis of what can be characterized as a 'cultural and symbolic life-world.' I use this phrase to call attention to the ways by which environmental protests are influenced by and connected to kinship ideology, popular religion, and customary practices within the settings of everyday life in village China.

Background information

After the most devastating floods in more than forty years hit the Yangzi River valley in the summer of 1998, Chinese officials acknowledged the contribution of human activity, even public policy, to the devastation. The settlements in flood plains had eliminated areas of water absorption for the expanding river, while excessive logging had removed forests that once helped check the rain's flow into the Yangzi. In 1950, about 25 percent of the river's middle section was forested. Since then, more than half of the forests have disappeared.

Deforestation, in fact a nationwide problem, leads to soil erosion and the consequent loss of arable land. But other forces are at play as well. From 1979 to 1986, about 19 million acres of arable land were lost under the combined assault of soil erosion, urbanization, and industrialization. Since then, another four million acres have been lost each year. Industrial projects alone claimed 1.5 million acres a year. The degradation of water and air quality is even more disturbing. A 1988 survey of 532 rivers found 436 badly polluted; 80 percent of the waste water discharged into these rivers was untreated. In 1993, roughly 8 percent of farm-lands received river water so polluted that it was unfit for use, leading to an estimated loss in grain production of one million tons. In major cities today, levels of total suspended particulates and sulfur dioxide are two to five times the World Health Organization's guidelines. Fouled air is responsible for 178,000 deaths a year, mostly in cities. Rural residents are also affected by air pollution, particularly since sulfur dioxide and nitrous oxide emissions react with atmospheric water and oxygen to form acid rain, damaging forests, crops, and human health.[3]

China's central leadership was first awakened to the hazards of environmental degradation in 1972, when Dalian Bay in the far northeast turned black with untreated industrial waste. In the same year, state authorities read the startling report that fish in a Beijing reservoir had been poisoned by heavy metal discharged from neighboring factories. But it was not until 1979 that China's first Environmental Protection Law was promulgated, on a trial basis. By 1989, it was revised for full implementation. During the intervening decade, the central government put unprecedented effort into environmental protection, adopting more laws, imposing heavier penalties for violations, and applying advanced technology to control pollution. One result of this effort was the creation of the National Environmental Protection Agency, established in 1979; its network of 70,000 employees has been extended to every county. More recently, a few non-governmental organizations have emerged in the larger Chinese cities. Of these, the best known are 'Friends of Nature' and 'Global Village of Beijing,' founded in 1994 and 1995, respectively. The priority of these citizens' organizations, usually led by intellectuals, is to raise public awareness of environmental issues through exhibitions, organized tree-planting trips, and tours of wildlife areas.

It was precisely during the experimental phase of China's Environmental Protection Law that environmental protests swept both urban and rural areas. Before this period, environmental protests were relatively rare, and they were often quickly suppressed by the government. Leaders of the few documented environmental protests prior to 1979 were treated harshly by local officials, and some of them were even thrown in jail and charged with a so-called 'counter-revolutionary crime.' Although subsequently removed from Chinese law, this charge was once used with devastating effect against organizers of different kinds of social protests. With the passage of the 1979 Environmental Protection Law, the government has become more tolerant of environmental protests, so long as they are not too disruptive. Most have been small-scale actions by people immediately affected by a local polluter or engineering project. These victim interest groups have almost always engaged in direct protests in the form of petitions, lawsuits, and even sabotage. Typical goals are compensation for damages, the installation of pollution-control technologies, and occasionally the relocation of serious offenders. The victim interest groups are the focal point in my discussion of the two rural cases of environmental protest examined here.

A village's struggle for clean water

The first case involves Dachuan, a village in Gansu province, northwest China, in a decades-long protest movement against a fertilizer factory. The village and the factory are separated by only a paved road and a railroad. Most of Dachuan's 3,600 residents earn their living from agriculture. The factory is run by the provincial government and produces urea. None of its 3,000 salaried employees is from Dachuan. Since it began operations in 1971, the factory has been discharging its waste water into a stream that runs through Dachuan's fields before entering the Yellow River. This section of the river, until 1981 the village's only source of drinking water, became severely contaminated.

Through repeated protests, the village made the factory build a pipeline to deliver clean water to six of the village's eight production teams in 1981 and another team in 1992. One team was left without clean water as late as 1998. By then, the factory claimed to have invested 16 million yuan in pollution control. That the river remained contaminated, the factory said, was caused by technical problems that it was doing its best to fix. No legal action was taken by the local county government's environmental protection agency, partly because the factory is a provincial-level enterprise whose jurisdiction extends beyond that of the local county government. County and township officials also discouraged Dachuan from filing a civil lawsuit, fearing that it would cost too much money and that Dachuan still might not win against a big business whose powerful connections extended from the provincial government to the court system. Dachuan's only choice was to engage in self-organized protests.

With legal avenues barred, villagers turned to social protest. I witnessed one protest action taken by Dachuan villagers against the fertilizer factory in 1996. A flash flood had swept down the 2-kilometer-long stream that runs from the factory to the Yellow River, destroying a bridge linking Dachuan with the local township seat. Dachuan's village head and a fish merchant led 200 local residents to the factory, blocked its entrance and demanded that the factory rebuild the bridge. The factory was held accountable for repairing the collapsed bridge because the stream had once been only 20 meters wide, but the factory's daily discharge of 360 cubic meters of waste water had widened it to 60 meters. This required Dachuan to build a longer bridge for the local people to go to the township seat. The village cadres of Dachuan held the factory responsible for rebuilding the bridge over the much widened and heavily contaminated stream.

As in previous protests, the villagers cited the factory's contamination of the water and its unfulfilled obligations to Dachuan. The protesters asked the factory's security guards to tell factory officials to come out with their wives and children to drink up ten plastic bottles of water the villagers had brought from the contaminated stream. They promised never to come back to demonstrate again if the factory's Party secretary, general manager, and their families came out and drank the foul water in front of the crowd. Similar demands had been made during previous protests, usually accompanied by accusing questions: If factory employees and their families dare not drink from the stream, how can management expect local villagers not to demand safe drinking water? Aren't the rural people as human as the factory workers? Are the lives of the village's children worth less than those of factory children? On this occasion in 1996, the factory's Party secretary and general manager, following what they had done in the past, refused to come out to talk with the agitated villagers. So a group of young people from Dachuan drove ten tractors up to the factory, each carrying a full load of contaminated water from the stream. Using rubber pipes, they shot the water over the factory wall. After 10 days of bombardment by demonstrators, the factory agreed to provide Dachuan with 150,000 yuan to build a new bridge and repair a pump to provide tap water to more than 600 people in the village's seventh production team who were still drinking from the polluted river.

The village's initial appeals to the factory had not been antagonistic. They evolved into fierce protests when the local people gradually came fully to appreciate the threat that the polluted water posed to human health and agricultural production, while the factory's corrective measures always fell short of the village's expectations. In retrospect, Dachuan's protests went through four stages. At first, the villagers were not acutely aware of how harmful the contamination was, although the factory's discharge of incompletely burned fuel already left on the water surface many patches of carbon black. They would wait for the carbon black to float downstream before drawing water for drinking and cooking. It was not until the mid-1970s, when a horse and thirty sheep went blind that the villagers began to realize that drinking from the river could be utterly harmful to human health too. Dachuan's village cadres went to the factory to voice their complaint. As a gesture of redress, one that left the problem of water pollution unresolved, the factory agreed to take a limited step of compensation by hiring temporary workers from the village and by providing the village with fertilizers at a below-market price.

The second phase of Dachuan's protest movement coincided with the breakup of agricultural communes in 1980–81, when farmland was distributed to individual households to manage. A stretch of cultivated fields along the polluted stream was turned over to households whose members numbered more than 100 people. But the stream was so contaminated that the crops along the banks were damaged from excess ammonia. When villagers working these fields demanded action to solve the problem, Dachuan's cadres led the villagers in a blockade of the factory gate, preventing the factory's trucks from making deliveries. This initial blockade lasted only one day, but then other villagers joined to demand the factory solve the drinking water problem. After three more days of demonstrations, the factory agreed to supply tap water to Dachuan's village proper.

The third phase of the village's protests began in the mid-1980s, within the context of China's birth-control policy. In a stepped-up effort, the county government restricted rural couples from having more than two children and imposed a 3-year interval between the first and second births. As forced abortions were performed, human reproduction became a dominant subject of anxious conversation among the villages. It was around this time that a fertility temple in Dachuan attracted a growing number of worshipers. Meanwhile, speculation about the causes of stillbirths and birth defects in the village increasingly focused on the factory, prompting the village to resume its protests.

The liberalization of the Chinese economy also had a direct impact on Dachuan's protests, as seen in the fourth phase of the village's struggle against the factory, from the mid-1980s to the mid-1990s. In this period, Dachuan demonstrated against the factory every year, in protests ranging from small rallies to major blockades. Resentment of the factory's threat to people's health grew along with concerns over the village's fish ponds. These had multiplied from a handful in the early 1980s to more than 300 by the early 1990s, mostly for raising Yellow River Carp. The fish ponds depended on drawing water from the Yellow River, which remained polluted.

The four phases of Dachuan's protests represent a 'cognitive revolution.' By that I refer to the process whereby the villagers' understanding of water pollution advanced at several critical points, as when dozens of domesticated animals went blind, when special health problems were recognized in response to the state's population policy, and when the village's economic development was put at risk by the factory. The cumulative effect of this process was a comprehensive understanding of the damaging consequences of water pollution, rather than just one aspect of the problem as in the past. Human health, however, remained the most contentious issue in each phase of the village's struggle against the factory. This issue will be fully explored after introducing the next case.

Petitions for a livable environment

This case is the first confirmed protest movement against officials in charge of local population resettlement for the Three Gorges Dam project on the Yangzi River. The petition movement unfolded in 1997 among more than 10,000 rural residents in Gaoyang township, Yunyang county (now under the municipality of Chongqing in China's southwest). Still gathering force at this writing, the Gaoyang petition movement began with accusations against local officials on three points. First, the petitioners blamed county officials for not distributing the full financial compensation that the central government already allocated for local people either to resettle on higher ground nearby or to move to other counties. Second, township officials were accused of embezzling resettlement funds. Third, the petitioners claimed that corruption among township officials and village cadres was responsible for a failed land reclamation project, which had been funded by the central government for local resettlers to move into a livable environment. The third accusation, dealing with the environmental aspects of the Gaoyang petition movement, is the primary concern of the case summary below. The relevant information is selected from three petition letters, ten government documents (including a police report), published studies of the Three Gorges Dam project, and two intensive interviews I had with the petition movement's organizers during my field research in the county of Yunyang in 1998.

The Three Gorges Dam project is unprecedented in terms of physical size and the number of people slated for relocation. The project, whose construction began in 1994, cost at least the equivalent of U.S. $25 billion, for capital construction and population resettlement. The government plan calls for the dam, whose construction began in late 1994, to be 185 meters high and 2,000 meters wide, holding back a reservoir extending 640 kilometers upstream. The dam's generating capacity of nearly 18,000 megawatts would be 50 percent greater than the world's current largest hydroelectric station, Itaipu in Paraguay. The first group of generators in the dam is to begin operating in the year 2003, requiring the reservoir water to rise to 135 meters above sea level. The entire project, scheduled for completion by 2009, requires the relocation of at least 1.3 million people. More than half of the resettlers, living in 1,352 villages, need new farmland to restart their lives.[4] An experiment for transferring some of the rural resettlers into factories to ease the pressures on land was dropped completely in 1997, as unemployment in the Three Gorges area rose to 20 percent of the industrial work force, a problem that also afflicted other parts of China in the aftermath of a government decision to restructure the state-owned industrial sector.

In Gaoyang, where the petition movement took place, the only way to find extra farmland is to build terraces on higher ground. But even the most successful land reclamation would fall far short of providing enough arable land. For Gaoyang has 25,118 rural residents and only 16,950 *mu* of arable land. This comes to just 0.6 *mu* of arable land per person, already an extremely low figure to sustain a livelihood from farming. The shortages of land are bound to become more severe in Gaoyang, considering that the Three Gorges project entails the inundation of 40 percent of Gaoyang's farmland and the resettlement of 60 percent of Gaoyang's rural residents. Since many of these people wanted to stay in the vicinity to be close to relatives and fellow villagers, they desperately looked to the land reclamation project as a way to rebuild the foundation of their livelihood.

The state provided land reclamation funds to township officials to manage and for village cadres to distribute as payment for labor. By 1995, the reclamation project was supposed to provide at least some of the relocating villagers with access to new land. But one village after another discovered that many of the so-called terraced lands were not flat, had little topsoil, and were too scattered to farm. Local officials, however, had reported to higher authorities that these were usable fields. Furthermore, village cadres and township officials were found to have falsely included in their reclamation reports already cultivated farmland and even some fields that did not exist at all. In total, the petition movement's organizers told the central government, nearly 1,000 *mu* of the allegedly reclaimed land were unusable or nonexistent. They charged that much of the land reclamation funds, amounting to three million yuan, had been embezzled by local officials.

The petitioners spelled out in their first letter to the central government what they thought would happen in Gaoyang if wrongdoing among local officials was not checked:

In the future, when desperate resettlers rush to government compounds begging for food, what then? And, what if these impoverished throngs decide to rush onto the streets of our cities and large urban areas to stage demonstrations to protest the embezzlement of compensation funds by local officials and to demand restitution of these monies? . . . If the central government takes no action until conflicts break out, the lessons to be learned will be learned too late.

To send this warning, the petitioners organized a village-by-village investigation into the so-called reclaimed lands that in fact had been never reclaimed or did not exist at all. They then wrote in the petition letter:

> According to our investigation, such false claims cover the following villages: 275 *mu* by Liutou, 285 *mu* by Hongmiao, 20 *mu* by Pailou, 25 *mu* by Lishu, 128 *mu* by Gaoyang, 70 *mu* by Tuanbao, 125 *mu* by Zouma, 130 *mu* by Mingchong, 25 *mu* by Tongxi, and 10 *mu* by Tianzhuang. Together, these add up to 993 *mu* of land that was falsely claimed as reclaimed and arable land.

After the first letter from Gaoyang reached Beijing by mail, officials in the city of Chongqing were told to investigate. Chongqing had been recently separated from the jurisdiction of Sichuan province and granted a special municipality status – joining Beijing, Tianjin and Shanghai – under the direct supervision of the central government. This move allowed Chongqing to incorporate smaller cities and rural counties in the upper part of the Three Gorges that had been part of Sichuan. All these cities and counties will be partially flooded once the dam is built. In fact, 80 percent of the people slated for resettlement live in these cities and counties. The remaining 20 percent are in the downstream province of Hubei.

The initial investigation by Chongqing authorities only scratched the surface of Gaoyang's problems. But it led to more investigations. Meanwhile, a second petition letter was sent to Beijing. By mid–1998, the Party secretary and five top officials of Gaoyang township were sacked. The Party secretary and one of the sacked officials were arrested and imprisoned. However, these officials were brought down not on charges related to land reclamation but because they were found to have taken bribes in the construction of Gaoyang's new township seat, which is relatively small and can accommodate only a few hundred resettlers. The failed land reclamation, by contrast, is politically explosive. It affects thousands of rural residents and its publicity may cast serious doubts as to whether the Three Gorges Dam project can deal effectively with the many problems of rural resettlement in an already bleak ecological environment.

With the reclamation problem still unsolved, local officials moved against the two leading petitioners. An internal county government document accused them of having been troublemakers during the Cultural Revolution (1966–76), adding that police should deal sternly with them if they engaged in any action that might constitute a criminal offense. To eliminate support for the petitioners at the village level, the county government launched, in August 1998, a 'laws and village security' campaign, and villagers were told to dissociate themselves from the petition movement. Fearing retaliation from local officials, the two men leading the petition movement hurried to Beijing to submit the third petition. There, they hand-delivered it to the 'Offices for Receiving People's Letters and Visits' operating under the State Council, the Central Committee of the Chinese Communist Party, and the Three Gorges Construction Committee.

The Gaoyang case shows that the petitioners were keenly aware that their challenge to official wrongdoings must be framed in terms acceptable to the central government, for their challenge raised serious questions on the feasibility of the politically glorified Three Gorges project. This case also demonstrates the strong consciousness of political and civil rights on the part of the petitioners. As the two leading petitioners told a sociology student who helped them type and print their third petition letter, their visit to Beijing was aimed at establishing an official record of their constitutionally protected right to write letters to national leaders to expose the wrongdoings of local officials.

Chinese culture and the nature of environmental protest

At the beginning of this chapter, it was mentioned that the two protest movements under discussion operated within a 'cultural and symbolic life-world.' To explain exactly what this means, I first suggest that an overtly political protest may achieve an immediate success but be incapable of further elaboration. I further argue that a protest is most effective when it resonates with a society's value system and its symbolic manifestations. Among the most important of these are death rituals, cosmological beliefs, or the telling and retelling of morality tales from history. To elaborate this point, I will analyze the Dachuan case of a descent group and the local worship of fertility goddesses. For Gaoyang, my analysis is concerned with funeral symbolism and its meaning for the petition movement. For both cases, I will underscore the relevance of Chinese culture to environmental protests.

Kinship and fertility goddesses: the Dachuan case

At first glance, it would seem that Dachuan's protests against the fertilizer factory were led by the village committee in cooperation with the leaders of the village's eight production teams. A closer look, however, reveals the indelible influence of a dominant lineage in the village's organized struggle for safe drinking water. More than 85 percent of Dachuan's households are surnamed Kong and trace their ancestry to Confucius (Kong Fuzi in Chinese).[5] Until the early 1950s, the Kongs were organized as a formal lineage. They maintained an ancestral hall, held an annual ceremony of ancestor worship, and used the incomes from more than 200 *mu* of land to finance rituals, local defense, and a primary school. Institutionally speaking, the Kong lineage collapsed in the Maoist era but made a partial recovery later, as embodied in the reconstruction of the Kong ancestor hall in 1991. The Kongs also dominated Dachuan politically. From 1958 to 1998, the village chief, the local Communist Party boss, and the accountant-general were all surnamed Kong, despite leadership reshuffles.[6]

So, given the lineage-grounded framework of Dachuan's organizational structure, it is no surprise that the village cadres tapped into the collective identity of the Kongs to mobilize protests against the factory. Above all, they emphasized the factory's threat to the ability of the Kongs to have healthy babies. This concern was a major catalyst for the reconstruction of four temples on a mountain behind the main residential area of Dachuan. Leveled by government decree during the Cultural Revolution (1966–76), these temples were fully rebuilt in the mid-1980s. Six goddesses and one male deity (a water-control god) were enshrined, in the form of elaborately painted clay statues of varying sizes. Each goddess is believed to possess the ability to help women give birth, protect young children, and cure life-threatening diseases.

The new enshrinement of the six goddesses merged together two types of anxiety-ridden experience: the effect of the Chinese government's population policy and the increasing awareness in Dachuan of the fertilizer factory's threat to people's health, especially the physical well-being of women and children. In Yongjing county, where Dachuan is located, a central government policy for birth control was implemented locally through much of the 1970s. Partly because of this policy, Yongjing county's birthrate of forty newborns per 1,000 population in 1968 declined to eighteen newborns per 1,000 population in 1978. By 1982, 3 years after the central government made its rural birth-limitation policy even tougher, the annual birthrate in Yongjing county declined to thirteen births per 1,000 population. To further reduce population growth, the county government adopted a stricter quota of two births for a rural couple and imposed a requirement of 3 years of spacing between the first and second births. A second child was allowed even if the first was a boy. To quell resistance to the birth quota, the county government organized officials, doctors, and policemen into special task forces to enforce the birth quota and the spacing of births. Dachuan became the target of one of these task forces, because government officials believed that Dachuan had too many *hei haizi*, or 'black babies.' That is to say, women in Dachuan found different ways to disguise their pregnancies and hide their unregistered newborns.

The implementation of the population policy was Janus-faced. On one side, forcible means were adopted. Using intrauterine devices was compulsory, routinely checked by sent-down doctors. Tubal ligations of young women who had given births to two or more children were performed at local clinics, by force when resistance was encountered. On the other side, persuasion was utilized. Blackboards were erected at a major intersection in Dachuan and a loudspeaker system was utilized by village cadres to publicize official recommendations for public health. These recommendations, in line with national campaigns, promoted what was described as 'scientific childcare' (*kexue yu er*). Through radio and television, simplified questions and answers were provided to why having fewer children is important to the rural family and the well-being of the next generation of young people. Specific recommendations covered pregnancy tests, breast feeding, weaning, and nutrition.

The impact of this combination of education and coercion was deeply felt in Dachuan. In interviews with six upper middle-age women who went from door to door to raise money for making deity statues, they said that local women did not associate miscarriages and stillbirths with the fertilizer factory's discharge of waste water until the government embarked on the education drive to promote scientific childcare. Moreover, they said that concerns for women and children's health were stimulated by an experimental program to immunize rural children against infectious diseases. This government-funded program brought a team of doctors from a county hospital to Dachuan every year. Local children stood in lines to receive the immunization shots while their mothers talked with the doctors and nurses. This was a perfect opportunity for village women to obtain free advice for the sake of their own and their children's health.

Repeatedly, the doctors told the inquirers that it was dangerous to drink from the polluted Yellow River. It could cause, the doctors said, miscarriages and stillbirths as well as mental retardation and stunted growth for children. The doctors' warning was made more alarming by the televised reports of environmental problems elsewhere in China. One report was about water pollution in south China and its effect on pregnant women. Among those who paid special attention to this report was the village's Party boss, who was the most powerful man in Dachuan but had no biological child of his own. His wife had suffered several miscarriages, after which the couple decided to adopt a little girl. No boys were available for adoption in Dachuan or in nearby villages. Convinced that his wife's miscarriages were caused by the fouled water, the Party boss played a leading role in the village's protests against the factory. His adopted daughter later married a Mr. Xi, a junior township official. Instead of moving out of Dachuan, she remained and her husband came to live with her. If they had two sons, the newlyweds promised at a witnessed ceremony, one would bear the surname Kong, after his mother's adoptive father, to prevent his patrilineal line of descent from breaking down.

Although Dachuan's Party boss stated in public that he did not condone the worship of fertility goddesses, he was once seen taking a portion of the food offerings from a goddess temple to bring home when most visitors had left after a midnight ceremony. The food offerings are considered blessed by the enshrined goddesses and are expected to enhance the health of children and adults alike. This expectation is based on the popular belief that people and deities enjoy a reciprocal relationship. Temple rituals suggest that deities depend on regular worship and offerings, which make them strong and powerful. So when food offerings to deities are ample and regular, supplicants can hope for a return, which includes the blessed foods to take home. There are many expressions of this belief. For example, new temple-goers in Dachuan were often told by regular visitors that they should let their children eat some of the food offerings to 'ensure peace and safety' (*bao ping an*).

Dachuan's most popular goddesses were known as *sanxiao niangniang*, or

'Three Heavenly Mothers.' Their half-life-sized statues in a temple called *bai zi gong* (the Palace of One Hundred Sons) were adorned with silk attire. Attached to their clothes, necks, and arms were homemade embroideries. Many of the embroideries were embellished with stylized fish, lotus flowers or half-open pomegranates. Because fish produce a multitude of eggs at one time and a pomegranate or a lotus flower contains many seeds, they became fertility symbols on these embroideries. Other embroideries had tiny human figures in the image of little boys, sitting atop a fish, playing with a lotus flower, or climbing out of a pomegranate. These religious artworks were constantly replaced by new embroideries from villagers seeking to have babies. After a simple rite of offering money and incense, the temple's embroidery could then be taken home. It was usually kept in a couple's bed for bringing in a boy in a timely fashion and for keeping the power of fertility goddesses inside the house to protect the baby to be born in the future.

In retrospect, the new enshrinement of fertility goddesses represented a pent-up sense of urgency to have babies quickly and safely, constituting a religiously grounded manifestation of the village's concerns over the factory's polluting water. It is hence by no means an accident that one of the major demands in Dachuan's protests against the factory was framed in terms of the continuity of the family line and the health of village women and children. More specifically, the village cadres vowed to end the protests only on one of two conditions. First, the whole village must have safe drinking water. Second, the protests could be ended if the factory's top leaders, their wives, children, and grandchildren would each drink one small bottle of the heavily polluted water fetched from the contaminated stream leading to the Yellow River. Considering that safe drinking water had been available to the families of the factory's own employees since the factory was founded, Dachuan's second condition for ending its protests was an especially stirring one. It was a demand that the factory leaders do for the villagers precisely what they had done for the protection of their own families.

Funeral symbolism and internal trust: the Gaoyang case

Organized protests in China and elsewhere in the world often embrace some culturally meaningful symbols and a politically adept language. In the Gaoyang case, this tendency was embodied in three petition letters, secret meetings to select the petition movement's leaders, and emphasis on loyalty. In the three petition letters, the central government's resettlement policies were lauded but described as being jeopardized by local officials. These letters included diplomatically phrased statements to win over central authorities by saying that the petitioners fully endorsed the goal of constructing a world-class dam to provide electricity for national development and understood that even though the project required local villagers to make considerable sacrifices, the state had designed sound compensatory measures in return. According to these letters, corrupt local officials had sabotaged central policies and had to be investigated by the state. In other words, the articulation of grievances in these letters echoed the rhetorical themes of popular protests throughout China's dynastic history: The emperor is just and kind but his benevolence is being thwarted by evil local officials.

By contrast, the manner in which local participants were mobilized to join the petition movement could be quite threatening to the state. In launching the petition movement, village meetings were held without the knowledge of township officials, and these secret meetings resulted in the selection of forty representatives from all the fourteen affected villages in Gaoyang to form a unified petition team. By secret ballot, this team chose three leaders, who then took an oath pledging fairly to represent the participating villages. One of the three leaders was Gaoyang's retired Communist Party head. He later quit the petition movement under government pressure involving his family, relatives, and former colleagues.

The petition movement leaders' oath also bound them never to betray their comrades and supporters even in the face of official persecution. Emblematic of this resolve and as part of the plan to deliver the first letter to Beijing, the forty-member team decided to make 100 white gowns inscribed with three slogans written in black characters: 'Resettlers Want a Meeting with Higher Authorities; Resettlers Want to Express Their Grievances; and Resettlers Want to Live.' The planned trip to Beijing was immediately exposed by an informer, and local officials responded quickly. The petitioners who had been selected to go to Beijing were ordered not to leave Gaoyang and were told to surrender their petition letter to county officials. Angry officials at the township level warned a rural businessman that if he paid to have the white gowns made, as he had promised at a secret meeting, he would forfeit his business license.

It is easy to understand why the officials did not want the letter to be delivered. But why were they enraged by the white gowns? Was it simply because they would display three protest slogans? To address these questions, it should be remembered that white is the traditional Chinese color of death and mourning. It is the color of funeral trappings such as wreaths, paper flowers, poetic couplets, and attire, including caps, gowns, and shoes.[7] The transfer of funeral symbolism to social protests actually is an important feature of China's political culture. In Beijing, popular demonstrations at Tiananmen Square in 1976 and 1989 usurped the official mourning for a national leader, turning it into a forum to express anger with the political regime.[8] At Hong Kong University in 1998, a sculpture of twisted human bodies was erected to honor those killed in the military suppression of the Tiananmen protests nine years earlier. In New York City, Chinese restaurant workers paraded white wreaths in a 1996 strike against an exploitative employer. In Taiwan, demonstrations against a nuclear plant engaged in what the local newspapers called a 'battle of the coffins' when protesters carried four coffins to the plant and set up a spirit altar.[9] Whatever the specific symbols of death and funeral used in these situations, the ultimate statement being made was that a serious crime had been committed.

The messages intended by such funeral trappings can vary, and the Gaoyang petitioners' plan to wear white gowns for delivering their first letter to the central government was meant not only to express grievances but also to convey their readiness to die for their cause. So high were the risks they were taking when they accused local officials and so unpredictable the consequences of their taking on the Three Gorges Dam project that the Gaoyang petitioners feared for possible imprisonment and even execution. The white gowns thus symbolized their preparation for martyrdom. In fact, as soon as she heard about the white gowns, the frightened wife of one of the petition leaders asked him for a divorce, as a way to protect herself and her children in case her husband were arrested or executed as a criminal.

The informer's disclosure of their plan to secretly visit Beijing and the withdrawal of one petition leader under pressure heightened the movement organizers' appreciation of the danger of betrayal. While speaking of their determination to go as far as dying for the petition movement, they tried hard to build internal trust by emphasizing the righteousness of their cause and the unspeakable nature of disloyalty. In so doing, they repeatedly made references to the unfortunate example of Song Jiang in *Outlaws of the Marshes*, an epic story about rebellions in the twelfth century that evolved from a written narrative from 1400 to an extended edition in 1641.

Largely a work of literary imagination based on the slightest historical evidence, the story features 108 bandit-heroes led by Song Jiang, a petty official who had numerous unpleasant encounters with the law but maintained a sense of loyalty to the throne. Even as a bandit chieftain who coined the popular slogan of 'Doing Justice in the Name of Heaven,' Song Jiang sought and received an imperial pardon; his decision to surrender his forces to the state and to lead them in government campaigns against other rebels was only grudgingly approved by his followers and set the stage for wrenching conflicts of loyalty. Song Jiang's respect for the throne rivaled his devotion to his sworn brother-rebels, who followed his lead only to meet tragic ends.

References to Song Jiang in Gaoyang's petition movement needed no elaboration; his legend had been recounted over the centuries by storytellers, portrayed in local operas, and more recently turned into television dramas. Every petitioner appreciated the irony of Song Jiang's death at the hands of corrupt officials who had him poisoned in the emperor's name. Every petitioner also knew that Song Jiang's surrender to the throne did not benefit his followers but instead led them to deadly situations from which they did not return alive.

It would be misleading to suggest, however, that the Gaoyang petitioners cited Song Jiang as a negative example while favoring other rebels in the novel who had little respect for state authorities. The petitioners wanted their grievances to be heard by the central government, which remained in their eyes the ultimate institution that might offer them real help. Like the symbolism of white gowns in confirming their willingness to die, reference to Song Jiang was an evocation of the petition movement's unpredictable consequences. In both instances, the petition leaders justified their actions by borrowing from China's cultural and historic legacies.

Conclusion: environmental crisis and local protests

To situate the Dachuan and Gaoyang cases in the broader context of similar protests, it is important to recognize that China's environmental problems evolved into a severe crisis in the 1980s and that that crisis persisted into the 1990s. Two major transformations of Chinese society under the rule of the Chinese Communist Party were responsible for this environmental crisis. From the 1950s through much of the 1970s, the Chinese government under the leadership of Mao Zedong pursued variants of the Soviet model of development so as to transform a largely agrarian country into an industrial society. Mao's economic program resulted in a basic infrastructure for development in favor of heavy, military, and chemical industries. The introduction of rural reforms in the late 1970s and the initiation of urban reforms in the mid-1980s started off the country's transformation away from a command economy to a market-oriented one. Official statistics show that between 1978 and 1995 China's per capita GDP growth averaged 8 percent a year; other statistics suggest a growth rate of 6–7 percent. Still, whatever the precise figure, China's economic growth in these years was almost unprecedented. Only South Korea and Taiwan had similar rates.

The development strategy under Mao that laid down China's industrial infrastructure and the unbridled growth in the post-Mao era that lifted at least 100 million people out of absolute poverty have turned out to be extremely damaging to China's natural environment. Take for example Guangdong province, home to one of China's fastest growing regional economies. In 1996 alone, the Guangdong provincial government had to shut down 739 factories so as to ease the excessive discharges of waste water and waste gas that had made the air and rivers in Guangdong dangerously polluted.[10] And in 1997, official delegations were urgently dispatched by the central government to the provinces of Henan, Jiangsu, Shandong, and Anhui to investigate and discipline 1,562 factories for turning the Huai River, the third largest waterway in China, into a belt of blackened water too polluted for irrigation and unsafe to drink.[11]

Although many studies and news reports on China's environmental problems are available, no scholarly or government surveys have been conducted on environmental protests. One source to locate some information on environmental protests in China is the official publications of what is known as "selected cases of environmental disputes." Chosen for their pedagogical effect and for use in environmental law enforcement, these documents reveal that petitioning government agencies, filing lawsuits, and staging demonstrations are the three leading forms of environmental protests in rural China. Urban areas are no exception either. In fact, urbanites may be quicker than rural residents to engage in blockades, sabotage, and even collective violence, which government and court officials identify as 'extreme action in environmental disputes.' Of eighty-eight environmental disputes in urban and suburban Shanghai recorded in a case-by-case publication released by the Shanghai Municipal Agency of Environmental Protection, forty-four of these predominantly urban disputes involved 'extreme action' and only five resorted to the judicial system.[12] Compare this with forty-seven disputes in rural areas recorded in two publications of the Chinese Environmental Science Press. Only eleven of these rural disputes involved 'extreme action,' whereas twenty-five were handled by the court, with verdicts rendered mostly in favor of the rural litigants.[13] Since these were selected cases rather than survey findings, the relevant court rulings should not be readily taken as evidence of the effectiveness of China's legal system in protecting the rural population against environmental damage. But they are indicative of the growing trend to take environmental issues to court.

The reasons behind the documented urban and rural differences with regard to the use of 'extreme action' – which often has involved collective violence – are complex and may have to do with a stronger sense of entitlement among urban Shanghai residents. Nonetheless, the use of violent means to retaliate against industrial polluters is still a significant form of protest in the rural disputes and a quarter of the recorded rural cases led to violence such as scuffles, sabotage, harassment and forceful detention of factory leaders.[14] The greater resort to the judicial system in the countryside, on the other hand, can be traced to the limited power of local, especially county-level, governments in imposing administrative penalties against violators of China's environmental laws. By these laws, a county-level government can punish only those enterprises operating under its administrative jurisdiction. These include county, township, village, and private enterprises. A county government, however, cannot resort to administrative penalties, such as imposing fines or shutting down facilities, to punish industrial polluters if they are beyond its administrative jurisdiction. In these situations, the power of administrative punishment, as written in environmental laws, is rendered useless.

An alternative is to ask the victims to file a civil lawsuit to be handled by the court system. That this has been done frequently explains why over half of the rural disputes I have mentioned above resulted in lawsuits. But even if a provincial-level enterprise is sued and held responsible by a county court, it would appeal and bring the lawsuit to a higher court where it expects to be judged more favorably than in the county court. This is certainly why in the Dachuan case I have discussed, the village cadres did not go to court, following the advice of township and county officials who claimed to have a better knowledge of how the judicial system would handle a lawsuit against the nearby fertilizer factory, which is a provincial-level enterprise.

And in other environmentally related protests such as that of the Gaoyang case, China's environmental laws can hardly be applied at all for political reasons or due to special government decisions. It is widely known, for example, that the construction of the Three Gorges Dam will further damage an already fragile ecological system along the Yangzi River, especially the middle and lower reaches. But since this is a state-sponsored construction project of unusual political importance, its devastating environmental impact is not subject to the possible scrutiny of the country's environmental laws. Instead, the problem has been treated by national leaders as a policy issue and as a matter of lesser importance than that of flood control and power generation.

The rise of environmental protests in China in the past 20 years is emblematic of the growing consciousness of community and individual rights among ordinary citizens as well as the cumulative effect of newly promulgated laws. In rural areas particularly, the inauguration of drastic economic and administrative changes in the 1980s and 1990s has led to a readjustment of state–society relations. Economic liberalization included agricultural decollectivization, marketization, and the legitimization of geographical mobility and the private sector. Administrative reforms were typified by the promulgation of the Organic Law of Villagers' Committees and the Administration Litigation Law, in 1987 and 1990, respectively.

These changes altered the power relations in village China, sometimes weakening the political base of rural cadres and leading to incidents in which ordinary villagers took upon themselves the task of organizing the local people to defend their community and individual rights. The Gaoyang case is an apt example of this trend, whereas the Dachuan case reveals the close cooperation of village cadres and local residents in a community struggle for clean water. Both cases demonstrate that Chinese villagers can become instant political activists when their livelihood is threatened. Of course, the concrete means of organizing themselves to engage in popular protests are dependent on other factors such as government policies, bureaucratic reactions, and state laws.[15]

On the basis of my study of the Dachuan and Gaoyang cases and my examination of forty-seven similar rural cases (as documented in the two official publications mentioned earlier), I suggest that environmentally related protests in the Chinese countryside display four characteristics that deserve to be emphasized. First, Chinese culture plays a central role in the mobilization of participants. This is often done through appeals to kinship ties, village unity, popular religion, and the security of the rural family. Second, economic grievances, health claims, or legal demands are accompanied by distinctly moral judgments and a remarkable sense of entitlement for a society with a poor record of human rights. Third, protest organizers not only appear highly aware of the country's environmental laws, they also know the importance of taking advantage of fissures within the government to find allies or at least sympathizers within the leadership. And finally, people in rural China who do not necessarily regard themselves as the state's adversaries are capable of launching well-organized and forceful protests against environmental abuses. But the ways they go around organizing their protests reflect the centrality of particular social values and moral concerns. These protests are not meant to save an endangered environment for its own sake, independent of its relevance to people. Rather, they are aimed at seeking social justice to protect the ecological basis of human existence.

Notes

1 Research for this chapter benefitted from the provision of a travel grant by the Research Foundation of the City University of New York in the 1998–99 academic year.
2 These official records are found in the following sources: Shanghai Municipal

Environmental Agency Protection, *Environmental Pollution, Conflict between Factories and Masses, and Conflict Resolution* (*Huanjing wuran changqun maodun yu chuli duice*), (Huangdong Politics and Law College Press: Shanghai, 1994); Xie Zhenhua (ed.), *Typical Cases of Environmental Violations and Guidelines of Environmental Law Enforcement in China* (*Zhongguo huanjing dianxing anli yu zhifa tiyao*) (China Environmental Science Press: Beijing, 1994); Zhao Yongkang (ed.), *Selected Cases of Environmental Disputes* (*Huanjing jiufen anli*) (China Environmental Science Press: Beijing, 1989).

3 For more information on China's environmental crisis, see He Baochang, *China On the Edge: The Crisis of Ecology and Development* (China Books & Periodicals: San Francisco, 1991); Vaclav Smil, *China's Environmental Crisis: An Inquiry into the Limits of National Development* (M. E. Sharpe: Armonk, 1993); World Bank, *Clear Water, Blue Skies: China's Environment in the New Century* (The International Bank for Reconstruction and Development: Washington, DC: 1997).

4 See Jun Jing, 'Population Resettlement: Past Lessons for the Three Gorges Dam Project,' *The China Journal*, Vol. 38, July 1997, pp. 65–92; Dai Qing (ed.) *The River Dragon Has Come: The Three Gorges Dam and the Fate of China's Yangtze River and Its People* (M. E. Sharpe: Armonk, 1998).

5 For a detailed social history of this Kong lineage, see Jun Jing, *The Temple of Memories: History, Power, and Morality in a Chinese Village* (Stanford University Press: Stanford, CA, 1996).

6 For additional information on the overlapping of kinship ties and village administration in the Maoist and post-Mao eras, see Edward Friedman, Paul Pickowicz, and Mark Selden, *Chinese Village, Socialist State* (Yale University Press: New Haven, 1991); Huang Shu-min, *The Spiral Road: Change in a Chinese Village through the Eyes of a Communist Party Leader* (Westview Press: Boulder, CO: 1989); Jack Potter and Sulamith Potter, *China's Peasants: The Anthropology of a Revolution* (Cambridge University Press: Cambridge, UK, 1990).

7 For a comprehensive analysis of Chinese funerals and mourning rites, see James Watson and Evelyn Rawski (eds), *Death Ritual in Late Imperial and Modern China* (University of California Press: Berkeley, 1996).

8 See Rubie Watson, 'Making Secret Histories: Memory and Mourning in Post-Mao China,' in Rubie Watson (ed.), *Memory, History, and Opposition Under State Socialism*, (School of American Research Press: Santa Fe, 1994), pp. 65–86; Joseph W. Esherick and Jeffrey N. Wasserstrom, 'Acting out Democracy: Political Theatre in Modern China,' in Jeffrey N. Wasserstrom and Elizabeth J. Perry (eds), *Popular Protest and Political Culture in Modern China: Learning from 1989* (Westview: Boulder, CO, 1992), pp. 28–66.

9 See Robert P. Weller and Hsin-Hung Michael Hsiao, 'Culture, Gender, and Community in Taiwan's Environmental Movement,' in Arne Kalland and Gerald Persoon (eds.), *Environmental Movements in Asia* (Curzon: London, 1998), pp. 83–108.

10 'Locals Long for the Return of Blue Skies to Guangzhou,' *China Daily*, June 5, 1997, p. 3.

11 Cai Haili, 'Can Environmental Protection Work in China?' *Harvard China Review*, 1998 1(1), 84–6.

12 Shanghai Municipal Agency of Environmental Protection, *Environmental Pollution*, op. cit.

13 Xie Zhenhua (ed.), *Typical Cases*, op. cit; Zhao Yongkang (ed.) *Selected Cases*, op. cit.

14 On the causalities of different forms of collective violence in the contemporary Chinese countryside, see e.g., Elizabeth J. Perry, 'Rural Collective Violence: the Fruits of Recent Reforms,' in Elizabeth J. Perry and Christine Wong (eds), *The Political Economy of Reform in Post-Mao China* (Harvard University Press: Cambridge, MA, 1985), pp. 179–92.

15 See Kevin O'Brien and Lianjiang Li, 'The Politics of Lodging Complaints in Rural China,' *China Quarterly*, No. 143 (Sept. 1995), pp. 756–83; Minxin Pei, 'Citizens vs. Mandarins: Administrative Litigation in China,' *China Quarterly*, No. 152 (Dec. 1997), pp. 832–62.

8 Religion as resistance

Stephan Feuchtwang

China contains a great many religious traditions, some ancient like Daoism, some very recent like the Protestant Chinese Little Flock denomination. All of them have been intimately affected and changed by their encounters with the Communist state and the economy which it has managed, through dramatic switches of policy. Popular religious imagery has provided some of the most evocative elements of mass campaigns. In the other direction, Chinese Communist heroes have become objects of religious veneration. Many local cadres have played a part in suppressing local traditions, others in rebuilding them. This chapter will follow some examples of this interplay. But the big question which this chapter addresses is whether we can understand revitalised religious traditions as political resistance.

One obvious 'yes' answer is where there has been a defence of religious traditions against political attacks, as during the Cultural Revolution or in present-day Tibet. But the more widespread and fascinating answer is far less obvious. It is the countless examples, some of which are described in this chapter, of preserving local identities and senses of history and of good conduct as a community, often in negotiation with local officials. In Buddhist, Christian, Muslim, sectarian, or local temple cults and their festivals, ways of judging government and everyday conduct are preserved which stand apart from current political ideologies. They are alternative arenas for telling or performing stories which reflect on the corruption, inequality and lack of security and support seen and experienced by the subjects of the Chinese People's Republic.

For the People's Republic of China (PRC), a crucial moment of resistance was the 3 years 1959–61 following the Great Leap Forward and the collectivization of agriculture.[1] Oversized communes, pressures to achieve hyperbolic production figures, and the consequent extraction of over-sized grain quotas, led to famine and widespread starvation. The 3 years of famine or of severe difficulty are a watershed in the social memory of virtually every village.

One man from Xicun, a pseudonym for a village within the hills of the southern part of Fujian province which was then one of the poorest parts of the country, had risen higher than any previous man born there.[2] He was accepted into the Party in 1955 and in 1959 he had become the second-in-command of the

Commune and of an attached state farm. No longer a cadre, he is now an organizer of religious renewal, having led the reconstruction first of the village's temples in 1988 and then of the ancestral hall of its major lineage, which is also his own, completed in 1994. I will call him Darkface (*wumiande*) because that is one of the ways he is known to fellow villagers, confirming his reputation as a bold and forceful cadre. The symbol of blackness, written with a different character (*hei*), was used as a label of condemnation in PRC political campaigns. Here dark (*wu*) is to be understood in terms of the iconography of the village guardian deity whose face is black and to whom Darkface is likened by fellow villagers. But note too that they and he combined this with being a good cadre, standing up for the people, administering justice and providing social security for which, in their eyes, the People's Republic stands or should stand.

The 3 years of hardship were a turning point for Darkface too. Like so many local cadres, he had to face in two directions: first, upward to his political masters, but consistent with his own enthusiasm for the revolutionary changes in which he had been a village-level activist. As the glowing hopes of the Leap yielded to disaster and famine, he also had to confront the dismay and eventually the anger of his fellow villagers. Many villagers respect him even now for the fact that he did not lose his loyalty to them as well as for the fact that he achieved high office, thereby bringing honour to the village.

The 3 years were a time of great hardship in which leadership blunders were exacerbated by natural disasters. A flood in 1961 destroyed the remains of the ancestral hall of the largest local lineage in Xicun. To the old, for whom the hall was a place for recreation and the lineage an organization which had provided them with a rare annual meal of meat at lunar New Year, the hunger of those difficult years was associated with hungry ancestors. In the words of Darkface himself, speaking sympathetically even as he distanced himself from such beliefs, a distance characteristic of a Communist cadre, to whom they are not religion but superstition:[3]

> collectivization led to failures of economic work and created a lot of difficulties. Because of this, villagers did not trust the state and cadres any more. Many elderly people who were in difficulties wanted to reorganize the lineage . . . and, in the face of natural disaster, many turned to superstition and called for the rebuilding of the ancestral hall.

Ancestral hall minutes show that Darkface not only approved but was present at the third of the three preparatory meetings and helped obtain some of the construction materials for the rebuilding in 1962. He risked being labelled 'superstitious' by his political superiors or by Party rivals, and gained the merit of a 'black cap' (*wushamao*), which is his own allusion to an older, imperial status. Feudal superstitions such as the honouring of ancestors were supposed by then to have been eliminated. But Darkface felt that the definition of superstition had been too sweeping.

To its participants, religious knowledge is true in a cosmological sense. It is by the cosmological scope of their claims to truth that religious practices are distinguished from other cultural practices. Religious culture links personal to collective truths which are large in potential scale, beyond the limits of a generational or a group identity or a particular period of a history, a government, regime or state. Such a large and authoritative stamp can challenge the practices of a state. Conversely, a state can consider itself sanctioned by the authority of a religious institution and can place it under its governmental authority. But by its own dependency on that authority, a state's sanctity is open to challenge by adherents of the religion which anoints it. To question a state is to question the legitimacy of a large and diverse set of supportive institutions, and not only the central apparatuses of government. But more diffuse kinds of challenge to state, regime or government can also be found, in which other senses of direction, other conceptions of the whole governed by a state and other ideas of its past gain legitimacy. Resistance of this kind may take such forms as the diffusion of knowledge, of stories and a sense of history and the direction of social forces, which may not directly challenge the state or regime, but which are autonomous from and alternative to its legitimating ideologies.

Darkface was an enthusiastic supporter of the revolution who retained a loyalty to the local temple, the lineage ancestral hall, and their festivals, which transmitted the village's history and identity. To put this in context I must turn to the larger religiosity of the People's Republic at this time.

The state decreed that civic ceremonies for schools and work units to honour revolutionary martyrs replace the cleaning of ancestors' ancestral graves. Burial was to be simplified and graves removed to marginal land and eventually replaced by cremation. The Spring Festival celebrating national accomplishments was to replace local temple fairs and pilgrimages at lunar new year. But the most ritualized and sanctified civil religion of the modern Chinese state was the cult of Mao which reached heights of enthusiasm in the Cultural Revolution.[4] Reinterpretations of its symbols and rites, as well as shelters from them in other cosmological truths, constituted religious resistance then and subsequently, as we shall see.

The Cultural Revolution and the cult of Mao; cultural transformation and its religious consequences

The Cultural Revolution must be one of the greatest attempts in any country to create a state-wide interpretative community of meanings.[5] Political rituals such as loyalty dances and daily reports to the leader, children's dances and songs, applause, sloganizing, drums, cymbals, red flags, memorizing, reciting from, and waving red books of Mao quotations, badges, great character posters and hoardings, all used in mass demonstrations, struggle meetings, executions, and the eight model revolutionary operas (but almost no other dramas or films) became the public culture of this era. Campaigns against the Four Olds (old ideas, old culture, old customs, and old habits) rallied young Red Guards and rural zealots. They sent underground or destroyed many central elements of the inherited public culture such as those associated with the rituals of birth, marriage, death, the worship of ancestors, festivals and holidays. Whatever the party's will, important elements of all of these were preserved, some even thrived, but nearly always behind closed doors within households. In rare cases, when a village was united and supported by its brigade leadership, when neither Red Guards or local rivalries could undermine it, religious buildings were left alone and not used for other purposes. Such was the case in a Hebei Muslim village whose mosque was untouched because, as I was told in 1991 by its *ahong* (imam), 'no one wanted to destroy it.' More typical was the series of events in Xicun.

Darkface could do nothing to prevent the destruction of the ancestral hall he had so recently helped to rebuild. In the factional strife which burst out at the beginning of the Cultural Revolution, Darkface was imprisoned. In 1967, an ambitious young man, at the head of the village militia, declared that as one of the old things it should be destroyed. Nobody would do it, out of fear of the offended and hungry ancestors. The brigade head was a member of another, minority lineage in the brigade. He and the militia forced bad class elements of Xicun at gunpoint to burn the hall down. Their next target was the village temple. But in this case, cadres of Xicun with whom Darkface was allied were able to prevent destruction by persuading the brigade leadership that it could be turned into an evening school. People took the statues of the gods into their homes. On festival days only the bravest among elders dared visit the homes where the gods were kept to burn incense together behind closed doors. The former public displays, processions, theatre and spirit-possession all ended.

Elimination of public religious meetings sometimes had a reverse effect. Those who wished to preserve their religion or even to find religion as a shelter from the political gales met in each other's homes, the bonds among believers perhaps even strengthened by the common risks of professing belief. It appears that the number of Christian 'house churches' (*jiating jiao-hui*) or 'meeting points' (*juhuidian*) grew during the Cultural Revolution.[6]

The Cultural Revolution was a series of mobilization campaigns (*yundong*) without a well-administered chain of command since the Party at all levels split into factions, as did the government and army. Peer pressure of enthusiasm, rivalry and suspicion had ample scope to proliferate rival orthodoxies about what it took to be revolutionary and to learn from the masses, always within the framework of pledging fealty to the supreme leader. Factional rivalry fed on vivid denunciation and hyperbolic praise. Tiger demons, saviour deities associated with stars, snake women, and other figures from popular religious imagery were transferred to campaign imagery, drawing on well known themes of the imperial era. Campaigns against the Four Olds eliminated the drum bands, musical troupes, and theatrical floats used in festival processions. These had been no mere displays, but were also for exorcising demons. At the same time, bands using some of the same drums and cymbals excited mass mobilization.[7]

In otherwise close-knit villages, long-defeated bad class elements were avoided by their neighbours for fear of being contaminated since they were bound to be the target of the next campaign of class struggle. Village officials could deflect accusations of political backsliding by viciously attacking these outcasts. A woman interviewed by Jonathan Unger more than a decade after the events provides a vivid glimpse of a demonic imagery of fear: 'I was scared of class enemies. It seemed as if they would harm us, would poison us, kill us and eat us. I took them as horrible, fierce. I dared not talk to them in case I got muddled up.' [8] The Party newspaper urged red youth to 'sweep away all ox ghosts and snake spirits.' The images retain a force of vivid evocation, which is why they were used in editorials and the posters which covered every wall and the new hoardings put up especially to carry them. Their force also invaded the class rhetoric of socialist revolution and mass mobilization, reminders of the myths and rituals from which they derived.

In addition, class rhetoric was sometimes used to mask historic rivalries. Inter-lineage and inter-communal struggle was inextricably mixed with attacks on old customs. Jonathan Unger provides an example from rural Guangdong, in which the temple of a village was burned down by rival villagers in the name of an attack on feudal superstition. Red Guards of the temple village retaliated by destroying an ancient tree near the temple-burners' village, likewise justifying their act as an attack on superstition. The temple was held to enhance the geomantic fortune (the *fengshui*) of the one village and the tree the fertility of brides who married into the other. The two villages had long engaged in violent disputes over water rights.

In sum, the Cultural Revolution in some of its ideals and mass actions, and strikingly in its rituals, itself constituted religious resistance to the previous, bureaucratic state. At the same time, old rivalries continued, using local religious symbols, even within proclaimed allegiance to Mao as the leader of the revolutionary faction of the Party, while the fervour of mass mobilization also drove the remaining popular rituals and cults and most of the public manifestations of what had been recognized religions behind doors and out of public life.

In the 1980s, some of the ritual language and practices of the Cultural Revolution have been transformed into the mythology of a bygone era, the era of Mao. Indeed, Mao himself has reemerged as a cult object in myriad ways, for example as an emblem of protection in countless cars and trucks, and as a design element in the arts. Mao also figures as the most dynamic element of a pantheon of religiopolitical figures. In northern Shaanxi, for example, temples honor the Three Sagegods (*San Sheng*): Mao Zedong, Zhou Enlai and Zhu De. Another temple to the three Chinese Communist leaders was built in Hunan province and attended by thousands a day until it was closed down in May 1995 because it encouraged superstition. The Reform state encourages a continuing cult of Mao by days of commemoration and veneration at his birthplace and in his mausoleum. Pilgrimage tourism in contemporary China features the birth and death places of Mao, Zhou, Zhu, and Deng Xiaoping along with Confucius and the Yellow emperor, founder of the Chinese nation. [9]

Drum bands once organized to promote mass mobilization from land reform to the Cultural Revolution now play for a Dragon god in a temple fair in Fan Zhuang village, Hebei province. Everywhere, the rhythm of the songs and anthems of the cultural revolution had in the 1980s already turned into a disco beat, and they remain favourites in the sales of tapes and discs. They were sung in the demonstrations of Spring 1989. In short, the performative community of cultural revolutionary rhetoric has been broken, but the songs retain a talismanic nostalgia for an era of certainty. In both cities and countryside there is now a double take on the Mao era. The songs are reminders of ideals which are still held and reflect back critically upon the current regime. In the countryside, when asked about their experiences from land reform to the end of the Cultural Revolution decade, many villagers speak of chaos, fear and hunger. But in relation to the present, the same speakers remember those years as a time of income security, straight dealing, and simplicity (*pusu*) which is itself a Maoist virtue, to be contrasted favourably with the self-seeking cadres of the reform era and enviously as a self-description compared with the rich textures of city life. Mao has become a means to criticize the present regime. Loyalty to fellow villagers can be associated with loyalty to revolutionary ideals, betrayed by the present Party.

In prison between 1966 and 1968, Darkface had considered the turn of events with the help of a fortune-teller with whom he shared a cell. History had become, for him, a change of fortune (*yun*) instead of a movement in which he had been active and successful. In 1994, reflecting on his time in prison, as he often did, he said:

> I tried to do my best to be good to the people as the Party taught me to be, and I did not do anything wrong according to the Party's principles. In the fifties, my good conduct was recognised by the Party and so I was promoted. Why should I be imprisoned?

In his view, his loyalty to his fellow villagers was central to his revolutionary leadership. The focal symbols of the village's identity, its hall and its temple, and the sense of history and morality which they embodied, were not just 'superstition.' They were also public works of the people whom he served. Serving the people (*wei renmin fuwu*) is what he said he had been doing and has continued to do. As Darkface put it: 'a good cadre should first know how to be good to his home place (*jiaxiang*) and to his elders (*fulao*).'

The reform state

A similar loyalty to local community can be found in Christian villages, neighbourhoods and networks which have come into the open and spread. Some go much further in comradeship than long-established localities and their religious institutions. Chinese church meetings are usually more generous and earnest in their mutual support and expressions of faith than Western ones. A very large proportion of Chinese Christians are members of movements which have a

Chinese origin, such as the Little Flock. Many of these have elements of exorcism, healing, and messianism, mixing earlier Chinese with newer Christian traditions. Perhaps some of the revolutionary idealism of socialism has also entered into the charismatic sources of the Protestant tradition, stressing lay leadership, participatory democracy and mutual support. Hunter and Chan visited a community of Apostolic Church members in the mountains of southern Fujian, more remote than Xicun. One member said their network of households was like stars, invisible when the weather is cloudy. Devout, quietist and very democratic, they are hostile to the system of registration under the officially sanctioned Protestant organization, the Three-Self Patriotic Movement (TSPM). They proclaim a higher spiritual regulation, the Kingdom of Heaven, and for that reason incur the hostility of local TSPM officials. But in most years this hostility is not cloudy enough to force them back into closed worship.[10]

The politics of mass mobilization campaigns has been abandoned in favour of a politics of regulation and directive, supplemented by law. The Party can still at times act with a heavy hand, for example in dispatching work teams to enforce birth control or the planting of a cash crop, or to deny urban registration to 'peasants' (*nongmin*). But the reform state's politics is as much one of permission as it is of prescription. A politics of permission, which includes the registration of associations and meeting places, is also a politics of response to the unforeseeable outcomes of its policies. Authorization is given to some, while strenuous and resourceful attempts are made to prevent the recurrence of others. Resistance may take the form of a reaction to suppression, or it may constitute a negotiated compromise with state agencies.

The revised Constitution of the PRC promulgated in 1982 included a provision (Article 36) protecting religious activities. Article 36 was anticipated in a thirty-page document circulated to leading cadres 4 years earlier. The circular spelled out protection against cadres attempting to force citizens to renounce religious beliefs. Cadres should respect the private nature of religious belief and not discriminate against believers in any way, with one exception. Members of the Party must be atheist. Article 36 also states that religion must not be subject to the control of foreign countries, and provides for prosecution in case religion is used for counter-revolutionary purposes, to foment disorder or to harm health and education. But the circular stressed that the campaigns of the previous era had not distinguished between patriotic and counter-revolutionary or harmful religious activities. It restricted itself to imposing on religious organizations the task of assisting the Party and government in raising patriotic and socialist consciousness. A subsequent policy study, conducted by the Institute of Religious Studies of the Shanghai Academy of Social Sciences, went further, pointing out that religious activities in themselves could raise social responsibility and be compatible with socialist society.[11]

Twentieth-century policy on 'religion' (*zongjiao*) – one of many neologisms brought into China via Japan – has met and tried to address major problems of definition. The burning of incense and divination in front of statues of gods, for instance, cannot be assigned to an institution, nor described as private belief.

Such 'superstitions' should be treated as the result of failures of schooling and of local cadres paying insufficient attention to ideological work. But they could just as legitimately in the Reform state be treated as part of a package of local heritage. The resolution of such conundrums hinges heavily on the political climate at the time, and on the inclinations of local cadres.

An important reform, rectifying the mistakes of the Cultural Revolution, was the return of religious buildings or their sites to religious use, but in general the state has sought, with mixed results, to prevent religious groups from building on new sites. So local administrations have restored numerous mosques, monasteries, temples and churches to their former use, though much more of the finance for restoration came from other sources including subscription by local believers and funds from linked organizations abroad. Religious practitioners were allowed to return to them and to train a new generation. The numbers of clergy and seminarians were, however, fixed, sometimes well below their numbers before 1949, and religious associations and their membership were registered. But what were cadres to do about local collections of funds and overseas donations for religious buildings beyond these sites? What were they to do about religious personnel beyond the specified number, and even more problematic, what to do about those not registered at all?

Rampant 'superstitious' temple-building and what was called the 'fever' (*re*) of Christianity were unintended outcomes of the new policy that local authorities have confronted since the 1980s.

Figures for numbers of religious believers are very unreliable, even for the recognized religions. Should we include all the population of ethnic minorities which have an Islamic heritage as 'followers' or 'believers' in Islam? If so, then we can conclude from the table compiled by Gladney that in 1990 there were 17.5 million Muslims out of a total population of over 1 billion, and the proportion is not growing. This does not include Muslims in the majority ethnicity, the Han.[12] In the case of registered and unregistered Protestants, estimates vary hugely, from 10 to 30 million in 1994, for example.[13] But what everyone agrees is that there has been a remarkable growth, from some 3 million in 1982. There is a similar variation for Catholics, also growing – if less dramatically – to estimates in 1994 of between 6 and 10 million. For the non-congregational religions of Buddhism and Daoism, official numbers (47,000 Daoists in 1994) are totally misleading for they are only of the ritual practitioners themselves, and even they are outnumbered by unregistered practitioners. It is from direct observations, interviews, and newspaper reports that we can get some idea of their rapid growth.

The responsible authorities are several, all linked to the Central Committee of the Party or to the State Council, but each with a different brief. Public Security bureaux are on the lookout for illegal activities, including unregistered associations and unauthorised temple building, while the secret Security Police probe for foreign subversion. Religious Affairs bureaux register and manage religious institutions, and in conjunction with the main national religious associations such as the Buddhist Association or the Chinese Catholic Patriotic Association seek to maintain compatibility with Party ideological work and policy, but have little control over the unregistered. Cultural bureaux are in charge of promoting local culture. This can be to preserve or at least tolerate what they consider to be the good aspects of superstition, as an official of Tong'an county, in southern Fujian, told me in 1988. The good aspects included unregistered temples, festivals and even spirit-medium displays understood as emblematic of local skills and entertainment, as well as contributing to the local economy. The United Front Work departments of Party branches are charged with aiding modernization by promoting links with religious organizations, and with foreign countries through them, not only to encourage investment and tourism but also to seal the unity of the Chinese nation and prevent mass disaffection.

This is no problem when the tourist attraction is a religious building, such as one of the Buddhist temples around West Lake in Hangzhou, many of which have been restored with finance from Japanese Buddhist foundations. But it comes into direct contradiction with the brief for Public Security bureaux when the temples are those of local deities and when festivals attract large gatherings for 'superstitious' practices. Some local compromises between them veer in the direction of stamping out superstition and unregistered religion, while others veer toward tolerance. Much depends on the involvement of local cadres in religious activities and on their own, personal balance of Party career and response to local pressures.

By the mid-1980s, the unpredictable outcomes of religious policy were evident in the reports of state agencies. For instance, the Ministry of Public Security reported in 1985 that:

> In every region and province of China with the exception of Tibet, acts of disruption by the reactionary sects and societies have occurred – most prominently in the provinces of Henan, Shaanxi, Sichuan, and Yunnan. The vast majority of these activities have taken place in the countryside, and particularly in remote mountainous areas along the borders between different counties or provinces.[14]

The assertion in such reports that revitalization of religious traditions was limited to remote border regions and among the least well educated was a fond wish, contradicted by other reports such as a 1986 *Sichuan Daily* report on excessive temple building in Shehong county on the northern edge of the central Sichuan plain, a rich land nowhere near a border.[15] Obviously, the provinces singled out by the Public Security are where its branches are most active. Tibet was not yet the problem it became two years later. But the report also left out other provinces, such as Guangdong, Fujian, and Zhejiang where 'superstitious' religious activity was as widespread as in the provinces mentioned but was tolerated as custom and as an attraction to the interest and investment of overseas Chinese compatriots, or as part of the free-play of market forces.

The 'reactionary sects' to which the Public Security report referred can be very widespread syncretic liturgical traditions which might be organized as societies for moral salvation through rituals and lectures on scriptures, but which are also sources for the annual cycle of festivals in large parts of northern China. One such is the Unity Sect (*Yi Guan Dao*) which also exists in Taiwan where it is described by Jordan and Overmyer as 'an ethical society devoted to the salvation of its members and ultimately of all mankind, in accordance with teachings claiming to incorporate Taoist, Buddhist, and Confucian traditions.'[16] Ethical societies present the world and, therefore, the current regime, as an order in need of moral renewal. They exercise an authority similar to that of unregistered, native Christian networks of communities. Because they are organized as congregations, they constitute an interpretative community defining meanings of the symbols and practices which they share with the festivals and temples of local cults, but which are not identical to the interpretations of official media and education.

The condemned sects can also be new ones led by someone claiming to be the possessor of secret powers in another tradition, identified by Barend ter Haar as 'the demonological paradigm.'[17] In this tradition, the world is seen as chaotic, a battlefield of demonic powers into which someone who can command them by secrets revealed through dream, vision or spiritual possession can bring about a new order. Demon commanders are treated as imposters by the officially sanctioned media, but the imposter also makes and therefore reflects back on the similar promises and impositions of the regime. The imposter is a new, messianic emperor who has entered into a blood covenant with a bestowing divinity to honour him or her and to save the world, in which humans are like hungry demons and are prey to the violent depredations of monster demons. The treasures include emblems and instruments, such as a peach and pennants coloured red and numbering nine, a sword, and a protective amulet which can be reproduced. But to these are added modern weapons. One report in *Democracy and Law* in 1987 describes an emperor claiming to have access to a hidden cache of nuclear weapons. Modern promises include the same consumer goods, such as the gifts of wristwatches and tape recorders from Hong Kong, which were the currency of favours in the early 1980s and sold by hawkers in Guangzhou. They were promised by another emperor whose story was reported at length in *The Chinese Peasant Gazette* on 6 June 1982.[18]

The imposture of a millennial promise of a good life activates an old story but is at the same time an alternative pretence to obtaining the good life which was promised by the Reform state but captured only by those who got rich first, through their already-made networks and social skills. Social skills include the performance of being a trustworthy and capable person, with the strategic knowledge of whom to contact and how to give them face, what gifts to present and which are appropriate to receive. The imperial imposture is the reverse of that performance and an exaggerated echo of entrepreneurial cadres as representatives of a modernising state.[19]

To adjust to the new reality, a 'Notice on further tackling certain problems of religious work' was issued by the Central Committee of the Party and by the State Council in February 1991, adjusting the balance of the 1982 document

from correcting the intolerance of cultural revolution policies towards emphasizing the warnings in the law on religious freedom against the use of religion by
foreign forces and as a cover for illegal activities. Even with this shift, there has
been no turning back the tide of temple- mosque- or church-building. Even in
places where it began after February 1991, suppression is sporadic. In some places
new religious buildings are tolerated, in others the Public Security forces periodically destroy them. For instance, in the village of Kaixian'gong in southern
Jiangsu province, in 1995 I saw that statues of deities had been moved from
homes to small shedlike buildings for the burning of incense and divination. In
1996 Public Security personnel had torn or closed them down.

Unregistered religions are treated as infringements of Article 36 of the Constitution, while activities in both these traditions are treated by public security
offices and the courts as criminal, citing the Criminal Law of 1979.[20] The
Criminal Law of 1997 has now replaced that of 1979. Article 300 in the new
Law's section on crimes disrupting public order now covers 'superstitious sects,
secret societies, and evil religious organizations' and the use of superstition to
sabotage state laws and executive regulations, to cheat others and lethally harm
them, to contrive illicit sexual relations with women, or to defraud money and
property. Article 105 on plots to subvert the political power of the state and
overthrow the socialist system could cover some sectarian activities, while article
294 on organised violence would cover secret societies such as the Triads. But
the most politically volatile are recognized religions in the autonomous regions of
minority nationalities, notably those in China's contested northern and western
borders including Tibet, Xinjiang, Qinghai, and Inner Mongolia.

Religious autonomy as community and ethnicity

In the areas where minority ethnicities are officially recognized and distinguished
from the majority Han nationality and from each other, there is recruitment of
minorities into Party membership to maintain unity. On the other hand, when
such members are found to be practising a religion closely associated and often
inseparable from their nationality, they may be exposed to re-education. As a
Party cadre said to Dru Gladney in Yinchuan, a county within an autonomous
region of the Hui nationality in northwestern China: 'The Hui are allowed to
maintain their ethnic customs that are influenced by Islamic traditions, but
religion and ethnicity are two separate matters and should not be confused'. On
the other hand, recognizing religion as ethnic tradition in the United Front work,
the Party encourages Hui to make the *haji* to Mecca and to establish relations
with Muslim countries. The effect is to create a separate hierarchy of religious
leaders from Party leaders. The Nationality Affairs Commission provides some
funds for the rebuilding of mosques and tolerates the collection of tithes in grain
and money, which amount to nine percent of average domestic income for the
maintenance of mosques and their *ahong* (imams).

To receive training to be imams, young men travel to famed centres of Islam
in China, and thus extend the reach of networks and of a sense of religious

community. Islamic devotees are developing a newly informed sense of religious community which goes beyond officially defined ethnicity.

A distinction between political and religious authority is evident outside the company of religious leaders. 'No matter which political winds blow, I am going to stick to Islam – the Quran doesn't change its mind,' a villager from the Sufi community of Na homestead told Gladney. This separates religion as an area of certainty from the world of changing politics, defining Islam as a retreat rather than as an opposition, in ways similar in spirit to the position of Christian meeting points. Both form local communities and in the process sharply differentiate themselves from non-believers. So the taboo on pork, extended to a taboo on any food cooked with utensils which might have been contaminated by pork, means there can be no reciprocal feasting by Muslims in non-Muslim households. A separate religious community led by imams but bound by social rules such as this isolates itself from neighbours and establishes itself under an authority and with a sense of direction beyond that of the Party.

What might not be resistance on its own, becomes potential resistance when it is categorized as illegal. Attempts at suppression produce resistance. The most extreme results of this escalating conflict are in Tibet and Xinjiang, where suppression has produced movements for greater autonomy verging on independence, in other words demands for a separate state.

In Tibet the policy of separating religion from ethnicity was used with respect to nuns and monks who resisted re-education after they had led demonstrations for Tibetan independence in 1987 and 1988. Their demonstrations had been among the results of the policy of greater religious tolerance allowing monks and nuns back into monasteries, and permitting them to lead such public rituals as the great prayer festival every March at the Jokhang temple in Lhasa. But they were also the result of official rejection of the union of state and religion that is at the heart of that Tibetan Buddhist doctrine in which the Dalai Lama is both a spiritual and political leader. Despite his attempts to negotiate greater autonomy without independence, the Dalai Lama is officially construed as someone seeking to break up the nation, attempting to split Tibetans from China.

The Religious Affairs bureaux and the Buddhist Association, the United Front Work department of the Party and the Nationalities Commission followed the 1982 constitution in distinguishing between those who can be treated as religiously faithful and have shown themselves to be patriotic members of the Tibetan minority nationality and those who are trouble-makers, splitting the unity of China. The dissident monks and nuns were branded troublemakers. The test of the success of their re-education into patriotic religious leaders by work teams sent to monasteries in 1987–89 and again in a campaign for patriotic education which began in 1994 was their willingness to denounce the 'Dalai clique.' Many nuns and monks refused to sign on the grounds that the Dalai Lama is their religious leader. To sign would violate their religious vows which are protected by Article 36 of the Constitution. At the same time they knew they were also refusing to do so on political grounds.

Tibetan (and other) Buddhist disciplines aim for a freeing of self to work for others and for a general release from the profanity of selfish or narrowly nationalist politics. But in the escalating dialogue in Tibet between two interpretations of political and religious unity, customary distinctions of diet, such as the eating of roasted barley called *tsampa*, religious practices such as the throwing of *tsampa*, the burning of juniper incense, and the clockwise circling of holy sites have become rituals of defiance. Retreats to havens of what might have been a transcendent politics of religion have been turned into an increasingly nationalistic intepretation of theocratic rule.[21]

Negotiated public space

More common than either of these instances of religion as resistance are the public spaces of temple and festival, which are the result of negotiation with political authority.

There is a by now famous ecological resort, the tree garden of the Black Dragon Pool (*Heilongtan*) in northern Shaanxi. In 1996 the Chinese Botanical Association held a meeting there and experts from several other countries have visited its rare trees and plants. In fact the land belongs to a temple rebuilt in 1981 (its first foundation was in the Ming dynasty). Temple land had been redistributed in the 1940s land reform. For its 1981 refoundation new land for the temple was donated by nine adjacent villages. The income from this new land goes into a fund which also receives cash donations which are offerings pledged to the Black Dragon god. Petitioners burn incense, announce a problem and draw lots for an explanation and hopes for a solution, then make an offering according to the importance of the problem. The fund is managed by what was officially sanctioned in 1988 as a Cultural Management Institute (*Wenhua Guanli Suo*), whose head is the head of the temple association. The fund finances education, care for the aged, electricity generation, and irrigation, as well as the upkeep of the temple and its largest annual festival. In short it is a welfare fund associated with a temple and not with the village administration and its committee. The head of the temple, the interpreters of lots, and workers in the temple garden are selected by villagers using religious criteria of authority: they must act out of responsibility to future generations, have gained hidden or otherworldly merit (*yin gong*) by altruistic deeds, and maintain good personal relations (*renqing*).[22] Through their own donations and control of the temple and its festival, the drawers of lots and their fellow villagers maintain an inner core of control over the temple, its garden and its annual fair which attract many times their number from all over China. The criteria of their relations to the god who is their authority are criteria which they also apply to the conduct of cadres and officials, in particular to their management of the irrigation system constructed since the Reforms. Theatrical performances for the annual festival and for rain, after the god's statue has been taken in procession around the dry land, always include plays about Bao Cheng the famous judge and sub-chancellor of the Song dynasty known for his unswerving integrity. In sum, temple and festival are officially treated and sanctioned as a cultural and ecological treasures, but within this official sanction villagers maintain a distinct set of criteria to judge the conduct of government. [23]

In some villages the political authority of village administration has been replaced by the institution of a lineage and its ancestral hall, which also funds and runs village welfare. Some village cadres trusted for their loyalty to the lineage-village may also be on the management committee of the lineage, but others are not.²⁴ In other words the ancestral hall and its committee in these instances provide an authority, with local resources, by which local government is judged and to some extent displaced. Such spaces for an alternative authority are open to a local leadership which if not elected has to prove itself by standards of local loyalty and is more accountable to neighbours than is the leadership of the local Party. An alternative authority of this kind emerged in Dachuan in Gansu province, a village of people surnamed Kong with a documented descent from Confucius, where the rebuilding of their Confucius temple and its management became the locus for effective village leadership. The temple and its management committee was a base from which was engineered the removal of the village Party Secretary who had opposed it as 'feudal superstition' and for further manoevres using county government connections to defend the temple and its very success-ful nursery school against other government cadres' threats to close it.²⁵

Religious spaces such as these are testing grounds for cadres who are in the Party but are judged by these local standards in the village elections run by the township government. In other cases the building of local temples or ancestral halls establishes separate senses of locality and authority which have to be accepted as accomplished fact by the local administration, but include none of the local cadres. In Xicun, because of his loyalty to his village and his public work for the hall and the temple since the Reforms, Darkface is the person whom villagers most respect and who can represent them in grievances against high-handed and self-seeking projects by the village Party Secretary and his superiors.

Religious resistance in these instances of temples, festivals and ancestral halls is more than a greater richness beyond the state's interpretative communities. It is the assertion of a determination by local residents to make their own history, in their own interpretation of the stories and heroes who are their deities and whom they treat as present through their own spirit media. In so doing it creates spaces and occasions to voice discontent with acts of government. This is not simply resistance to the regime's policy on religion and superstition. It is the establish-ment of a more general local authority, often capable of mounting local welfare projects and networks in their own defence and advancement. In this respect it constitutes a local community comparable to those of Islamic and Tibetan Buddhist communities, but not associated with ethnicity. Rather it offers its own definition of local Chinese identity and history.

Notes

1 In many Chinese eyes, the first ten years of the People's Republic (1949–58), from the redistribution of land to the formation of cooperatives for agricultural produc-tion in the countryside, were the heroic years of the People's Republic. This first decade of the new state's achievements of equity and security continues to enjoy respect.

2 Research in Xicun was conducted mainly by my colleague Wang Mingming in 1992, 1994 and 1995.

3 The distinction is one of convenience to a state, though it leads to confusion for local cadres. Officially 'superstition' (*mixin*, literally 'errant thoughts') is not protected, because it is a belief overtaken by scientific knowledge. That can often be applied to religious faith. But a religion is officially protected by the Constitution. It is a discipline and an ideology which can be named as one of the known, universal faiths, including Daoism, each of which has a distinct set of texts and institutions which can be registered and collected, whose adherents can be counted, and the training of whose practitioners can be kept under supervision. Unregistered practitioners, syncretic sects, or religious practices which are parts of everyday life, like the cults of local deities or the many different kinds of divination, are lumped together as 'superstition.' But the same practice can as well be called 'custom' and treated as part of local culture.

4 The height of mass mobilization and volatility was the years 1966–68, but the politics of mobilization, prescription, and Mao ritual stretched into the next 8 years until the death of Mao and, in weaker form, for some years thereafter.

5 Robert P. Weller, *Resistance, Chaos and Control in China: Taiping Rebels, Taiwanese Ghosts and Tiananmen* (University of Washington Press: Seattle, 1994) uses this idea of an interpretative community in an instructive approach to cultural resistance in China. I have added the concept of a peformative community. The Cultural Revolution was an attempt at forming a strict interpretative community, but it turned into an indefinite number of performative communities, with factional and sectarian divides.

6 Meeting points not only resisted the attempts at repression by the campaigns of the cultural revolution. Before and since, they have refused the authority of the official hierarchy of the Protestant church in China. Similarly, an underground Catholic movement refuses the authority of the Chinese Patriotic Catholic hierarchy although it retains the authority of the Pope in Rome. The underground churches have been the most lively basis for the spread of Christian communities under the Reform State. See Alan Hunter and Kim-kwong Chan, *Protestantism in Contemporary China* (Cambridge University Press: Cambridge, 1993) and J. Dunn, 'The Protestant Church in China' in Julian F. Pas (ed.), *The Turning of the Tide; Religion in China Today* (Oxford University Press: Hong Kong, Oxford, New York, 1989), pp 243–58, and Richard Madsen, *China's Catholics; Tragedy and Hope in an Emerging Civil Society* (University of California Press: Berkeley, CA, 1998) for detailed information.

7 A policy of transformation and cleansing from within the songs and dances collected by folklorists and troupes of revolutionary performers had been implemented from the time of the Yan'an revolutionary base area in the early 1940s. Some folk theatre was ready made. One such, the Red Lantern Dance, from long before the Communist revolution had a rebellious song to accompany it, containing the lines: 'With one blow I chop to bits the Demons' Gate./Don't pay rent, don't make contributions,/Don't give them hay, don't hand over money'. But, as David Holm *Art and Ideology in Revolutionary China* (Clarendon Press: Oxford, 1991), nicely points out, rebelliousness could not be left as such; it had to be turned into celebration of a successfully complete revolution. What should be done with the 'Demons' gate'? Bad class elements and their children, carrying the labels given them in land reform or assigned to them in campaigns to weed out rightists, had by the mid-1960s become the celebratory opposite. They were the rubble of the Demons' Gate, but were still portrayed as threatening. At the other end of the scale, Holm observes that in the most celebratory anthem The East is Red (*Dongfang Hong*) Mao is a star of salvation (*jiuxing*) which made the imperial connection between earthly emperors and astral deities such as that of the north pole star (1991: 333).

8 Jonathan Unger, 'Cultural Revolution Conflict in the Villages,' *The China Quarterly* 153 (1998), p. 98.

9 Thanks to Lo Hong-guang, personal communication, and to the following for the information contained in this paragraph: Geremie Barme, *Shades of Mao; the Posthumous Cult of the Great Leader* (M. E. Sharpe: Armonk and London, 1996) figures 3, 21, 22, 45 and pp. 211–14; Dachang Cong, *When Heroes Pass Away* (University Press of America: Lanham, NY, 1997). Stephan Lansberger, 'Mao as the Kitchen God: Religious Aspects of the Mao Cult during the Cultural Revolution', *China Information* vol. 11 nos. 2/3 (1996), pp. 196–214.

10 Further details and other cases are to be found in Hunter and Chan (1993, pp. 185–218). Another, but much more Christian partisan source of examples from the 1980s, is Tony Lambert, *The Resurrection of the Chinese Church* (Hodder and Stoughton and Overseas Missionary Fellowship, 1991), pp. 117–42.

11 Luo Zhufeng *et al.*, *Zhongguo Shehui Zhuyi Shiqi de Zongjiao Wenti* (Problems of religion in the period of Chinese socialism) (Shanghai: Shehui KexueYuan, 1987).

12 Dru Gladney, *Muslim Chinese; Ethnic Nationalism in the People's Republic* (Harvard University Press: Cambridge, MA and London, 1991).

13 All the following figures are taken from Chan Kim-kwong 'Bringing Religion into the Socialist Fold' in Lo *et al.* (eds), *China Review 1995* (Chinese University Press: Hong Kong, 1995), pp. 17.1–27.

14 PRC Ministry of Public Security No. 1 Bureau, 'An Introduction to the Reactionary Sects and Societies' (Qunzhong Chubanshe: Beijing, 1985) in Robin Munro (transl. and ed.), 'Syncretic Sects and Secret Societies: Revival in the 1980s,' *Chinese Sociology and Anthropology*, vol. 21 no. 4 (M. E. Sharpe: Armonk, 1989), pp. 49–50.

15 Thomas Hahn, 'New Developments Concerning Buddhist and Taoist Monasteries' in Julian F. Pas (ed.) (1989), pp. 87–89.

16 David Jordan and Daniel Overmyer, *The Flying Phoenix; Aspects of Sectarianism in Taiwan* (Princeton University Press: Princeton, 1986), p. 213.

17 Barend ter Haar, 'China's Inner Demons; The Political Impact of the Demonological Paradigm,' *China Information*, vol. 11 nos. 2/3 (1996), pp. 54–88.

18 The first is translated by Robin Munro (1989), pp. 35–48, the second translated and analysed by Ann Anagnost, 'The Beginning and End of an Emperor: A Counter-Representation of the State,' *Modern China*, vol. 11 no. 2(1985), pp. 147–76.

19 This point is made at greater length and with more examples, by Ann Anagnost 'Politics and Magic in Contemporary China,' *Modern China*, vol. 13 no. 1(1987), pp. 40–62.

20 Article 99 of the 1979 law is on using or organizing 'feudal superstition or superstitious sects and secret societies to carry on counter-revolutionary activities.' Article 165 covers 'sorcerers or witches who use superstition to engage in the activities of rumour-mongering or swindling articles of property.' When exorcisers of demons harm their patients, other crimes of injury are relevant.

21 On Tibet see Robert Barnett, 'Symbols and Protest: The Iconography of Demonstrations in Tibet, 1987–1990' and Ronald Schwartz, 'The Anti-splittist Campaign and Tibetan Political Consciousness' in Robert Barnett and Shirin Akiner (eds), *Resistance and Reform in Tibet* (Hurst & Co: London, 1994). See also Ronald David Schwartz, *Circle of Protest: Political Ritual in the Tibetan Uprising* (Hurst & Co: London, 1994). In other parts of China, Buddhist retreat simply remains a haven from which the world of politics can be refused and scorned. From such reclusive teachers, as from the teachers behind the film and tourist scenes of such better-known centres as the Shaolin monastery famous for martial arts, spread networks of disciples. In these networks a version of reality is sustained which is at variance with the scientific, political and economic realities of the state.

22 This information comes from Lo Hong'guang, 'Quanli yu Quanwei – Heilongtande Fuhaotixi yu Zhengzhe Pinglun (Politics and authority – on the symbolic system and politics of Heilongtan)' in Wang Mingming and Wang Sifu (eds), *Xiangtu Shehuide Zhixu, Gongzheng, yu Quanwei* (Order, Justice and Authority in Rural Chinese Society), (Zhongguo Zhengfadaxue Chubanshe: Beijing, 1998).

23 For another instance of compromise between official and local versions of a temple, first revived in disgust at government neglect of flood control in Sichuan see John Flower and Pamela Leonard, 'Defining Cultural Life in the Chinese Countryside: The Case of the Chuan Zhu Temple' in Eduard Vermeer, Frank Pieke, and Woei Lien Chong (eds), *Cooperative and Collective in China's Rural Development: Between State and Private Interests* (M. F. Sharpe: Armonk and London, 1998). Negotiated compromises between the two kinds of authority, governmental and religious, are not always so well established. Just outside the capital city of Jishou autonomous prefecture of Miao people in western Hunan, a temple has been built by the Minority Affairs Bureau not to sanction but to replace and eliminate a temple to the same gods which had been built by local Chinese-speaking people. The people on the plain where the temple was built are probably of mixed Miao and Han descent, while Miao-speaking people live in the hills of the prefecture. The research on this temple was carried out by Mary Rack, a PhD student in the Department of Anthropology at Edinburgh University. I am most grateful to her for letting me read and use her paper presented to the 1998 conference of the European Association for Chinese Studies. The temples celebrate three military heroes called Celestial Kings who are local guardian gods. The temple had been destroyed during the Cultural Revolution. Local people had rebuilt it and the Public Security bureau destroyed it several times before officials decided to build what they wanted the temple to be. The official replacement was far larger, and built in front of the one local people had built, effectively walling their temple up. A fee was charged for entry into the new temple and collected by employees of the Minority Affairs Bureau who laughed at the people who could afford it but came in to pray rather than to tour and photograph displays of Miao ethnic costume and drum dance. People from the hills stopped coming because the fee had made it something other than a temple for them. Soon a spirit medium was said to have transmitted the dissatisfaction of the celestial kings and their mother with the large official temple and not long after that on a new site another ramshackle temple was being built by local people claiming that the land belonged to their home village. They flouted the regulation that all new building must have permission because the state owns the land. This act of repossession was not just in anger against the imposition of the Minority Affairs temple and to being slotted into the government's version of ethnicity. It was also a reaction to the building of a new road, a rice spirits factory, and a university campus on purchased village land as the prefectural city expanded.

24 See Ku Hok-bun, *Defining Zeren: Cultural Politics in a Chinese Village*, University of London, unpublished PhD dissertation, 1999; and Stephan Feuchtwang, 'What is a Village?' in Vermeer *et al.* (eds) (1998), p. 68. Both of these instances are from villages with remunerative overseas Chinese connections.

25 Jing Jun, *The Temple of Memories: History, Power, and Morality in a Chinese Village* (Stanford University Press: Stanford, 1996), pp. 89 and 96 and a personal communication, for which I am most grateful.

9 Ethnic resistance with socialist characteristics

Uradyn E. Bulag

Drawing on examples from Inner Mongolia, this chapter argues that ethnic resistance in socialist China can hardly be understood as a Manichean struggle against the Chinese state or Communism. Better insight is gained by examining such behavior in relation to the state's construction of *minzu* (nationality), a discursive category that enables both resistance and complicity on the part of minorities. The history of socialist China has been punctuated by ethnic conflict over land appropriation, linguistic deprivation, and exploitation of economic resources. But Mongol resistance has been predicated on the socialist state's moral hegemony; it has not questioned the state's legitimacy in ruling the Mongols, only its methods of rule. The chapter pays particular attention to internal processes among the Mongols and their implications for resistance in the post-Mao market economy. Under market competition, a *minzu* is no longer a society in its own right, but a location within the political economy of a nation-state. Ethnic resistance in the post-Mao period has seen a breaking of the *minzu* boundary by both Han and minorities.

Introduction

Ethnic unrest is among the myriad social problems confronting China in the era of reform. In recent years, Chinese leaders have warned of ethnonationalist insurgencies in Tibet, Xinjiang and Inner Mongolia. While launching ambitious affirmative action programs, they have not hesitated to deploy military and security forces to suppress nationality resistance and unrest. The high international profile of the exiled Dalai Lama has propelled ethnic issues, including questions of national self-determination, to the world stage, puncturing official Chinese claims of harmonious unity, and elevating the question of Tibet to a central place in US–China relations and global human rights discourse.

What has been the Chinese record overall in nationality affairs, and particularly in the 1980s and 1990s accompanying the reform agenda? How do we understand the ethnic resistance and the state repression that characterize China's volatile ethnopolitics? Scholars have noted profound contradictions in the Marxist–Leninist theory of nationalities, which holds that nationalities are only one of the stages in human social development. The Chinese Communist government has added this theory to the age-long Chinese mistrust and bias towards non-Han as barbarians. The trajectory of Chinese nationality policies is reflected in discrimination against minorities, the weakening of minority autonomous institutions in the 1950s, the attack on minority cultures and autonomy during the Cultural Revolution in the 1960s, and finally the modernization agenda featuring the centralizing and assimilating power of education and propaganda systems since the 1980s. This approach, reinforced by the fact that minority populations are scattered over vast areas and together constitute less than 10 percent of the population, has led many observers to conclude that assimilation and the loss of cultural integrity were inevitable. In the 1980s and 1990s, in light of the disintegration of the Soviet Union and Yugoslavia along ethnic lines, ethnic minorities have been pinpointed by some analysts as being comparable in importance to issues of Greater China, including the global Chinese diaspora, in shaping China's future.

There is however a profound theoretical, let alone practical, problem with the dominant approach in the West that pits ethnonationalism against the communist party-state. Such an approach tends to frame ethnic consciousness and goals in Manichean categories of power and resistance. It invariably portrays ethnic consciousness and identity as sovereign, never colonized by power. Ethnic identity is invested with primordialism, *für sich*, even if circumstances of power require temporary acceptance of subordination. This is the source of much of the celebration of ethnic resistance against Communism. I suggest that such a perspective is deeply flawed, above all because it essentializes ethnicity as the exclusive definition of identity, and because it isolates ethnicity from the complex and fluid socio-economic and political contexts of ethnic relations, including intraethnic divisions and diverse aspirations of minority peoples.

Anthropologists and sociologists have recently highlighted the flexibility of ethnic identities and boundaries. Instead of positing an ineluctable conflict with the state's communist or modernist agenda, this perspective is attentive to the fact that the Chinese state has classified numerous subject groups, often in hierarchical order, with different spatial and temporal relationships to the state's agenda for social transformation. Not only has the Chinese state invented many ethnic groups, including the supreme category 'Han' used to define the hegemonic position of the majority, but all nationalities, and their subcategories such as women, workers, villagers and intellectuals, actively bargain with the state to secure their own advantage. These analysts point to the multiplication of ethnic groups from five in the Republican period (Han, Manchu, Mongol, Tibetan and Muslim) to a number that has fluctuated between fifty-four and fifty-six during the Socialist period. They call attention to the fact that the officially registered minority populations have increased dramatically in the post-Mao era, thanks to affirmative action policies that have given certain material advantages to minorities, such as exemption from the policy of limiting each household to one child, greater political representation in their own titular autonomous units, and privileged access to higher education and to official positions.

The role of the state in inventing and classifying ethnic minorities and the latter's response to the state have led Dru Gladney, the foremost proponent of this new perspective, to argue for a dialogical interpretation of ethnicity in China. He notes that established ethnic groups and the state are engaged in ongoing processes of social and political negotiation mediated on the basis of relations of power and hierarchy. Ethnic resistance in this view is thus a product of the state's own making, yet one that it cannot completely control: 'the role of the state must not be over-privileged. Even the most totalitarian of regimes has its limits. Ethnicity has a power and resilience of its own that acts in dialectical fashion with the state apparatus'.[1]

Although not all non-Chinese peoples were invented by the Chinese, the fact that they now exist as a category of ethnic minority *vis-à-vis* the state and the majority Han Chinese testifies to the fact that they no longer live in a closed community. Ethnicity in China, as it is everywhere in the twentieth century world, is thus relational in the multiple senses that its boundaries and social position are in constant flux and its perceived sovereignty is an invention by the state. Yet, this invented sovereignty may take on a life of its own, even challenging the state on its own ground. This chapter takes inspiration from Gladney's theory to examine contradictory aspects of social production of Mongolian identity in contemporary China. A focus on both the 'contradictions' of socialism in its approach to minorities and the peculiarities of 'socialism with Chinese characteristics,' will enable us to capture fluctuating political and ideological dynamics of ethnic 'resistance' and complicity. In this paper, I approach this issue historically by alternating ethnography with theoretical analysis.

A brief picture of ethnicity in China

China is a multinational state whose minority nationalities constitute 8 percent of the population and occupy approximately 60 percent of the national territory, including its most sensitive border areas. The classification of fifty-five minorities indicates, however, that ethnic minorities are fragmented and that each is numerically insignificant *vis-à-vis* the one billion strong majority 'Han Chinese': the largest minority, the Zhuang, number over 15 million, while the smallest number only several thousand. There is no uniform pattern of minorities, as each has its distinct history, culture, language, and territorial association. Nor are ethnic minorities unified by any single religion. Tibetans and Mongols, for example, are Buddhist, but they are geographically separated from one another, despite strong cultural affinity. China's Muslims are widely scattered throughout large areas of the nation. It is possible to suggest, nonetheless, that most of the minorities in southwest China are 'enclosed groups' with little irredentist aspiration, whereas Mongols, Tibetans, Uyghurs, and Koreans are groups with external orientations: toward Mongolia, the West, Central Asian republics, and Korea, respectively.[2] We might say, moreover, that many Muslims have some form of 'external orientation' toward other Islamic nations and the Holy Land in the Middle East. The nationalities differ, moreover, in their assimilation or distance from the dominant economic and cultural premises of the Han.

Despite this seemingly 'hopeless' situation of minority fragmentation, over much of its long imperial history China was ruled by non-Han peoples, such as the Mongols and Manchus. Not until early in the twentieth century was China reborn as a nation-state with 'Han', a term invented explicitly to isolate the ruling Manchus and their Mongol allies, claiming to be the guardian nationality while incorporating non-Han minorities in an ethnic hierarchy based on the state's new enumerative technology. China's march to Han nationalism at the expense of minorities might have been more devastating had it not been both for external circumstances and the Communist revolution. After almost a century of post-Empire trauma, characterized by ethnic rebellions, revolutions and independence movements, in 1949 China proclaimed itself a people's republic, a multinational state, promising autonomy for ethnic minorities.

China's ethnic autonomy system is as much a projection of the Chinese Communist Party's (CCP) ideological commitment to equality as it is a concession to Mongol and other non-Han demands to recognize difference and autonomy. The latter goals emerged as the product of strategic alliances with the CCP in defeating the Chinese Nationalist Party, which espoused and implemented a blatantly racist agenda directed toward creating a pure Han nation-state. Of course not *all* nationalities played such a role in determining the outcomes of civil war leading to the proclamation of the People's Republic; among those who did, there was often deep division across Communist–Nationalist lines, and in some instances loyalties were also owed to the Japanese.

One group that made important contributions to the Communist victory and managed to bargain for some form of 'autonomy' as a result was the Mongols in Inner Mongolia. The critical role played by native Mongol communists in the consolidation of CCP power, and their strategic geographical location on the border of the Mongolian People's Republic and the Soviet Union, as well as their ethnic affinity with the independent Mongolian People's Republic, were central to this outcome. A dramatic change in China's political ethnoscape was first instituted in relation to Mongols in May 1947, a model that was subsequently applied to other non-Han peoples in the form of establishment of autonomous territorial institutions at the provincial level in Tibet, Xinjiang, Guangxi, and Ningxia, and lower levels within Chinese provinces. However, socialist China was far from proving to be an ethnic safe haven. A nationality (*minzu*)-building project was soon launched that resulted in mixed fortunes for ethnic minorities.

Grassland identity as resistance symbol for Mongols?

Minzu is part and parcel of Chinese nation-state building, which is marked by what Michel Foucault has called governmentality – the application of techniques of surveillance and control to a whole range of institutions of a political economy and moral community. China's *minzu* building project can be understood as a boundary-producing project predicated on Stalin's four criteria defining nationality: common territory, common economy, common language, and common psychological make-up (Stalin's lexicon for culture). In determining the ethnicity of a group, one criterion may play a larger role than another, depending on the group's cultural proximity to the Chinese. The mode of production, including the nature of economic enterprise and class structure, pivotal in the Marxist binary thesis of base and superstructure, is deemed of primary import- ance in demarcating Mongols from Han. Pastoralism, an economic practice adapted to the ecology of the grasslands and dating back to antiquity, became the ultimate cultural symbol defining the core of Mongol identity. The *minzu* building project is simultaneously a purifying process, designed to make ethnic traits congruent with the qualities said to define Mongolness. In this process, other economic activities, such as agriculture, although practiced by a large proportion of the Mongol population, including pastoralists, came to be associated with memories of Chinese colonization and thus were seen by Mongols as alien to Mongolness.

For three and a half centuries pastoralism was preserved and agriculture purged among Mongols in order to maintain Mongol military prowess that could be used in the service of the Manchu rule of China. Mongols, for all their military prowess, were thus unprepared for the avalanche of Chinese immigrants and agricultural expansion as well as cultural assimilation as a result of the Qing dynasty's New Policy in 1902. Subsequent Chinese agricultural and military colonization of Inner Mongolia brought increasing clashes with Mongol herders who lost pastureland. Defending pasture against Han agricultural colonization then became a battle cry that was the driving force behind Inner Mongolian nationalism and communism. Numerous Mongol uprisings occurred between 1910 and the 1940s, including clashes with Mongol nobles for selling land, as well as resistance against Chinese land grabbing.

In light of this history, agricultural expansion was an extremely sensitive issue in Inner Mongolia, and it continued to be so after the founding of the Inner Mongolian Autonomous Region in 1947. In 1958, in a major turn of policy towards ethnic minorities, the Chinese state began a massive colonization program that turned a large part of Mongol pasture into military farms along the northern borders with the Mongolian People's Republic and the Soviet Union. This was a blatant offense to the sensibilities of the Inner Mongolian army, led primarily by Mongol commanders who had supported the communist-led fight against the Japanese and the Nationalist Party and who were proud of their contribution to the founding of the People's Republic of China. Military farming and civilian agricultural expansion were informed by Chinese disdain toward pastoralism, a perspective which denigrates pasture as wild land (*huangdi*) as well as by the socialist evolutionary hierarchy, which conveniently placed agriculture above pastoralism. Mongol herders were enjoined to abandon pastoral production in favor of agriculture under the slogan 'Herders should not eat grain with a guilty conscience' (*mumin bu chi kuixin liang*). In the frenzy of the leap, the Chinese exercised domination over Mongols, attacking pastoralism, and the associated Mongol way of life, continuing a process of large-scale Chinese migration to the Mongol homeland.

The famine disaster of the Great Leap Forward and the Chinese admission of mistakes provided the first opportunity for Mongols to negotiate a settlement of the military farms directly with Beijing. By 1962, most of the military farms were returned to pasture. Chinese immigration was also temporarily halted. This move earned Ulanhu, the Mongol leader of Inner Mongolia (1947–66), huge popularity among Mongol herders, and his feat remains legendary today when opening grassland for agricultural use can no longer be resisted effectively. The success of this resistance in the early 1960s was predicated on the counter-critique developed by Mongols who argued that expansive military farming at the expense of grassland violated the Party's nationality policy and showed disrespect for nationality autonomy.

It is possible that interethnic confrontation between agriculture and pastoral economy in Inner Mongolia only strengthened ethnic polarization between these two modes of production in socialist China. The Mongol emotional tie linked to pastoralism may be described, following Fujitani, as a Mongolian 'mnemonic site', referring to a 'material vehicle of meaning that helped construct a memory . . . or that served as a symbolic marker.'[3] Similarly agriculture is a 'mnemonic site' of the Chinese. Each side struggles to invest positive meaning to its side, and negative meaning to the opposing side.

We should be cautious not to invest Mongol ethnic resistance with too much romanticism. The binary ethnic divide between agriculture and pastoralism ultimately shaped a socialist Mongol identity pivoting on the image of the herder, and yet as Almaz Khan has shown, this hegemonic herder symbolism marginalizes the majority of eastern Mongols who have long been farmers.[4] Since agriculture is excluded from the cultural repertoire used to construct a socialist Mongol nationality in China's Inner Mongolia, Mongol farmers become an unnamable category.

Nor were there other possibilities for forging Mongol identity, in contrast, for example, with Tibetans. Categories such as monks and aristocrats had long been purged from the newly imagined Mongol community, having been held responsible for collusion with Han colonizers or incompatible with socialism. Buddhism was denounced by Mongol communists not only for supporting the Manchus and the Chinese Nationalists against Mongol interests, but also for reducing the Mongol population as a result of the imposition of celibacy on the clergy, thereby weakening Mongol prowess. This combination of exogenous ideological factors and endogenous nationalist sentiment had especially devastating consequences for Buddhism. This may explain why the Mongols, who were almost as devout Buddhists as Tibetans before 1947, and indeed were responsible for originally setting up the Dalai Lama and Panchen Lama institutions, have largely abandoned Buddhism. Tibetans view Buddhism as the core of their identity and culture, turning it into a symbol of resistance and empowerment, while Mongols are deeply ambivalent about it.

Attempts were made in the 1950s to create different modernist categories, such as the industrial working class, but they ultimately failed not only because the numerically small number of workers was soon engulfed by the sheer numerical supremacy of the Han migrant population, but above all because industry came to be appropriated by the Han, in both practice and image. It was not modernization *per se* that was responsible for this outcome but its concurrent sinicization that has exacted a heavy toll on Mongols. Urbanization and modernization have led to loss of Mongol language and culture, as urbanity is defined as Chinese because of the overwhelming Chinese predominance in the cities. For example, over 90 percent of the residents of the capital, Huhhot, are Han. The image of a Mongolian industrial working class never developed. In the mythology of the Mongol *minzu*, urban intellectuals and cadres, who are themselves products of the *minzu* project, devote their lives to serving the Mongol people – herders (*malchid*).

Herders, grassland, and livestock thus became the primary markers of Mongol ethnicity during the socialist period. The grasslands now represent more than a homeland; they stand for pure 'nature' (*baigal*), filled with fresh air and familiar smells, herds, yurts, and mobility. This makes for the strongest possible contrast to Chinese culture, which is sedentary and agricultural with the predominance of grain, pig farming, commercial guile, and dirt. The Mongol herder symbol is strategically boundary setting, and all its attributes can be summed up in a single factor: difference from the Chinese. It is an essentialist symbol, naturalized, ahistoricized, and sanitized.

This grassland identity, whatever its romantic nationalist overtones, offers a paucity of other attributes that modern Mongols individually aspire to, i.e., productivity, progress, social mobility, creativity, technological skills, and excitement. Nevertheless, and precisely because of this, upwardly mobile elements of the Mongol population continue to move to the cities, and few aspire to return 'home,' that is to the grasslands.

There is an extreme disjuncture of increasing urbanization and sinicization together with the increasing romanticization of the pastoral. Few bridges are available to connect the two, which remain separated by the state's household registration system (*hukou*). This only intensifies the rhetoric of Mongol 'intellectuals' claiming to defend their 'Mongol' identity in the grasslands. They sing songs, drink, and cry, celebrating their pastoral identity. They also dream and yearn for power, re-imagining an 'underground' Mongol identity, based on military prowess and the moral qualities of the fighter symbolized by Chinggis Khan, the world conqueror.

In short, the *minzu*-building project necessarily delineates, strengthens and distorts ethnic consciousness. It also defines what constitutes a member of a nationality, frequently blithely disregarding contemporary social reality and aspirations that may be independent of, or at odds with, stereotypical minzu categories. A *minzu* is no longer a 'society' in its own right, but a location or positioning within the political economy of a nation-state.

Ethnic resistance with socialist characteristics

Resistance, especially ethnic resistance in China, therefore must not be romanticized in terms of reflexive categories of class conflict, colonialism, national liberation and revolution. Rather, searching to understand what 'creates' ethnic resistance, we must examine the social and political conditions that *impel* ethnic groups to 'resist' certain policies or discriminatory behavior. According to John Comaroff, ethnic consciousness is generated not by cultural symbols or primordial loyalties but by the relationship to the state and the position of ethnic groups as a result of 'asymmetric incorporation of structurally dissimilar groupings into a single political economy.'[5]

Chinese socialism has simultaneously fostered ethnic consciousness and replicated and reinforced patterns of ethnic discrimination. The Chinese revolutionary notion of 'liberation' (*jiefang*) has been applied to minorities, 'recognizing' their exploited and colonized status and encouraging them to transcend it. Yet the Party's own developmental discourse creates hierarchies both of class and ethnicity through an official social evolutionist schema that tortuously justifies the superiority and inferiority of different groups. In China, Han are anointed as the nationality of destiny, equated with the Chinese Nation (*zhonghua minzu*), while all minorities are classified as being located at various lower stages and exhorted to 'catch up' with the Han precisely by becoming Han themselves, in values, social customs, class structures, and developmental praxis. And these differences, both real and imagined, *ipso facto* make the non-Han suspect. These contradictory features of Chinese socialism have to be understood in historical context.

Central to the Chinese Communist ideology is the notion of equality, which is also the core of the enlightenment project globally. But enlightenment, a Chinese modernist commitment since the May Fourth Movement of 1919, has constantly been sidelined by Chinese nationalism. China's modern experience of humiliation in the era of imperialism shaped national ambitions to pursue wealth, power, and autonomy or independence. Communism in China thus became a means to empower China in the world community.

The slogan 'Only socialism can save China' is perhaps the most condensed expression of Chinese determination to give priority to national survival and to making China equal to any western power. Laden with notions of power and hierarchy, China's communism/socialism naturalizes the rhetoric of nationalism, and sees the minority demand for equality with the Han not in terms of enlightenment goals of equality, but in terms of harm or benefit for China's quest for equality with the West.

To simplify, this combination of Communism and Nationalism was responsible for putting the Dalai Lama and tens of thousands of Tibetans to flight in 1959, for the exodus of over 60,000 Kazaks to the Soviet Union in 1962, and for genocidal attacks against Mongols during the Cultural Revolution. The result in each instance was abandonment of socialism's lofty ideals of enlightenment and equality in favor of resort to the murderous battle cry of patriotism, chauvinism, and racism.

The demise of nationalities was not so simple, of course, nor was it limited to the above notable failures. The ostentatiously generous policies of permitting and preserving minority languages and cultural forms were geared to expressing Chinese 'socialist' ideas – a socialist civilizing project captured by the arcane maxim: 'national in form, but socialist in content.' It is precisely this exaltation of *minzu* as a classificatory unit, and, simultaneously the state's ultimate desire to eliminate it through assimilation, that provides the central paradox of China's 'nationality policy'.

It should be noted that communist ideology mystified and justified Chinese national ambition with regard to ethnic minorities. To be sure, the Communists never justified their violence against ethnic minorities without the holy claim to bring them enlightenment and equality. Theirs was a 'civilizing mission', one that would enhance equality and eliminate serfdom or slavery *for* minority nationalities. They mobilized arbitrarily classified oppressed elements of the nationality for self-liberation, and they oversaw the violent overthrow of one class by another, thereby promoting the 'friendship' of the 'proletariats' of the Han and the minorities.

What is problematic is not the analysis directed toward elimination of inequality *within* the minorities, but the new 'inequality' established *between* Han and minority as a consequence of the 'civilizing mission'. This is the irony of the Chinese discourse and practice of equality. Although all proletarianized nationalities were proclaimed to be equal politically, minority cultural customs, religious practices, and modes of production were deemed not just different and hence incompatible with Chinese visions of a socialist society, but inferior, hence requiring active Chinese 'elder brotherly' help. Or worse, they were seen as 'false consciousness', mystifying the subordination of some groups within the minority population by others, hence requiring their destruction. It was precisely this discrepancy between declared *de jure* equality and *de facto* inequality that the minorities could draw strength from in order to bargain with the Chinese party–nation-state and resist many Chinese practices.

Resistance does not exist in a vacuum, nor does it exist in pure opposition; it emerges within the discursive space shared by both sides. Minority resistance in China derives from and is shaped by the meta-narrative of the Chinese state: realization of equality by eliminating exploitation and achieving modernization, science, and national unity through ethnic harmony. Since these constituents of the meta-narrative are not always mutually compatible, and the end result often deviates from the lofty ideal, they provide fertile ground for ethnic resentment at being 'betrayed'. For their part, the theoretical and practical poverty of the communist leadership in handling minority resistance compels the majoritarian state and its convinced majority Han subjects to label minorities as (local) nationalists. As local nationalists, minorities are marginalized and their alleged subversions need to be smashed ruthlessly. Below I illustrate both ethnic resistance and complicity with socialist characteristics, drawing on linguistic examples from Inner Mongolia.

Linguistic resistance within Marxist discourse

Language is another important criterion for defining a *minzu*. In the Chinese *minzu*-building project, the Chinese state even went so far as to invent scripts for some minorities that had no written language. But Stevan Harrell detects a serious problem associated with such an equality project – Han chauvinism and the dominance of the Chinese political economy have consistently sabotaged the *minzu* project.[6]

Chinese had no need to invent the Mongol written language, which has long existed, but after 1949 language was invested with special saliency. Previously Mongol nationalists regarded not language, but territory, as the central issue. Following the 1947 founding of the Inner Mongolia Autonomous Government, in 1952 the seat of government moved to Huhhot, originally a monastic town divided between Manchu (army), Han (merchants), and Mongol (monks and pilgrims) quarters, that quickly became overwhelmingly Han with the migration of tens of thousand of workers and officials from north China. Very soon, the children of Mongol cadres and intellectuals lost their language because of the combination of peer pressure from Han children and classroom instruction in Chinese rather than Mongol. The rapid loss of language stirred strong resentment among Mongol officials and intellectuals who voiced their criticism in the Hundred Flowers Movement in 1957. If, in old China, Mongols had lost their language because of the oppression of Great Han Chauvinists, they asked, what could account for the loss of Mongol language in the New China in which ethnic oppression was supposed to have been eliminated and all nationalities were equal? It was agreed that Mongol language use had to be strengthened. However, one month later, this officially sanctioned criticism was targeted as a veiled attack on the Party and the Chinese Nation. Language became an issue precisely because it was one of the defining principles of Mongol nationality. Coupled with this was the fact that Mongolian was defined as the first language of the Inner Mongolia Autonomous Region, and it was decreed as early as 1947 that official documents must be prepared in Mongolian and Chinese. The failure to maintain the dual language policy after 1949 was resented by Mongols, not only because it inconvenienced many Mongol cadres and intellectuals, but also because the Mongol language was a powerful symbol of their status and identity. To be deprived of that status had profound political implications: it was a sign of the assimilation of the Mongols, one which could warrant rescinding of Mongolian autonomy, the very basis of their status, authority, and position. Ethnic autonomy was, after all, based on difference.

Mongol language, one of the symbols of Mongol political equality, from the founding of the People's Republic was challenged in the state's new discourse. Chinese (Mandarin) was privileged, becoming the direct medium not only for the transmission of Mao's doctrine but in virtually all government activities from administration to education to the military, even in the Inner Mongolia Autonomous Region. This association of political correctness and linguistic chauvinism posed a stark choice to Mongols: to remain politically and scientifically 'backward' (thereby inevitably subjecting themselves to the Han civilizing mission), or to 'catch up', in the first instance by incorporating key loan words from Chinese but ultimately losing the Mongol language in favor of Chinese. While a few Chinese-leaning Mongol linguists advocated taking in not only borrowed words from Chinese, but even sounds and grammatical components, most Mongol officials resisted this by forming a committee to borrow words from Cyrillic Mongolian used in the Mongolian People's Republic. They rejected the idea that only Chinese was an appropriate source of loan words. Their unique link to the Mongolian People's Republic, where a Communist government was established in 1921, the very year that the Chinese Communist Party was founded, provided a proud alternative. Mongols then not only resisted in terms of cultural difference, but also from an ideological and political highground.

Mongol linguistic resistance was poignantly demonstrated in 1957 by Ulanhu, the leader of Inner Mongolia, who deliberately spoke Mongolian on the tenth anniversary of the founding of the Inner Mongolia Autonomous region. Many Mongols were moved to tears, and could not forget it even after his death in 1988. Mongols interpreted his Mongol speech as defiance against increasing Maoist and Han chauvinist onslaught against Mongol culture. It was sensational because Ulanhu could not speak Mongolian, as he belonged to the Tumed Mongol group which had lost Mongolian language a century ago. He read his speech from a text written in Cyrillic that was translated from his original Chinese (he spoke Russian fluently). The subsequent Chinese assault on the Mongolian language, charging that demands for its use were manifestations of a divisive nationalism, generated defiance.

On the occasion of the fifteenth anniversary of the founding of the Inner Mongolian Autonomous Region in 1962, a new local regulation was passed making Mongolian the official language of Inner Mongolia. That regulation required that Han learn Mongolian, too. Prior to the Cultural Revolution, Ulanhu developed his own 'theory' to justify this language policy. Rejecting the view that the Mongol language was backward and thus useless, he maintained not only that Mongols should continue to write and speak Mongolian, but that Chinese, especially Chinese cadres working in Inner Mongolia or among Mongols, should also learn and use it. Mongols, he argued, were the masses (*qunzhong*), thus they were a class that cadres should serve. 'I want to ask, are the Han cadres working in Inner Mongolia to serve the Han or the Mongols? I say you should serve the Mongols, but if you can't speak the language, what can you do if you can't communicate feelings?'[7] So, it was essential that Han cadres show their sincerity, differentiating themselves from earlier Chinese Nationalist Party chauvinists, exhorted Ulanhu. He himself had begun learning Mongolian, and signed his name in Mongolian.

This delicate ideological balance which Mongols desperately sought to maintain was crushed in 1966. The Cultural Revolution provided a perfect pretext for the Chinese, long frustrated at the persistent criticism by and resistance of the Mongols, to crack down on the entire Mongol people. Over 16,222 people were killed by official Chinese count and hundreds of thousands more were tortured in perhaps the bloodiest episode of the Cultural Revolution. Along with this physical onslaught, Chinese was vigorously promoted as the 'unified motherland language', and Mongolian was prohibited in many areas.

Such a language change policy was counter-attacked by Mongols after the Cultural Revolution as a policy of assimilation that denied Mongol autonomy. Mongols used Marxist–Leninist theory to combat the blatantly national-chauvinist practices disguised as Marxism by quoting the classics, insisting that, according to Stalin, 'the policy of assimilation is unreservedly excluded from the arsenal of Marxism–Leninism, as an anti-popular and counter-revolutionary policy, a fatal policy.'[8]

Western scholars have noted that after the Cultural Revolution, the Chinese state began to encourage minorities to revive their culture. I argue that this change of policy was not a voluntary gift on the part of the party-state, but a response in part to minority efforts. Post-Mao minority 'resistance' is not simply a 'hidden transcript', but in many instances it directly challenges the Han to make policy and practice commensurate and to make amends for the terrible injustices suffered by minority nationalities during the Cultural Revolution.

As a result of the traumatic experience of the Cultural Revolution, Mongols, perhaps more than any other ethnic minority, sought to control the classificatory power of the state. Their Communist experience and the relatively high position of leading Mongols in the regional and central government and party organs, put them in a position to translate certain Inner Mongolian practices prior to the Cultural Revolution into national laws, providing a foundation for improved ethnic relations respectful of minority rights. It prepared the ground for a new phase of ethnic cultural revival that many scholars have mistakenly attributed to enlightened Chinese national policy alone. The personal involvement of Ulanhu, then China's Vice-president, in drafting China's Regional Autonomy Law for Minority Nationalities (passed on 1 October, 1984), boosted efforts toward cultural revival, greater political representation, and affirmative action for minorities throughout China. Although the Law was far from satisfactory in granting genuine autonomy to minorities, it did lay the ground for a dramatic popular movement from below and above to revive Mongol language teaching and to establish schools and universities that offer courses in Mongolian, undertakings that have been linked to the exercise of rights integral to regional nationality autonomy. The same is also true for other regions of China. It is apt to suggest that the Law provided a discursive space that worked to the advantages of both the state and minorities. To a large extent, ethnic minorities have collectively spearheaded the demand for 'rights' from the state, a notion that was nevertheless remarkably absent in other spheres. However, this 'golden' time for minority cultural revival proved to be short-lived. China's rapid economic development and political turmoil quickly sabotaged this effort.

The competition for indigeneity: redefining state–minority relations

The Tiananmen Incident of 1989 had repercussions not only for political liberalization, but also for delicate ethnic relations. In the wake of this political failure, the Party turned to the combination of brute force and promotion of economic growth in an effort to retain its political monopoly. This strategy was facilitated by the economic and political disintegration of the former Soviet Union and eastern Europe, suggesting by comparison the far greater achievements of the Chinese state. Post-1989 'National Situation Education' (*guoqing jiaoyu*) launched by the Party unambiguously held that China was not ready for political change and raised the slogan: 'Only China can save socialism!' Since 1992, however, this slogan has been changed to 'Only economic development can save socialism', or in Deng Xiaoping's words '*fazhan caishi ying daoli*' (Only development can win an argument).

Of particular importance here is the structural damage to the minority regions as a result of the national and international implications of the Tiananmen Incident and the drastic change of China's developmental course that was designed to 'win an argument'. The post-Tiananmen period saw minorities increasingly marginalized even in their own homelands. China's new regional economic development, particularly following Deng Xiaoping's agenda-setting 1992 trip to Shenzhen, initiated processes that linked the minority regions with the coastal areas in a new relationship that is best described as internal colonialism. This reversed earlier trends that substantiated economic and political claims that the minority regions were 'autonomous' in their own right, and state claims that it was attempting to create a 'socialist' *minzu*. Heavy industrial complexes including steel and nuclear industries, were built in Inner Mongolia and other remote inland regions before 1966, justified by the claim that these industries were to help develop both national and local industry, and that they would simultaneously elevate minority regions as integral and equal parts of China. However, as suggested, this ostensibly egalitarian pro-*minzu* state project was subverted by Han chauvinism. Mongol efforts to create a large and technically advanced Mongol working class utterly failed. In post-1992 China, minority regions became precious areas whose primary purpose is to serve the dynamic coastal regions and the Chinese nation as natural resource bases. The redefinition of the minority regions as natural resource bases, however, has the potential to delegitimize the state's entire autonomous *minzu* project.

Along with this development, minorities began to be seen ever more negatively. They have been redefined in terms of their ability to exploit natural resources in the service of accelerating market forces. And that alone determines their 'nationality quality' (*minzu suzhi*). Against this trend, Fei Xiaotong, China's foremost anthropologist, lamented the deeply rooted Chinese disdain for 'wilderness' and the instinct to turn pasture into farmland. He enjoined them to change their mentality:

> The Han nationality that thrived on the advantage of agriculture is now challenged to change its economic composition. The compact communities in which they live are suitable for agriculture, but are short of resources needed for industry. But the areas inhabited by minority nationalities, previously unattractive to the Han, are precisely where industrial resources are abundant. Meanwhile, industrial development requires science and

technology and cultural knowledge, but in this respect the levels of minority nationalities are below those of the Han. It would be extremely difficult for minority nationalities to use their *local* resources to develop *local* industry.[9]

Fei's seeming criticism of discrimination against minorities turns out to be a call to replace the minorities by the Han to develop 'local industry' in minority regions. Fei in effect promoted a predatory policy at the expense of minority nationalities in the name of meritocracy. But apparently even the frontier Han prove no match for the coastal developers equipped with capital and blessed with the State's favorable policies. This inequality seems to have affected the material wellbeing of the local Han, who now actively call for more state investment and policy change, allowing them direct access to domestic and international markets. They would sometimes encourage limited minority protest to add to their bargaining strength with the Center. In Inner Mongolia, the subdued Mongols are often jokingly rebuked by the local Han for losing Chinggis Khan's fighting spirit and admonished to learn from the Tibetans. It is pointed out that the gush of capital flow to Tibet in recent years was a response to the Tibetan unrest.

Curiously, one of the ways of mitigating the inequality between the coastal Han and the frontier Han has been to promote and manage tourism in the latter's 'homeland' – minority areas. Ethnic tourism has become a bonanza in many areas of China, bringing in greater revenues than the new rural industries. Although some minority élite also view tourism as a channel to promote their identity and visibility in and out of China, they often fall prey to exploitation of Chinese managers and tourist voyeurism, resulting in a profound cultural change.

The party-state has begun a process to systematically remove the foundations of minority autonomy by assertions of native status for Han everywhere, including in minority autonomous regions. Ever since the removal of Ulanhu from Inner Mongolia in 1966 at the start of the Cultural Revolution, the Party Secretary, the highest authority of Inner Mongolia, has been Han, a pattern found in all autonomous regions. Since 1994, in Inner Mongolia the top positions of both the People's Congress and the Party have been held by Han, making an open mockery of claims of 'ethnic autonomy'. A new attempt to allay Mongol concerns resulted in a 1994 appointment to the post of party secretary of a Han from Shandong province with familial ties in Inner Mongolia, presenting him as a local 'Inner Mongolian' (*Neimeng ren*), a new identity that is based more on territorial location than ethnicity.

The result was an acrimonious political drama in Inner Mongolia in 1993–94 when Han began to claim that they are also indigenous in the autonomous regions, indeed, perhaps more indigenous than the Mongols. A Han party leader delivered a lecture at the Inner Mongolia Party School asserting that Han rather than Mongols are indigenous to the region. His assertion of a 5,000-year Chinese history and extensive documentary sources and archaeological science have been deployed to prove beyond a doubt that Mongols settled in Inner Mongolia only 700 or 800 years ago, when they began to expand from their Siberian 'homeland', whereas the Han settled there before the Han dynasty 2,000 years ago. His lecture handouts were quickly retracted in the face of strong protest by Mongol leaders.

This is not an isolated case peculiar to Inner Mongolia, but a concerted effort by local Han party leaders and academicians. He Jihong, a Chinese scholar, wrote that before the Han dynasty, only the Qiang, Saizhong, Dayueshi, Wusong, Yilan and Han were indigenous (*tuzhu*) to Xinjiang. All of these indigenes except the Han subsequently disappeared without a trace. The Uigurs, Mongols, and other nationalities in Xinjiang, according to this view, only migrated there after the Han.[10] He further asserted that China would never suffer the same fate of dismemberment as the former Soviet Union, not only because the Han were 'aborigines' in Xinjiang, but because Han and minorities in Xinjiang are bound by blood relations nurtured through centuries of inter-marriage.[11] This claim to indigenous status is the basis for asserting Han contributions to the 'development' and 'prosperity' of the region.

We are witnessing in China a form of settler colonialism reminiscent of patterns found in the Commonwealth nations. The indigenized Han are now able to 'legitimately' enter areas previously reserved for 'autonomous' minorities, not only as the defenders of the nation, but also as co-developers or even as original developers of the frontier. In this context, we witness competing claims to indigenous status by both Han and minorities, a struggle whose outcome will shape the survival or the demise of the autonomous system.

As a substitute for minority political and economic autonomy, a multiculturalism (*duoyuan wenhua*) has recently been promoted, celebrating the colorful and diverse cultures of the Chinese Nation. Minority cultures and arts, symbols precisely of their inferiority in an era of modernization, have been invested with intrinsic value in this multiculturalism. Minorities and their cultures, in this new multicultural discourse, do not exit in their own rights, but as part of the Chinese Nation. They now occupy prominent positions in specialized theme parks concocted for national and international consumption in Beijing, Shenzhen, and Florida.

We now enter a new phase in the three stage trajectory of ethnicity in China, which some Chinese scholars have identified as history, politics, and culture. In this new celebratory mode of multiculturalism, history and ethnopolitics are conveniently forgotten, instead sanitized ethnic cultures are selectively deployed as the new property of the Chinese Nation.[12] This particular brand of multi-culturalism in China signifies the failure of political claims to equality, and that the *de facto* ethnic inequality unresolved in the economic and political domains are now to be evened out in the celebration of their cultural colorfulness and their contribution to the great culture of the Chinese Nation.

Market economy and the moral dilemma of ethnic minorities

Dru Gladney recently argued that China's economic reform has brought profound ambivalence to the Han due to a powerful construction of Han cultural identity as agrarian, egalitarian and Confucian anti-commercialism, while providing an historic opportunity for ethnic minorities such as the Hui (Muslims) to advance their religious and hence ethnic interest. According to Gladney:

> their explicit motivations for economic prosperity are often described in terms of religious and ethnic goals. To some extent, the Hui are essentialized by the state and broader public as entrepreneurs and in turn essentialize themselves this way; this is to their advantage and, eventually, to the advantage of the state as well.[13]

Although economic reform has worked to Hui advantage, this experience is rare among other minorities, with the possible exception of the Koreans. I argue that it is difficult to posit an absolute dichotomy between the perspectives of Han and minorities; many Han feel ambivalent about the market economy while some minorities seize it as an opportunity to enhance their ethnic and personal status and position. Insofar as Han ambivalence is rooted either in Confucian ethics or Communist communitarianism, it is equally true that the cultural heritage and socialist *minzu* characteristics affect the performance of minorities in the market economy. Mongols have historically been deeply hostile to commerce due to earlier painful experiences with Han merchants. In the Mongol language, commerce or business – *hudaldaa*, means cheating. Socialist *minzu* building did not cultivate Mongols' 'entrepreneurial spirit', as trade was both restricted and monopolized by the state. Hence, this anti-commercial sentiment persists. Nor was the herder image a positive one for entrepreneurial development. Therefore, we have to take into account cultural sedimentation from the past and its shaping of ethnic consciousness, factors which may or may not help a nationality to 'swim' in the 'sea' of market economy.

Despite these handicaps, Mongols have embraced market reform. Plunging into the sea of commerce signifies new hopes and dangers. The survival of the minorities will be determined by 'scientific' market principles that naturalize losers and winners. Not all Mongols drown in this market sea, but on the whole they have experienced the loss of formal positional power even as a small number of adept individuals with social capital manage to achieve marginal success. Market economy demands the ability to translate dwindling Mongol social capital into economic capital, to use French sociologist Pierre Bourdieu's handy terms.

This context sets in motion many processes. These include a unique 'voluntary' drive to shed ethnic identity, leading many Mongols to intensify efforts to learn Chinese in their determination not to be left behind. Those who have forgotten Mongolian are admired, since they seem equipped, at least linguistically and socially, to join directly in economic development. In a 1997 tour of a banner in western Inner Mongolia, which is predominantly pastoral, and where local people speak Mongol and have only stammering proficiency in Chinese, I noted that a Mongol cadre who was trained from primary school to university in Mongolian felt at ease explaining technical matters and policies in Chinese to herders who could barely understand him. In a township level middle school, 10 percent of the Mongol students applied to join Chinese language class, hoping to secure a factory or commercial job. The party secretary of the township complained to me that he did not write Chinese well. Not only did this hamper promotion, he also understood that the reports that he and fellow leaders wrote in Mongolian were ignored at the higher level. As a result, there was scant hope that much needed financial support for alleviating poverty would ever be allocated to his village.

A striking example is provided by Mongol language researchers and professors in several elite universities in Huhhot, the capital of Inner Mongolia, who send their own children to Chinese language schools. Ironically, these teachers instruct students to read and write Mongolian, yet make sure that their own children learn Chinese and specialize not in Mongolian studies but in science or computer courses taught exclusively in Chinese. Many of them now regret that they stayed on as teachers not because they loved it, but because they knew nothing else. They spoke as victims who had suddenly awoken from a bad dream. Through the combined weight of diverse institutions and social processes, people speaking non-Chinese languages are now induced, as Bourdieu puts it, 'to collaborate in the destruction of their instruments of expression.'[14]

But it is not inevitable that the Mongol language deprives its speakers of opportunities for advancement. This is the outcome of processes whereby the *minzu* project is subverted by chauvinism. Because of this subversion, Mongols have lost the political and linguistic capital they had long accumulated. Nor can hard work enable them to re-accumulate this capital. As Bourdieu advises, capital is related to the specific field or arena in which a form is utilized. Political capital and linguistic capital take their form from the arena within which they are utilized. Since the 'arena' has changed from socialist *minzu*-building to a capitalist market economy, in which *minzu* is more an obstacle than an advantage, and in which individualism is prioritized, it requires different forms of capital. The socialist Mongolian *minzu* subjects suddenly found themselves 'bankrupt' in this transition initiated by the reformist Chinese party-state. Bankruptcy requires a radical restructuring and 'new' ways of thinking.

Kaifa, as the new ideology of 'opening up and development', targets the ever-shrinking pastureland in Inner Mongolia. 'Opening up' in fact takes the form of enclosure of pastureland, allocating pasture for each individual household and then fencing it in with barbed wire, which Dee Williams perceptively calls 'barbed walls.'[15] This is the transplantation of intensive agricultural management upon pastoralism that requires wider space to avoid grassland degradation. Fencing in grassland is now rationalized as efficient resource management. However, the result has been the promotion of agriculture, including growing fodder to compensate for the deficient grass yield. Growing fodder to feed the malnourished livestock is praised as 'pluralism', as a form of civilization, and effective use of pasture, ignoring the historical fact that it is a product of Han colonization, and a necessity because of the shrinkage and enclosure of pastureland. It destroys the delicate topsoil, leading to wide-scale desertification. Whereas in the past, Mongols blamed Han for causing environmental havoc, now it is the Han who criticize Mongols' unscientific management.

Shortage of labor, cultural 'resistance' to farming, and the pressure to maintain sound ecological balance with increased productivity have forced many Mongol households to hire Chinese labor to tend the crops. Nowadays almost every Mongol herding household, rich or poor, has one Chinese laborer, who is normally paid half the yield of the crop, plus housing and food from spring to fall. This seeming ethnic cooperation often leads to inter-ethnic tensions. There have been Mongol reports of rape and even murder committed by migrant Han laborers not registered with local administration. Chinese laborers, in turn, also resent that they have been exploited by Mongols.

Kaifa also captured the imagination of many Mongol officials who had once opposed turning pastureland into agricultural land. Many of them are now active 'developers'. Some retired Mongol officials also plunged into the 'sea'. Since the prime resource they could lay hands on is grassland (they have little say on the matter of coal mines, forests, or other industries, which were long ago lost either to central ministries or to local Han), this became the target in their attempted *kaifa*. Many households now rent their leased pasture to urban companies, brokered by such cadres, in order to obtain urban '*hukou*' permits and realize a dream of becoming urban residents. For local Mongol cadres in the pastoral area, the only way to benefit is to contract out land with urban centers, in and out of Inner Mongolia.

This *kaifa* is reminiscent of the 1902 'new policy' which started Han colonization, leading to ethnic clashes. Today, towards the end of this century, *kaifa*, the new hegemonic concept, apparently charmed people into ethnic cooperation. Agricultural expansion need not be conducted just by the Han, for Mongols have also become active developers. Does Chinese capitalism now override and liquidate ethnic hierarchies and create equal citizens of the state? Or is something more profound at work here? How do we come to terms with this alternation of resistance and complicity of minorities that appears to be leading inexorably to 'the destruction of their instruments of expression'?

Conclusion

The central thesis of this chapter is that ethnicity in socialist China cannot be reduced to Han-nationality conflict because members of each group have a variety of complex interests that transcend ethnic opposition, yet reflect their subject positions *vis-à-vis* the Communist state. I have argued that socialism with Chinese characteristics has a propensity to reify ethnic consciousness along lines specified in the *minzu*-building project. It should now be clear that *minzu* building is not just a state project; it is also, in this and many other instances, one that is enthusiastically embraced in diverse ways by the *minzu* subjects or fractions thereof. These amount to colonizing operations within the majoritarian Han society that is simultaneously colonizing minorities. The socialist 'subjects' like '*funü*' (women) or '*nongmin*' (peasantry), constitute the constituencies for special citizen-forming projects that create categories which energize certain elements while suppressing others. Resistance and complicity of these groups with the state may produce a range of outcomes including heavy-handed suppression, affirmative action, and even massacre, as happened during the Tiananmen incident in 1989.

Minzu highlights central contradictions of socialist nation-building. *Minzu* is to be constructed for the ultimate purpose of its destruction. Having made its contribution to national unity and economic development, its mission is complete. Although the state's leading propaganda journal on minorities still retains its original Chinese name *Minzu Tuanjie*, it is notable that the English translation has recently been changed from Nationality Unity to Ethnic Unity, 'ethnic,' connoting more of a cultural character. The Chinese state has devoted substantial resources to build up *minzu* regional autonomy and solidify it through affirmative action, while at the same time devoting almost commensurate energy to 'solve the nationality problem' (*jiejue minzu wenti*) in ways that ultimately assume integrating minorities into the Chinese Nation, politically and culturally.

Deng Xiaoping's reform project, and that advanced by his successor Jiang Zemin, promotes a multiculturalism that constitutes not socialist subjects but *Chinese* subjects. Minorities are evaluated by meritocratic criteria, i.e., their service to the Chinese nation. Unlike the worker subject who is forever dreaming of resuming center stage, or attaining some kind of autonomy from the state, but who nevertheless constitutes the national citizenry (albeit a powerless 'national citizenry' now facing unemployment), *minzu* has only two options for the time being: it becomes a foil to the Han Chinese nation-state, displayed in the human zoo theme park, or it becomes the antithesis of the Han, serving to unite the Han, as reflected in the denunciation and suppression of minority secessionism of recent years.

Acknowledgements

I thank Mark Selden, Elizabeth Perry, Caroline Humphrey and Pan Jiao for insightful comments and advice. Mistakes are mine alone.

Notes

1 Dru C. Gladney, *Muslim Chinese: Ethnic Nationalism in the People's Republic* (Council on East Asian Studies, Harvard University: Cambridge, MA, 1991), p. 332.
2 Alan P. L. Liu, *Mass Politics in the People's Republic: State & Society in Contemporary China* (Westview Press: Boulder, 1996), pp. 190–92.
3 Takashi Fujitani, 'Inventing, Forgetting, Remembering: Toward a Historical Ethnography of the Nation-State', in Harumi Befu (ed.), *Cultural Nationalism in East Asia: Representation and Identity* (Institute of East Asian Studies, University of California: Berkeley, 1993), p. 89.
4 Almaz Khan, 'Who are the Mongols? State, Ethnicity, and the Politics of Representation in the PRC', in Melissa J. Brown (ed.), *Negotiating Ethnicities in China and Taiwan* (Institute of East Asian Studies, University of California: Berkeley, 1996), pp. 125–59.
5 John L. Comaroff, 'Of Totemism and Ethnicity: Consciousness, Practice and the Signs of Inequality', *Ethnos*, vol. 52, no. 3–4 (1987), p. 307.

6 Stevan Harrell, 'Linguistics and Hegemony in China', in Carol M. Eastman (ed.), *Language in Power*, a Special Issue of the *International Journal of the Sociology of Language*, no. 103 (1993), pp. 97–114.

7 Ulanhu, 'Ulanfu zai qingzhu ershi zhounian chouwei hui zhaokai de zuotanhui shang de jianghua' (Speech by Ulanhu on the Forum of the Preparatory Committee for Celebrating the 20th Anniversary), *Duwuji. Ulanfu Fangemin Yanlun Xuanbian*, vol. 3 (1967 [1965]), p. 37.

8 Joseph Stalin, *Marxism and Linguistics* (International Publishers: New York, 1951), p. 53.

9 Fei Xiaotong, 'Zhonghua minzu de duoyuan yiti geju' (Plurality and unity in the configuration of the Chinese nation), in Fei Xiaotong *et al.* (eds.), *Zhonghua Minzu de Duoyuan Yiti Geju* (Zhongyang minzu xueyuan chubanshe: Beijing, 1989), p. 34, emphasis added.

10 He Jihong, *Xiyu Lungao* (Treatise on the Western Territory) (Xinjiang renmin chubanshe: Urumqi, 1996), pp. 14–26.

11 Ibid., pp. 53–63.

12 This is the unifying theme of the Southwest China Study Series launched by the Yunnan Education Press in 1991.

13 Dru C. Gladney, 'Getting Rich is Not So glorious: Contrasting Perspectives on Prosperity among Muslims and Han in China', in Robert W. Hefner (ed.), *Market Cultures: Society and Morality in the New Asian Capitalisms* (Westview Press: Boulder, CO, 1998), p. 121.

14 Pierre Bourdieu, *Language and Symbolic Power* (Harvard University Press: Cambridge, MA, 1991), p. 7.

15 Dee Mack Williams, 'The Barbed Walls of China: A Contemporary Grassland Drama,' *The Journal of Asian Studies*, vol. 55, no. 3 (1996), pp. 665–91.

10 The revolution of resistance

Geremie R. Barmé

China's economic reforms have not only been about the growth of an entrepreneurial business sector. The privatization of public debate, intellectual life and cultural activity has been a process that has also unfolded over the past twenty years. Availing themselves of state resources, which were the product of plunder in the name of nationalization in the 1950s and 1960s, groups and individuals have arrogated to themselves both the *matériel* and prerogatives to develop alternative intellectual and cultural activity in China. Due to the nature of the Kong-Tai (that is Hong Kong and Taiwan Chinese language) media and its involvement with the mainland and with international media networks, it is this culture that has generally achieved a global profile, construed as being representative of the latest version of 'New China'.

The present chapter attempts a review of the incipient growth of these activities in the 1980s and their significance during the second radical phase of party-initiated reforms in the 1990s. It raises questions about the nature of resistance within the intellectual–cultural urban elites, and offers an overview of who is resisting what and why.

Revolution. To revolutionize revolution; to revolutionize the revolution of revolution; to rev . . .[1]

In late December 1991, Zhou Lunyou, a poet of the 'Not-not' school in Sichuan, produced a manifesto entitled 'A Stance of Rejection'. Written in response to what he saw as being the cultural capitulation that had followed in the wake of the 4 June 1989 Beijing massacre, Zhou called on his fellows to resist the blandishments of the state. 'In the name of history and reality,' he wrote,

in the name of human decency, in the name of the absolute dignity and conscience of the poet, and in the name of pure art we declare:

We will not cooperate with a phoney value system –

- Reject their magazines and payments.
- Reject their critiques and acceptance.
- Reject their publishers and their censors.

- Reject their lecterns and 'academic' meetings.
- Reject their 'writers' associations', 'artists' associations', 'poets' associations', for they are all sham artistic yamen that corrupt art and repress creativity.[2]

The stifling of cultural experimentation and intellectual debate that occurred in the wake of 4 June was neither as extreme nor as widespread as anti-liberals in Beijing had hoped (or, indeed, as overseas dissidents and exiles claimed). That purge came after a decade of radical economic policies that had undermined the ideological certainties of high socialism and fostered, among other things, an environment of intellectual and cultural debate outside the stifling confines of political agitprop. The scope and effect of the 1989 purge was circumscribed by many factors: a revulsion of the spectre of Cultural Revolution-style denunciations, internal dissension within the party, the impact of administrative reforms and weakening of the mechanisms of social and political surveillance, widespread public disinterest, political fatigue and opposition, as well as the stark economic imperatives of the party's own program.

Zhou Lunyou's romantic call for resistance itself came at an intriguing and crucial moment for Chinese culture. It was on the cusp of Deng Xiaoping's vaunted 'tour of the south' of early 1992. During his inspection of economic reformist centres in Guangdong province, Deng made a series of speeches and comments that not only had a radical impact on the economic life of the nation, but also further transformed the nature of cultural dissent and intellectual opposition to the party.

In the years prior to Zhou's appeal to reject the state-sanctioned arts world, cultural practitioners and activists had evolved complex relationships with the official overculture that made any simple gestures of rebellion seem quixotic, if not nugatory. Egregious oppositionist acts, while sometimes meaningful if not heroic, were generally also part of a larger, highly-nuanced skein of activity that could not be easily classified in terms of clumsy dichotomies. Furthermore, from 1989 mainland Chinese cultural and intellectual discord more than ever before developed an international dimension. The 1989 protest movement and its bloody denouement served to globalize further the debate and dissent in many ways, a process that, not surprisingly, worked in tandem with the internationalization of the economy.

Hong Kong, Taiwan, as well as international media attention was now fixated on the issues related to the 1989 protests and subsequent massacre, the fate of activists, any hints of a change in official government policy and the possibility of further mass unrest. Key participants in the movement escaped, or were subsequently sent, into exile, and some continued agitating for political change in China, while many turned their energies to other, often business, pursuits from 1990–91. The Chinese government and its avowed opponents throughout the 1990s engaged in a 'mimetic violence' against each other – rhetorical attacks, purges and dissident resistance – that entrenched their mutual opposition. Meanwhile, in the larger realms of intellectual, cultural and commercial life debate flourished. New Chinese-language forums (newspapers, magazines and semi-academic journals) strengthened an environment for discussion and contention within the 'Chinese commonwealth'. This involved mainland writers, as well as offshore and overseas commentators, in a direct dialogue about future scenarios for China and the region in a manner – as some pointed out – that was reminiscent of the 'internationalization' of political dissension in late-Qing China at the end of the nineteenth century when the frustration of the 1898 reforms of the Guangxu Emperor had forced his supporters into exiled activism overseas.

The economic boom of the 1990s challenged thinkers and critics of all schools to re-evaluate the modern history of the Chinese party-state; it also drew scholars and activists into a series of discussions about the impact of the party's program on issues of official corruption, condoned cronyism, the growth of a new underclass, commodification–consumerism and globalization, as well as media freedom and democratization. Some of these issues were central to the inchoate protests of 1989; however, a decade later they were being debated in the mainland media in unprecedented detail and with considerable candour. In the 1980s vague and wispy reformist visions had been at the centre of much intellectual and political debate, during the 1990s the integration of China's economy into the global system (and the global system's infiltration into China), as well as the cut-throat commerce of the decade, confronted intellectuals with an impetus to the revolution of resistance.

Also after 1989, the romantic posture of failed resistance achieved a certain social and commercial eclat. This was particularly true in the cultural sphere where transgressive activities – that is, actions that were 'naughty but not dangerous'[3] to the entrenched power holders and new élites – flourished. A number of successful careers in cinema, art, theatre and literature were launched on the basis of alternative cultural activity, sporadic state repression, and offshore investment in avant-garde cultural activities. The crushing of flagrant dissent gave these more anodyne activities a highly visible media profile. Non-official arts activists continued to plunder state resources in a fashion not dissimilar to the vampirization of state (that is 'public') sector assets by bureaucratic cronies and the super-rich, thereby giving them access to new markets and opportunities. Film-makers and artists who joined the international exhibition and cultural carnival circuit during the 1990s, for example, were generally trained in state institutions, cultivated alliances with associates and used (or 'privatized') state and semi-official resources (equipment, locales, networks) to pursue their activities. The works of film-makers like Zhang Yuan (director of MTVs and feature films like *Beijing Bastards* and *East Palace, West Palace*) and a slew of painters were in the artistic avant-garde of those diverting state resources to their private (and often profitable) ventures. The arrest or harassment of activists who attempted to organize a concerted opposition to one-party rule, or who petitioned the government to undertake democratic reform, to reassess the events of 1989, or at least to honour the national constitution, continued. This was yet more evidence that political confrontation, rather than image marketing, was regarded by the power-holders as being both illegitimate and dangerous.

For a time after 1989, consumerism was viewed popularly, and among many segments of the political and intellectual élite, as possessing a near revolutionary significance[4] – and many of the most celebrated cultural fads drew upon revolutionary images.[5] The romance of resistance included now a belief that quotidian activities were the site of struggle and cloaked sociopolitical retail therapy (that is, shopping for new lifestyles and accessorizing the self in contradistinction to the official nation-state inculcated guise of identity). It was a development acceptable to economic reformers, the business elite, crony cadres, wannabe rebels, kids with 'tude, and the displaced literati (displaced in so far as many members of the caste felt they had been sidelined by economic developments and political stability in the 1990s) alike. The rise of this discourse of consumer-as-revolutionary also dovetailed neatly with a liberal teleology that now saw the ascendancy of the middle class and the democracy of Taiwan as part of the overall trajectory of Chinese modernity, and not just as a hotly contested alternative. While ballot-box democracy might be deferred until a sizeable middle class existed, the free-range republic of shopping could be realized immediately.

Along with cultural transgression, consumption was also a key zone for the affirmation of avant-garde scouts. Consumption directs desires and enlists resistance within itself as product promotion and placement usurp edgy non-mainstream, or state-sanctioned, phenomena. Cultural or social developments that once seemed antipathetic and threatening could, in the guise of marketing strategies or sound street commercial sense, be incorporated in the domain of product and purchase. Some might well claim that this did not necessarily 'make commodified resistance "packaged", tame or lame. It simply makes it tactical and potentially effective.'[6] But, such optimism surely begs the question: effective for what? Arguments about shopper-as-rebel and promoter-as-revolutionary are certainly suggestive if the seditious subaltern or canny consumer was chiefly construed as existing and acting in some closed system embraced by the market-party-state. If viewed within the larger, multipolar environment of the Kong-Tai (Hong Kong and Taiwan) world, as well as in the thrall of the international media and transcultural sphere, however, the 'new ways and new things "to market", consume, subvert, rebel against or steal'[7] so noteworthy on the mainland during the 1990s, could also be appreciated in terms of promotion, positioning and as part of a redefinition of elitist norms in the guise of subaltern strategies. For the mavens of international academic theory, China was fallow territory, a 'blank page' as Chairman Mao would have it, on which new texts could be written or at least divined.

After 1992, it was initially the old 'Maoist-style' left[8] which, through internal lobbying and public propagandizing, continued to articulate most coherently a position of opposition to the reformist status quo. From the middle of the decade, however, a number of 'new-leftist' thinkers joined pro-party conservatives to respond both to the predicament of mainstream social and political thinking, and to the glaring inequities resulting from the economic libertarian agenda. Many of these thinkers – who were based both in the US and China – emphasized the threats posed by the twin dangers of the declining fiscal viability of the Beijing authorities and the growing social inequities that had resulted from decentral-ization and marketization. They envisaged a range of dire scenarios that invoked the plangent fate of the former Yugoslavia or Soviet Union and grudgingly argued that a strong and economically competent Communist Party was perhaps, for the moment at least, a necessary bulwark against national collapse.

The post-1976 period of the officially-sponsored 'movement to liberate thinking' (*sixiang jiefang yundong*) from Maoist strictures was a time during which official ideology underwent a transformation that freed the authorities from past dogma while also providing a rationale for economic reform and new directions for social growth. In a retrospective analysis of the intellectual developments on the mainland over the two decades from 1978 to 1998, Xu Jilin, a leading scholar of twentieth-century intellectual history based in Shanghai, observed that the party's previous reliance on a utopian political program was gradually replaced by theoretical justifications for the 'secular socialism' (*shisuhua shehuizhuyi*) of the economic reforms.

The next phase in this process – or rather the continuation of it – was a complex intellectual and cultural mutation that extended far beyond the earlier limited aims of pro-party revisionists. From around the middle of the 1980s, the mainland experienced a cultural effervescence that was called by some 'another "May Fourth" movement', a 'Chinese Enlightenment'.[9] Like that earlier period of cultural and political debate and furore during the 1910s and 1920s, this post-Cultural Revolution 'New Enlightenment' was supposedly witness to an initial period of broad agreement among thinkers who rejected the old state ideology and propounded instead various alternative models for modernization; there was an active reappraisal of political systems and cultural paradigms that empha-sized economic growth, as well as potential political and cultural freedoms. It was a period in which intellectual traditions were invoked, invented and reclaimed as part of intellectuals' attempts to define themselves within the Chinese polity and claim a role in its evolution. This supposed consensus, however, also contained within it a critical response to the various international discourses that were being introduced piecemeal through translation projects, young scholars studying overseas, conferences, seminars and a wealth of publications; and it was a response that carried also the seeds of a major reassessment of China's 1980s and 1990s fascination with the West (or global commercial and political culture) itself.

Moreover, the debates of the 1980s were influenced by an intermittent series of cultural and political campaigns, or purges, in particular the nationwide attacks on 'spiritual pollution' and 'bourgeois liberalization' in 1980–81, 1983–84, 1987, and 1989–90.[10] These administrative and ideological condemnations included attacks on official Marxist-style humanism and the efforts by loyalists to construct a new rationale for the party beyond the confines of its economic program. The purges more often than not had the effect of silencing establish-ment intellectuals (*tizhinei zhishifenzi*) and critics who stepped out of line, or resulted in their isolation within or banishment from its ranks. In conjunction with economic reform and more general social transformations, however, a semi-independent sphere of intellectual activity gradually blossomed, and found outlets in the deregulated publishing market. At the same time, a revival of the educational sphere and academic standards saw a rapid increase in tertiary enrolments and a college-trained urban stratum that enjoyed unprecedented (in post-1949 terms, at least) access to information and a range of media. As a consequence, they provided a ready audience for the products of the *Kulturkampf*.

The period of the 1980s New Enlightenment was, to use Xu Jilin's description,

> A major historical turning point for Chinese intellectuals in that through cultural debate they gradually withdrew from and, in some cases, entirely broke free of the politico-ideological establishment and the state system of specialized knowledge production [that is, the strictures of official academia]. This enabled them to create intellectual spaces and attain a new cultural independence.

It was a kind of autonomy more akin to the situation that had existed prior to the founding of the People's Republic in 1949.[11]

Although they avoided direct confrontation with the official ideology, these intellectuals in effect began to challenge its dominance in every field of thought. The public realm for intellectual debate was to flourish in the 1990s although the consensual environment shared by different schools of thinkers and cultural activists was ruptured first by the 1989 protest movement and the subsequent purge of élitist activists, and then again by the effects of the economic boom that followed in the wake of Deng Xiaoping's 1992 'tour of the south'.

In the 1980s, intellectual contestation had generally centered on debates about abstract ideas and theoretical issues; there was a renewed belief that it was through cultural and national transformation that China would be revitalized. Educated urbanites long excoriated under Maoist cultural policy presumed that this new 'Enlightenment project' was their responsibility, and members of the intelligentsia were anxious to play the role of patriot–savant supposedly central to the identity of the traditional educated caste. Following the successes, and excesses, of the economic reforms during the 1990s, however, engaged intellectuals related their disagreements more directly to economic and political programs, as well as to class or caste differences. In an age during which much of the 'capital accumulation,' that is, superficial economic prosperity, that had been the goal of earlier reforms and revolutions seemed to have been realized, the nature of this affluence and the inequities it presented now came to the fore as issues of pressing importance. The intelligentsia had, throughout the twentieth century, argued bitterly over the merits of a dizzying array of developmental theories, political programs, economic systems and cultural paradigms. Now, at the century's end, debates and intellectual programs began to revolve around not simply how to achieve power and prosperity, but the dilemmas of power and prosperity *per se*.

In this environment ideas were not mere abstract formulations; economic wealth and the vision of a strong and prosperous China – or even the reverse, the looming menace of an economically imperilled, crisis-ridden and socially divided nation – made the debates about the history of modernity in China and the future it faced both relevant and urgent. Although past controversies had been launched from a common ground, and a general wariness of monopolistic party rule had existed among diverse cultural and intellectual worlds from the late 1970s, now questions were disputed on the basis of vastly different, even mutually exclusive, academic and theoretical frameworks, as well as social experiences.

While open intellectual debate in the style of the 1980s was quelled for a time after 4 June, the broader cultural sphere was witness to considerable resilience. During 1990 the pall of the Beijing Massacre still hung over artistic life in the capital in particular as well as much of the rest of the country. It was, however, also a time of considerable ebullience for alternative culture. For example, the rock'n'roll scene enjoyed unprecedented activity and growth. Similarly, in 1989–91, independent painters developed on the diversity of the 1980s arts scene and began creating work that would gain an international audience and, through high-profile exhibitions and reviews, came to represent more than any other aspect of mainland culture the face of the new 'New China' overseas. Despite a number of bans on authors directly involved in the 1989 protests, controversial and younger novelists and poets who were not aligned with the establishment, along with essayists and cultural critics, continued to publish in leading provincial journals or, when the opportunity arose, in the pages of Hong Kong and Taiwan publications. And, just as Zhou Lunyou published his *cri de coeur* (quoted at the beginning of this chapter), Beijing TV aired *The Editors*, a sitcom set in a magazine editorial department that lambasted the official overculture with unprecedented, and ill-concealed, glee.[12] Zhou's *A Stance of Rejection* itself appeared in a samizdat poetry journal that subsequently ceased publication because its contributors found they could readily get their works into mainstream literary magazines.

The growth of these popular market spaces was not as revolutionary *vis-à-vis* the ordained cultural order as many observers would claim. Nonetheless, the rise of a local rock and pop (dubbed by some 'Mandopop' – that is, Mandarin rock-pop[13]) scene, the mass publishing market with its plethora of entertainment and lifestyle journals, mainland commercial and party advertising, and so on, did constitute an active response by local culture producers, both mainstream and alternative, to the incursion of off-shore cultural forms and capital. However, in the years following Deng Xiaoping's 1992 tour, during which he openly criticized 'leftist' thinking (that is, political opposition to the accelerated market reforms, the privatization of state industries, the 'outsourcing' of state functions, and so on), the most vocal and concerted attacks on the Communist Party's reformist agenda and its socio-political impact came not from the semi-independent intelligentsia, or fringe cultural figures, but from within the party itself.

The hostility of the official left, a group of establishment thinkers and writers who were derided by their public critics as 'red fundamentalists' (*yuan hongzhizhuyizhe*), also found expression in a number of public forums that had been created following 4 June. As they were routed by policy shifts and marginalized during the 1990s, many of the true believers decamped to institutions and publications on the fringes of power. Their journals covered both cultural and ideological issues and, throughout the decade, they produced a constant stream of criticism – and in many cases vitriol – aimed at the most divisive elements of the party's program.[14] They also launched attacks on an array of ideological soft targets, in particular individuals whom they regarded as being dangerous revisionists, the chief object of their spleen being Wang Meng, the writer and former Minister of Culture (1986–89).

In 1995, the Australian-based Chinese journalist and oral historian Sang Ye questioned one retired high-level cadre about his views of the degeneration of the revolution and his opposition to the reform policies. He said that,

> . . . starting with the Third Plenum of the Eleventh Party Congress in 1978, we have pursued a dangerous rightist policy. We've now gone so far to the right that we've abandoned the basic principles of Marxism and the objective rules of social development.
> . . . [W]e still talk about revolutionaries being people who struggle valiantly their whole lives for the cause of liberation, and no matter what difficulties we encounter we should just tough it out. But things have reached a point that anyone with a conscience, anyone who cares about the fate of our nation, just has to weep at the dire predicament we are in.[15]

Retirees like this former government minister muttered glum condemnations in private while some of their colleagues memorialized the Central Committee through secret petitions, but from the mid 1990s a number of writers chose to speak out publicly against the market reforms that they believed (or at least argued) were undermining what remained of both the ethos and the rationale of the revolution.

Their protests were aired in a media debate about what was called the 'humanist spirit' and 'kowtowing to the vulgar'. The burgeoning of mass-market popular culture led to despair among people who had only recently regained their faith in (and affirmed their identification with) the tradition of the Chinese literati-scholars, the political and cultural mandarins of the past. It was a self-identification reinforced by an abiding belief in the socialist dogma of the artist as prophet. Having borne witness to the decay of the cultural welfare state over the past decade, they now saw their own influence waning. They felt that writers who profited from the tide of commercialization were prostituting their talents and betraying the cause of a revived literati culture.

Among the most outspoken critics of the new marketplace and its advocates were two ex-Red Guard novelists, Liang Xiaosheng and Zhang Chengzhi. They issued dark warnings about the effect that mass commercial culture was having on the 'soul of China.' As Zhang wrote in an alarmist hyperbole partially inspired by Samuel Huntington's writings on 'the clash of civilizations':

I've been thinking. After the war of the civilizations, they should at least find in the rubble of the defeated a few bodies of intellectuals who fought to the death. I despise surrender. In particular, in this war of civilizations, I loathe intellectuals who have made a vocation out of capitulation.[16]

Appeals for a moral rearmament that would find its ordnance in the Maoist past were part of a strategy used by writers like Zhang to carry out their critique of contemporary social, political and artistic realities. To question the status quo, the incursion of capital and the consumer tendencies of the society was a shrewd tactic in an avowed 'war of resistance.' Opponents to this approach, however, were deeply suspicious of the presumption of intellectuals to harangue their fellows. Of these the most noteworthy was the novelist and essayist Wang Xiaobo (d. 1997), an important figure who perhaps, more than any other 1990s writer, represented the urbane scepticism of people both weary and wary of intellectual afflatus. 'I respect your high-sounding ideas,' he wrote, 'but I'm less than anxious to have them shoved down my throat.' Or as he remarked on the habits of the educated caste: 'Chinese intellectuals particularly enjoy using moralistic paradigms to lecture others.'[17]

Indeed how useful or reliable were the tainted resources of high-socialist 'leftism', ones that were by the very nature of their place in contemporary Chinese life unreliable, compromised and disingenuous? Or was 'leftist' political and cultural history being adapted with the help of various theories that authorized the use of a past that was fragmentary, piecemeal and ad hoc, to serve élites in their creation of an expansive critical unanimity in the mainland? Was the objectivization of the past simply distorted and clouded by the subjectivist caste of those who lived it/remember it, or needed to use it to justify themselves in the 1990s? Again, a number of writers were equivocal about intellectual grand-standing and instead turned their attention to the detail of the past and attempted, through the writing of local histories for a general readership, to fill in some of the gaps of public knowledge.[18]

Not all critics of either the moral revivalists or the 'new leftists', however, were as phlegmatic as Wang Xiaobo. The ideological control of the party had been such that many had suffered, or continued to suffer, directly from its manipulations, or at the hands of the people's democratic dictatorship (the main organs of which were the police, the penal system, the armed police, the army and the judiciary). There were those who had been arrested for their unorthodox activities or views, denied publishing opportunities, or chances to travel, or refused improved housing conditions and promotion, as well as those who had been jailed, harassed by the police, and placed under surveillance. They were emotionally and intellectually determined to see the one-party state weakened and undermined no matter what the cost. For them the marketplace was a welcomed ally in their quest. They would prefer an enfeebled party-state that permitted direct resistance even if it meant that the new dominant market might well make that resistance little more than cosmetic.

For some publishers and editors the sense of trepidation about the continued ability of the CCP to maintain national integrity, as well as to shore up its ideological and cultural hegemony, was virtually on a par with fears about the inundation of overseas capital and the multinational corporations that were energetically expanding into the Chinese cultural market. As one publisher remarked to me in late 1998: 'If you are a responsible intellectual you have to consider whether you are willing to live with the consequences of your opposition to the relatively free-wheeling status quo.' Such an opposition could see local cultural institutions (publishing, the media, the sports entertainment industry, cultural activities, and so on) overwhelmed by foreign capital, know-how and new forms of commercial and capital repression that could well prove to be more insidious than those typical of the chaotic environment of late-socialism. Individuals like my interlocutor contemplated a future ruled by the kind of Great Leader that the American journalist P. J. O'Rourke encountered during his late 1990s 'worst of both worlds' sojourn in *fin-de-siècle* Shanghai,

> ... omnipresent amid all the frenzy of Shanghai is that famous portrait, that modern icon. The faintly smiling, bland, yet somehow threatening visage appears in brilliant red hues on placards and posters, and is painted huge on the sides of buildings. Some call him a genius. Others blame him for the deaths of millions. There are those who say his military reputation was inflated, yet he conquered the mainland in short order. Yes, it's Colonel Sanders.[19]

Modernization and prosperity had been central to the aspirations and public discourse not only of the Chinese intelligentsia but also to the concerns of the broader population throughout the twentieth century. When, during the 1990s, the economic reforms created a version of modernization as well as its attendant problems in the urban centres of the nation, the debates about it took a new turn.

As we noted earlier, the 1980s saw intellectuals and broad segments of the population gradually breaking away from the thrall of the socialist nation-state to articulate visions of the society and its future at variance with the official world. In the 1990s, a gradual reformulation of controversies and issues that had first resurfaced in the intellectual and cultural worlds (resurfaced in the sense that they found a lineage in pre-1949 cultural debates, as well as being a reformulation of issues directed by the state since the founding of the People's Republic) took place. The topics of political reform, Enlightenment values and modernity were now interrogated in more comprehensive terms and in relation to the history of modern Chinese history, conventionally dated from the Opium War of 1840.

A number of the key intellectual critics of the 1990s – as well as some of the most controversial participants in the debates – were themselves historians, or specialists in aspects of intellectual history. Their number included academics like Xiao Gongqin, Lei Yi, Wang Hui, Xu Jilin, Qin Hui and Zhu Xueqin. They were thinkers who constantly shifted between their studies of sociopolitical issues of the past, the development of historical narratives during the century, and an engagement in contemporary polemics. Although these individuals were attracted to different academic schools of thought, from the early 1990s they were all active as media cultural commentators. Writers like Xu Jilin recognized that even though the intelligentsia no longer enjoyed its previous prominence, there was still a place for the socially engaged cultural commentator.

> One can take on the role of observer, a person who from their particular intellectual and cultural standpoint attempts an independent critique of various social phenomena. You try to participate actively in the cultural evolution of your world . . . and try to use the mass media to give voice to one's conscience.[20]

After 4 June, various divisions within the intellectual and cultural worlds laid the basis for the conflicts of the 1990s. One group of intellectuals, academics, writers and propagandists tended to devote its energies to developing theoretical approaches and formulating practical policy strategies to serve the party-state, to participate in what was called 'systemic renewal' (*zhidu chuangxin*). Supporting the secular socialism of post-totalitarianism, these strategists and academic thinkers-cum-advisers concentrated their efforts on aiding the existing market–socialist state to modernize itself, augmenting its efforts at legitimacy as well as helping it respond effectively to the problems and issues that the reforms (as well as its disavowed utopian socialist project) had created. Their aim was to achieve some form of 'ideological hegemony' for themselves while also helping buttress the legitimacy of the Communist Party.[21] Beyond the calculated good-will and efforts of these image and policy consultants, non-aligned critics were more generally drawn to ponder the questions of whether the party leadership could renew itself effectively, or if it was simply fatally burdened with the political talents of what John Maynard Keynes would have recognized as 'third-generation men.'

Some thinkers, who were not necessarily unconditional supporters of the status quo wrote advice papers both for the political and the new economic elites. Their motivations were complex, they combined a sense of duty to the nation-state with the hope of achieving a public profile while at the same time providing a rationale for the activities of (or a reasoned limitation on) the power holders. They were latter-day advocates of 'disinterested opinion' (*qingyi*) if you will.[22] The issues that many of these thinkers tussled with concerned the balance between equity and liberalism, market power and political stability, national sovereignty and global capital. Concocting strategies that could help the party renovate itself and possibly move towards greater plurality was, for many of these activists, the best way China could avoid going through another revolution and suffering the social dislocation, mass deprivation and political confusion that was felt would inevitably result from it. National crisis was not some distant or inchoate fear, but an overshadowing spectre reinforced both by China's history from the 1840s onwards and the more recent collapse of the former socialist countries to the West.

For many other writers, however, the fate of the party and its immediate future were no longer issues of particular moment, or relevance. Broad-based political, social and cultural criticism became one of the fundamental ways in which circumspect dissent was expressed throughout the decade. Authors of historical tracts, as well as publishers, took advantage of the commercial market to help fill in the 'white spots' of history and inform contemporary debates. By the late 1990s, as a range of analysts within China warned that the economic reform strategy in its present form had all but run its course, many publicly-active intellectuals – that is academics and writers who engaged in the major intellectual and cultural disputes of the decade in the print media and at specialist forums – were tending to form into two different camps. These were divergent, even opposing, groups insofar as they identified themselves as being at least rhetorical opponents in the debates surrounding the central issues of twentieth-century Chinese cultural and political polemics: modernity, Enlightenment values, science, democracy, class and the nature of the state. Added to this were contentious questions more peculiar to the 1990s in general: the 'level playing field' of the marketplace, commodification, crony-communism, official racket-eering, the rise of both a middle class and the super-rich (*baofu jieceng*), the impoverishment of the proletariat and agricultural workers, the degradation of the environment, the complex impact of the fiscal crisis in Asia, Russia and Latin America, and the systemic quandaries of the market–socialist state.

Here it may also be worth pausing to speculate on some of the other, more pragmatic, causes for the increased and open acrimony between contending schools of cultural and socio-political thought. The 1990s was a time generally described by local commentators as being one of 'ideological retreat' (*yishi xingtai tuichao*) or, more neutrally, a 'period of transition' (*zhuanxing shiqi*). That is to say, the formerly dominant state-sponsored ideology was going through further transformation; a time when the fusty party credo still maintained a notional media hegemony, even though the actual pursuit of political cohesion was increasingly limited to party organs and official discourse. In administrative terms, the aging and retirement of staunch traditional propagandists left the way open to a cadre of younger men and women who functioned more as party PR people than political watchdogs. The downsizing (or 'rightsizing') of the party apparatus also meant that there were fewer reliable apparatchiki devoted to the persecution of clandestine or even egregious ideological errors. Added to this was the ravenous publishing market hungry for new books and periodicals, as well as the commodification of transgressive thought. As a result writers and thinkers had to contest openly for the approval of like-minded activists, a share of public attention, media success and even official approbation. All of these developments had a significant impact on the commercialized controversies of the 1990s. This was certainly true of the clash over humanistic values of 1993 onwards, the strife regarding the 'kowtowing to the vulgar' a few years later (mentioned earlier), and the furore surrounding pop nationalistic screeds like *China Through the Third Eye* and *China, Just Say No!* As the decade drew to a close, a number of factors gave a focus to the last major intellectual clash of the century: a previously buoyant economy coupled with a looming fiscal crisis and social upheavals; concerns about the agendas of the entrenched party bureaucrats and its big business allies; US hegemony and the impact of global capital; and, the effects these were having on the population at large.[23]

The mainland characterization, or even assumed self-description, of the two major opposing groups of independent intellectuals that developed from the mid-1990s was that they consisted of neo-liberals and neo-leftists, or to follow Xu Jilin's early 1999 appellation of the latter group, the new left-wing.[24] The initial public conflict between these schools of thought was sparked by Wang Hui, the editor of *Reading* and a prominent intellectual historian.[25] In a lengthy analysis of the post-Cultural Revolution Chinese intelligentsia and its relationship to the question of modernity published in late 1997, Wang interrogated the ability of contemporary mainland thinkers to respond to the complex issues related to China's modernization and involvement in the global economy.[26] A year later, he further challenged his fellows by issuing a theoretical discussion of scientism, the accepted sociopolitical and historical paradigms of modernity, and the nation-state in twentieth-century Chinese intellectual history.[27] It was from the publication of Wang's 1997 essay in particular that the two polemical groupings developed contending public positions and thereafter engaged in what could perhaps be described as a high-profile 'confrontation of caricatures.'

An extensive and widespread theoretical interest in liberalism had developed from the 1980s. This body of thought and theory was influenced by the introduction, or popularization, of the writings of a range of thinkers from James Locke and Jean Jacques Rousseau, to Karl Popper and F. A. von Hayek, as well as by the efforts of writers in Beijing, Shanghai and elsewhere to 'unearth' and write about Chinese proponents of liberal thought from earlier in the century.[28] By the mid 1990s, there was, as Xu Jilin observed, a *de facto* 'thorough-going victory of liberalism in the realm of popular ideas. The word "liberalism" itself had achieved a cultural cachet previously enjoyed by such terms as democracy and science.'[29] Writers of all backgrounds and persuasions, philosophers, historians, as well as literary critics, were gradually drawn in to considering the impact of these ideas and employing them, as well as other theoretical models, to come to terms with the vast changes China was experiencing.

Finding inspiration in particular in the neo-classical liberalism of von Hayek, thinkers and writers advocated the pursuit of an Enlightenment agenda: their concern was to see the project of modernization in China fulfill its promise to allow for independent thinking and democratic reform, as well as providing a legal framework for the protection of property rights and economic freedoms. As ideological policing waned for a time in 1997–98, writers in this camp gave voice to their opposition to the Communist Party and called for further market reforms. They talked directly of the need for a program of political change, along with democratic and legal reforms, that would bring the nation into line with what they identified as accepted international practice.[30]

Many thinkers entered the fray, and their writings covered a range of positions that reflected a spectrum of opinion that actually belied the overall impression that there was agreement even within these avowedly opposing groups. A number of observers remarked that they thought the controversy between neo-liberals and neo-leftists rather bizarre, given the fact that, as they put it: 'In you there is a little bit of me, and in me there is a little bit of you' (*nizhong you wo, wozhong you ni*). Be that as it may, while the neo-liberals were more than willing to be identified as such, the neo-leftists generally shied from the label of leftism; it was a reluctance influenced by the negative connotation that 'the left' had acquired in China due to its historical associations with the extremism of the Maoist past.[31] And here we should be mindful of the fact that all participants in the intellectual debates of 1990s China were functioning in an environment that was both less ideologically confrontational (the authorities were generally reluctant to interfere directly) and more commercially driven than ever before. In other words, well-articulated intellectual positions could accrue dividends in a range of ways within academia, the media and in terms of public exposure and intellectual profile.

The symbiotic relationship of dissenting individuals and groups could also be evaluated in terms of both group dynamics and long-term 'outcomes' and credibility. That is to say, many individuals were sorely aware of how it would subsequently appear to their fellows if they were not active during such a period of political and cultural ferment. A person's status and position during the next period of liberalization could be influenced if one had not performed in a manner acceptable to one's intellectual–cultural peers during the previous phase of activism and repression. While we should be alert to the need to avoid assertions that there was some crude collective mentality at the heart of this performative activism, it would nonetheless be naive to ignore the realities of group dynamics when considering the style as well as the content of cultural and political apostasy.

The thinkers identified as the left-wing had first found their voice among overseas scholars and writers based in particular in the US. Although they initially published their views in Hong Kong journals like *Twenty-first Century*, which was founded in 1990,[32] gradually they came to enjoy overt support among mainland-based writers. Their stance, one particularly informed by their position in US academia, provided 'a vigorous critique of the liberal ideology of the West and a call to transcend socialism and capitalism by developing a strategy for "systemic renovation" based on China's particular path of modernization.'[33] Their credentials and post-colonial superiority did not impress everyone, however, and in 1995 the voluble philosopher Liu Dong dubbed their writings as a product of a 'pidgin academic style.'[34]

As they gradually formulated a general position in the Hong Kong and mainland media from the mid 1990s, the left-wing writers were particularly attentive to what they saw as being the collaboration between the socialist state and international global capital. Some of their number analysed how intellectuals had been disarmed by their acceptance of an economic (and ideological) program that, they argued, would not necessarily lead to a real social and market liberalization, or a democratization that could be enjoyed by all equally. They stressed that the reforms would foster extreme inequalities, inequities both of class within China and in relation to international geopolitics in which the mainland would be dominated by overseas capital. What they were witnessing was a new form of mass dictatorship by a cartel of international capital, the super-rich oligarchy, or 'monopoly élite' (*longduan jingying*) of China and party cronies. According to these thinkers, all the indications were that the liberal intellectuals would, by default, provide a cultural and historical justification for the power holders as this process unfolded.

If the neo-liberals championed the middle class and the 'level playing field' of the market, aiding (as their critics saw it) the interests of both domestic and international capital – and saw in the rise of the market the possibility for equit-able modernization that would eventually benefit the society as a whole – then the new left wing was deeply skeptical about the democratizing benefits of market reforms. They increasingly took a position in defence of 'mass participatory democracy' (*quanmian minzhu*), a vague formulation that notionally favoured the exploited masses and the rapidly growing underclass. As Cui Zhiyuan, an outspoken thinker of the 'new left' based at the Massachusetts Institute of Technology, put it, 'The real struggle today is between reformers out for the people as a whole, and reformers out for themselves.'[35] Some on the left stressed the need for a stronger state that could effectively limit inequities, prevent domination by foreign/private capital, and shore up national unity. According to the Qinghua University historian Qin Hui, himself an active participant in the debates, the irony of the situation was that both sides in this rhetorical stand-off should have been able to find common cause in opposing extremist positions; that is to say, the liberals should have concentrated on opposing authoritarian-ism, while the left-wing 'social democrats' should have been on guard against populism. Instead, they identified a common enemy in each other.

Something that added an edge to these increasingly acrimonious debates was the crucial issue of perceived political impotence. Communist Party monopoly rule effectively deprived participants in the rancorous intellectual exchanges from utilizing any direct political or systemic mechanism through which they could implement their ideas, other of course than exercising a measure of influence on party leaders. The hegemony of the one-party state both frustrated the intelligentsia and at the same time it afforded them an unprecedented freedom to debate the abstract issues central to twentieth-century Chinese intel-lectual life. The left-wing, while energetic in its critiques of liberalism and the market, was until the time of writing at least, unenthusiastic about joining forces or openly advocating any concrete political program or strategy to deal with what they perceived as being a parlous situation. Certainly, some of their number advocated a reinvigorated central government and putting a brake on the market and foreign capital, while expanding the state's redistributive role. Similarly, the spectrum of liberal thinkers actively advocated change within the context of the existing political system – and their demands in this context were not that different from the protesters of 1989, or the small number of public dissidents during the 1990s[36] – but they shied away from direct political action or the forming of public lobby groups.

Han Yuhai, a professor of literature at Peking University, became one of the most extreme public opponents of liberalism. His critiques were so splenetic that one was reminded of the 'gunpowder stench' (*huoyaowei*) of Cultural Revolution-period denunciations. Han declared that the market liberals' support for social and political stability for the sake of economic development (and, theoretically, long-term societal transformation) was little more than a justification for market rapaciousness; it served to protect and further the interests of entrenched elites, mitigated against majority political participation and indeed frustrated attempts at bona fide democratization. In one particular screed entitled 'Behind the "liberal" pose', Han stated that 'liberalism has enjoyed ascendancy because it proffers a theoretical framework that allows right-wing politics to overcome its legitimacy crisis.'[37] According to this view, liberalism and the intellectual mandarins who espoused it were giving succour to the party-state and the status quo; stability was essential for economic prosperity, and the threat of a collapse in China was being used by *soi-disant* liberals as an argument against democratic rebellion, concerted and organized opposition, or radical resistance.

Han Yuhai proclaimed the so-called liberal intelligentsia of China to be bankrupt; he said they had lost any claim to legitimacy themselves and a role in the (presumably more democratic and egalitarian) future of the nation. But even for extremists like Han not all liberalism was bad – even if, as a label, it was useful for tagging one's opponents and condemning them holus-bolus. In the same article Han referred positively to Isaiah Berlin, the political philosopher whose death in 1997 evoked widespread commentary in China, on a 'great herald of liberalism'. Indeed, in Berlin's writings we find a clear articulation of the issues that hound Chinese intellectual debate,

> Both liberty and equality are among the primary goals pursued by human beings throughout many centuries; but total liberty for wolves is death to the lambs, total liberty of the powerful, the gifted, is not compatible with the rights to a decent existence of the weak and the less gifted. . . . Equality may demand the restraint of the liberty of those who wish to dominate; liberty – without some modicum of which there is not choice and therefore no possibility of remaining human as we understand the word – may have to be curtailed in order to make room for social welfare, to feed the hungry, to clothe the naked, to shelter the homeless, to leave room for the liberty of others, to allow justice or fairness to be exercised.[38]

Although both sides could quote Berlin at each other, something that made a dialogue between the contending camps problematic was the glaring disparity in the intellectual underpinnings of the groups. The neo-liberals identified with the post-May Fourth tradition of cultural renewal in China and basically accepted mainstream views of the Western Enlightenment and late-twentieth century Euro-American market democracy. For their part, the neo-leftists were generally imbued with a range of theoretical paradigms that drew on post-modernist, post-colonial and neo-Marxist theories, as well as on more conventional

Marxism–Leninism and Mao Thought. While they may have questioned international capital, some of their number were also deeply concerned with global issues and had points in common with the internationalism of an earlier age. Be that as it may, by the end of the decade, neither side was willing nor, to a certain extent, even able to talk to the other.

Critics like Xu Jilin were intent on maintaining independence from these two, notionally opposed, polemical camps. In 1989, Xu had written an essay on the 'vicious cycle of the May Fourth movement,' in which he reviewed the history of the first decade of the reform era and expressed concern that the nation was entering another period similar to that of the May Fourth when the opposing forces of iconoclasm and conservatism had led to bitter intellectual and cultural infighting. The strife of the 1920s had become endemic to public debates thereafter, and politicized academic life in China for decades.[39] Writing again in 1998, this time in retrospect over the intellectual history of the past twenty years, Xu concluded,

> A unified intellectual sphere in which people can engage in profitable dialogue no longer exists. The consensus of the New Enlightenment [of the 1980s] has collapsed, very much in the way that it did during the original May Fourth movement. Does this mean we are to experience some inescapable historical destiny?[40]

Although I would be tempted to question whether such a consensus ever really existed,[41] a nightmarish vision that predicted that the present would itself disappear in such a circular motion made for an appealing cultural trope. But confinement to this kind of historical 'intellectual panopticon' only tended to serve entrenched intellectual gambits. Confrontations could aid and abet ideological opponents in a media environment still circumscribed by the Communist Party. Indeed, the public clash of competing views tended to enhance extreme positions and led to 'a certain idiom of outrage and vituperation that belongs to the levels of escalation at which debate is no longer possible.'[42] During the late 1990s, each side in the dispute became more extreme in its critique of the other, where a middle ground existed it was often undermined by rhetorical overkill. Both sides felt that their opponents were conspiring (*hemou*) with the authorities. Thus, 'leftists' were identified as being part of the party–state status quo; while the 'rightists' were seen as serving the interests of international capital and new commercial élites within China.

In early 1999, a number of non-aligned Shanghai-based scholars including Xu Jilin gathered to discuss the contest between the new left and the new right. Xu in particular pointed out that there were traditional intellectual resources, a lineage of liberalism dating back to the 1920s, that could perhaps help foster a new environment for rational disputation.[43] What was required was, and here Xu referred to the political philosopher John Rawls, an 'overlapping consensus,' that is to say, an 'overlapping consensus of reasonable comprehensive doctrines.'[44]

Just where that consensus could be found could not easily be articulated in public. As Joseph Brodsky observed in an open letter to the former Czech dissident Václav Havel shortly after the latter's rise to political power in the early 1990s, 'in the police state absolutes compromise each other since they engender each other.' For one point of commonality among the disputants described above appeared to be a shared opposition to the one-party state as it was presently constituted. And although writers would meditate in their long analyses on the multifarious crises facing China, direct confrontation with the authorities was still limited to a small, and at times highly public and vocal, coalition of dissidents. Again, as Brodsky noted about dissidents in socialist Czechoslovakia, overt opponents to the powers-that-be were often a 'convenient example of the wrong deportment and thus a source of considerable moral comfort, the way the sick are for the healthy majority.'[45] Their existence cautioned others not to catch cold.

In the left-wing stance, however, there was also an explicit critique of the monism of globalization and liberalism current in China from the early 1990s. It was a critique that went back to the origins of the 1970s reform policy itself when the incipient economic policies were justified not only as a necessity, but as part of a continued effort to link the nation with the grand trends of market-oriented developmentalism. The 1990s left-wing questioned the new holism, the view that there was one program or rationale that promised through its realization the resolution of the myriad of problems of contemporary life – political, social, cultural and economic. Thus the loose collective of Chinese left-wing thinkers came to articulate an opposition to democratic capitalism and the ideology of a universal civilization, what John Gray identified as the 'last false Utopia of the twentieth-century:' globalization. Perhaps, like Gray, they would feel that,

> The belief that prosperity drags liberal democracy in its wake is an article of faith, not a result of disciplined inquiry. Often it is little more than a neo-liberal variation of the Marxian tenet that the development of capitalism generates a growing middle class. The recent experience of many states supports a different Marxian view: that uncontrolled, slash-and-burn capitalism impoverishes and shrinks the middle class.[46]

But to accept on face value the wholesale (perhaps even ritualistic) condemnation of liberals by writers like Han Yuhai is easily misleading. Liu Junning, for example, was a prominent Beijing-based advocate of liberalism and the editor of the main liberal journal, *Res Publica*. In his editorial introduction to a collection of essays on pre–1949 liberalism and the history of Peking University published at the time of the school's centenary in 1998, Liu noted that, although the Chinese intelligentsia had been captivated by holistic projects from the 1920s, when it came to the economic realities of their own environment they were often at a complete loss. Throughout the century they shared a skepticism regarding the role of free markets and the need for the growth of a strong middle class. For them 'the allure of totalitarian patterns of thought was paramount.' Liu argued that although the intelligentsia had at times shown itself to be passionately interested in cultural liberalism and a measure of political freedom, in regard to socioeconomic realities the disparate members of the nation's liberal thinkers had always 'been basically out of touch with their environment. They have never really been part of the normal Chinese community, rather they have been sequestered in an ivory tower.'[47]

Intellectuals debating these issues in the pages of learned journals, often employing the guarded language required by an environment of official censorship, was one thing. But change would not necessarily come from the refined 'wonking' of the chattering classes or *trahison des clercs*.[48] Dissidents felt that only popular agitation would allow disparate social forces to have a say in the direction and protection of their own lives, as well as in national politics. Other nonaligned intellectuals and social activists attempted in a myriad of ways – through private, small-scale charity projects, covert foundation activities and so on – to engage actively in civic actions that would benefit their fellows. However, for those imbued with the ideologies of national salvation and participation, to be materially well-off but politically dispossessed, a member of the underclass or itinerant labour force, or being engaged but compromised within a system that would allow the acquisition of capital but maintained electoral disenfranchisement and political impotence, was deeply frustrating. The hope, follies and failure of 1989 and the quest for systemic change and political reform that was central to the concerns of thinkers, cultural activists, progressive politicians and people of conscience at the time remained issues central to the political agenda ten years on. Enforced political impuissance and the internecine warfare obsessed the intelligentsia, and for moderate thinkers like Xu Jilin and his fellows, it was increasingly evident that when major changes did come the niceties of political discussion could once more be overridden by restive mass sentiment.

At the end of the millennium, as the People's Republic celebrated its fiftieth anniversary, here was the dilemma that the intelligentsia and cultural activists faced once more. Was the role of the independent critic or feisty artist enough to satisfy participants in the bitter debates about the state of the nation and its future? Was the 20th-century tradition of political agitation and commitment to remain obscured by the Communist Party's purges of the early 1950s, the repression of the Hundred Flowers, the 'mass democracy' of the Cultural Revolution, the crushing of the Democracy Wall dissidents, and the purges of the 1980s, as well as the bloodshed of 1989, and the quelling of dissidents in late 1998? Would élite intellectuals who proffered analyses of the nation's woes find fellowship with dissidents who were willing to confront the government, or workers and peasants whose outrage at exploitation increasingly led them to rebel? Or was the reconstitution of the intellectuals' mission something that encouraged circumspection and inactivity? This 'cult of transgression without risk'[49] found adherents at all points of the political spectrum, while a cult that did not really transgress, like that of the Buddho-Daoist Falun Gong meditational sect that was outlawed in mid-1999, did ironically pose risks for its adherents.

In his 1991 manifesto, 'A Stance of Rejection', Zhou Lunyou had advocated cultural disengagement and disobedience. In the following years, market reforms as well as expanding areas of civil debate and social agitation blurred the simple cultural antagonisms of the past. By the end of the decade, the romance of resistance may still have appealed to observers of the mainland arts scene (both Chinese and foreign), but for prominent participants it was often easier to ignore the state than to resist the discreet charms of offshore capital. In the revolution of resistance, outspoken members of the intelligentsia found themselves variously on the defensive and on the offensive, participants in and opponents to the reforms that had given them a new lease on life. At the *debut de siècle*, the domain of intellectual politics on mainland China was quickened not by an overlapping consensus, but by issues and debates that divided and confronted at every turn.

Acknowledgements

During 1998, I profited from discussions with the following individuals in Shanghai and Beijing: Chris Buckley, He Ping, Li Shulei, Liang Xiaoyan, Liu Naiyuan, Liu Qing, Lu Yuegang, Tang Xiaodu, Wang Dingding, Wang Hui, Wang Xiaoming, Xu Jilin, Yan Bofei and Zang Di. My thanks also to the editors of this volume for their numerous useful suggestions, as well as to Chris Buckley for his comments.

Notes

1 Lu Xun, 'Xiao Zagan', *Eryiji*, collected in *Lu Xun quanji* (Renmin wenxue chubanshe: Beijing, 1981) vol. 3, p. 532. From the translation by Simon Leys in his *The Burning Forest: Essays on Chinese Culture and Politics* (Holt, Rinehart and Winston: New York, 1985), p. 222. The first part of the quotation is:
   Revolution, counterrevolution, nonrevolution.
   Revolutionaries are massacred by counterrevolutionaries. Counterrevolution-aries are massacred by revolutionaries. Nonrevolutionaries are sometimes taken for revolutionaries, and then they are massacred by counterrevolutionaries, or again they are taken for counterrevolutionaries, and then they are massacred by revolutionaries. Sometimes, also, they are not taken for anything in particular, but they are still massacred by revolutionaries and by counterrevolutionaries.
2 Quoted in Geremie R. Barmé, *In the Red: On Contemporary Chinese Culture* (Columbia University Press: New York, 1999), p. 37. For more on the 'Not-not' poets, see G. Barmé and John Minford (eds), *Seeds of Fire: Chinese Voices of Conscience* (Hill & Wang: New York, 1988), 2nd edn, pp. 405–06; and 'Feifei Zhuyi Zhuanji' in *Jintian* (1998) 3, no. 42, pp. 55–96.
3 This is W. J. F. Jenner's gloss on the term 'transgressive'.
4 After 1989, a number of dispirited cultural activists turned to money making in the south. It was a trend also obvious in intellectual discourse from around 1992, at first particularly in Shanghai where a number of intellectuals began playing the stock market and speculated on the real estate boom.
5 Evinced in the new Mao cult, revolutionary *karaoke* numbers, popular interest in pre–1966 feature films, and so on.
6 Michael Dutton, *Streetlife China* (Cambridge University Press: New York, 1998), p. 282.
7 Ibid.
8 That is, ideocrats who supported elements of traditional Marxist–Leninist–Maoist theory, although few of the public, or internal, pronouncements by these figures was 'Maoist' in the pre–1976 or high-Cultural Revolution sense of the word.

9   Xu Jilin, 'Qimengde Mingyun – Ershi Nianlaide Zhongguo Sixiangjie', *Ershiyi shiji* (1998) 12, no. 50, pp. 4–13, at p. 5. For a detailed study of the 1980s cultural foment, see Chen Fong-ching and Jin Guantao, *From Youthful Manuscripts to River Elegy: The Chinese Popular Cultural Movement and Political Transformation 1979–1989* (Chinese University Press: Hong Kong, 1997).

10 For an overview of responses to the intellectual and cultural ructions of the late 1980s, see *On The Eve: China Symposium '89, Bolinas, California, 27–29 April, 1989*, edited and annotated by Geremie R. Barmé, 1996 cyberpublication at <http://www.nmis.org/gate/film/Bolinas1.html>.

11 Xu Jilin, op. cit., p. 6.

12 For the published version of this series, see Wang Shuo, Feng Xiaogang, *et al.*, *Bianjibude Gushi – Youmo Dianshi Gushi* (Shenyang chubanshe: Shenyang, 1992), 2 vols.

13 'Mandopop' was promoted in competition to Canto pop, or Cantonese pop music from the mid 1990s. Mandarin language rock/pop had flourished in Taiwan from the early 1980s with the success of singer-songwriters like Lo Ta-yu (Luo Dayou).

14 Two leading oppositionist journals were *The Pursuit of Truth* (Zhenlide zhuiqiu) and *Currents in Contemporary Thought* (Dangdai sichao).

15 From the interview 'The Non-dissident', in Sang Ye (Geremie R. Barmé, ed.) *Chairman Mao's Ark: The People on the People's Republic* (University of California Press: Berkeley, forthcoming). Although the 1999 Hong Kong edition of Sang Ye's book contained this interview, the editors deleted it from the mainland version.

16 Zhang Chengzhi, *Wuyuande sixiang*, edited by Xiao Xialin (Huayi chubanshe: Beijing, 1995), pp. 24–25, quoted in Barmé, *In the Red*, p. 308. Samuel P. Huntington's controversial work *The Clash of Civilizations and the Remaking of World Order* (Simon & Schuster: New York, 1996), had an inordinate impact in China.

17 Wang Xiaobo, 'Zhishifenzide Buxing', in his *Wode Jingshen Jiayuan: Wang Xiaobo Zawen Zixuan Ji* (Wenhua yishu chubanshe: Beijing, 1997), p. 18; and 'Zhongguo Zhishifenzi yu Zhongguo Yifeng', in his *Siweide lequ* (Beiyue wenyi chubanshe: Taiyuan, 1996), p. 21.

18 An example of this kind of work was the journalist Lu Yuegang's work on the state-induced famine in Fenghuo Village, Shaanxi Province. See Lu, *Daguo guamin* (Zhongguo dianying chubanshe: Beijing, 1998).

19 P. J. O'Rourke, 'How to Have the Worst of Both Worlds: Shanghai', in his *Eat the Rich: a Treatise on Economics* (Atlantic Monthly Press: New York, 1998), pp. 220–21. For a discussion of the impact of another US food giant, Ronald McDonald, in the north, see Yan Yunxiang 'McDonald's in Beijing: the localization of Americana', in James L. Watson (ed.), *Golden Arches East: McDonald's in East Asia* (Stanford University Press: Stanford, CA, 1997), pp. 39–76.

20 Meng Meng (ed.), *1999 Dubai (Juan Yi)* (Shanghai yuandong chubanshe: Shanghai, 1998), pp. 57–58.

21 Xu Jilin, 'Qimengde Mingyun', p. 11.

22 The *qingyi* scholar-officials of the late-nineteenth century were both spokesmen for public conscience and reformers of the status quo. See Luke S. K. Kwong, *A Mosaic of the Hundred Days: Personalities, Politics, and Ideas of 1898* (Harvard University Press: Cambridge, MA, 1984), pp. 68–73, esp. p. 70.

23 For an articulate presentation of these issues by well-informed mainland analysts, see Zhongguo zhanlüe yu guanli yanjiuhui shehui jiegou zhuanxing keti zu, 'Zhongguo Shehui Jiegou Zhuanxingde Zhongjinqi Qushi yu Yinhuan', *Zhanlüe yu guanli* (1998) 5, pp. 1–17; Yang Fan, 'Zhongguo Jingji Mianlinde Weiji yu Fanweiji Duice', *Zhanlüe yu guanli* (1998), 5, pp. 18–27; and He Qinglian, *Xiandaihuede Xianjing – Dangdai Zhongguode Jingji Shehui Wenti* (Jinri Zhongguo chubanshe: Beijing, 1998).

24 The terms in Chinese are *ziyouzhuyipai*, *xinzuopai* and *xinzuoyi*, respectively.

25 *Dushu*, produced by Sanlian Publishing in Beijing, was founded by Fan Yong in the late 1970s and, for twenty years, was a leading forum for public intellectual discussion.

26 Wang Hui, 'Dangdai Zhongguode Sixiang Zhuangkuang yu Xiandaixing Wenti', *Tianya* (1997), 5, pp. 133–50; translated by Rebecca E. Karl as 'Contemporary Chinese Thought and the Question of Modernity,' in *Social Text 55* (1998), 16, pp. 9–44.

27 Wang Hui, 'Kexuezhuyi yu Shehui Lilunde Jige Wenti', *Tianya* (1998), 6, pp. 132–60.

28 During the 1980s, prominent works on this subject were translated from English, and writers like the journalist Dai Qing and Xu Jilin, among others, began introducing the reading public to the variety of liberalist thought and leading pre–1949 liberal activists.

29 Ibid. Xu identifies the idolization of the Cultural Revolution-period writings of Gu Zhun (both essays and diaries). For reactions to Gu Zhu's posthumous literary debut, see Ding Dong and Chen Minzhi (eds.), *Gu Zhun Xunsi lu* (Zuojia chubanshe: Beijing, 1998). The best-seller status of the 1997 translations of von Hayek's *The Road to Serfdom* and *The Constitution of Liberty*, as well as the influence of *Res Publica* (Gonggong luncong), a journal edited by Liu Junning, aided the theoretical and public rise of liberalist thinking in China.

30 See, in particular, the introductory essays of Li Shenzhi and Liu Junning in Liu Junning (ed.), *Ziyouzhuyide Xiansheng: Beida Chuantong yu Jndai Zhongguo* (Beijing: Zhongguo renshi chubanshe), 1998, pp. 1–5; and the essays by a range of prominent thinkers in Dong Yuyu and Shi Binhai, eds, *Zhengzhi Zhongguo: Mianxiang Xintizhi Xuanzede Shidai* (*Jinri Zhongguo* chubanshe: Beijing, 1998).

31 Xu, op. cit., p. 13, note 14. See also Ren Jiantao, 'Jiedu "Xin Zuopai"', *Tianya* (1999) 1, pp. 35–46.

32 Based at The Institute of Chinese Studies, The Chinese University of Hong Kong, *Twenty-first Century* was edited by Liu Qingfeng and Jin Guantao. Throughout the decade this journal, which was increasingly available on the mainland, was one of the major forums for intellectual and cultural debate in the Chinese-reading world.

33 Xu Jilin, op. cit., p. 11. These writers included, in particular, Gan Yang, Cui Zhiyuan, Sheng Hong, Wang Shaoguang and Hu Angang. For details of their early writings, see Xu, op. cit., p. 13, note 15. See also Xudong Zhang's introduction to 'Intellectual Politics in Post-Tiananmen China,' in *Social Text 55*, op. cit., pp. 1–8.

34 *Yangjingbang Xuefeng*. See Liu Dong, 'Jingti Renweide "Yang Jingbang Xuefeng"', *Ershiyi Shiji* (1995), 12, pp. 4–13, and a response from Gan Yang, 'Shei shi Zhongguo Yanjiuzhongde "Women"?', *Ershiyi Shiji* (1995), 12, pp. 21–25.

35 Quoted in Erik Eckholm, 'Detour on Capitalist Road: Die-hard Maoist Collective', *The New York Times* 7 January 1999.

36 For a range of the opinions regarding media freedom, as well as legal and democratic reform, see the 1998 volume of essays by leading liberal thinkers edited by Dong Yuyu and Shi Binhai, *Zhongguo zhengzhi*, op. cit.

37 Han Yuhai, 'Zai "Ziyouzhuyi" Zitaide Beihou', *Tianya* (1998), 5, p. 17.

38 Isaiah Berlin, 'The Pursuit of the Ideal', in his *The Crooked Timber of Humanity: Chapters in the History of Ideas*, Henry Hardy (ed.) (Fontana Press: London, 1990), pp. 12–13. See also David Kelly, 'The Chinese Search for Freedom as a Universal Value' in David Kelly and Anthony Reid (eds.), *Asian Freedoms: The Idea of Freedom in East and Southeast Asia* (Cambridge University Press: New York, 1998), pp. 99–114.

39 See Xu's comments as translated in Geremie Barmé and Linda Jaivin (eds), *New Ghosts, Old Dreams: China's Rebel Voices* (Times Books: New York, 1992), pp. 345–50.

40 Xu Jilin, op. cit., p. 12.

41 In regard to the 1980s, for example, one thinks of the overlapping but often antagonistic agendas of various intellectuals and cultural figures. There were also those dissidents, old and young, who rejected the elitist consensus entirely.

42 J. M. Coetzee, *Giving Offense, Essays on Censorship* (University of Chicago Press: Chicago, 1996), p. 134.

43 See, for example, Xu Jilin, 'Shehui Minzhuzhuyide Lishi Yichan – Xiandai Zhongguo Ziyouzhuyide Huigu', *Kaifang shidai* (1998) 4, pp. 13–20; and Jerome B. Grieder, *Hu Shih and the Chinese Renaissance: Liberalism in the Revolution, 1917–1937* (Harvard University Press: Cambridge, MA, 1970).

44 John Rawls, *Political Liberalism* (Columbia University Press: New York, 1993), p. 43. See also, pp. 140, 144ff. The Qinghua University historian Qin Hui was, in particular, an advocate of such an 'overlapping consensus'.

45 Joseph Brodsky, 'Letter to a President', written as a response to a speech by Václav Havel published in *The New York Review of Books*, 27 May 1993. For these quotes, see Brodsky, *On Grief and Reason: Essays* (Hamish Hamilton: London, 1996), pp. 214 and 215, respectively.

46 John Gray, *False Dawn: The Dilemmas of Global Capitalism* (Granta Books: London, 1998), pp. 3 and 191 respectively.

47 Liu Junning, 'Beida Chuantong yu Jinxiandai Zhongguode Ziyouzhuyi', editor's preface to *Beida chuantong yu jindai Zhongguo*, p. 9.

48 Those whose interests, and jobs, were concerned with formulating policies like the Anglo-American Third Way in the 1990s were called members of the 'working classes'. What they did was 'to work'.

49 This formulation comes from Pierre Bourdieu. See his *Acts of Resistance. Against the Tyranny of the Market* (The New Press: New York, 1998), p. 12.

11 Suicide as resistance in Chinese society

Sing Lee and Arthur Kleinman

According to recently available statistics, China has by far the world's largest number of reported suicides: more than 300,000 each year, comprising 42 percent of all suicides world-wide and 56 percent of all suicides in women. Although there are substantial inter-regional differences, about 90 percent of suicides in China are rural, and of these young women are affected two times more than young men. This pattern of high suicide rates in young rural women is unique. It is not only against the Confucian value of filial piety (*xiao*) and the Daoist philosophy of inaction (*wuwei*), but is also counter to virtually everything written about suicide in the West, from Durkheim to the present.

Although psychiatrists frequently attribute suicide to mental illness, suicide can also be viewed as a social indicator. Because there are no long-term data available, it is not certain if the rate is increasing (as it is at present in many countries worldwide); the very low rates of depression and substance abuse documented in community epidemiological studies in China render psycho-pathology a grossly inadequate explanation for the disturbing number of suicides. There are numerous anecdotal accounts of suicide from the Maoist era of political chaos, affecting particularly intellectuals and 'rightist' cadres in urban China. This seems to suggest that high rates of suicide may well represent a long-term trend in that country. However, the fact that a disproportionately high percentage of rural women commit suicide speaks to the working of a particular conglomeration of social factors specific to contemporary rural China. These include, among others, long-term patriarchal influences, recent economic reforms and their adverse consequences for certain susceptible families, state-imposed birth control policy, preference for sons over daughters, and the easy availability of pesticides as a lethal method of suicide.

In this paper, we submit that suicide may be considered a strategy of resistance (in James Scott's sense) by women who feel powerless in situations of political and social domination. We also set out a model for understanding suicide and other social health problems as a result of the effects of largescale social forces (global and national) transforming local moral worlds (villages, neighborhoods, communities) in such a way as to alter the interconnection between the moral, political and medical underpinnings of social and individual experience.

For Gentlemen of purpose and men of benevolence, while it is inconceivable that they should seek to stay alive at the expense of benevolence, it may happen that they have to accept death in order to have benevolence accomplished.

Analects, Book XV.9[1]

In the West we ask of a suicide, 'Why?' In China the question is more commonly, 'Who? Who drove her to this? Who is responsible' . . . for a woman it is the most damning public accusation she can make of her mother-in-law, her husband, or her son.

Margery Wolf (1975: 112)

Introduction

Suicide is a universal phenomenon of humankind that has been shown to have different causes and consequences. When 33-year-old Kevin Carter, a celebrated South African photojournalist, killed himself only several months after winning the highly prestigious Pulitzer Prize for photographing a starving toddler in the southern Sudan (who had, in one of the Sudan's civil war-created famines, fallen down alone in a stubble field with a huge vulture nearby, an icon of African misery), his suicide could be attributed to a number of different things: remorse over letting the child die and appropriating the image of her death for fame and fortune to begin with, but also substance abuse, break-up of his marriage and separation from his own small daughter, and to be sure his manic–depressive disorder.

Depending on the observer's disciplinary bias and discursive context, the life of a suicide examined microscopically can support different causal interpretations – thick craniums or excess phosphorus in the brain for physicians in the nineteenth century (Farberow 1975), depression and/or borderline personality disorder for a modern psychiatrist, negative cognition for a psychologist, anomie for a sociologist, patriarchy for a feminist, or change of meaning for an anthropologist. The death certificate, however, does not have space or authorization for the complex account of a life, rather a local term or at most a phrase is assigned to indicate the cause of death. In addition, political and economic factors may affect how readily a death is ascribed to suicide. For example, authoritarian regimes typically have suppressed the reporting of deaths as suicide and prohibited the disclosure of suicide statistics because of concern that such data will be used to critique the state. Thus, until the late 1980s, data on suicide were embargoed in China. In market economies, the need to seek compensation from insurance companies may make the suicide's family prefer a disguise of accidental death.

At the collective level of social statistics, nonetheless, it has been repeatedly shown that suicide rates can serve as an index of societal problems, such as economic downturn, political violence, social chaos, and the current phase of global capitalism (Desjarlais *et al.* 1995). Emile Durkheim (1897), the great French sociologist and anthropologist who was active early in this century, described kinds of suicides which represented, he surmised, responses to anomic tensions of social breakdown and others that responded to socially approved opportunities for altruistic action. Nowadays, suicide is two to five times more common in men in Europe, North America, Africa, and Latin America. This gender ratio is less pronounced in Asian countries, being 1.3 in Hong Kong and Singapore, 1.7 in Japan, and 1.3 in India respectively. The ratio between youth and elder suicide also varies with respect to society (Desjarlais *et al.* 1995). And, even if two societies have the same suicide rates, the local causes, meanings, and impacts of suicide can still be quite different (Baechler 1979). As a social index, suicide may therefore be indexing different things across societies.

Suicide in traditional Chinese society

For complex historical, political and social reasons, suicide in China has not gone through a period of critical social science inquiry as in the West. Nonetheless, there is ample evidence that suicide has a long history and ancient provenance in Chinese culture. In a scholarly dissertation on suicide in pre-modern China, Lin (1990: 7) has even suggested that 'suicide is a hallmark of Chinese culture.' Suicide was connected, for example, with changing of dynasties (*gai chao huan dai*), wars, corrupt emperors, and inauspicious family situations. It was variously described as an act of ardent loyalty toward an emperor (*zhong chen bu shi er zhu*), as a moral protest, and as a strategy for dealing with exploitative and oppressive social relations (Da 1993; He 1996). Mass suicide, involving at times hundreds and even thousands of people, and affirming moral commitment to a leader, was part of the record of Chinese history (He 1996: 187). This moral grounding of suicide is salient for social analysis because it explicates the downside of the society that the suicides may be criticizing.

When transposed into the female life world, suicide was available to women as a way of defending their loyalty and chastity (*zhen jie*). More commonly, it was an ultimate means of escape (*jie tuo*) from life situations they found to be more unbearable than death (*sheng bu ru si*), such as forced remarriage, brutal bondage as a kind of slave and producer of sons in miserably oppressive family situations, accusations of adultery or incest, marriage to abusive husbands who squandered the family fortune, took concubines and other wives, abuse by in-laws, and the like.

It needs remembering, of course, that suicide is not simply authorized in the Chinese tradition. As an unnatural death it was to be avoided and the *felo de se* was in some texts not to be mourned for. Suicide was polluted and polluting. It also entails economic loss by diminishing productive and/or reproductive power. Whatever the individual motives involved, suicide represents a rejection of everything in society on the level of cultural production, and compels the members of society to doubt its core values. Confucian teachings, too, do not simply encourage suicide as a way of fulfilling virtue (*sha shen cheng ren*) or choosing righteousness (*she sheng qu yi*). There is, for example, the filial notion that 'Our bodies, in every hair and bit of skin, are acquired from our parents, and must not be injured or damaged' (*shenti fa fu shou zhi fumu, bu ke wei shang*). Suicide notes left by dead persons typically convey a deep sense of apology and of unfulfilled filial responsibility towards their parents or other family members (Liu and Li 1990: 41). To die and become a solitary spirit with no one to depend on (*gu hun wu yi*) is, in fact, against the Confucian emphasis on family solidarity. Likewise, by propounding naturalness (*zi ran*), non-action (*wu wei*), and contentment with ordinariness (*gan ju zhong you*), Daoism does not advocate suicide either (Zhai 1997: 289). Buddhist responses to suicide are multi-sided, but there is much in Buddhism as well that does not authorize it.

Unlike the Christian churches' explicit anti-suicide stance (Farberow 1975), the Chinese cultural tradition generally and Confucian doctrine more narrowly are somewhat ambiguous, and can be used either to support suicide as prosocial, or discourage it as antisocial. This is not surprising as Chinese have been shown to appropriate the Confucian past both as a moral ideal and for solving practical problems in daily life (Lin 1990). When these uses are not in agreement, then the tension between them allows for creative ambiguity as well as the difficulties of normlessness and hypocrisy. At turbulent times when it was necessary to choose between loyalty to the country (*zhong*), the husband (*zhen*) and the father (*xiao*), women who killed themselves emulated and defied Confucian teachings at the same time. For this reason, the larger community, the clan, and the family might react to their death differently.

Suicide in modern China

Suicide rates in Hong Kong and Taiwan are relatively stable and comparable to the global average, being 10.6/100,000 and 10.0/100,000 per year (1981–94), respectively (Yip 1996). This may suggest that Chinese people are not particularly prone to suicide.[2] But data made available in China since the early 1990s have suggested a very different picture. These data have come from a variety of sources: Chinese Ministry of Health, World Health Organization (WHO) (based on figures from the Chinese Academy of Preventive Medicine's county level reporting system), and the World Bank, as well as from Chinese investigators and others.

According to the World Bank's *The Global Burden of Disease* study (Murray and Lopez 1996), there were 343,000 suicides in China in 1990, about three times the global average, making suicide the fifth most important health problem in the country. Among women it is a greater source of lost workdays than common diseases such as diabetes, heart disease, or cancer. This study also found that although China has 21 percent of the world's population, it accounts for 44 percent of all reported suicides worldwide and for an astounding 56 percent of all female suicides worldwide.[3] Young rural females are at particularly high risk: for those 15–35 years of age suicide accounts for more than 20 percent of all deaths (Phillips *et al.* in press). Using data from the thirty-nine countries that provide suicide statistics to the WHO, we and other colleagues at Harvard Medical School compiled the World Mental Health Report (Desjarlais *et al.* 1995). This found that China has the second highest suicide rate amongst young adults aged 15 to 24 (after Sri Lanka), and the third highest rate amongst the elderly (after Hungary and Sri Lanka). Moreover, China is the *only* country in the world that reports higher rates of suicide in women than in men. It has also been predicted that suicide rates will continue to rise in the next two decades (Murray and Lopez 1996). Although Chinese researchers' estimates are invariably, and perhaps rightly, lower than those made by Western researchers (e.g., Da 1993: 22.8/100,000; He 1996: 17.1/100,000),[4] it is almost certain that China still has the world's largest number of reported suicides by virtue of its 1.2 billion population – 800 (or at least 600) people are killing themselves each day.

Data on suicide in China have challenged a number of entrenched facts and theories in the West. One of these is gender ratio. In most Western countries, male suicides outnumber female suicides by three to five times. This gendered pattern has promoted views of womanhood that we do not endorse. For example, Jean Baechler (1975: 291) wrote that:

> women endure misfortune better than do men. Their social roles require them to face unbearable problems less frequently. . . . As daughters, wives, and mistresses, and conforming to the dependency which nature and culture encourage, women have a greater tendency to reach their ends by the *threat* (emphasis is ours) of trying to kill themselves. . . . Dangerous and aggressive behavior generally is not characteristic of women.

In more recent years, psychiatrists have trivialized female suicidal behavior as 'manipulative', 'hysterical', or 'pseudocidal'.

Suicide in China also casts doubt on the notion that social isolation, crowding, and laxness of social control lead to more suicides in urban than rural areas. For example, Halbwacks (1930, cited in Taylor 1988: 16) suggested that 'suicide was relatively higher in urban areas because the urban way of life was more transitory and impersonal, and left increasing numbers of individuals socially isolated from their fellows and hence vulnerable to suicide'. But the rural idyll is a myth in China. Although suicides may be less likely to be reported in rural than urban regions, the rural rates of suicide are three-fold the urban rates (Phillips *et al.* in press).

Suicide in China disputes Western assumptions in yet another way, namely, that it is predominantly a result of psychiatric disease. What we do know is that even though the rates of depression and substance abuse are going up in China, they are much lower than in the West. The latest community epidemiological studies indicate that the rates of mood disorder may be more than 200 times lower in China than in the US (Lee 1999).[5] Yet, the rate of suicide is three times higher in China than the US (Murray and Lopez 1996). Likewise, alcoholism remains, for China as a whole, relatively uncommon. Thus, unless new research were to show that our current epidemiological and clinical data are completely wrong, it is hard to imagine that depression and alcohol are largely responsible for China's suicides.

Suicide is also notable in our time because the rates are going up in many developing societies together with rates of alcohol abuse, illicit substance abuse, violence, sexually transmitted diseases, and depression and anxiety disorders, as what our colleagues and we have called 'the downside of capitalism' and the traumatic social health consequences of global social change (Desjarlais et al 1995). Although all these rates have been going up in China, too, we cannot be entirely sure over the long term if the suicide rate in China is going up or coming down, because the only valid data are from the last 10 years. Tellingly, He (1996) cited one study which estimated that the annual suicide rate among the faculty at 'one well-known university' in China was 87.4/100,000 during the Cultural Revolution (1966–76), and as high as 532/100,000 for the year 1970. The cause of suicide was reported to be political in 95.2 percent of cases (p. 191 and p. 292).

Given this estimate and other anecdotal information from the Cultural Revolution, there is reason to suspect that the rate during that chaotic and destructive time may well have been even greater than it is at present, though the subgroups of people most affected could be different in the two periods.[6] Although psychiatric epidemiologists speak of baseline rates, this idea is of dubious validity from the standpoint of anthropology. It assumes a societal state of changeless equilibrium that is contradicted by the experience of Chinese in this century, which has been one of near constant but different societal change.

Suicide as resistance

Unlike Durkheim's classic theory of suicide which has been criticized for leaving out individual motives and their relationship with social values (La Fontaine 1975; Baechler 1979), recent anthropological theory emphasizes that human experience is *intersubjective*: people live in close relation to others in local worlds (villages, clans, neighborhoods, networks, work units, families) and what is at stake in those worlds affects what is at stake for individuals (Kleinman and Kleinman 1997). Large-scale economic, political and cultural transformations – such as the global changes of our era – can alter or threaten what is at stake. People's actions are influenced not only by what individuals think and feel, but by the values and practices that characterize the local worlds in which they live, struggle, and die. Indeed, what people feel and what they value is so closely linked that moral processes and emotional processes interfuse. That is to say, collective delegitimation experiences are associated with subjective states of demoralization; relegitimation at the social level realizes remoralization at the level of individuals.

Seen in this anthropological way, suicide can be understood as a means of resisting social power and thereby as a strategy in the intersubjective struggles of everyday social experience. The phenomenologist Max Scheler (1971[1928]) argued that resistance is a part of ordinary existence. The social and natural worlds resist our purposes and plans; and we in turn resist the imposition of authority, especially when it threatens what is most at stake for individuals in their local worlds. Thus, for example, the political scientist James Scott, in several publications (e.g. 1990), has shown how villagers – who are responding to a change in the moral economy in which they live that alters what they expect from others and what is expected from them – may resort to foot-dragging, rumor, non-compliance, and even sabotage, to indicate their unwillingness to go along with changes in everyday life conditions that they now regard as unacceptable, and to resist the power of those who coerce them. Likewise, Lucien Bianco

(1978) has demonstrated a range of peasant resistance in Republican China, from tax protest to rent strikes to crowd violence and revolt. He cautions, however, that such anti-fiscal riots were usually non-coordinated and presented no major threat to the authorities. Albeit common, they also did not depict the claims of the most disadvantaged layers in the rural population. Bianco then notes that 'one of the most popular ways to take revenge upon a pitiless creditor is to commit suicide before his door' (p. 280). Even though this is 'a roundabout way of expressing aggression towards the exploiter' (p. 301), it could serve to make the landlord lose face.

The question we want to examine is: under what conditions do ordinary Chinese men, and women in particular, embody (or strategically employ) suicide as a form of social resistance? What kind of resistance is it? What consequences does it have? How should we respond to it?

Suicide as social resistance has been interpreted as occurring in different Asian societies; the classical examples cited are certain, though by no means all, instances of suttee in India and seppuku in Japan. Although China is often left out of such interpretation, there are, in fact, various historical examples of suicide as resistance in the Chinese tradition. Of course this is only one of different kinds of suicide among the Chinese (Lin 1990). Thus, the suicide of Qu Yuan (340–278 BC) as told in *Li Sao* may be a quintessentially Chinese example of the right of a scholar-bureaucrat to criticize the policies of a government by taking his life. Compared to the adversarial style of faultfinding, by drowning himself in the Miluo River (on 5 May, lunar calendar), Qu Yuan was engaging in a mode of criticism that did not upset the rules of social harmony and hierarchy so much underscored in Chinese culture.

But his suicide needs also to be seen as an active moral act inasmuch as it was meant to show that even death is preferable to living under unacceptable political conditions. For just this reason, Qu Yuan's example has traditionally been valued by Chinese, who persevere in the rituals of dragon boat racing, and of throwing glutinous rice in lotus leaves into the river/sea, symbolically preventing his body from being eaten by hungry fish, and feeding his hungry ghost. Thereby they celebrate, remember, and reaffirm resistance as a part of their cultural identity. In other words, the scholar–bureaucrat in the Chinese tradition was expected to be an independent source of moral authority who had the right to criticize and respond to the times in which he lived. Suicide for Qu Yuan was both a criticism and an act of resistance. In this way, it has the paradoxical effect of 'living by killing' – living not at the physical level but in the moral and cultural plane (*jingshen bu si*).

Chinese history also has many examples of scholar–bureaucrats who withdrew from public life, with excuses like age, sickness, madness, eccentricity and the like, because they did not want to serve a particular emperor or his regime. These acts could be considered social resistance as well, and might even become examples of 'dying to achieve virtue' (*sha shen cheng ren*), as when officials of the last Ming emperor refused to serve the new Qing dynasty. But this concept of social resistance does not have to involve the political domain alone. It can occur inside an institution and, perhaps most commonly, in the family. For example, Chinese history contains innumerable accounts of women who committed suicide to resist intrafamilial oppression and exploitation. Some did so to avoid forced marriages that they found unacceptable. Others were resisting the over-bearing brutality of husbands and in-laws. Yet others were responding to miscarriage, involuntary female infanticide, polygamy, and forced prostitution. In these pernicious patriarchal contexts, suicide provides both subjective escape and, intended or not, a means of social resistance. Etymologically, the word 'resist' was borrowed from Old French *resister* and directly from Latin *resistere*, meaning to 'stand still' or 'stand against' (Barnhart 1995: 657). Hanging (*shangdiao*), the most common method of suicide in traditional Chinese society and in contemporary Japan, was the final, but unequivocal, way of standing still against and above oppressive authorities, often with the suicide ceremonially dressed prior to the ultimate act.

In these cases suicide created social consequences which made it a powerful action, even though a desperate and final one for the dead person. For example, daughters-in-law who rebelled against degrading oppression in highly authori-tarian families by committing suicide caused the family to lose the social production and reproduction of an important member. It also menaced the family's prosperity with the inauspiciousness of the death and with the threatening presence of a hungry ghost, which could attack family members, causing illness or misfortune (Wolf 1975). There are texts that show that the *hun* of the person who committed suicide by hanging polluted the ground under the body, and the dirt had to be removed as another example of the dire consequences for the family of this sociomoral form of death.

Case studies in contemporary China

Can the concept of social resistance help us understand the distinct pattern suicide takes in China nowadays? Though no substitute for detailed ethnography, reports of suicide from contemporary China provide, in a modest way, stories that do sound like social resistance. For example, there have been newspaper reports of group suicides of Chinese farmers in Hunan to protest enforcement of laws preventing burials of family members in ancestral lands that the local state now regards as too valuable for agricultural purposes. Other suicides have protested corruption, injustice, and the laying off of hundreds of thousands of workers at moribund state owned enterprises. Liu and Li (1990), among others, described a number of cases which, fragmented as they are, suggest that suicide may constitute resistance against the exploitative components of traditional culture and the downside of China's economic reforms (He 1998).

A young rural woman, Chen, had a 3-year relationship with young man, Li. They had sex several times, resulting in pregnancy. When Li demanded separ-ation, Chen pleaded many times in vain. Feeling hopeless and too ashamed to face people (*wu lian jian ren*), she swallowed a large amount of pesticide. She then walked to the Court and died there (He 1998: p. 91). This should not be understood only as an impulsive act by an individual that followed broken love, or a woman's way of freeing herself from the terrible shame of premarital pregnancy in rural China. It can also be interpreted as a premeditated act based in the intersubjectivity of social experiences that constituted a moral accusation against Li's irresponsibility and resistance against patriarchy. While compelling evidence for either interpretation is not presently available, the confluence of other stories and sources of data make the issue of resistance at least as salient as the cliched common sense intuition of impulsivity.

Unlike in ancient times, for example, young rural women nowadays are aware that choice in marriage is possible, especially in urban China. Yet the custom of 'matches are to be arranged by parents' order and on the matchworker's word' (*fumu zhi ming, mei shuo zhi yan*) remains influential. The anomic gap between expectation and actuality then intensifies young women's frustration over arranged (and often mercenary) marriage. The latter is typically of low quality and high stability, and causes fatalism which classically has been considered a psychological antecedent to suicide (Durkheim 1966). Liu and Li (1990: 112) described cases of group suicide among young rural women in Fujian, where they literally formed a suicidal 'alliance' (*tongmeng*) to protest against arranged marriage. The story of three such girls all with the surname of Chen is instructive:

> Chen[1] was 18 years old. Under her parents' arrangement, she was engaged when she was only 12. Although she was supposed to have been 'in love' with this man for 6 years, the two of them never spoke. Their relationship consisted only of 'casting a sidelong glance' at each other occasionally. Chen[2] was engaged even earlier, at the innocent age of 10. On growing up, she became very dissatisfied with the prospect of a loveless marriage. Chen[3] was a lively girl who was good at singing and dancing. She was engaged at an early age, but fell in love instead with a young male actor from the village's theatrical troupe. Although she wanted to break off the engagement, her parents were insistent that she should comply. Being similarly afflicted and feeling much pity for one another, the three girls decided to emulate a scene in a play by choosing to die together in protest against the arranged marriage. It was two days after they died that people discovered their bodies at a secluded hillside.

Similar incidents have been reported from other rural provinces such as Jiangxi, where fifteen young women dressed themselves in choice clothes and threw themselves in group into a lake. Some of them were reported to believe that after they died they might return to live better lives as urban girls (*South China Morning Post*, October 15, 1988, cited in Phillips *et al.* in press). In more traditional times and in other rural areas, these girls might have prayed for spiritual release and heavenly happiness.[7] Their longing for an urban status tallies with the widely demonstrated fact and the everyday perception among Chinese people in China that urban and rural lives are now as unequal as heaven and hell (*tian yuan zhi bie*). Of course, many more women, who would comply with their parents' arrangement for fear of incurring gossip (*ren yan ke wei*) and chastisement, hold out against a lifetime of 'sharing the same bed but dreaming different dreams' (*tong chuang yi meng*).

Suicide may, of course, occur after marriage. Zhou was arranged by her parents to marry a man she did not love. Despite her resentment, she was forced to accept the marriage. Afterwards, she tried hard to develop feelings for him, and did everything she could to be a good wife. However, her husband was a habitual gambler who scolded and quarreled with her all the time. Feeling utterly helpless, she chose an alternative way of escape and protest that was suicide (Liu and Li 1990: 93). This case demonstrates that suicide may be the last strategy used by disempowered women in oppressive marriage situations.

Work-place harassment, though not necessarily recognised as such, can also trigger suicide. For example, after being raped and then continually tormented by her supervisor, a 17-year-old temporary worker at a supply and marketing agency left home to kill herself. Before she died, she left her parents the following note (Liu and Li 1990: 41):

> Dear Dad and Mom:
> Forgive me for doing this. I hate myself! Why am I a woman?! Why is the world so unfair to me?! Although I am only 17, I find my life not worth living any more. Instead of having beautiful dreams, I am suffering . . . I am tormented by a wolf disguised as human. He scares me, but I dare not complain as he is so powerful. I cannot lose my dignity as a woman but if I don't comply, I will lose my job. Then neither you nor society will sympathize with me – I cannot stand such contempt (*bai yan*). You may not believe it, the person who makes me take this path is my supervisor – Wang X.X. Mom, after I am gone, please redress the injustice and seek revenge for me and have him punished. . . . This is the only way I can reduce my mental pain. Forgive your non-filial daughter. Mom, don't come and find me, and don't cry for me. Take care, Dad and Mom. Let me repay all your love and care from childhood in my next life!'.
>
> Your daughter's last words (*jue bi*)

Teenage suicide may represent yet another form of resistance against rural parents who, being socially disadvantaged themselves, invest heavily and hold high expectations of their children's academic performance. For example, poor peasant Fu and his wife in Sichuan, having suffered from illiteracy themselves, held high hopes for their 14-year-old daughter (*wan zi cheng long*). They saved up money in order to send her to school, with the long-term hope of changing their family's rural status. Unfortunately, Miss Fu failed the entrance examination for junior high school in 1987. Her parents then paid a good sum of money to allow her to resit the examination. Later they warned her, 'if you fail the examination next year, even our ancestors will lose face!' Feeling overburdened, Miss Fu wrote in her room on 9 June, 1988: 'A large number of students are sitting the examination this year, but only a small number will be accepted into high school.

I really don't have the courage to walk into the examination hall'. She then poisoned herself to death (Liu and Li 1990: 110).

Over nine-tenths of parents in urban China now have only one child, while rural couples are usually allowed to have a maximum of two children. This birth control policy has beneficially reduced the risk of population explosion, but has made a poignant impact on young rural women, whose only opportunity to improve their lowly status may be to produce sons rather than daughters. Tellingly, a study of sixty-five young rural women (age 20–30) whose first born had been a girl showed that as many as 67 percent of them reported suffering from neurasthenia[8] (Zhou 1988). The great majority (82 percent) of them experienced a loss of face for having produced female babies, and some felt they were prematurely forced into sterilization, which crushed their longing to give birth to another child. Specifically, they were fearful about not carrying on the lineage, the loss of extra labour power, and not having someone to provide for them in old age. These collective fears were compounded by the abrupt change in attitude of their husbands and parents-in-law, who likewise felt a loss of face, became apathetic, and called them 'the devil who extinguishes the family' derogatorily. Physical abuse and threats of divorce were common.[9] Hostile attitudes were also shown by their neighbours, who shared the patriarchal belief that since daughters would eventually 'marry out', they were *pei qian huo* ('commodities on which the seller stands to lose') – a metaphoric phrase in which rural women's powerlessness finds its most succinct expression. In Zhou's study, one rural woman had the following to say about her oppressive local world:

I was sterilized after the birth of two girls. My mother-in-law condemned me by saying: 'I have only one son who married a bitch like you. You have extinguished our family. Get out of here and get yourself killed; otherwise we will never turn around.' My husband abused me, beat me, and threatened to divorce me every day. He angrily reproached me: 'If I can get rid of you, you ugly woman, I'll get another woman who can bear me a son. I'll kill you if you don't clear out.'

The birth-control policy may also interact with marital problems in leading to suicide. For example, elder sister Liu killed herself with poison after discovering that her younger sister had an improper relationship with her husband Zheng. After her death, younger sister Liu cohabited with Zheng illegally. She got pregnant later and desired to keep the child. Since Zheng already had a son, he was reluctant to accept this future child for fear of being punished. She reacted by poisoning herself (Liu and Li 1990: 93).

Phillips and coworkers (in press) cite one more example of how the low status and limited options of rural women contribute to suicide. A 38-year-old illiterate rural woman killed herself by taking insecticide in 1994 after protesting uselessly against her husband's extramarital affair with another woman in a neighboring village. Her heavy household responsibilities then fell on their 16-year-old daughter who was unable to stand the hard work and her father's physical abuse.

After making seven pairs of cloth shoes for her younger brothers as a parting gift, she 'joined her mother' by taking pesticide as well. Sadly, the main community response to the tragedy was to find the elder son a wife who would then once again take up the onerous household chores.

Rural women may use suicide to resist despotism outside of the family as well. One issue of *Democracy and Law* (*Minzhu yu Fazhi*, 1988, volume 1) described such a young woman whose wheat wagon accidentally tumbled over and killed a chicken of the wife of the deputy head of a town. She was subsequently tortured until she was unable to work again. She tried many times to lodge a complaint to the authorities concerned but was invariably ignored. In the end, she killed the 4-year-old boy of the deputy head and then committed suicide herself. It would seem that this woman was legally liable to provide compensation for the chicken. The tragic act of self-killing can, nonetheless, be understood as a form of rebellion against oppressive officials (*guan bi min fan*).

Another adverse consequence of economic reform in China is the decline of family solidarity, filial values, and status of aging people, though the weakening of these core commitments is a much longer term process that reflects the destructiveness of this century in China, especially the ruinous political movements under radical Maoism. Li and Wan (1987) described a 60-year-old illiterate rural man with three daughters and two sons, all of whom were married. He lived alone as none of the children wanted to support him. They also quarrelled frequently over the responsibility of caring for him, and complained that he simply 'ate the bread of idleness' (*chi bai shi*). After another such quarrel, he killed himself by ingesting pesticide. While there is a historical tradition, supported in the Confucian classics, of the elderly committing suicide as an altruistic act of saving limited resources, in this instance the issue seemed to be angry resentment.

Inequitable access to health care is now a major problem in China. Because economic reforms have drastically limited the state budget for health-care financing, health care is now organized less by the socialist spirit of equity than the language of cost. The rural health-care financing and delivery system of the Maoist years has disappeared. Being predominantly uninsured, rural people have to pay for medical services out-of-pocket. To do this, however, may be for them to invite a financial catastrophe (Lee 1999). In the face of competing needs, sick parents may be the first party in the family to be sacrificed. This is illustrated by the case of a 47-year-old rural man with a debilitating neurological disease that required medical treatment. In order to save money (that would otherwise be spent on medical care) for his daughter to enter university (an unusual achievement for a rural female), he killed himself by taking insecticide in 1995. His death as a loving father (*ci fu*) mobilized the local community to help pay his daughter's education (Phillips *et al.* 1999). From a family-centered perspective perhaps, his suicide can be considered a triumphant strategy of resistance against inequitable access to health care and limited education for rural people as much as an act of filial concern. Resistance in this sense need not connote resentment or recrimination, but a practical strategy to protest and mobilize resources.

Although the above case descriptions are selective, lack ethnographic detail of a vital nature, and may be biased toward clinicians' psychosocial framings, they can be rethought as social resistance. To do so means that the infrapolitics of the local world be given primacy over the stereotypes routinely applied to individuals. The issue of resistance against the vicious bonds of patriarchal subjugation should perhaps come as little surprise, as it has long been suggested that the weakest part of the Chinese social fabric is the insecurity in the life of a woman before she establishes her own 'uterine' family (Wolf 1975). Nonetheless, the nature of patriarchal mistreatment in the above cases is not exactly the same as those classically described in traditional China, such as a woman following a husband loyally in death instead of remarrying (*cong yi er zhong*) and being awarded with tablets of honor because of the familial cohesiveness her death displayed socially, or a woman killing herself in order to become an avenging spirit. The woman worker who was raped (see p. 230), for example, requested in her suicide note that her mother should seek revenge for her. This does not suggest that she operated with the belief that she would become a malicious ghost after her own death. Her suicide cannot be attributed, therefore, to the traditional belief in a vengeful *hun*. Rather than being based on ghostly vengeance (Jeffreys 1952), it suggests an active strategy of soliciting familial retaliation.

Instead of being viewed as 'feudal remains' of religious and moral traditions, as often happens in the ideology of Chinese communism, suicide in contemporary Chinese women can be interpreted in the context of the poignantly gendered impact of economic reforms on a changing patriarchal society. For example, although arranged marriage of an even more oppressive kind was normative in traditional China, the opportunity for more education and the media that glamorize urbanity have raised young rural women's expectations about marriage and life-styles. According to Rubinstein (1992), who studied extremely high rates of suicide among *male* youth in a matrilineal community in Micronesia, the growth of aspirations and the concurrent blocking of opportunities would lead to a retreatist anger and eventually suicide among the powerless, be they male or female. Such suicide, as Counts (1980) also demonstrated in an ethnography of the suicide of a young Kaliai girl in northwest New Britain, Papua New Guinea, may be institutionalized as a realistic strategy of shaming and revenge against those who drive the powerless to self-killing.

Is social resistance of any use at the macrosocial level? The high rates of suicide among young rural women and the substantial disease burden they engender have begun to draw the attention of the media, women's associations, the Chinese government, Befrienders International, and people around the world (e.g., *The Economist*, 8 November, 1997: 39; *South China Morning Post*, 3 May, 1997: 5; *TIME*, 26 January, 1998: 21). Higher rates of suicide among Chinese than Western elderly have also been used as a critique of policy toward old people in East Asian countries (Hu 1995). Thus far, four national conferences on crisis intervention and suicide have been held in China. This was hardly conceivable during the pre-reform era. Research institutions such as the Chinese Academy of Preventive Medicine too have begun to look into suicide as a health and social problem. In China's large cities, limited resources have been made available for suicide prevention, such as the setting up of counseling hotlines and crisis intervention centers. The Chinese Association for Crisis Intervention was established in 1994. Whether these limited efforts will, in the absence of a free press, lead to policies that improve the structural disadvantages of vulnerable people remains uncertain.[10] But the fact that suicide is on the agenda and that the search is on for its causes points to a kind of macro-societal efficacy that none of China's suicides could have imagined. As a collective process and cultural production, then, whatever the intentions of individuals, suicide has resisted the societal forces that for so long have silenced alternative histories of people's despair.

Resistance from a wider perspective

There can be no universal theory of suicide, and one needs to be cautious of overgeneralizing in a society as many-sided and complex as China. Suicide is not always social resistance, and may be associated with remorse, disgrace, and serious mental disorders (Phillips *et al.* 1999). Despite its high rates, suicide afflicts only a tiny portion of rural Chinese people nowadays. A far more common alternative form of resistance adopted by rural people is, in fact, rural–urban migration.

Driven by a sense of inequality *vis-à-vis* urbanites, as well as a rational search for income maximization, many Chinese peasants have re-oriented their funds to non-agricultural enterprises, while others have abandoned their fields and streamed to both state and non-state firms in the major urban centers and nearby townships. Currently estimated to have reached 100 million, these migrant workers leave home with a firm destination in mind, and often follow 'chains' set up by fellow villagers that minimize search and transition costs and maximize the probability of success (Solinger 1997). Though treated as bumpkins in the cities and often maltreated at work, many of the migrants bring home modern urban ideas, skills and, above all, earnings that strengthen township enterprises and alleviate the poverty of their places of origin (Zhou 1996). Far from being 'blind drifters' (*mangliu*), they are calculating agents that have created one of the largest and most active markets in the world.

Nor do all rural women succumb to arranged marriage. Apart from work migration, Gilmartin and Lin (1997) found that women have increasingly used marriage migration as a means of effecting upward social and economic mobility, and many of them have indeed been successful. Migration in post-reform China may therefore be considered a collective strategy for several different things. Is resistance among these? We think it is. Resistance against institutionalized mechanisms of discrimination that have been rationalized within state socialism and that place peasants at a great disadvantage create new options and also hearken back to traditional methods of peasant action. They can be thought of as a thoroughly modern means of taking full advantage of the economic reforms by artfully dodging state barriers, which themselves have become unsupportable, so that the state in turn has come to depend on peasant initiative in the construction industry, for example (Solinger 1997). Zhou (1996) has argued that this endogenous action for empowerment is not merely defensive; by undermining China's socialism as well as the *danwei* system, it is reshaping the very structure of power in Chinese society.

Thus, suicide may be considered one of many forms of institutionalized courses of action that rural people use to resist, criticize, and revise rural–urban inequity (He 1998). It would appear that those who are better educated, more skilled, and/or have more connections in their *guanxi wang* choose different strategies of resistance from the much smaller numbers of people who choose to take their own lives. Recent studies in China have indeed found that suicide is more common in 'illiterate' and 'uneducated' women (Da 1993; He 1996). Although psychiatrists would generally label these women as 'being at risk for ill health', the lack of education (and social connections) must be seen as one of many kinds of social marginalization. Suicide may then be understood as a rational, if still filled with pathos, means of resistance and an expression of power by otherwise powerless people (Counts 1980).

Resisting medicalization

Family conflict, especially involving in-laws or spouses, is the most commonly cited cause of suicide among both lay and professional people in China (Li and Wan 1987; Liu and Li 1990; Da 1993). As reflected in the popular sayings that 'even an upright official finds it hard to settle a family quarrel' (*qing guan nan duan jia wu shi*) and 'domestic shame should not be made public' (*jia chou bu ke wai yang*), state, medical, or other external interventions in suicide are exceptional in Chinese society. Viewed in this light, the medicalization of suicide may enable helping professionals to secure resources for establishing suicide treatment and prevention services. For authoritarian regimes that suppress the study of suicide, because of fears of its political implications, medicalization may be the only (albeit still limited) way of bringing about otherwise prohibited social actions, such as the dissemination of more accurate official suicide statistics, research, conferences, media publicity, and the promotion of general awareness of the problem.

But even if it accomplishes some of these objectives, medicalization is not without its own distorting effects. For example, while attesting to the social origins of suicide, it emphasizes individual pathology and thereby diverts needed attention from the wider political, economic, and cultural forces that need to be targeted for intervention to reduce the high rates of suicide. And the gendered social forces in rural China are easily submerged in the homogenizing psychiatric discourse of 'major depression'. When psychiatric diagnostic criteria are applied to disempowered rural women, they rewrite their social experience in medical terms, and thereby destroy the moral exigencies and infrapolitics of personal suffering in public life. In this process psychiatry supplies the bureaucratic apparatus and expert culture for transforming what is at stake in society into the medical management of individual pathology (Kleinman and Kleinman 1997).

But not all social sources of suffering and suicide among rural women can be drugged away by antidepressants. In some societies, in fact, madness would preclude suicide because only a sane person is supposed to be able to choose rationally between life and death (La Fontaine 1975). Although Chinese psychiatrists have begun to liberalize their concept of depression, they have, unlike psychiatrists in the West, attributed only a minor proportion of suicide to depression (Lee 1999); this is one of only a very few major conceptual differences with psychiatry in North America and Europe. In the CCMD–2-R, which is the latest national system of psychiatric classification used in China, it is stated that 'suicide may be motivated by hopelessness, protest against injustice, fear of punishment, superstition and mental disorders. . . . Most people who commit suicide do not suffer from mental disorders' (Chinese Medical Association and Nanjing Medical University 1995: 135). Ironically, for the argument developed here, this is only one of very few times in the Chinese diagnostic system that an attempt has been made to offer *resistance* to what otherwise has been an inexorable Westernization of Chinese diagnostic categories.

Even where depression is present, and even where suicide is impulsive, the act itself needs to be seen as a social process that requires different kinds of social interventions aimed at structural causes, such as rural women's powerlessness. Likewise, the high rates of suicide among Chinese elderly (e.g. 145/100,000/year for rural males 75 years old and over) compel us not to find another new antidepressant but to re-examine how such Confucian values as filial piety and respect for the elderly lose their salience in the new political economy of the reform era, and may have lost it decades before owing to the delegitimation crisis of the Chinese tradition that radical Maoism brought about. Thus, a study of 1,021 cases of elderly suicide in Changde county, Hunan, found that the common causes were chronic diseases (23.6 percent), desertion by family members (20.3 percent), anger due to abuse by children (12.2 percent), and pessimism caused by children's gambling (9.4 percent) (Zhang and Zhang 1998). Clearly, what biomedical research has identified as 'risk factors' and 'causes' of 'successful' suicide are a mere starting point for anthropological research.

Methodological issues

Lin (1990) has suggested that from the angle of vision of the suicide, the act is always 'weightier than Mount Tai' (*zhong yu Taishan*), even if others may consider it 'lighter than a goose feather' (*qing yu hong mao*). This view tallies with the anthropological emphasis on subjectivity and local meanings.

However, suicide is typically enveloped by layers of privacy and equivocality. Its study is a challenge in the sense that we can never interview the persons who successfully kill themselves. Current methods in particular make it difficult to ascertain whether 'resistance' was itself an intention held by the person who kills him or her self, or whether this can only be an analytic category for the researcher to interpret a collective intentionality. What is needed, as a complement to the standard interview with family members and friends that makes up the psychological autopsy, are ethnographies of the social processes that culminate in, and the local impact of, a person's self-killing. Such an ethnography will require an anthropologically trained person to spend a period of time in a region containing several communities where suicides are recent and relatively numerous. Taking advantage of China's increased openness toward suicide statistics and by making the appropriate local connections, the ethnographer will need to get to know people in the local world, so that he or she can describe what is at stake in the particular settings of local experience, and how those things at stake influence the lives of suicides and members of their networks.

This means interviewing many different types of people from family and neighbors and friends to local authorities, knowledgeable community members, and so forth, so that various positional perceptions, local myths, legends, gossips, and reconstructions of the suicide can be combined in a more validly trans-positional manner. The researcher would also need to understand things that are not (and perhaps cannot be) stated openly because of social sensitivities, and to deliberate carefully the culture of such reluctance as well. That is why cursory answers to survey research on such a sensitive topic, which are obtained when lengthy questionnaires are used outside of relations of trust, cannot be regarded as adequate data. Additionally, we believe that it is possible to find evidence of social resistance in suicide attempters too, and their acts may sometimes be enough to effect changes in local worlds. Because of the unrestrained availability of pesticides and the inaccessibility of medical resuscitation facilities, the distinction between completed and attempted suicide may be particularly blurred in rural China. Unlike those who commit suicide, these 'survivors' of 'unsuccessful' suicide along with their significant others can be interviewed and may make for valuable sources of information on subjectivity (emotions, memory, self-evaluation, other self-processes), motives (whether, for example, belief in Buddhist reincarnation or malicious ghosts before they make the attempt are actually operative in decision making), interpersonal dynamics, varied local impacts, and other ethnographic issues.

By developing a mini-ethnography, the researcher can come to terms with the variety of economic, political, familial, and interpersonal issues that may (and usually do) make for complex, multi-sided grounds for suicidal action. The ethnographer is also in a position to determine the social effects of suicide, including whether the resistance it engenders makes an impact at individual and collective levels. In this way, they perform more of a social analysis than psychological autopsy.

We believe that ethnographic research, which is only now being applied to this subject, is important and practicable for understanding suicide as social resistance, and that must be the first step before we develop effective programs and policies to reduce the numbers of cases and to respond to what it is that drives people – especially elderly people and young women – to it. And, given that Chinese people constitute over 20 percent of the world's population, the more suicide data from China can be introduced into, and thereby problematize and destabilize, taken-for-granted theories in the Western social and medical sciences, the more cogent will be our grasp of what suicide signifies generally about the values of life and death, suffering and resistance, and the relationship between collective and individual levels of experience across societies.

Notes

1 Translated by D. C. Lau, *Confucius: The Analects*, XV.9 (The Chinese University Press: Hong Kong, 1983), p. 151.
2 In lay usage, the term *zisha* refers to both completed and attempted suicide. In the health field, *zisha* is completed suicide whereas *zisha weisui* is attempted suicide.
3 Note that reliable suicide data from Central and South America, Africa, Middle East, and huge Asian countries such as India and Indonesia are still lacking.
4 The higher estimate (by as much as one third) is due to the ascription of a percentage of accidental deaths of unknown cause to suicide by the Western researchers. This assumption has been questioned.
5 This huge discrepancy is partly a result of the difference in diagnostic criteria and in the cultural acceptability of experiencing depression.
6 Young rural women, for example, were unlikely to be the predominant group affected during the Cultural Revolution.
7 This can still be interpreted as resistance, inspired by hope as well as by despair, against the current life in favor of an imagined future paradise.
8 Neurasthenia (*shenjing shuairuo*) is a popular illness label for a varying mixture of anxiety, depressive and physical symptoms (Lee in press). It is a common form of sociosomatic connections in Chinese society that can express disguised criticism and recrimination in bodily terms.
9 Liu and Li (1990: 88) noted that 50 percent of women who commit suicide because of marital strife do so after being cruelly beaten by their husbands.
10 A case of suicide as protest that does impact on social policy in Hong Kong is unambiguously exemplified by a 76-year-old jade seller, Mr. Wang, who set himself ablaze in court on 7 Dec, 1998 while he was tried for hawking illegally and obstructing the streets. The judge ruled that he should pay a fine of HK$400 (US$50) and have all of his 251 pieces of jade confiscated. Mr. Wang pleaded guilty but begged that he should be allowed to keep the jades for his livelihood. When this was turned down, he poured inflammable liquid onto himself and ignited it. As he quickly became a fireball, he walked toward the judge, but soon fell onto the floor (*Ming Pao*, A5, 8 December, 1998). Having sustained a 70 percent deep burn, he died 2 days later. This incident hit the headlines for several days, and aroused unanimous support from politicians and academics as well as strikes from many hawkers, demanding that the law pertaining to illegal hawking be reviewed and implemented humanely, especially at a time of high unemployment rates. The government then made a positive preliminary response to the collective request.

References

Barnhart, R. K. (1995) (ed.) *The Barnhart Concise Dictionary of Etymology* (HarperCollins: New York).
Baechler, J. (1979) *Suicides* (Basil Blackwell: Oxford).
Bianco, L. (1978) 'Peasant Movements', in J. K. Fairbank and A. Feuerwerker (eds), *The Cambridge History of China*, volume 13, *Republican China 1912–1949* (Cambridge University Press: Cambridge), pp. 270–328.
Counts, D. A. (1980) 'Fighting Back is Not the Way: Suicide and the Women of Kaliai,' *American Ethnologist* 7, 332–51.

Da, D. (1993) 'A Preliminary Inquiry into Suicide in China', in J. Peng (ed.), *Social Observation in a Special Zone* (Haitian Publishing House: Shenzhen), pp. 492–510 (in Chinese).

Desjarlais, R., Eisenberg, L., Good, B. and Kleinman, A. (1995) *World Mental Health: Problems and Priorities in Low-Income Countries* (Oxford University Press: Oxford).

Chinese Medical Association and Nanjing Medical University (1995) *Chinese Classification of Mental Disorders*, second edition, revised (*CCMD–2-R*) (Dong Nan University Press: Nanjing) (in Chinese).

Durkheim, E. (1897/1966) *Suicide* (Free Press: New York).

Farberow, N.L. (1975) 'Cultural History of Suicide,' in N. L. Farberow (ed.), *Suicide in Different Cultures* (University Park Press: Baltimore), Chapter 1.

Gilmartin, C. and Lin, T. (1997) 'Where and Why Have all the Women Gone? Women, Marriage, Migration, and Social Mobility in China,' paper presented at The International Conference on Gender and Development in Asia, 27–29 November, 1997, The Chinese University of Hong Kong, Hong Kong, China.

He, Q. L. (1998) *Pitfalls of Modernization: Economic and Social Problems in Contemporary China* (China Today Press, Beijing) (in Chinese).

He, Z. X. (1996) *Suicide and Life* (Guangzhou Publishing House: Guangzhou) (in Chinese).

Hu, Y. H. (1995) 'Elderly Suicide Risk in Family Contexts: A Critique of the Asian Family Care Model,' *Journal of Cross-Cultural Gerontology 10*, 199–217.

Jeffreys, M. D. W. (1952) 'Samsonic Suicide or Suicide of Revenge Among Africans,' *African Studies*, September, 118–22.

Kleinman, A. and Kleinman, J. (1997) 'Moral Transformations of Health and Suffering in Chinese Society,' in A. Brandt and P. Rozin (eds), *Morality and Health* (Routledge: New York and London).

La Fontaine, J. (1975) 'Anthropology,' in S. Perllin (ed.), *A Handbook for the Understanding of Suicide* (Jason Aronson Inc: Northvale), Chapter 4.

Lee, S. (1999) 'Diagnosis Postponed: Shenjing Shuairuo and the Transformation of Psychiatry in Post-Mao China,' *Culture, Medicine and Psychiatry* in press.

Li, J. H. and Wan, W. P. (1987) 'An Investigation of Suicide in Puning County, Yunnan,' *Chinese Mental Health Journal 1*, 73–75 (in Chinese).

Lin, Y. H. (1990) *The Weight of Mount Tai: Patterns of Suicide in Traditional Chinese History and Culture* (PhD Thesis, The University of Wisconsin, Madison).

Liu, J. C. and Li, Y. Z. (1990) *Unravelling the Suicide Riddle* (Sichuan Publishing House of Science and Technology: Chengdu) (in Chinese).

Murray, C. J. L. and Lopez, A. D. (1996) *Global Health Statistics: a Compendium of Incidence, Prevalence, and Mortality Estimates for over 200 Conditions* (Harvard University Press: Cambridge).

Phillips, M., Liu, H. Q. and Zhang, Y. P. (1999) 'Suicide and Social Change in China,' *Culture, Medicine and Psychiatry 23*, 25–50.

Rubinstein, D. H. (1992) 'Suicide in Micronesia and Samoa: A Critique of Explanations,' *Pacific Studies 15*, 51–75.

Scheler, M. (1971 [1928]) *Man's Place in Nature*, trans. H. Meyerhoff (Noonday Press: New York).

Scott, J. C. (1990) *Domination and the Arts of Resistance: the Hidden Transcripts* (Yale University Press: New Haven).

Solinger, D. (1997) 'The Impact of the Floating Population on the *Danwei*: Shifts in the Pattern of Labor Mobility Control and Entitlement Provision,' in X. B. Lü and

E. Perry (eds), *Danwei: The Changing Chinese Workplace in Historical and Comparative Perspective* (M. E. Sharpe: New York), pp.195–222.

Taylor, S. (1988) *The Sociology of Suicide* (Longman: London).

Wolf, M. (1975) 'Women and Suicide in China,' in M. Wolf and R. Witke (eds), *Women in Chinese Society* (Stanford University Press: Stanford), pp.111–41.

Yip, P. S. F. (1996) 'Suicides in Hong Kong, Taiwan and Beijing,' *British Journal of Psychiatry 169*, 495–500.

Zhai, S. T. (1997) *Crisis Intervention and the Prevention of Suicide* (Publishing House of People's Health: Beijing) (in Chinese).

Zhang, H. L. and Zhang, J. C. (1998) 'Analysis of 1,021 Cases of Elderly Suicide in Chang De County,' *US Chinese Psychosomatic Medicine Journal 2*, 185 (in Chinese).

Zhou, J. H. (1988) 'A Probe into the Mentality of Sixty-five Rural Young Women Giving Birth to Baby Girls, *Chinese Sociology and Anthropology* (Journal of Translations) *20*, 93–102.

Zhou, X. K. (1996) *How the Farmers Changed China: Power of the People* (Westview Press: Boulder, CO).

Index

abortion 107; sex-selective 111, 112–13
Administrative Litigation Law 33, 34, 36,
    121, 122, 159; land cases brought
    under 128
agriculture: decollectivization of 2–3, 89,
    159; effect of pollution on 145;
    expansion into Mongolia 182, 194–5;
    grain harvests 93; prices and incomes
    93; reforms and rural mobility 88–9
All-China Alliance for Seeking Civil
    Damages from Japan 29
All-China Federation of Trade Unions
    (ACFTU): and economic protest 17,
    46; role in disputes at foreign-owned
    enterprises 50–1; weakness of 55;
    Women Workers Department 69–70
April Fifth Movement 43
arbitration committees 17, 42; and labor
    disputes 47–8; regional variations 48

Bao Ge, activist 29, 34
Beijing: UN Conference on Women
    (1995) 70; workers' protest march
    (1989) 51; Zhejiang Village 90, 93, 94
Beijing Workers' Autonomous
    Federation 56
Berlin, Isaiah 213
birth control policies 12, 103–4; fines
    for unplanned births 110; officials
    attacked 107, see also single-child
    policy
birth permits 104, 105; sale of 109
Black Dragon Pool (Shaanxi province)
    173–4
Blair, A., UK Prime Minister 31
Brodsky, Joseph 215
Buddhism 168, 180; in Mongolia 180,
    183; and suicide 223; in Tibet 172–3,
    180, 183

cadres see local authorities
Chen Xitong, trial for corruption 28
China: economic growth 1, 44, 93;
    ethnicity in 180–1, 190–2, 196; and
    international community 30–2;
    perception of national crisis (1990s)
    208, 209–10; reform program 1, 2–7;
    suicide in modern 224–6; suicide in
    traditional 223–4
China Democracy Party (CDP) 29, 31;
    formation (1998) 28
China Development Union 30, 57
Chinese Academy of Preventive
    Medicine, and suicide 233–4
Chinese Association for Crisis
    Intervention (suicide prevention) 234
Chinese Communist Party (CCP):
    attacks on revisionism 204–5;
    continuing controls 6, 10–11, 13,
    170–1, 212; and debate on economic
    reform 202; and direct village elections
    121–2; effect of legal and political
    reforms in 11; ethnic policies 181,
    184–6, 190–2; ideological control 206,
    209; ideology of equality 181, 185;
    and reaction to resistance 21; residual
    strengths of 14, see also State
Chinese Constitution (1982 revision) 23;
    protection for defined religious
    activity 167–8; right to strike removed
    49
Chinese Nationalist Party, racism of 181
Chinese Women's News, The, UN
    Conference on Women 70
Christianity 166–7; Catholicism 168;
    Little Flock Protestant denomination
    161, 167; suicide condemned in 224;
    Three-Self Patriotic Movement 167
cinema 200

civic organizations, lack of 139–40
civil disobedience, in urbanization
    protests 133, 135, 136, 138
civil procedure law 33
class, in popular protest 7–8
class polarization 14
Clinton, W., US President 31
collective acts of resistance: against
    development 122–3; by ordinary
    people 25, 125; by workers 45–7, 57;
    environmental protests 158; migration
    as 234; toleration of 24
collectives: arbitrated disputes 48;
    managerial role of 3
collectivism, in rights concept 23, 37
commodification: of *hukuo* 92; of welfare
    system 44–5; of women 73
communications, dissidents' use of
    modern 30
community service, jobs for unemployed
    women 77–8
conflict, on-going 2
Confucianism, and suicide 223
consumerism 200–1; and
    commodification of women 73
consumers, complaints by 36
contract law 121
corruption: dissidents' focus on 28; in
    HRS system 92–3, 95, 99–100; in
    suburban land market 128; workers'
    protests against 49, 52
crime: by workers 53; rise in organized
    10
criminal code, revised 33
Criminal Law (1997), and secret societies
    and superstitious sects 171
criminal procedure law 33
Cui Zhiyuan, 'new left' thinker 212
Cultural Revolution (1966-76) 7, 43;
    attacks on minorities 179, 185–6;
    attacks on Mongol people 185, 188–9;
    and cult of Mao 163–6; and death of
    Lin Biao (1971) 2; and gender equality
    67, 70; mobilization campaigns 164;
    and status of workers 42, 43; suicide
    rate 226; worker discontent 43, 45–6
cultural tradition: and local loyalties 174;
    patriarchal 111–12, 115; role in
    protest mobilizations 159; single-child
    policy as threat to 107, 111; suicide in
    223–4, 227; suppressed 163–4;
    transferred to cult of Mao 164, 165–6;
    use of Song Jiang legend 156; women's
    social role in 63, 67, 112

culture: 1989 purge 199–200, 204;
    alternative 204; mass-market popular
    205

Dachuan (Gansu province): Kong lineage
    151–2, 174; water pollution case 146–8
Daoism 168; and suicide 223
Daqing oil fields, strike 49
deforestation 144
Democracy Movement (1989) 21, 25, 55,
    57
Democracy Wall movement (1978–81)
    24, 57
Democratic Progressive Association, and
    rural protest 125, 127
demonstrations 16–17; against
    development projects 120–1; against
    water pollution 146–7; by workers
    51–2
Deng Xiaoping: economic reforms 5, 48,
    196; and single-child policy 104; tour
    of South China 25, 199
Deng Xiaoping Theory 6
deportation, of migrants 97
depression, as cause of suicide 225,
    235–6
detention, of migrants 97
development: 'externalities' of 120–1,
    122–3; in Mongolia 194–5, *see also*
    urbanization
Diaoyutai Islands, Japanese occupation
    of 28
dissident movement: and autonomous
    trade unions 55, 57; causes favoured
    by 28–9; Democracy Wall Movement
    (1978–81) 24; economic resources of
    29–30; and intellectual debate 209,
    216–17; international support for
    29–30, 31; and rights consciousness
    20; Tiananmen Square Movement 25,
    see also intellectuals
dissident resistance: compared with
    ordinary 25–7; long-term effects of
    37–8; peaceful nature of 26–7
dissidents: in Czechoslovakia 215;
    families of 23
Durkheim, Émile, theory of suicide 226

East Asia: birth sex-ratios in 114; Newly
    Industrializing Economies 1
economic growth 1, 44, 67, 93; and
    population growth 103–4, 116
economic protests 17; and arbitration
    committees 17, 42; toleration of 42,

53–4; wage arrears 48, 51, *see also* labor disputes

economic reform: Deng's introduction of 5, 25, 48; effect on ethnic minorities 192–5; intellectual debate on 201–2

education: migrant 'work shed' schools 98; of rural women 79, 80; of urban women 75–6

education campaign, on legal reforms 5

elections: fraud in 125; for village committees 6, 11, 33, 121–2, 139

élite, divided 58

Engels, Friedrich, concept of women's liberation 63

enlightenment: as goal 185; post-Cultural Revolution 202, 203, 209, 210, 214

enterprises: bankruptcy among 44; growth of 3; increased autonomy 44; rural 88–9, *see also* foreign-invested; private; state-owned

entertainment industry, and 'rice bowl of youth' phenomenon 72–3

environmental protection: dissident support for 28, 29, *see also* pollution

Environmental Protection Law (1979) 145

environmental protests, nature of 143, 157–9

ethnic minorities 178–9; and autonomous states 181; and Han claims to indigenous status 191–2; and *minzu* (nationality-building project) 181–2; and regional policies 190–1; and religion 171–3; state classification of 179–80, *see also* language; nationality

ethnic resistance, and Chinese socialism 184–6

family farming 3

Fang Lizhi, dissident 25

farmers, as migrant workers 87

femininity, discourse of 68–71, 81

fertility rate, decline in (from 1970) 103, 104

fertility temple, and water pollution (Dachuan) 147–8, 152–4

financial services 54

foreign capital investment 44, 207; in small enterprises 3

foreign trade 2

foreign-invested enterprises: arbitrated disputes 48; labor conditions 50; strikes 50–1; women in 74–5

foreigners, higher profile in China 12

free markets *see* market reforms

Free Trade Unions of China 57

French Revolution 21

funeral rites, under Communism 163

funeral symbolism, in environmental protests (Gaoyang) 154–6

Gaoyang (Chongqing municipality): Three Gorges Dam resettlement project 148–51; use of funeral symbolism 154–6

gender: and discourse of femininity 68–71, 81; ratio of suicide 222, 224–5; and unemployment 8, 64–6; in work hierarchy 63–4, 71–2, 76, 79, *see also* women

gender equality laws 69

George Orwell 20

global markets 11–12

globalization 215; and localization 16

Gray, John, on globalization 215

Great Leap Forward 104; crisis and famine following (1960) 84, 161–2, 182–3

Guangdong province: labor disputes 47; pollution 157

Guangzhou, work stoppages 46

Guo Ruoji, lawsuit against Communist Party 29–30, 33–4

gynecological examinations 105

Han people: claim to be indigenous to Mongolia 191–2; claims to modernizing 'civilization' 8, 187, 190–1; cultural identity 192–3; and Mongol linguistic resistance 188–9; in Mongolia 183–4, 187, 193–5; supremacy of 179, 180, 181, 185

Han Yuhai, opponent of liberalism 213, 215

Heavenly Soldiers Fraternal Army 9

Hired-Hands Workers' Federation 57

homeowners, temporary housing for displaced 134–6

Hong Kong 201; media 199, 204, 211; suicide rate 224

Hong Xiuquan 9

household registration (*hukou*) system (HRS) 84–7; 'non-agricultural' status 85, 86–7, 92; relaxation of 4, 12, 99; sale of permits 92–3, 95; 'urban registration with self-supplied grain' 90–1

Household Responsibility System (HRS) 3
housing: for migrant workers 96–7; for
    workers 46, 48–9
Hu Ping, Democracy Wall dissident 24
Hu Yaobang, CCP General Secretary 25,
    33
Hui people (Muslims) 171–2, 193
hukuo see household registration system
human rights, international covenants 31,
    32, 178
Hundred Flowers Movement (1956–57)
    7, 43, 187

identity, and ethnicity 179
ideology, official 6
individual rights: in 1982 Constitution
    23; in legal reforms 32, 159
Indonesia, ethnic Chinese in 28–9
industrialization: heavy industry 54, 84;
    in Mongolia 184, 190; and pollution
    145, 157
industry, growth (1980–97) 44
inequality: economic 5; social 5, 13,
    see also gender
infant abandonment 111, 112
infanticide, female 111, 112
Inner Mongolia, labor disputes 47
Inner Mongolian Autonomous State 47,
    178, 181, 182, 187; Han–Mongol
    relations 193–5
intellectuals: attempts to renovate state
    ideologies 208, 212; criticism of
    205–6; debate on economic reforms
    201–2, 203–4; growing independence
    202–3, 207–8; and liberalism 210–12,
    213, 215–16; 'new leftists' 201–2, 206,
    210, 211–14, 215–16; official tolerance
    of 6, 211; support for dissidents 28;
    and trade unions 56, *see also* dissident
    movement
international law and institutions 20, 32;
    human rights covenants 31, 32,
    see also UN
international support: for dissidents 30;
    for unions 57
internationalization 11–12, 199–200
Internet, dissident use of 30
Islam, among Hui people 171–2
IUD devices 107, 109

Japan: finance for Buddhist associations
    169; ownership of factories 50;
    protests against 28, 29; suicide in 227,
    228; women's domesticity 67

Jiang Zemin, President 3, 196; speech at
    UN Conference on Women 70
job referral services, for women 70, 77, 78
joint venture companies 3; women in
    74–5
Jospin, Lionel, French Prime Minister 31

kaifa (ideology of development), in
    Mongolia 194–5
Kazaks, driven out (1962) 185

labor activism 41–2, 43, 57–8
Labor Bureau, role in disputes at
    foreign-owned enterprises 50–1
labor conditions: contract reform 44, 47,
    55; for migrant workers 44; in private
    and foreign owned firms 41; in
    state-owned enterprises 43, 44–5
labor disputes: and arbitration 47–8;
    regional variations 47–8, 54, 55, 56
Labor Law (1994), women's employment
    rights 69
Labor Law (1995) 47
labor market 44; gendered nature of 71–2
labor mobility 4, 44, 64, 89–90, 99,
    see also migrant workers
labor stoppages 48–51
land, marketization of suburban 127, 128,
    129
land disputes 123–4
Land Management Law (1986) 128
land ownership 3
language, Mongolian 184, 186–9
Law on Protection of Rights and Interests
    of Women (1992) 69
lawsuits: against Communist Party
    29–30, 33–4; against government
    offices 132–3
League for the Protection of Rights of
    Working People 57
legal community, growth of 33
legal reforms 5–6, 32; contract law 121;
    and labor arbitration 47; rights
    protection laws 57, 69, *see also* legal
    system; litigation
legal system: and cases of rural protest
    126, 132–3, 134–5, 136, 140–1;
    dissident use of 20, 32–5; and
    environmental protests 157–8; 'rule
    by law' 122, 140, *see also* petitions
legality, weakness of sense of 123, 127,
    140
Li Weiping, administrative litigation suit
    34

Liang Xiaosheng, novelist 205
liberalism, theoretical interest in 210–12
Lin Biao, death (1971) 2
Lin Hai, use of Internet 30
lineage loyalties 8, 174; Dachuan example
    151–2, 174
litigation, growth of 33, 34, 35–7
Liu Junning, editor of *Res Publica* 215
Liu Shaoqi, and population control 104
Liu Yufen, woman entrepreneur 72
local authorities: abuse of power 124–5;
    collusion in evasion of birth limits 108,
    109–11; Gaoyang petition movement
    against 149–51; and jurisdiction over
    environmental violations 158; and
    land disputes 123–4; relations with
    village committees 159, 174; role in
    protests 10, 134–5, 136, 153
local taxes, protests about 124

managers: attacks on 52–3; increased
    powers of 44, 45; status of 42, 49;
    support for workers' protests 53;
    young women as 75
Manchu ruling nationality 181
Mao, cult of 9–10, 163–6
Mao Zedong: Great Proletarian Cultural
    Revolution (as class struggle) 7–8;
    and labor revolts 43; view of
    population control 103–4
Maoism 7; reappropriation of rhetoric of
    57; status of urban workers under
    42–3; women's employment policy
    63–4, 66–7
market reforms 2–3, 44, 193, 212;
    protests arising from 124
markets: farmers' 89, 99; in suburban
    land 127, 128
marriage: age limits raised 103, 104, 109;
    suicide to avoid arranged 228–30
Marxist theory of women 69
Marxist-Leninist theory of nationalities
    178–9
May Fourth Movement (1919) 56, 185,
    213–14
media: Hong Kong 199, 204, 211;
    international 199; and rights
    consciousness 137; role in dissident
    resistance 38; role in rural protests
    125, 127, 135–6, 138–9; Taiwan 199,
    204; television 139
mediation committees, and labor disputes
    47–8
medical personnel, bribery of 109

middle class, championed by neo-liberals
    212, 215
migrant workers 5, 12–13, 55, 85–6;
    construction workers 95; forms of
    resistance 95–6; housing for 96–7;
    industrial workers 95; labor protests
    49–50, 57–8; native-place ties 50, 97–8;
    organizations of 97–9; restrictions on
    80, 89, 93, 95–7, 100; self-employed
    95; and unemployment 91, 100;
    young rural women 44, 74, 78–80
migration: 1978–84 period 88–90; 1985–
    8 period 90–1; 1989–91 period 91–3;
    1992–7 period 93–5; classification of
    86; control *see* household registration
    system; 'guerrilla birth corps' 108;
    'migrant flood' (*mingongchao*) 87–8,
    91–2; as public order issue 84, 85, 92;
    as resistance 234–5
mingong (rural labor migrants) 86
Ministry of Civil Affairs, view of
    economic protest 17
minority parties 6
Minzhu yu fazhi journal: and corruption in
    land market 128; data on rural
    petitioning 123–7, 137–8
minzu (nationality-building project) 181–2,
    184, 195; and language 186–9
'modernity': and debate on women's
    employment 66–7, 68–9, 71–6, 81;
    intellectual debate on 204, 207
Mongol pastoralism 8, 182–4, 194–5
Mongolian People's Republic 188
Mongols: efforts to learn Chinese 193–4;
    farmers in east Mongolia 183;
    genocidal attacks against (Cultural
    Revolution 1966) 185, 188–9; hostility
    to commerce 193; as imperial rulers
    181; loss of language 184, 187–8,
    see also Inner Mongolia
moonlighting 46
multiculturalism 192, 196
Muslims: as ethnic minorities 180;
    external orientation of 168, 180

Nanchong (Sichuan), worker's protest
    52–3
Nanjing, urbanization case study 129–31
National Environmental Protection
    Agency 145
National People's Congress, strengthened
    33
National Situation Education (from 1989)
    190

nationalism, Chinese 185, 190–2
nationality: in Chinese culture 178–9;
    and ideology of equality 181, 185;
    Stalin's defining criteria 181–2,
    see also ethnic minorities
native-place connections, important
    among migrant workers 50
New Social Movement Theory 15–16
non-governmental organizations,
    environment issues 145
North China Agricultural Conference
    (1970) 2
Northwest Medical Instruments plant,
    strike 49

oppression, relationship with resistance
    20–1
Organic Law of Villagers' Committees
    (1987) 159
O'Rourke, P. J. 207

Party Congresses, Eleventh (Third
    Plenum 1978) 2, 88; Fifteenth (1998)
    100; Fourteenth (1992) 93
pastoralism, as defining Mongol identity
    182–4
patriotic causes, dissident support for
    28
Peng Ming, China Development Union
    30, 34
pension arrears and cuts 51–2
personal rights 36
petitions 122, 137–8; cost of filing 125; as
    first step 134; Gaoyang movement
    148, 149–51; rejection of 125;
    workers' use of 48
police, armed (*wujing*) 7
Polish Solidarity Movement, influence of
    48, 49, 55
political reforms 6–7; and new
    institutions 121–3, *see also* elections
political rights, curtailed by 1982
    Constitution 23
pollution 144–5, 157; and birth defects
    12, 145, 146–8
popular protest *see* public protest
population: control as state policy 102–3,
    114–15, 116–17; decline in fertility
    rate 103, 104; demographic effects of
    policies 115; prospects for voluntary
    control 115–16; sex-ratio skewed
    113–14; target limits 103, 104, 110,
    see also single-child policy
population mobility *see* migration

postmodernism 213–14; as fragmented
    15–16
private enterprises 3; arbitrated disputes
    48; owned by women 72; rural
    women employees 79
production, mode of 181, 182
property rights 36
prostitution 74
psychiatry, and diagnosis of depression
    235, 236
public protest: historical precedents 7;
    use of Cultural Revolution slogans 9,
    see also demonstrations
Public Security bureaus, religious
    controls 168, 169–70
publicity: for strikes 50, *see also* media
publishing market, deregulated 203, 204,
    206–7

Qin Hui, historian 212
Qin Yongmin, Wuhan dissident 30
Qing dynasty, New Policy (1902) (in
    Mongolia) 182
Qu Yuan, suicide (278 B.C.) 227

Rawls, John 214
Re-employment Project, for women 76–7
reciprocity, of rights 23
Regulation on Handling Labor Disputes
    (1993) 47
religion: and autonomous ethnic
    minorities 171–3, 180; imperial
    imposture 170; official associations
    168–9; reform policies on 166–71;
    sects 170; and state definition of
    religious belief 167–8; state
    responsibility for 168–9; temple-
    building 168; temples as tourist
    attractions 169; Unity Sect 170;
    unregistered 171
religious traditions 161; and cult of Mao
    9–10, 165; and dilemmas for
    Communist cadres 162–3, 164; driven
    underground 164; fertility goddesses
    152–4; funeral symbolism 154–6;
    temples to Communist leaders 165–6
repression: alternated with toleration 18;
    as response to interconnected
    movements 16, 42
residence permits: temporary 96, *see also*
    household registration (*hukou*) system
resistance: by migrant workers 95–7;
    dissident compared with ordinary
    25–7; forms of 20, 106, 234–5;

invisible 2, 95; labor mobility as form of 80; nature of 226–7; non-compliance 45–6; relationship with oppression 20–1; relationship with rights 22–4; religion as 172–3; and rights consciousness 35–7; as single-issue conflicts 15; and threat to state 21; use of litigation 34–5, *see also* collective acts; single-child policy; Tiananmen Incident

retirees, effect on urbanization on financial security of 132–3

'rice bowl of youth', and women in entertainment industries 72–3

rights: Chinese conception of 22, 23, 36, 37; international covenants on 6, 20; relationship with resistance 22–4; source of 36, 37; as state-centered 22; subsistence 52

rights consciousness 20, 23; among villagers 127, 137, 143, 159; and legal recourse 37, 137–8; and resistance 35–7

rights practices, inconsistencies in 22

Robinson, Mary, UN Human Rights Commissioner 31

rural areas: agricultural reform 88–9; development of rights consciousness in 127, 137; effect of urbanization on 129, 130; hostility to single-child policy 105; and industrialization 84; migration from 83–4; non-agricultural occupations 90; protests about development 123–36; rustication to (1968) 88; strategies to resist single-child policy 107–14; and use of media 138–9

Rural Women Knowing All journal 79–80

rural workers: discrimination against 64, 78–9; 'rural' as stigma 79, *see also* migrant workers

Scheler, Max, phenomenologist 226

security system 6–7

service industries, protests in 54

service sector, female qualities for 78

Shanghai: call for independent unions 49; labor disputes 47; women in foreign companies 75; women's retraining 77

Shenzhen SEZ, strikes 50

single-child policy 5, 12, 114–15; accommodation strategies 111–14; confrontation strategies 107; and education of only daughters (in urban areas) 76; evasion strategies 108–11, 113; introduced 104–5; prospects for modification 116–17; resistance to 105–6, 115; and second chance for a son 112; and suicide 231–2; and water pollution in Dachuan 152 4, *see also* population

single-issue conflicts 15

small towns, welfare entitlements in 90–1, 100

socialism: in charismatic Protestantism 167; and ethnic consciousness 184–6, 195–6

socialist market economy, term coined (1992) 93

Song Jiang, legend of 156

South Korea, sex ratio at birth 114

Soviet Union, resistance to collective reforms 4

Special Economic Zones (SEZs), migrant labor in 12, 50

Stalin, Josef, definition of nationality 181

State: adaptation of religious ceremonies 163; capacity to administer 14; Chinese obsession with weakness of 22; and classification of ethic minorities 179–80; and economic protests 17, 42; fear of independent organizations 139; strategy for labor reform 58–9; suppression of autonomous unions 57, 58, 85; view of migration as public order issue 84, 85–6, 92

state-owned enterprises (SOEs) 4–5, 63; arbitrated disputes 48; bankruptcy among 44, 51; reforms in 41–2; unemployment in 44–5; workers' congresses 55

state–society relations, as zero-sum 10, 106

sterilization 107, 110–11

strikes 48–51; by migrant workers 50; constitutional right removed 49; use of publicity for 50

students: and trade unions 55–7; withdrew from politics (late 1990s) 27

subsistence rights 52

substance abuse 225

suicide 222–3; by elderly 232, 233, 236; by workers 53; case studies 228–34; ethnographic research into 236–8; gender ratio 222–1; as indicator of social problems 222, 225, 226; inter-regional differences 221; medicalization of 235–6; in modern

Suicide (*continued*)
   China 224–6; resources to prevent
   233–4; result of depression 225, 235,
   236; as social resistance 227, 228,
   236–7; as strategy of resistance 221,
   226–8, 230–1; in traditional Chinese
   society 223–4; young rural women
   221, 224, 228–34

Taiping Rebellion 9
Taiwan 201; media 199, 204; suicide rate
   224
Taiyuan steel mill strike 48–9
taxes, local 124
technology: access to 12; dissident access
   to 30
temporary residence permits 96
temporary workers: in state-owned
   enterprises 43; and urban *hukou*
   registration 91
The Little Red Book (Mao Quotations) 10
Three Gorges Dam project 8, 158;
   population resettlement protest
   148–51
Tiananmen Incident: cultural repression
   after 198–9, 204; heaviest sentences
   for workers 49, 56–7; as rare event 21;
   repercussions on ethnic relations
   189–90; use of funeral symbolism 155
Tiananmen Square dissident movement
   see Democracy Movement
Tibet 178, 181, 191; Buddhism in 183;
   Chinese purge of 185; politics of
   religion 172–3
Tocqueville, Alexis de, on oppression and
   resistance 21, 23
tourism: Black Dragon Pool (Shaanxi
   province) 173; ethnic 191
township and village enterprises (TVEs)
   3, 100
trade unions: independent 42, 49, 55–7;
   international connections 57; Union
   Law (1992) 55; workers' congresses
   55, *see also* All-China Federation of
   Trade Unions (ACFTU)
training, and retraining for women 70,
   76–7
transport system 91–2
Triads 171

Ulanhu, Mongol leader of Inner
   Mongolia (1947–66) 183, 188, 189, 191
ultrasound technology, for sex-selective
   abortion 112–13

UN Conference on Women (Beijing
   1995) 70
UN Covenant on Civil and Political
   Rights 31
UN Covenant on Social, Economic and
   Cultural Rights 31, 57
UN Fund for Population Activities
   (UNFPA) 115
UN International Conference on
   Population and Development (1994)
   116
UN Security Council, China's place on
   (resumed 1970–71) 2
unemployment: from state-owned
   enterprises 4–5, 54, 64; gendered 8,
   64–6; off-duty 44; protests against 49,
   54; and Re-employment Project for
   women 76–7; registered 44; and
   restrictions on migrant labor 80
unemployment allowances 44
Union Law (1992) 55
United States, diplomatic links with 2
urban areas: environmental protests in
   157; floating populations of migrants
   94, 108; labor shortages 90, 91, 99;
   rustication from 88; single-child policy
   105; small town welfare entitlements
   90–1; welfare benefits 5, 62–3, 78–9,
   84–5, *see also* migrant workers; rural
   areas
urban industry: slower changes in 4;
   workers' benefits in 62–3
urbanization: effect on Mongol language
   and culture 184; effect on retirees
   financial prospects 132–3; protest case
   studies 129–36; protests against
   127–9; and temporary housing for
   homeowners 134–6
urban–rural differences: single-child
   policy 5, 76, 105; welfare benefits
   62–3, 78–9, 84–5, 99–100
utilitarianism, in rights concept 23

Vietnam 4
village committees: elections for 6, 11, 33,
   121–2, 139; relations with local
   authorities 159
violence: against birth planning officials
   107; in collective protests 26, 125; in
   workers' protests 52–3
von Hayek, F. A., interest in 210

wage arrears 48, 51
Wang Hui, editor of *Reading* 210

Wang Meng, Minister of Culture (1986–89) 205
Wang Xiaobo, novelist 206
Wang Youcai, China Democracy Party 31, 32
water pollution 145, 146–8
Wei Jingsheng, Democracy Wall dissident leader 24
welfare, religious connections 173–4
welfare system: commodified 44–5; need to strengthen 59; small towns 90–1; urban–rural disparity 62–3, 78–9, 84–5, 99–100
Wenzhou, migrants from 87, 94
women: blamed for low economic growth 67; as entrepreneurs 72; escorting girls (*sanpeinü*) 74; as foreign language students 75–6; in foreign-owned companies 74–6; gendered employment 63, 64; insecurity of 233; Maoist employment policy 63–4, 66–7; as migrant workers 44, 64; 'modernity' and employment 71–6; Re-employment Project 76–7; and 'rice bowl of youth' 72–5; social expectations of 63, 67; strategies for gender justice 70–1; suicide among (traditional) 223, 228; suicide rates (modern) 224–5, *see also* gender; single-child policy; women, rural
Women of China, on women's unemployment 65
Women Entrepreneurs Friendship Association 72
'women return home' proposals 68, 71; 'home economics' retraining 77
women, rural: continuing disadvantages 64; 'maiden workers' 79–80; as migrant workers 44, 74, 78–80; migration as resistance 234–5; suicide among 221, 224, 228–34, *see also* single-child policy
women, urban: employment advantages under Maoism 63–4; rise of professional 72–6

Women's Federation: and feminist discourse 70–1; forecast of shortage of wives 115; and rural 'maiden workers' 80; and women entrepreneurs 72; and women's unemployment 68, 69–70
work permits, fees for 96
Workers' Autonomous Federations 56
workers' congresses 55
working class: and democratic movements 56; divisions among 58; enhanced status of urban 42–3, 44; lack of support for dissidents 28; unemployment 4–5, 45, 57, *see also* intellectuals; middle class; peasants; urban–rural differences; women

Xinjiang 48, 181, 192; ethnonationalism in 178
Xiong Zhifu, anti-corruption campaigner 28
Xu Jilin, writer 207, 208, 210, 214
Xu Wenli, Democracy Wall dissident leader 24, 35

Yangzi River: flood disasters 29, 144, *see also* Three Gorges Dam
Yuan Hongbing, lawsuit against Communist Party 34

Zhai Meiqing, woman entrepreneur 72
Zhang Chengzhi, novelist 205–6
Zhang Yuan, film director 200
Zhao Ziyang, CCP reformer 33
Zhejiang province, cotton mill strike 49
Zhejiang Village, Beijing 90, 93, 94
Zhou Enlai, Premier, and population control 104
Zhou Lunyou, 'A Stance of Rejection' 198–9, 204, 216–17
Zhu Houze, CCP propaganda chief 25
Zhuang minority people 180
Zhuang Weihong, 'Mama Zhuang Vegetable Service' 78